the cinema of MICHAEL HANEKE

DIRECTORS' CUTS

Other titles in the Directors' Cuts series:

the cinema of
MICHAEL HANEKE

europe utopia

edited by Ben McCann & David Sorfa

 **WALLFLOWER PRESS** LONDON & NEW YORK

A Wallflower Press Book
Published by
Columbia University Press
Publishers Since 1893
New York • Chichester, West Sussex
cup.columbia.edu

A complete CIP record is available from the Library of Congress

ISBN 978-1-906660-30-7 (cloth : alk. paper)
ISBN 978-1-906660-29-1 (pbk. : alk. paper)
ISBN 978-0-231-50465-2 (e-book)

Series design by Rob Bowden Design

Cover image of Michael Haneke courtesy of Studio Canal+/Centre National
De La Cinematographie/The Kobal Collection

Columbia University Press books are printed on permanent
and durable acid-free paper.
This book is printed on paper with recycled content.
Printed in the United States of America

c 10 9 8 7 6 5 4 3 2 1
p 10 9 8 7 6 5 4 3 2 1

CONTENTS

ACKNOWLEDGEMENTS

This book had its inception in the Film Criticism module we ran jointly at Liverpool John Moores University in 2004.

Our thanks, first and foremost, must go to Yoram Allon at Wallflower Press, whose enthusiasm during the project's formative stage encouraged us to broaden our scope and ambition. Thanks must also be extended to Jacqueline Downs at Wallflower Press, who expertly shaped and sharpened the manuscript in its final months.

We are grateful to Professor John Orr, who stepped in at the last minute to provide a wonderful piece on *The White Ribbon*.

As this book was going to press, John Orr died suddenly.
We wish to dedicate this book to him.

CONTRIBUTORS

LISA COULTHARD is Assistant Professor of Film Studies at the University of British Columbia. She is working on a book on film sound and the films of Quentin Tarantino and she has recently published articles on Michael Haneke, Bruno Dumont and Catherine Breillat.

NEMONIE CRAVEN RODERICK is completing a PhD on love and war in the work of Emmanuel Levinas at Queen Mary, University of London. She has contributed to the *Blackwell Encyclopedia of Literary and Cultural Theory*, *Sight & Sound* and *Filmwaves*, and is creator of the How to Live project.

RICARDO DOMIZIO is a Senior Lecturer in Film Studies at London South Bank University. His research interests are in philosophy and film, Italian cinema and filmic representations of the city. He is currently undertaking a PhD in Gilles Deleuze and digital cinema.

MATTIAS FREY is Lecturer in Film Studies at the University of Kent. His writings have appeared in *Cinema Journal*, *Screen*, *Quarterly Review of Film & Video*, *Literature/Film Quarterly*, *Framework*, *Film International* and *Senses of Cinema*, as well as numerous anthologies and reference works. He is currently finishing a book on the new understanding of national history in German film, *Goodbye, Hitler: Postwall German Cinema and History*.

ALEX GERBAZ works in the Department of Film & Television at Curtin University of Technology, Western Australia. He has been a Research Fellow at the National Film and Sound Archive, Canberra and received the 2008 Margaret George Award for Emerging Scholars at the National Archives of Australia. Recent publications include work on the Experimental Film Landscapes of Paul Winkler, and Errol Morris's *Interrotron*.

PAULA GEYH is Associate Professor of English at Yeshiva University, New York. She is the author of *Cities, Citizens, and Technologies: Urban Life and Postmodernity* (2009) and the co-editor of *Postmodern American Fiction: A Norton Anthology* (1998). She is currently working on a project on the interrelationships between literature and avant-garde art movements of the early 20th century.

DEBORAH HOLMES is Researcher at the Ludwig Boltzmann Institute for the History and Theory of Biography in Vienna. She has published on Austrian, German and Italian literature and culture in the period 1860 to the present day, including *Ignazio Silone in Exile* (2005) and (with Lisa Silverman) *Interwar Vienna: Culture between Tradition and Modernity* (2009). She is currently working on a biography of the educationist and philanthropist Eugenie Schwarzwald.

KATE INCE is Reader in French Film and Gender Studies at the University of Birmingham. She has co-edited books on French women's erotic writing, Samuel Beckett and Marguerite Duras, written studies of the performance artist Orlan and the French film director Georges Franju, and edited a volume of essays on contemporary Francophone auteurs, *Five Directors: Auteurism from Assayas to Ozon* (2008). She is currently working on feminist philosophical approaches to the films of Agnès Varda and Sally Potter.

CHRISTOPHER JUSTICE is a lecturer at the University of Baltimore and its Director of Expository Writing. Recent book chapters have explored the sexploitation films of Edgar G. Ulmer, the political rhetoric of Robert Zemeckis and radicalism in Joseph H. Lewis's *Gun Crazy*. He is currently writing about depictions of the Arctic in eco-trauma films. His monthly column, 'The Tackle Box', appears in *PopMatters* and explores the confluence of fishing and popular culture.

TARJA LAINE is Assistant Professor and Program Director of Film Studies at the University of Amsterdam. She is the author of *Shame and Desire: Emotion, Intersubjectivity, Cinema* (2007) and has published widely on emotions and sensations in cinema. She is currently writing a new book on cinematic emotions.

BEN MCCANN is Senior Lecturer in French at the University of Adelaide. Amongst other work, he has contributed to both editions of *The Cinema of Terrence Malick* (2003, 2007) and has recently completed a study of *Le Jour se lève* (1939). He is currently writing a book on the set designs of Alexandre Trauner.

BENJAMIN NOYS is Reader in English at the University of Chichester. He is the author of *Georges Bataille: A Critical Introduction* (2000), *The Culture of Death* (2005) and *The Persistence of the Negative: A Critique of Contemporary Continental Theory* (2010).

JOHN ORR was Professor Emeritus in the School of Social and Political Studies at the University of Edinburgh and has published widely in many areas of Film Studies and Modern Culture. His books include *Cinema and Modernity* (1993), *Contemporary Cinema* (1998) and *Hitchcock and Twentieth Century Cinema* (2005). His most recent work is *Romantics and Modernists in British Cinema* (2010).

LANDON PALMER is the co-editor and co-founder of the interactive media studies e-journal *Movement*. He is a columnist for *FilmSchoolRejects.com*, where he writes 'Culture Warrior', a weekly examination of recent movies and their discursive role within popular culture at large. He received his MA in Cinema Studies from New York University in 2009 and is now enrolled in the PhD program in Communication and Culture at the University of Indiana-Bloomington.

WILLY RIEMER is Assistant Professor Professor of German at the University of Delaware. He is the author of *After Postmodernism: Austrian Literature and Film in Transition* (2000).

DAVID SORFA is Senior Lecturer in Film Studies at Liverpool John Moores University and managing editor of the journal *Film-Philosophy*. He has published on Michael Haneke, Jan Švankmajer, Czech cinema and a wide variety of other film-related subjects.

OLIVER C. SPECK teaches Film Studies at Virginia Commonwealth University. His work focuses on narrative strategies and the representation of memory and history in French, German and other European cinema. He has written *The Under-written Gaze: The Problem of Subjectivity in Film* (1999), while recent projects include *Funny Frames: The Filmic Concepts of Michael Haneke* (2010) and the co-editing of *New Austrian Film* (2010).

TEMENUGA TRIFENOVA is Assistant Professor Professor of Film Studies at York University. She is the author of *The Image in French Philosophy* (2007) and *European Film Theory* (2008). Her research interests include film and philosophy, film theory, European Cinema, American Cinema, film remakes and aesthetic theory. She is currently working on a book entitled *Warped Mind: Madness and Cinema.*

FELIX W. TWERASER is Associate Professor of German at Utah State University. He is currently working on a monograph – *Vienna and Hollywood: Dream Factories and Cultural Transfer* – which traces the contributions of Central-European émigrés to the American film industry and Hollywood's Golden Age.

IULIANA CORINA VAIDA has a PhD in philosophy from the University of Miami and is currently teaching philosophy at the College of William & Mary. She has published an article on aesthetic qualities (1998) and co-authored a review of *Mulholland Drive* (2005), based on Freudian dream analysis. She is currently working on several papers on Kant's transcendental idealism, the third antinomy, freedom and moral agency, based on her dissertation, 'How Kant Needs to Interpret Free Will'.

CATHERINE WHEATLEY is currently a Research Associate at the University of Southampton, where she is working with Dr Lucy Mazdon on a history of French cinema in Britain since the advent of sound cinema. She is a regular contributor to *Sight & Sound* and is the author of the first English-language monograph on Haneke – *Michael Haneke's Cinema: The Ethic of the Image* (2009).

INTRODUCTION

Ben McCann and David Sorfa

Michael Haneke (b. 1942) is one of the most important film directors working in Europe, and arguably the world, today. His films and earlier television productions examine the ethical dilemmas of our era with forensic clarity and merciless insight. His films look at their audience as much as the spectator considers them and that audience is very often found wanting. There is nevertheless a dark strain of optimism that runs throughout Haneke's work and elevates it above fashionable nihilism. In this collection we have gathered a group of essays to celebrate, explicate and sometimes challenge the *Weltanschauung* that Haneke presents in his film world. Amos Vogel sums up the inherent contradictions in Haneke's filmmaking thus:

> All filmmaking inevitably entails control over the spectator; it is the degree and the kind of control that will vary from filmmaker to filmmaker, from film to film. Haneke's stated intention to have the viewer come to his own insights and explanations presupposed, in its purest form, a level playing field that cannot exist. (1996: 75)

It is perhaps not surprising that his films have a strong critical focus, considering Haneke's studies in psychology and philosophy at the University of Vienna and his subsequent work as a film and theatre critic. After a period as a theatre director in Germany and Austria, Haneke began to make television programmes in 1973 and his first feature film, *Der siebente Kontinent* (*The Seventh Continent*), appeared in 1989. At the time of writing Haneke has released eleven feature films, including *Das Schloß* (*The Castle*, 1997), a version of Franz Kafka's novel, made originally for the television channel Arte. His latest film, *Das weiße Band* (*The White Ribbon*), won the Palme d'Or at the 2009 Cannes Film Festival.

Within a European filmmaking context Haneke's productions are closely allied to what we might call 'critical realism'. By this we mean that his films engage not so much with 'reality', although being very much involved with historical events, but with the problems and possibilities of presenting such a reality through a fictional, normative medium. In this sense, he can be allied to the work of Bertolt Brecht in theatre and Rainer Werner Fassbinder in the cinema.

We could also consider his films as being a forebear and contemporary of what has been called the French New Brutalism of the late 1990s and early 2000s. Film-makers such as Gaspar Noé (*Seul contre tous* (*I Stand Alone*, 1998), *Irréversible* (2002)), Catherine Breillat (*Romance* (1999), *A ma soeur!* (2001), *Anatomie de l'enfer* (*Anatomy of Hell*, 2004)), Virginie Despentes with Coralie Trinh Thi (*Baise moi* (2000)), and François Ozon (*Sitcom* (1998), *5x2* (2004)) combine sex and violence to an almost unbearable degree and, more or less, implicate the – usually bourgeois – protagonists and audiences as being the guilty architects of their own misfortunes. Ozon in partic-ular deals more generally with the artifice of cinema and its ability to manipulate real audiences in a way that talks to Haneke's films in a very productive manner. However, his camp sensibility draws his work towards a more carnivalesque exuberance than is evident in Haneke.

Perhaps Haneke's most significant contemporary is the Danish provocateur Lars von Trier. Von Trier's films exhibit a similar interest in cinematic formalism and in the current political state of Europe. Von Trier often characterises this as being a condition of amnesia, disaffection and complete lack of purpose. His Europa trilogy (*Forbrydelsens Element* (*The Element of Crime*, 1984), *Epidemic* (1987) and *Europa* (1991)) imagines a Europe in which the past is always the hidden and inaccessible truth of the present. For example, in *The Element of Crime* the protagonist-detective is unknowingly guilty of the crimes he is himself investigating. In these films there is a sense of paranoid dread, a Heideggerian *angst*, which characterises contemporary Europe as unhinged and unmoored; floating into the future with little or no sense of direction and there-fore being unable to prevent the repetition of past mistakes. This, of course, is the theme that structures Haneke's *Caché* (*Hidden*, 2005).

Critical Reception

We are now on the cusp of a publishing wave surrounding Michael Haneke. Catherine Wheatley's monograph *Michael Haneke's Cinema: The Ethic of the Image* (2009) has appeared and a number of other edited collections focusing on Haneke are now in print. Wheatley's earlier article on *Hidden* in *Sight & Sound*, 'Secrets, lies & videotape', appeared in February 2006 and it was this film that seemed to particularly capture the contemporary audience. Aside from the popular press, there has been a steady increase in the number of articles dealing with Haneke in academic journals with *Screen* presenting six pieces in its 'The *Caché* Dossier' in 2007.[1] This amount of critical interest in a single European auteur is almost unprecedented since the 1960s.

While Haneke's films of the early 1990s had attracted some critical attention, especially with *The Seventh Continent* and *71 Fragmente einer Chronologie des Zufalls* (*71 Fragments of a Chronology of Chance*, 1994) being selected for the Cannes Film Festival, the two early seminal studies were the collection *Der siebente Kontinent:*

Michael Haneke und seine Filme (1991) edited by Alexander Horwath and Amos Vogel's detailed 1996 analysis in *Film Comment*. It was, however, with the release of *Funny Games* in 1997 that Haneke came to international attention. The film engendered a cult following as well as fierce critical debate. Mark Kermode's review in *Sight & Sound* demonstrated particularly well the criticisms that were aimed at Haneke. Kermode characterises Haneke's position in *Funny Games* as a belief that 'sanitised media violence has inured us to the realities of pain' and that this film is 'designed to appal, revolt and traumatise those who have come to watch a violent film' (1998: 44). Kermode argues that Haneke wishes to punish those who have come seeking visceral pleasure in the pain of others. He sees the film as being too academic and not at all original. He cites *The Texas Chainsaw Massacre* (Tobe Hooper, 1974), *Henry: Portrait of a Serial Killer* (John McNaughton, 1986) and more facetiously *Gremlins 2: The New Batch* (Joe Dante, 1990) as more worthy forebears. Kermode asks the question: 'Why … would anyone wish to continue to endure an intentionally unendurable work of art? Why would anyone wish to stay when the film so explicitly challenges them to leave?' (1998: 45). This, of course, echoes Haneke's own assertion that 'Anybody who leaves the cinema doesn't need the film, and anybody who stays does' (in Falcon 1998: 11). It would seem to be the explicitly didactic nature of the film, or at least Haneke's spoken formulation of its didactic intention, to which Kermode objects.

Kermode's criticism accuses Haneke of being a 'humourless Austrian' (1998: 45) and while obviously meant itself to be humorous, this rather odd nationalism is echoed in Kermode's later review of Haneke's 2007 shot-for-shot remake of the film in the US. In an *Observer* review headlined, 'Scare us, repulse us, just don't ever lecture us', he describes the experience of watching the new version at Cannes as 'being told off for two hours. By an Austrian. In France' (2008). What Kermode exhibits here, apart from the assumption that Europhobia is amusing, is that he dislikes the clarity of Haneke's moral thesis in the film. Perhaps rightly Kermode pours scorn on the 'post-graduate postmodern gimmicks' of the film in contrast to more 'accomplished adult fare such as *The Piano Teacher* and *Hidden*', but he ends the review on a grudging note of admiration for *Funny Games U.S.*: 'And for me, there was a perverse masochistic pleasure in enduring the damned thing over again, just to remind myself how cross it made me the first time round.' Masochism as the willed and pleasurable experience of suffering is what Haneke overtly takes as his theme in his films and perhaps Kermode's criticism is an acknowledgement of just this. Kermode's accusation of humourlessness is an interesting one, however, since serious cinema is very often defended as ironic in order to avoid accusations of being actively denunciatory. Haneke's films are not ironic – the evil tends to be unambiguously, if rather diffusely, evil. The only problem lies in deciding who exactly is or is not evil. It is the aim of Haneke's cinema to bring this question to the fore without necessarily providing a definitive answer.

Thematic Concerns

It is possible to identify a number of distinct thematic concerns that run through many of Haneke's films. In the broadest terms, his works are involved with three closely inter-related elements: ethics, audiences and power. Again, perhaps there might be a broad purpose quotation here that can link all of these competing ideas together. Firstly, if we understand ethics to be the arena within which moral choices are made, that is, that the ethical is the structure that allows us to decide whether a choice is morally right or wrong, then Haneke's ethical universe is a complex one that seldom yields an easy moral stance. Films such as *Funny Games* and *Hidden* explicitly address the nature of evil and its ethical counterpart: guilt. David Sorfa argues in 'Uneasy Domesticity in the Films of Michael Haneke' (2006) that it is the bourgeois guilt of the holidaying family in *Funny Games* that calls forth the righteous retribution of the inter-diegetic killers. In *Hidden* it is the consequences of hardly remembered actions as a six-year-old that bring about the near-destruction of the television talk-show host, Georges Laurent (Daniel Auteuil). For Haneke, the past is inevitably linked to the present and, almost as inevitably, that temporal movement involves a repression of one sort or another. In this reading, Haneke could be considered as an almost classical Freudian psychoanalyst who knows that hysteria as the return of the repressed is a form of reminiscence. The related theme of alienation, famously explicated in his 'emotional glaciation' trilogy of *The Seventh Continent, Benny's Video* (1992) and *71 Fragments of a Chronology of Chance*, also exists within the hazy world of Haneke's ethics. The issue of familial glaciation reappeared forcefully in Austria in 2007 with the discovery of a suburban dungeon in which a father had kept imprisoned a part of his family for over twenty years (see Bradshaw (2008a) for an explicit comparison of this to *The Seventh Continent*).

The central place of the audience in Haneke's films is one that is often commented on in the secondary literature and Haneke sees the contemporary cinema spectator as being in a position of culpable responsibility: there is no viewer who can claim innocence in the face of the cinema before them. Spectators are almost mindlessly influenced by the media they consume and it is perhaps here that there is a weakness in Haneke's analysis of the almost entirely passive spectator. It is difficult, as Kermode points out, to imagine what Haneke wishes for us to do – other than to renounce cinema in its entirety. Haneke says:

> My films should provide a countermodel to the typically American style of total production to be found in contemporary popular cinema, which, in its hermetically sealed illusion of an ultimately intact reality, deprives the spectator of any possibility of critical participation and interaction and condemns him from the outset to the role of a simple consumer. (In Vogel 1996: 75)

Haneke is also interested in the relationship between high and low culture and, as is perhaps most obviously seen in his choice of classical composer John Zorn's pastiche death metal music in *Funny Games*, refuses to make an easy distinction between the two. In *La Pianiste* (*The Piano Teacher*, 2001) Erika Kohut's (Isabelle Huppert) sublime, but deeply disturbed, pleasure in both Schubert and hardcore pornography appears to equate the two. In this world almost everything is always already corrupt. Fundamentally, Haneke does not imagine that an audience creates meaning from cultural texts but strongly insists that there is a power dynamic between text and consumer. However, this dynamic appears to condemn both parties equally. There is perhaps a joy in this uncompromising position.

Haneke explicitly addresses the problem of the unequal distribution of power in society and highlights the complex relationship between the weak and the strong, the exploited and the exploiters, but typically shows that neither unambiguously inhabits either position. The very existence and structure of exploitation makes all parties co-conspirators in their own unhappiness. Haneke highlights the position of other, immigrant cultures in Europe, particularly effectively in *Code inconnu: Récit incomplet de divers voyages* (*Code Unknown: Incomplete Tales of Several Journeys*, 2000), and is interested in the way in which these cultures relate to the colonial history of imperial Europe. His scrutiny of the family and its dissolution is ongoing and it is never clear whether the family is a protection against the blind might of the state or whether it is the family itself which is the locus of oppression. It does seem, however, that Haneke's views on the problem of the family have been changing somewhat from his very first films in which suicide and murder are offered as the only solutions to family life. It is in *Le temps du loup* (*The Time of the Wolf*, 2003) that the small family unit, perhaps significantly fatherless, represents a viable possibility of a new future: the utopia of the title of this volume. In a related area, Haneke explores the relationship of the self and society to the land and to agriculture. In *Code Unknown* a farmer kills all his cattle in a fit of depression and it seems evident that there is no rural skill available to deal with the apocalypse in *The Time of the Wolf*. Haneke appears to exhibit a vague nostalgia for a subsistence autonomy in contrast to a broader embedding within larger economies. Haneke's solution to differential power is to try and remove oneself from the situation. This is, however, a hopeless and short-term resolution, lasting for only as long as the sleeping pills that Georges takes at the end of *Hidden*.

One of the power games to which Haneke returns over and over again in his films is the relationship between actor and director. The scene in *Code Unknown* where Anne Laurent (Juliette Binoche) is tortured, or at least acts being tortured, by a film director seems to be an appropriate *mise-en-abyme* of Haneke's own view of himself and his work. In the cinema of Michael Haneke, there is a dystopian view of his own practice as a filmmaker just as much as there is one of the general functioning of contemporary society. And yet there is something in this almost nihilistic analysis that allows us to consider the possibility of future in which this terrible and (almost) inescapable guilt might not necessarily be true. It is this contingent and unlikely future that we find in Haneke. We find in his films a vision of Europe Utopia.

Mapping the Terrain

The first section of the book reveals several of the structural, thematic and artistic complexities of Michael Haneke's films, and, through a diverse range of approaches and objectives, explores multiple aspects and perspectives. In 'Domestic Invasion: Michael Haneke and Home Audiences', Catherine Wheatley argues that Haneke's films engage with popular genres in order to create a self-reflexive audience. She discusses *Funny Games* (1997) and its use of the conventions of the thriller film, paying close attention to the formal properties of Haneke's style. She goes on to examine the relationship between the film and the audience in the context of home, rather than cinema, viewing. She discusses threatening domestic spaces and the ubiquitous appearance of the droning television set in terms of the illusion of control. Drawing attention to the importance of actors and performances, Ben McCann considers the ways in which the actors in Haneke's films are directed and the extent to which one of Haneke's stated influences, Robert Bresson, has influenced his understated style. Like Bresson, Haneke rejects the conventional 'safe' co-ordinates of film stars and the superficiality of psychologically-driven performances in order to reach a pared-down visual and performative 'truth'.

Lisa Coulthard explores the complexities of suicidal gestures in Haneke to deliberate on their status as ethical acts and analyses the relations of such acts to the structures of the family, the social and the political. For Coulthard, these violent gestures offer an ethics of suicide similar to Jacques Lacan's notion of the authentic 'Act'. Coulthard ultimately argues that suicide in Haneke's films implicates and interrogates the audience itself.

Oliver C. Speck's chapter, 'Thinking the Event: The Virtual in Michael Haneke's Films', traces the way in which Haneke has been accused of a nostalgia for the bourgeois values he explicitly criticises, leaving only a space of guilt-ridden self-loathing for his audience. Using Guy Debord and Gilles Deleuze, Speck argues that Haneke offers something more than this through the self-reflexive style of his filmmaking and the point-of-view shot in particular. In a brilliant move, Speck links the virtual and the acousmatic in Haneke's films.

Referring to the work of Georg Simmel and Siegfried Kracauer, Temenuga Trifonova's chapter on the politics of film form highlights Haneke's use of the trivial and everyday in his films. Trifonova argues that Haneke's films revive a specifically modernist aesthetic (characterised by an emphasis on fragmentation, indeterminacy, endlessness, chance, multiplicity and ambiguity) and a certain uncompromising, almost punitive, moralism that appears 'untimely' from the point of view of the affected affectlessness that constitutes the privileged postmodern stance.

The second section opens with Kate Ince's chapter, 'Glocal Gloom: Existential Space in Haneke's French-Language Films'. Ince tackles Haneke's presentation of the relationship between the local and the global, arguing that the liberal dream of multiculturalism has failed. Haneke is defined as a transnational filmmaker and *Code Unknown*, *The Piano Teacher*, *Hidden* and *The Time of the Wolf* are discussed in terms of their use of existential space.

Space is also the subject of Christopher Justice's chapter, which outlines the way in which Haneke sees the holiday and travel as failed attempts to escape the ethical dilemmas of Europe. Justice suggests that Haneke's characters force us to question our own travel experiences and transform them from quick excursions devoid of ramification into thoughtful, consequential explorations of identity, culture and spirituality.

Paula E. Geyh uses Jacques Derrida's work on cosmopolitanism to explore issues surrounding hospitality and the foreigner in *Code Unknown*. For Derrida, the contemporary global city is a city of refuge, not least because it mediates relationships between exterior and interior hospitality through its inside and outside spaces, and also through our experience and conceptualisation of these spaces. If we are to make the heterogeneous, globalised city of Paris in *Code Unknown* work, Geyh argues that we require a balance of ethical and political hospitality.

The next section concentrates on Haneke's lesser-known work in television. In 'The Early Haneke: Austrian Literature on Austrian Television', Deborah Holmes considers Haneke's television work in the 1970s and 1980s with particular reference to his adaptation of Ingeborg Bachmann's *Drei Wege zum See* (*Three Paths to the Lake*) in 1976, *Die Rebellion* (*The Rebellion*, 1993) and *The Castle*. For Holmes, Haneke's literature for the small screen is not only a self-conscious reflection on the process of reading and adapting literary texts, but proof that Haneke can be seen as a 'literary' director when filming his own screenplays, and a cinematic director when working for television.

The practices of literary adaptation are also central to Willy Riemer's analysis of the differences between Haneke's *The Castle* and Kafka's *Das Schloß*. He looks particularly at the problems of loss of identity and communication that are central to both artists' work, and underlines how Haneke's 'televisual' techniques anticipate the stylistic approaches he adopts in his later feature films.

The fourth section explores Haneke's 'glaciation trilogy', the now standard term applied to *The Seventh Continent*, *Benny's Video* and *71 Fragments of a Chronology of Chance* after Haneke's claim that the films were intended as a reflection on the 'progressive emotional glaciation of Austria'. In 'Attenuating Austria: The Construction of Bourgeois Space in *The Seventh Continent*', Benjamin Noys not only highlights the specific 'Austrian-ness' of Haneke's first feature film, but also analyses the way in which subjects are alienated by deterritorialised capital and argues that Haneke moves this figuratively into the real space of the family.

Mattias Frey develops Marc Augé's ideas around supermodernity and non-places in his discussion of *Benny's Video*. He also seeks to situate the film in the context of other strands of contemporary French thought, and by focusing on Jean Baudrillard's simulcra and Deleuze's actual/virtual distinction, Frey argues for a new consideration of agency in the supermodern world.

The final sections of the book focus specifically on five films – *Funny Games* (1997, 2007), *The Piano Teacher*, *Hidden* and *The White Ribbon*. In 'The Ethical Screen: *Funny Games* and the Spectacle of Pain', Alex Gerbaz examines the ethical and social aspects of film spectatorship. In particular, he explores how the ethics of 'direct address', watching others suffer and the ways in which the relationship between viewer and suffering object/subject are negotiated through entertainment by Haneke in *Funny Games*.

Closely analysing the two versions of *Funny Games*, David Sorfa links the repetition of the *Funny Games* to an internal repetition which evokes the Freudian structure of the Superego, Ego and Id. Sorfa sees Haneke as moving beyond both Freud and Žižek's subject topographies; instead, Haneke's films are fundamentally based on the logic of inexorable repetition.

Landon Palmer discusses Haneke's use of music in *Funny* Games and *The Piano Teacher* and looks at the way in which he utilises music both to comment on the formulaic codes of film music and underpin notions of oppression and possible freedom. For Palmer, the bourgeois strictures of aesthetic beauty and classical music are linked to violence and sexual perversion.

Felix W. Tweraser's 'Images of Confinement and Transcendence: Michael Haneke's Reception of Romanticism in *The Piano Teacher*' is a close reading of *The Piano Teacher* that pays particular attention to confined spaces and themes of imprisonment, while Iuliana Corina Vaida analyses the same film by using Deleuze's conception of masochism. In both chapters, there is an emphasis on the adaptation from Elfriede Jelinek's novel to Haneke's film.

There then follows three different readings of one of Haneke's most critically-acclaimed and oft-discussed films, *Hidden*. In 'Subject to Memory? Thinking after *Hidden*', Nemonie Craven Roderick argues that the film critically engages conceptualisations of history and memory, as the past re-emerges as a question and a power in its movement through various individuals and groups of individuals (including the viewer) who become subject to interrogation or subject to memory.

Ricardo Domizio uses *Hidden* to investigate the question of cinematic ontology in the digital age in relation to Gilles Deleuze and Felix Guattari's concept of schizophrenia in late capitalism. For Domizio, Haneke's previous decodification of middle-class life is taken even further in *Hidden* into areas of history, memory and subjectivity. Haneke's digital images multiply, perplex and haunt, and as such represent the great potential of the digital image.

Tarja Laine, in her chapter 'Hidden Shame Exposed: *Hidden* and the Spectator', interrogates the strategies the film uses to confront the viewers with their own engagement with visual displays. Through a close reading of *Hidden*, Laine explores the concept of 'reciprocal alteration', found so often in Haneke's films, that requires mutual recognition between both film and spectator.

Finally, John Orr explores Haneke's most recent film, *The White Ribbon*, and shows the relationship between this film and the work of Robert Musil and Thomas Mann, particularly as inflected through the New German Cinema of the 1960s and 1970s. Orr describes *The White Ribbon* as a 'revisionist Heimat film' and highlights Haneke's elliptical and elusive style which is perhaps one of the filmmaker's most distinctive formal practices. Orr sees the film as finally fulfilling Haneke's insistence on a 'moral spectatorship' and claims that this mature work focuses more fruitfully on mystery rather than un-pleasure. *The White Ribbon* has been greeted with almost unanimous critical praise and it is Haneke's relentless uncovering of the dystopic centre of utopia that heralds him as the European director that this century deserves and needs.

Notes

1   See Ezra & Sillars, '*Hidden* in plain sight: bringing terror home'; Cousins, 'After the end: word of mouth and *Caché*; Beugnet, 'Blind spot'; Gilroy, 'Shooting crabs in a barrel'; Khanna, 'From Rue Morgue to Rue des Iris'; Silverman, 'The Empire Looks Back'; *Screen*, 48, 2, 211–49.

References

Beugnet, M. (2007) 'Blind spot', *Screen*, 48, 2, 227–31.

Bradshaw, Peter (2008a) 'Haneke's House of Horrors', *Guardian*, 30 April. On-line. Available at: http://www.guardian.co.uk/film/filmblog/2008/apr/30/hanekeshouseofhorrors (accessed 28 November 2008).

Cousins, M. (2007) 'After the end: word of mouth and *Caché*, *Screen*, 48, 2, 223–6.

Ezra, E. and J. Sillars (2007) '*Hidden* in plain sight: bringing terror home', *Screen*, 48, 2, 215–21.

Falcon, R. (1998) 'The discreet harm of the bourgeoisie', *Sight & Sound*, 8, 5, 10–12.

Gilroy, P. (2007) 'Shooting crabs in a barrel', *Screen*, 48, 2, 233–5.

Kermode, M. (1998) '*Funny Games*', *Sight & Sound*, 8, 12, 44–5.

_____ (2008) 'Scare us, repulse us, just don't ever lecture us', *Observer*, 30 March. On-line. Available at: http://www.guardian.co.uk/film/2008/mar/30/features.horror (accessed 28 March 2009).

Khanna, R. (2007) 'From Rue Morgue to Rue des Iris', *Screen*, 48, 2, 237–44.

Silverman, M. (2007) 'The Empire Looks Back', *Screen*, 48, 2, 245–9.

Sorfa, D. (2006) 'Uneasy Domesticity in the Films of Michael Haneke', *Studies in European Cinema*, 3, 2, 93–104.

Vogel, A. (1996) 'Of Nonexisting Continents: The Cinema of Michael Haneke', *Film Comment*, 32, 4, 73–5.

Wheatley, C. (2006d) 'Secrets, lies & videotape', *Sight & Sound*, 16, 2, 32–6.

CHAPTER ONE

Domestic Invasion:
Michael Haneke and Home Audiences

Catherine Wheatley

From the outset of his feature-making career, Michael Haneke has defined his work against the dominant conventions of mainstream (Hollywood) movies. He describes the trilogy of *Der siebente Kontinent* (*The Seventh Continent*, 1989), *Benny's Video* (1992) and *71 Fragmente einer Chronologie des Zufalls* (*71 Fragments of a Chronology of Chance*, 1994) as 'a polemic against the American cinema of distraction' (1992: 89) and in his notes to *71 Fragments of a Chronology of Chance* he writes:

> I attempt to provide an alternative to the totalising productions that are typical of the entertainment cinema of American provenance. My approach provides an alternative to the hermetically sealed-off illusion which in effect pretends at an intact reality and thereby deprives the spectator of the possibility of participation. In the mainstream scenario spectators are right off herded into mere consumerism. (2000: 172)

In my own book on Haneke, and again in a number of articles, I have posited that both the content and the form of the director's work are shaped by a concern with the ethics of dominant film-viewing practices.[1] My argument throughout is that the director deliberately draws on Hollywood convention (most prominently genre forms) in order to encourage emotional engagement with narrative, only to rupture this engagement by deploying self-reflexive devices which stall the pleasure-drive and give rise to a position of rational awareness that centres around two points of knowledge. At once, the spectator becomes aware of the film as a construct – the product of a director. But at the same time, he becomes aware of himself, sitting in the cinema, as a consumer of the film. In this way, I have argued, the films are able to make their spectators aware of certain desires and motivations that may be less than admirable.

Haneke's *Funny Games* (1997) provides the most pronounced illustration of my thesis. The film was promoted as a 'thriller', right down to the fact that when it premiered at the 1997 Cannes Film Festival tickets to the screening were issued with a red warning sticker (a measure previously only taken with one film – Quentin Tarantino's *Reservoir Dogs* (1992)). Even before entering the cinema, audiences were primed to expect, as Jonathan Romney puts it, 'a blood-soaked nail-biter' (1999). And indeed, in the opening thirty minutes of the film, Haneke deliberately heightens these expectations: cutting is moderately paced, speeding up at points of high tension; shot/reverse-shots, point-of-view shots and lingering close-ups of various objects (a knife left on a boat, a set of golf clubs, the family dog, all of which will play an important role later in the narrative) function as generic signposts. As the director states:

> Elements from the history of the suspense thriller appear as quotes – the classical opening, the scene when the boy escapes to the villa – very classical, like Hitchcock. And the audience only engages with the film when they don't know what's going to happen, when they allow themselves hope. (In Falcon 1998: 12)

Once the spectator of *Funny Games* is engaged with the narrative, once they 'allow themselves hope', the film draws on a repertoire of self-reflexive techniques, ranging from long, drawn-out shots in which little happens, to direct audience address, to the film's now infamous diegetic rewind in order to break any sense of intactness, and force the spectator to acknowledge his participation in (ostensibly) violent spectacle.

In my understanding, then, cinematic viewings of *Funny Games* are characterised by a tension between a pleasurable absorption in the film's narrative and unpleasurable awareness of the film's constructedness. At this point of tension, the spectator is invited to enter a thought space, in which he or she engages with the ethical implications of mainstream film consumption. While I stand by this argument, I must nonetheless concede here that it is based upon a rather problematic premise: that the spectator of *Funny Games* – or indeed, any of Haneke's other works – is viewing the film in a cinema. And yet with the growing popularity of DVDs and downloads and the concomitant decline of theatrical attendances, such an assumption can at best be rather presumptuous. At worst, it may fail to account for the vast majority of spectators of Haneke's films: according to the distributors of *Funny Games*, roughly five thousand viewers saw the film in US cinemas and even fewer in the UK, yet the film has seen steady video sales in both countries.[2]

Since the experience of home viewing is widely recognised to be significantly different from that of watching a film in a cinema, some consideration of this viewing context is pivotal to a full understanding of how Haneke's films relate to their spectators. In what follows, I would like to examine the transition which the films undergo when viewed on the small screen rather than in the cinema, and in particular to suggest some ways in which the shift in viewing context might reframe the self-reflexive devices which Haneke employs.

Mediated Reality

In an interview with Michel Cieutat for the journal *Positif,* Haneke explains that he has been witness to the television's invasion of the domestic sphere and its hijacking of the cinema's unique pleasures:

> I am part of a generation which was able to grow up without the continual presence of television. So I was therefore able to learn about the world directly, without any intermediary. Today, by contrast, children learn how to perceive reality through television screens, and reality on television is shown in one of two ways: on the one hand there are documentary shows, and on the other fiction. I think that the media has played a significant role in this loss of any sense of reality. (In Cieutat 2000: 28)

Over the course of his lifetime, Haneke has seen television supplant cinema – and eventually transform it. Much has been made in scholarly literature of Haneke's allegiance to modernist filmmaking traditions, and yet he is working in a postmodern period (or perhaps even a 'post-postmodern period'): a time when the joys of the cinema, as celebrated by François Truffaut and the young Jean-Luc Godard are passed; when the ideologically pernicious potential of the cinema has been discovered, dismantled and discussed; when critics such as Jean Baudrillard and Slavoj Žižek can write of the disruption between the 'virtual' and the 'real'. The very etymology of media suggests something of the mediation of perception that has now become a norm. Cine-tele-visual representation is no longer a new and exciting phenomenon, but something quotidian: we take for granted its presence in homes, hotels, aeroplanes and arenas, public houses and public spaces.

Of course, cinema and television are not the same thing, but they influence each other, ape each other. The brute power of the impression created by the larger-than-life dimensions of the screen upon a one-off visit to the cinema has been matched and indeed overtaken by the mass of impressions and their permanent presence in which both television and DVD play a role. The rapid editing and jump cuts that were so innovative when Godard first introduced them, when Arthur Penn and Sam Peckinpah developed them into their cinema of 'ultraviolence' (Prince 1998), are now the hallmarks of MTV and television shows such as *ER* (1994–2009). Likewise, Peckinpah's slow-motion montages are now a standard means of stylising gunplay in film and television alike. Little matter that when Peckinpah first introduced this aesthetic of violence into cinema it was intended to shock audiences into a realisation of violence's true horror; it has now become the norm. Television can take what is most strange, captivating and unique from the cinema and turn it into something domesticated, ordinary, even *boring*, simply through its ubiquity.

Within Haneke's oeuvre, *Benny's Video* offers the most extended treatment of this perceived mediatisation of reality. Based on a real-life incident, in which a young man videotaped his murder of another teenager, the film provides us with a wealth of incidental detail to suggest how, for Benny (Arno Frisch), perception comes to be mediated by the technology with which he is surrounded. As Brigitte Peucker points out, visual discernment takes place chiefly through a video camera, and the sounds of television and rock CDs form an aural space that envelops him (see 2000: 180). Benny spends his time watching the choreographed violence of action movies and the restrained, 'normalising' television reportage of scenes of death in Bosnia (Peucker 2000: 181). In these news programmes, images of carnage are accompanied by voices of commentators carefully trained to exclude all emotion, thus rendering a sanitised version of the real precisely where the spectator has come to believe he has access to its immediacy (see ibid.).

If the realism of film is conceptualised in spatial terms, Mary Ann Doane has argued, the realness of television lies in its relation to temporality, to its sense of 'live-ness'.[3] The temporal dimension of television would seem to be 'an insistent "present-ness" – a "This-is-going-on" rather than a "That-has-been"' (Doane 1990: 222). Televi-sion, Doane claims, deals 'not with the weight of the dead past but with the potential trauma and explosiveness of the present' (1990: 225). But while Doane connects the liveness of television to trauma, to Haneke's mind, the medium works hard to keep the shock of catastrophe at bay. Perhaps what is more important than the liveness of the instant of filming is the way in which the very fact of filming automatically consigns its subject matter to the past, packaging it up neatly and sealing it away. For as Doane continues:

> Insofar as a commercial precedes news coverage of a disaster which in its own turn is interrupted by a preview of tonight's made-for-TV movie, television is the pre-eminent machine of decontextualisation. (Ibid.)

The very sense of liveness that characterises televisual information as part of the present means that it effaces the past. Television, as Doane puts it, inhabits a moment in time and then is lost to memory: it 'thrives on its own forgettability' (1990: 226). Urgency, enslavement to the instant and hence forgettability are the attributes of televised infor-mation and catastrophe; Benny's demeanour in the face of his crime reflects the calm detachment of a news commentator.

If television is characterised by its liveness, Laura Mulvey (2006) has suggested that video may be characterised by its deadness. In *Death 24x a Second*, Mulvey argues that the digital frees the viewer from the dictates of narrative continuity and cinema time. For Mulvey, in the cinema of moments or, as she refers to it, 'delayed cinema', where the pause button stills movement at will, 'a film's original moment of registra-tion can suddenly burst through its narrative time … the now-ness of story time gives way to the then-ness of the time when the movie was made' (2006: 30–1). Moreover, she posits that the modes of nonlinear viewing permitted by video – rewinds, fast forwards and so forth – reveal to the viewer the inherent stillness behind the moving image in the form of the single frame. Mulvey connects the tension between the individual frame and the moving image to cinema's capacity to capture the appearance of life and preserve it after death. The constant flow of images vomited forward by television is countered by the film still, itself highlighted by the pause button: an image of death. In Benny's case, this equation of the video image with death is literal. By filming his murder of the young girl, Benny captures it in a constant present, a present without history or consequence – as demonstrated by his replaying and rewinding of the video cassette, reducing and deflating through its overpresence, the murder's shock value.

At a narrative level we might say that *Benny's Video* functions as a critique of how the cinematic conventions of mainstream film and television can contribute to the Debordian 'Society of the Spectacle',[4] a point echoed formally through Haneke's use of varying levels of cine-televisual 'reality', which render the film extremely self-reflexive. As the film's title and opening scenes suggest, the boundary between the ongoing diegetic video and the so-called 'reality' of the film narrative is repeatedly called into question, and at various junctures the spectator is only retrospectively made aware that the footage he or she has been watching is actually part of Benny's video (as opposed to Haneke's film). One of the most effective of such moments within the film occurs at its end, when we see footage shot from the darkness of Benny's bed into the brightly lit room beyond. The spectator does not recognise the image, but the soundtrack is familiar: it is a conversation in which his parents discuss how best to dispose of the body of the young girl (Ingrid Stassner) that Benny has killed. This sequence, out of temporal order, is momentarily confusing: although the image is unfamiliar, the viewer has heard the dialogue before, and gradually realises that Benny had asked his parents on that occasion to leave the door of his room open because he had meant to videotape (or rather, as it is dark, to record) their conversation. It is not long before the spectator becomes aware that Benny's video is once again being viewed within the diegesis of Haneke's film: this time the soundtrack consists in a voice-over conversation about the footage, a conversation that Benny holds with the policeman with whom he is viewing it. As Brigitte Peucker points out, we are well aware that, deprived of a context and without the image of his parents' suffering to which he had initially been privy, their dialogue on tape will, in all likelihood, serve to indict Benny's parents for the murder that their son has committed. Hence the videotape functions not only as a document of violence, but as its instrument as well (see 2000: 184).

Reflexivity in the Home

The trope of the threatening tape resurfaces within Haneke's work – in *Caché* (*Hidden*, 2005). Much has already been written on this subject (and indeed, *Hidden* seems to have captured the critical imagination in a way that Haneke's other works are yet to do), so I will say little about it here – although I will return to the matter of the violent video cassettes in my concluding remarks.[5] Suffice it to say here that while *Benny's Video* may be Haneke's most extended treatment of television's impact on contempo-

The recurring image of the diegetic television: *Caché* (2005)

rary modes of perception, the subject materialises in mitigated forms throughout his work. In fact, it is striking that while a diegetic cinema appears in only two of his films (*La Pianiste* (*The Piano Teacher*, 2001) and *Hidden* – in fact the exterior of a cinema), the diegetic television is an image that recurs throughout Haneke's oeuvre. At the time of writing, Haneke has made ten feature films (eleven if we include his adaptation of Kafka's *Das Schloß* (*The Castle*, 1997), originally filmed for television but subsequently given a cinematic release; eleven if we include the remake of his own *Funny Games*, released in 2007 under the title *Funny Games U.S.*). Discounting the Kafka adaptation, almost all of these films features a television set.[6] At the close of *The Seventh Continent*, the television screen, filled with snow, is the last thing we see; in *Benny's Video* it is the first; in *71 Fragments of a Chronology of Chance* a news bulletin bookends the narrative. It also forms a backdrop to the (violent) action in several scenes of the latter, as it does too in *Code inconnu: Récit incomplet de divers voyages* (*Code Unknown: Incomplete Tales of Several Journeys*, 2000), *Funny Games* (both versions) and *Hidden* – in which the protagonist is a television presenter. In *The Piano Teacher*, the heroine's flat is persistently bathed in its flickering light and gentle drone.[7] In *Le temps du loup* (*The Time of the Wolf*, 2003), a post-apocalyptic vision of society in crisis, the sole screen we come across is broken – but then, it is perhaps appropriate for a film in which neither we nor the characters can gain a purchase on the events taking place that our primary source of information about the world is remarkable by its absence: indeed, the same might be said about *The Castle*.

The apotheosis of Haneke's fascination with the diegetic screen is perhaps his one-minute segment for the portfolio film *Lumière et compagnie* (*Lumière and Company*, 1995), which consists of a static shot of – what else? – a television, showing news footage including a space shuttle launch, the Queen of England, a bombing and sports and weather news, all broadcast on 19 March 1995, one hundred years to the day since the first 'official' cinematic exhibition. But while here the shape of the screen, its containment within the plastic structure of the 'box', are made evident, other diegetic screens are not always given to us as such – at least not immediately. Just as watching *Benny's Video* we are often unsure as to whether we are seeing Haneke's film or one of Benny's tapes – *Benny's Video* or Benny's video, as Brigitte Peucker puts it (2000: 179) – so in Haneke's other films the status of the image is frequently unclear. We are often only made aware retrospectively that we have been watching a diegetic image sequence, when offscreen characters talk over the tape (*Hidden*), when a cut reveals the television's place as part of a much larger scene (*71 Fragments of a Chronology of Chance*), when the actors within the scene drop their façade (*Code Unknown*) or the technicians editing the footage shout (*Hidden*). Most frequently, we become aware that we have been watching a film-within-a-film when the footage onscreen is manipulated by an unseen hand, which pauses, rewinds or fast-forwards the action.

This latter device holds particular significance for domestic audiences of Haneke's films. For the tell-tale white lines which signal the manipulation of the screen image are a phenomenon peculiar to home viewing. In a cinema, the option to skip through scenes which disturb us, to go over parts to which we have paid insufficient attention, is not open to us. Watching a film on VHS or DVD, however, it is. As Laura Mulvey writes:

Once the consumption of movies is detached from the isolation of absorbed viewing (in the dark, at 24 frames a second, in narrative order and without exterior intrusions), the cohesion of narrative comes under pressure from external discourses, that is production context, anecdote, history. But digital spectatorship also affects the internal pattern of narrative: sequences can be easily skipped or repeated, overturning hierarchies of privilege, and setting up unexpected links that displace the chain of meaning. (2006: 28)

Watching a film at home, the spectator thus has more control over the onscreen image, or at least they have a greater potential for control – and they therefore arguably have a greater responsibility for their relationship to these images. No longer at the mercy of the film text, they are its master. Hence the importance of the rewind, the pause and the fast forward: where scenes such as those in *Hidden* and *Code Unknown* for example (which see the makers of a film or television show interrupt its filming) foreground film's *construction*, the use of what we might call 'remote control' moments on the other hand calls attention to its *consumption*, to practices of film viewing – and more significantly to film viewing within the home.

While the impact of other forms of self-reflexivity such as the long take and the distance shot may be mitigated by alternative viewing contexts, then, the impact of diegetic images of television and video spectatorship may in fact be redoubled courtesy of a *mise-en-abyme* effect. This has certainly been the case in my own experience. The first time I saw *71 Fragments of a Chronology of Chance*, it was on a VHS copy recorded from a television screening. The film's opening scene – a mock news broadcast covering events contemporary to the film's action such as the Bosnian war, the arrest of Michael Jackson on suspicion of sex offences – confused me profoundly, and for a brief period

I thought I was watching the end of the previous emission. It was only at the film's close, which consists of a matching news sequence, that I came to understand the significance of the opening passage. Immediately following a massacre that involves most of the film's characters, the closing sequence features this event amongst the real-life stories it mentions: a simulated news report of the killing in which witnesses express their horror and incomprehension. Maximilian Le Cain (2003) infers from these scenes that Haneke is pointing out the manner in which real lives and real people so easily become just another news story in a parade of media images, the actual state of their lives becoming lost as they – like the family at the end of *Benny's Video* – become subject to a relentlessly impersonal image system: in a world already saturated with images, they become just another. Haneke's film therefore suggests to Le Cain that television reportage has anaesthetised our capacity to respond to scenes of suffering. It is a conclusion that echoes Mary Ann Doane's thoughts on television's lack of a past, of a significance aside from its liveness: such rapidly-edited news bulletins dull our perception and foreclose any visceral engagement with the real traumas that take place around the world on a daily basis. With this final gesture, the film contrasts the 'realistic' perception of an event that it offers with the more conventional manner in which the televised news would distil this information into a 30-second newsbite: easily consumable, but ultimately meaningless. I have subsequently attended several theatrical screenings of *71 Fragments of a Chronology of Chance*, and the device retains an unarguable potency in this setting, but its effect was enhanced by the home context in which I first viewed the film. We might say that the bookend scenes profited from a heightened realism which emphasised the film's proximity to its spectator: the world which it depicted seemed dangerously close to my own.

Reviewer and BBFC censor Richard Falcon relates a similar shift between the experience of watching a Haneke film at the cinema and watching it at home. Of viewing *Funny Games* on tape, he states that the domestic viewing context 'added a layer of oppressiveness to a film dealing with a family trapped and tormented within a domestic environment' (1998: 11). Falcon's comment highlights a further way in which Haneke's films create a *mise-en-abyme* of domestic viewing situations: for as David Sorfa has noted, the home environment is the central site of violence in all of Haneke's films (see 2006: 98). And nowhere is the connection between violence, mass media and the domestic more in evidence, Sorfa rightly claims, than in *Funny Games*, where two young men have complete control over a family because they are able to move between the diegetic and non-diegetic worlds of the film in a way that their three victims cannot (see Sorfa 2006: 99). These two young men are ultimately triumphant because they, like Benny, have learned to successfully manipulate media: they control the remote. However, *Funny Games* is replete with imagery not only of the domestic screen and its capabilities (we will learn of one victim's death by the traces of blood splattered across a television's surface), but also of the home viewing context. Shots repeatedly feature both protagonists and antagonists lined up on sofas, either facing the spectator in a mirror image of their presumed position, or with the backs to the camera, so that we peer over their shoulders as if in the same room. On a couple of occasions, Haneke positions the camera alongside the characters: we literally seem to be watching alongside them.

Domestic Invasion

The protagonists of *Funny Games* lock themselves in a prison of their own design. The fence intended to keep out intruders hinders their escape; the phone is out of reception, the golf clubs and expensive knives purchased as status symbols are used to injure and maim them, their boat provides a getaway for the villains. As Haneke explains: 'The fact that the family can't escape is due to the way they've tried to insulate themselves from the world with their money, they've locked themselves in' (in Falcon 1998: 12).

The stronghold of objects and technology that the Schöber family create for themselves is what Umberto Eco might term a 'Fortress of Solitude'. Eco's explanation of these citadels, cited in Barbara Klinger's excellent study of domestic viewing practices, *Beyond the Multiplex*, is as follows:

> In America there are many Fortresses of Solitude, with their wax statues, their automata, their collections of inconsequential wonders. You only have to go beyond the Museum of Modern Art and the art galleries, and you enter another universe, the preserve of the average family, the tourist, the politician. (2006: 1)[8]

Klinger contends that more than any other location, it is the contemporary household that most closely approximates the Fortress of Solitude. Today, the home is a place 'where viewers are increasingly armoured by technology' (Klinger 2006: 9). Moreover, it is a getaway, a location where, 'stocked with an array of devices for audiovisual entertainments', individuals and families can sequester themselves and seek refuge from the world, engaging in 'private shows and reveries via the playback of cinematic and other images' and controlling the ebb and flow of media within the comforts of a self-defined refuge (ibid.).

The cinema has long been theorised as offering a form of escapism. For Stanley Cavell, for example, the peculiar appeal of cinema lies in the fact that it grants us not the power of the pornographer, but *respite from our complicity in the structuring of the world* (see 1971: 40). In his discussion throughout *The World Viewed* of issues concerning the troubling of epistemic relations to each other and to the rest of the world, both our desires and the blocks to their gratification are given by Cavell as *ours* – all of ours, as inhabitants of the modern, Western world, sharers of a particular culture. Cinema relieves us of this burden, granting 'not a wish for power over creation … but a wish not to need power, not to have to bear its burdens' (1971: 40). Cavell's theory of cinema's appeal underlines the spectator's agency as a consumer of films – a point which goes to the very heart of Haneke's filmmaking agenda – and it is a point elegantly illustrated within *Hidden*: following the suicide of his childhood acquaintance Majid, we see Georges Laurent enter a cinema. The implication is clear:

in Jonathan Romney's words 'we can use film to deny reality or to face it head on' (2006: 65).

But what of the 'home cinema' (and I use the term here in its widest sense, to indicate domestic film viewing in all its forms)? Can that, too, provide an escape from reality, open as it constantly is to interruption and intrusion from the outside world – from telephones and tea breaks? Given that we are so familiar with the benefits of the remote control, is it not true that film exhibition via television in the casual setting of the home still cannot help but constitute a break with the mesmerising power of the cinema in the motion picture theatre?[9] Perhaps so, but any reduction in the quality of attention that we give to a film when viewing it in the home rather than in the cinema is perhaps counterbalanced by the perceived 'benefits' of the location itself. As Klinger points out, 'the home has often represented a haven from the pressures of work and other aspects of private life' (2006: 23). She notes the developments in the rhetoric of media companies in the wake of 9/11, when travel and attendance at public events declined and a stay-at-home mentality gained ground: the act of installing a home cinema system was referred to by some as 'bunkering the house' or 'post-9/11 cocooning' (Klinger 2006: 25). The image of the home as fortress assumes then an almost literal meaning as media comes to provide 'self-sufficiency and refuge from the hazards of the public sphere at a time of national crisis' (ibid.).

Haneke's films directly refute this vision of the home as fortress, however, calling attention at a narrative level to the permeability of the home, as well as to the dangers that lurk within. It is perhaps no coincidence that the children who rise up against their parents and their surrogates – Benny, the Laurents' son Pierrot in *Hidden*, the unnamed killers of *Funny Games* – are white, well-to-do, adolescent males: one of the key demographics for DVD retailers, if not *the* key one (see Klinger 2006: 64). They embody the insinuation of the media into our homes, they are the generational pratico-inert to the praxis of self-protection that their forebears perpetuate.[10] If seeking refuge in the cinema is, to Haneke's mind, a withdrawal from our responsibilities to the world, surely seeking refuge in the home cinema is worse still? Just so, the threat of violence from the outside is frightening, but the thought that it comes from within the home is more terrifying yet. The self-reflexive devices that hit the spectator of the cinematic versions of his films with an unforeseen force are rendered more sinister, more creepy, in the home context, as the spectator becomes aware gradually that he is looking into a skewed mirror of his own situation.

While the total absorption in the narrative on which I predicated my earlier theory of Haneke's critical aesthetic finds itself attenuated within the home viewing context, the spectator's attachment to the film is no weaker, but merely different. That is, where once the viewer entered the darkened space of the theatre and submitted himself to the film, now he cocoons himself in his comfortable living room, in which the television is one of numerous accoutrements which offer something familiar, safe, knowable: if cinema offers respite from the world by allowing us to forget about ourselves for ninety minutes, television and video provide an ongoing blanket of white noise which dulls perception. They render everything safe, logical, anodyne.

During home viewings, then, the purpose served by devices such as the rewind and the set-ups which replicate the viewer's position, function to bring their attention back to the film, causing not a break in our involvement with the film, but a reconsideration of it. In both the case of the cinema and of the home viewing, the 'standard' position is disturbed via the same means. But the experience is rather different, since for the televisual viewer, the aim is not to force a step back from the image, but one towards it. Self-reflexivity concentrates and brings about concentration, allowing the spectator a heightened awareness of himself as a viewer, and prompting him to consider his own behaviour as a casual, rather than a considered, consumer of images. Thus the entry of the unexpected, via self-reflexive techniques, retains the power to discomfort, perhaps all the more so since it has entered into our private citadel. Through the media of VHS, DVD and television Haneke's films, like the protagonists of *Funny Games*, are able to invade both our homes and our minds.

A Coda: Haneke and DVD Technology

Earlier in this chapter, I examined how, within *Benny's Video*, footage taped by Benny with his video camera is distinguished from fictional reality by being manipulated from within the narrative – rewound, put into slow-motion, paused – just as we see within *Hidden*. However, in the earlier film, this footage is also visually coded as amateurish documentary: it is grainy, unedited, marked by hand-held effects. *Hidden* sees Haneke's first use of high-definition video cameras which allow him to set up a narrative device that will mix the images from the videotapes with the images from Georges' life. In this way, the director formally achieves the maturity of a meta-linguistic style he has long been developing which makes the image itself a central character of his films. The video sequences are generally marked out from the filmic 'reality' by the use of static cameras, but even this does not allow the viewer any purchase on what kind of images we are seeing as the line is blurred not only between film and life but between whether we are seeing an image in the process of being filmed or played back. The only indicator which makes this crystal clear is the use of 'remote control' devices.

However, while Haneke has stepped into the digital age on the production side, it is striking that at a narrative level he remains tied to analogue. The threatening tapes which haunt Georges are precisely that – tapes – not discs: the visual coding of the image is heavily reliant on the white lines which have no place in a digital film.[11] Describing the impact of the remote control scenes in *Hidden* on home audiences, Martine Beugnet posits that 'those who first discover the film in its DVD version will probably reach for the remote control', presumably to verify that something has not malfunctioned (2007: 229). But this is in fact unlikely to be the case, since there is a mismatch between the diegetic and extra-diegetic technology (or screen and screening technology). In one of the very few deviations from the original, however, the 2007 remake of *Funny Games* sees the white lines excised from the rewind scene, which simply shuttles backwards, in an imitation of the manner in which DVDs reverse. It is perhaps a small indication of an increasing recognition, on Haneke's part, of home audiences.[12]

Notes

Unless otherwise stated, all translations are by the author.

1 See Wheatley (2009). See also Wheatley (2006a; 2006b; 2006c).

2 This information comes from the press notes to *Funny Games U.S.*, Haneke's 2007 English-language remake of the same film.

3 I am deeply indebted to Brigitte Peucker for calling my attention to the connection between Benny's world view and Doane's theory of televisual viewing.

4 For an extended reading of *Benny's Video* within the framework of Baudrillard's philosophy, see Mattias Frey (2002; 2006). Frey extends his vision to encompass Haneke's work in general in 'A Cinema of Disturbance: The Films of Michael Haneke in Context' (2003).

5 The body of academic writing on *Hidden* is already too vast to give a comprehensive list of articles here. One might point to the dossiers on the film in both *Framework* (see Price 2006) and *Screen* (see Ezra & Sillars 2007) as exemplifying the diversity of responses to the film, however.

6 Discussing *The Castle*, Haneke states that, 'My attitude is that TV can never really be any form of art because it serves audience expectations. I would not have dared to turn *The Castle* into a movie for the big screen; on TV, it's okay because it has different objectives' (in Cockrell 2006: 26).

7 The source material for Haneke's film, Elfriede Jelinek's *Die Klavierspielerin*, describes Erika's relationship to the television thus: 'Every fibre in Erika's body longs for her soft TV armchair behind a locked door ... This is her Never-Never Land, where nothing ends and nothing begins' (1989: 74).

8 The original quote comes from Umberto Eco, *Travels in Hyperreality* (1990).

9 The binary opposition that tends to dominate thinking about film and video, whereby the 'big-screen performance is marked as authentic, as representing bona fide cinema', and 'video is characterised not only as inauthentic and ersatz but also as a regrettable triumph of convenience over art that disturbs the communion between viewer and film and interferes with judgements of quality' (Klinger 2006: 2) is, as Klinger points out, a problematic one, which fails to account for phenomena such as the drive-in cinema. While the limits of this essay preclude a full examination of viewing Haneke's films in all their contexts (although I think it is safe to say that a drive-in is an unlikely exhibition space for his works), I am nonetheless aware that some reductionism is inherent to my argument.

10 One might think here of the scene in *Hidden* in which Pierrot is thought to have gone missing, which is dominated visually and aurally by a diegetic television showing news footage, to which his parents Georges and Anne remain oblivious.

11 Garrett Stewart offers an intriguing – although perhaps overambitious – interpretation of the status of the analogue tapes in *Hidden*. Comparing them with the digital footage of Georges' television show, he argues that the 'home video' quality of the tapes 'with their streaked indications of tampered temporality, can be taken to assault the media professional as the clumsy return of a technological repressed'

(2007: 197–8). I would offer the rather less imaginative reading that they offer a point of contrast between home media and professional media, the latter being rather in advance of the former. It is not until the 2007 version of *Funny Games* that DVD becomes accepted into the home.

12   It is interesting to note, too, that subtle references to gaming – 'Player One, Next Level'/'You've failed' – appear, while the admonition that the action has not reached 'feature length' yet has also disappeared.

References

Beugnet, M. (2007) 'Blind spot', *Screen*, 48, 2, 227–31.
Cavell, S. (1971) *The World Viewed.* New York: Viking Press.
Cieutat, M. (2000) 'Entretien avec Michael Haneke: La fragmentation du regard', *Positif*, 478, 22–9.
Cockrell, E. (2006) 'Michael Haneke', *Guardian International Film Guide 2006.* London: Guardian Books, 23–8.
Doane, M. A. (1990) 'Information, Crisis, Catastrophe', in P. Mellencamp (ed.) *Logics of Television: Essays in Cultural Criticism.* Indianapolis: Indiana University Press, 222–39.
Ezra, E. and J. Sillars (2007) 'The *Caché* Dossier', *Screen*, 48, 2, 211–49.
Falcon, R. (1998) 'The discreet harm of the bourgeoisie', *Sight & Sound*, 8, 5, 10–12.
Frey, M. (2002) 'Supermodernity, Capital, and Narcissus: The French Connection to Michael Haneke's *Benny's Video*', *Cinetext*. On-line. Available at: http://cinetext. philo.at/magazine/frey/bennys_video.pdf (accessed 10 October 2008).
_____ (2003) 'Michael Haneke', *Senses of Cinema*. On-line. Available at: http://www. sensesofcinema.com/contents/directors/03/haneke.html (accessed 10 October 2008).
_____ (2006) '*Benny's Video, Caché*, and the Desubstantiated Image', *Framework*, 47, 2, 30–6.
Haneke, M. (1992) 'Film als Katharsis', in F. Bono (ed.) *Austria (in)felix: Zum öster-reichischen Film der 80er Jahre.* Graz: Edition Blimp, 89.
_____ (2000) '*71 Fragments of a Chronology of Chance*: Notes to the Film', in W. Riemer (ed.) *After Postmodernism: Austrian Film and Literature in Transition.*Riverside, CA: Ariadne Press, 171–5.
Jelinek, E. (1989) *The Piano Teacher*, trans. J. Neugroshel. London: Serpent's Tail.
Klinger, B. (2006) *Beyond The Multiplex: Cinema, New Technologies, and The Home.* London and Berkeley: University of California Press.
Le Cain, M. (2003) 'Do the Right Thing: The Films of Michael Haneke', *Senses of Cinema*. On-line. Available at: http://www.sensesofcinema.com/contents/03/26/haneke.html (accessed 17 January 2008).
Mulvey, L. (2006) *Death 24x a Second: Stillness and the Moving Image.* London: Reaktion.

Peucker, B. (2000) 'Fragmentation and the Real: Michael Haneke's Family Trilogy', in W. Riemer (ed.) *After Postmodernism: Austrian Film and Literature in Transition*. Riverside, CA: Ariadne Press, 176–87.

Price, B. (ed.) (2006) 'Dossier on Michael Haneke', *Framework*, 47, 2, Fall, 5–36.

Prince, S. (1998) *Savage Cinema: Sam Peckinpah and the Rise of Ultraviolent Movies*. Austin: University of Texas Press.

Romney, J. (1999) *Notes to Funny Games*. Artificial Eye VHS release.

____ (2006) '*Hidden*', *Sight & Sound*, 16, 12, 64–5.

Sorfa, D. (2006) 'Uneasy Domesticity in the Films of Michael Haneke', *Studies in European Cinema*, 3, 2, 93–104.

Stewart, G. (2007) *Framed Time: Towards a Postfilmic Cinema*. Chicago: University of Chicago Press.

Wheatley, Catherine (2006a) 'Unseen/Obscene: The (Non)Framing of the Sexual Act in Michael Haneke's *La Pianiste*', in L. Bolton, G. Kimber, A. Lewis and M. Seabrook (eds) *Framed!* London: Peter Lang, 127–44.

____ (2006b) 'Ideology, Ethics and The Films of Michael Haneke', in B. G. Renzi and S. Rainey (eds) *From Plato's Cave to the Multiplex: Contemporary Film and Philosophy*. Newcastle: Cambridge Scholar's Press, 63–73.

____ (2006c) 'The masochistic fantasy made flesh: Michael Haneke's *La Pianiste* as melodrama', *Studies in French Cinema*, 6, 2, 117–27.

____ (2009) *Michael Haneke's Cinema: The Ethic of The Image*. Oxford: Berghahn.

CHAPTER TWO

Acting, Performance and the Bressonian Impulse in Haneke's Films

Ben McCann

In January 2008, the following announcement was published on www.naomi-watts. org, a fan site dedicated to the actress:

> Naomi Watts struggled to work under 'difficult' director Michael Haneke because he forced her to go against her acting instincts. The Australian actress teamed up with Haneke on new movie *Funny Games U.S.* and she soon discovered his reputation as a controlling taskmaster was wholly justified.
> She says, 'He's very connected to everything, Michael. He's very specific about every detail: when to pick up the glass, when to move it, when to say the line. It's a very difficult way for an actor to work. It feels like it goes against my instincts in a way, because you want to intuit your performance, discover it as you go. But I trust Michael. He's one of the directors everyone will remember. I wanted to learn from him, I wanted this new experience, as different and as awkward as it was.'[1]

Reading this, one cannot help but be reminded of similar fastidious working methods and attitudes towards actors employed by the French director Robert Bresson. Bresson inaugurated a radical approach to acting, whereby he rejected the conventional 'safe' co-ordinates of stars and the superficiality of psychologically-driven performance in order to 'strip away the layers of self-defence masquerading as self-projection' (Reader

2000: 5). Writing in *Notes on Cinematography*, his influential treatise on the film-making craft, Bresson renounced the conventional schemas of gesture and perform-ance, arguing instead that 'It is not a matter of acting "simple", or of acting "inward" but of not acting at all' (1977: 49). His performers – he called them 'models' rather than 'actors' – approached a degree-zero standard of acting by turning away from conventional mimetic acting to reinforce the sincerity of Bresson's desire to apprehend the existential reality of authentic human figures capable of 'eluding their own vigi-lance, capable of being divinely "themselves"' (1977: 36). This 'acting without acting' was achieved by working strictly with non-professional actors who were stripped of self-masquerading gestures and theatrical mannerisms, and who expressed themselves through a steady, unmelodic delivery of lines without inflection or emotion. The move-ments of the 'models' were strictly controlled by Bresson – walking from point A to point B necessitated a precise number of steps; the angle of a tilted head or a turned wrist was mathematically calibrated – and performers in a Bresson film would only ever be given their own lines shortly before filming began, and never a complete overview of the script. While such performance practices are relatively common in contemporary cinema, they are generally employed either to encourage the emergence of a natu-ralistic performance married to a wider search for 'truth' and emotional integrity or to showcase the particular perfectionism of individual directors.[2] For Bresson's actors, on the other hand, this utter yielding of motion to their director limits the intention and purpose of their action to one single point in time and space, or, more simply, 'life'. He writes 'models who have become automatic (everything weighed, measured, timed, repeated ten, twenty times) and are then dropped in the middle of the events in your film – their relations with the objects and the persons around them will be *right*, because they will not be *thought*' (1977: 12; emphasis in original). This paring away is emblematic, then, not just of Bresson's visual and narrative schemas – once described by Susan Sontag as 'cold, remote, overintellectualised, geometrical' (1967: 179) – but also of his approach to his actors. François Truffaut described Bresson's treatment of actors as 'holding them back from acting "dramatically", from adding emphasis, forcing them to abstract from their "art". He achieves this by killing their will, exhausting them with an endless number of repetition and takes, by almost hypnotising them' (1978: 192–3). Truffaut recognised that for Bresson, performance is not an ostentatious projection of physical or vocal aptitudes, but instead the steady incorporation of a series of heavily choreographed movements that the audience would interpret as the film progressed.

This chapter will suggest how, in his emphasis on performance and gesture, Michael Haneke incorporates Bresson's ideas on the status of performance into his films. Whereas Haneke's oeuvre is generally analysed in terms of its cool *mise-en-scène* (compositional austerity, absence of non-diegetic music, anonymous tracking shots), its elliptical and fragmentary narratives, its provocative engagement with the televisual/ cinematic apparatus, and its nihilistic appraisal of contemporary European society, understanding the complexities of acting and gesture in Haneke's films are impor-tant because performance is frequently the site onto which his thematic concerns are projected. Haneke states that he tries 'to make anti-psychological films with charac-ters who are less characters than projection surfaces for the sensibilities of the viewer;

blank spaces force the spectator to bring his own thoughts and feelings to the film. Because that is what makes the viewer open for the sensitivity of the character' (quoted in Donner 1993: 35). He offers up de-psychologised and de-subjectivised characters whose actions and motivations cannot be easily explained, precisely because those performance registers that encourage identification (close-ups, voice-image matches, improvisation, self-expression) are traditionally absent in Haneke's films. As Libby Saxton suggests, Haneke's 'traumatised, vulnerable protagonists are often driven by a desire to forge new connections and a search for new forms of intimacy' (2008: 86). Saxton's optimistic appraisal finds its clearest indication in climactic performative gestures – a man saves a child from self-immolation in *Le temps du loup* (*The Time of the Wolf*, 2003), a deaf boy mimes a bird fluttering skyward in *Code inconnu: Récit incomplet de divers voyages* (*Code Unknown: Incomplete Tales of Several Journeys*, 2000) – which recall similarly Bressonian 'transcendental' actions at the end of *Pickpocket* (1959), when Michel unexpectedly kisses Jeanne through the prison bars and *Quatre nuits d'un rêveur* (*Four Nights of a Dreamer*, 1971), where Marthe walks away with her lover and Jacques retreats to his artist's studio.

'I am, of course, a fan of Bresson ... I think he's the *ne plus ultra*', proclaimed Haneke in an interview (Eisenman 2008).[3] This admiration for Bresson has been consistently revealed in interviews with Haneke: in 1993, he lauded Bresson's 'truthfulness' alongside Andrei Tarkovsky, Michelangelo Antonioni and John Cassavetes (in Nevers 1993: 68); his 1998 essay for a retrospective on Bresson praised the director for his 'absolute unity of content and form' (1998b: 553); and when *Sight & Sound* polled directors in 2002 for their Top Ten films, Haneke began his own list with two Bresson works, *Au hasard Balthazar* (1966) and *Lancelot du lac* (*Lancelot of the Lake*, 1974).[4] Trace elements of Bresson's style permeate Haneke's work: from the emotional detachment and unwillingness to psychologise and the focus on isolated individuals and understated relationships, to the pared-down yet painstaking visual detail and the minimising of narrative causality. When Anthony Lane admits that watching a Bresson film feels 'like a pupil approaching the principal's door, wondering what crimes I may have committed and how I must answer for them' (1999: 82), he might well be referring to Haneke: the ascetic naturalism and stark visual style favoured by Bresson has been adopted and modulated by Haneke throughout his career, explicitly placing Haneke within a community of modernist filmmakers that begins with Bresson, Antonioni and Jean-Luc Godard and continues through to Jean-Marie Straub, Danièle Huillet and Chantal Akerman. Broadly speaking, these filmmakers all display an aversion to traditional cinematic narrative properties such as identification, transparency, goal-oriented protagonists and the restoration of equilibrium. Instead, they seek to imbricate the binary opposites of these values (narrative opacity, multiple protagonists, open-ended conclusions) into their film narratives, not just as a counter-strategy to the dominant codes and conventions of mainstream Hollywood cinema, but also as a means of foregrounding the potential of contemporary cinema to express narratives of fragmentation and ambiguity that move away from the certainties of coherence and totality. Thus, Richard Roud's appraisal of Bresson's *Pickpocket* – that we 'must make the connections; we participate in the final meaning of the film' (1980: 148) – is exemplified in Haneke's own thoughts on narrative ambiguity and uncertainty: 'I can lead a character in a story in such a way that the sum of his behaviour does not give sufficient explanation for his decisions. The audience will have to find one' (in Engelberg 1999: 34). In *Code Unknown* and *The Time of the Wolf*, Haneke's use of the long take, the refusal to generate character identification through the close-up, and the interstitial cuts to black allegorise an approach to storytelling that rejects reductive interpretation or facile moralising. This in turn has implications for both films' acting and performance praxis: the reduced camera movement and obscure chronology in *Code Unknown* and the disorientating visual palette of *The Time of the Wolf* postpone emotional involvement and dictate that the nominal stars – Juliette Binoche and Isabelle Huppert – be incorporated into a de-subjectivising visual and narrative framework in which no single person is privileged.[5]

It is perhaps in their treatment of actors that the affinities between Bresson and Haneke most evidently converge. *Notes on Cinematography* contains numerous pronouncements on acting and performance that reverberate across Haneke's films. Bresson wrote that film can be a true art 'because in it the author takes fragments of reality and arranges them in such a way that their juxtaposition transforms them … each shot is like a word, meaning nothing by itself … [it] is given its meaning by its context' (quoted in Sontag 1967: 185). Hence the repetition in Bresson's films of shots of feet, legs, stairs, hands, glances, wheels, doors and doorknobs that reveal fragments of a world connected through the interaction of his characters and their movements between, through and across places. These insertions of quotidian ephemera are not designed to depict naturalistic behaviour, for truthfulness cannot be intensified or captured merely by recording things. Rather, as the camera frames these gestures and movements, the protagonists' soul is fathomed. In *Au Hasard Balthazar*, a girl reveals her change of feelings for her childhood sweetheart by imperceptibly moving her hand away from his while they sit on a bench; in *Pickpocket*, the camera focuses fetishistically upon hands as they slip into pockets and remove wallets; *Un condamné à mort s'est éschappé ou Le vent souffle où il veut* (*A Man Escaped*, 1956) is replete with multiple close-ups of hands that refrain from intercutting with a shot of Fontaine's face. This decision to back away from a psychological approach coupled with the rejection of panoramic or wide shots to locate action and spatially anchor the spectator to a recognisable environment epitomises Bresson's 'anti-cinema' and his abrogation of conventional performance praxis. It is for this reason that Haneke admires Bresson; for his unremitting omission of 'the pretence of any kind of wholeness, even in the depiction of people. Torso and limbs come together for only scant moments, are separated, are treated like and at the mercy of objects, the face is one part among many, an immobile, expressionless icon of melancholy' (Haneke 1998b: 559).

The passivity of the protagonists and the heightened importance of the close-up on body parts are thoroughly amplified at the start of *Der siebente Kontinent* (*The Seventh Continent*, 1989). Haneke reveals in partial and fragmented ways the mind-numbing repetitiveness of middle-class existence by showing ritualistic gestures that focus on hands making coffee, tying shoes, reaching for toast and cleaning teeth. These actions reinforce the psychological paralysis at the core of the film and emphasise the de-subjectivised status of human interaction. Later on, as the family prepare for suicide, Haneke again focuses on hands – money is flushed away, photographs are ripped and the fish tank is smashed – and continues to film these actions with the same resolute objectivity as the earlier mundane acts of domesticity. Tactility, here in conjunction with static compositions and a flattened-out image, effects a deeper connection in the surrounding environment, but also – through the lack of any identificatory presence – suppresses the imposition of a facile, expository psychological realism that would conventionally seek to explain or interpret.

Just as faces in Bresson's films epitomise 'the extreme of impassivity, their materiality one of non-intervention, their sensuality undeniable and unchanging, frozen amid a quiet frenzy of signals and actions' (Thompson 1998), so too does Haneke's work insist upon micro-gestures. Bresson and Haneke seek both to instigate a more immediate and deeper response to their films by concentrating on facial movements, and also to elicit more truthful renditions of particular emotions by imposing upon their actors a more rigorous performance style at odds with a more customary demonstrative or mannered approach. Writing on *Caché* (*Hidden*, 2005), Philip French (2006) praises Daniel Auteuil and Juliette Binoche's skill of 'expressing their emotional upheaval through the slight movement of an eye or the flicker of a lip', and Helen Macallan and Andrew Plain (2007) note how Auteuil's gestures 'reveal his suppressed anxiety and ... belie his otherwise impassive countenance'. In both cases, it is the physicality of the body rather than the vocality of the voice that is privileged, with micro-movements functioning as modes of communication that bypass an excessive reliance upon performance mannerisms and learned technique.

This truthfulness encapsulated in micro-gestures is frequently explored by Haneke, and can, like Bresson, lead towards a near-sadistic treatment of his actors. The intruders in *Funny Games* (1997) declare that they are after 'the truth', and will not be satisfied 'until they have replaced the contented smiles of the bourgeois family with twisted grimaces and eyes reddened and puffy from crying' (Vicari 2006). Likewise, in his treatment of Binoche's Anne in *Code Unknown*, Haneke recalls Bresson's thoughts on his models that the 'thing that matters is not what they show me but what they hide from me and, above all, *what they do not suspect is in them*' (Bresson 1977: 2; emphasis in original). Anne is a film actress, and the offscreen director at her audition wants to break her down using a succession of coercive tactics not dissimilar from those put forth by Bresson. 'Show me your true face. Not your lies or tricks. A true expression', he says. Here the role of director and sadist align, with an insistence on debilitating repetition and the stripping away of layers in order to extract a more 'truthful' performance. Justin Vicari (2006) suggests that such strategies are all part of Haneke's rationale; that we have become so inured to consensus and have experienced a deficiency in personal identity, that we 'must be broken down still further, until [we] remember what humanity is, at an exact distance from which [we] can become aware of what is lost'.[6]

Haneke subverts stars in his films, denying audiences the chance to 'bask in their starshine' (Matthews 2003: 65). Although his career can be divided into two parts – the Austrian films from 1989–97 featuring lesser-known actors and the post-2000 shift towards more trenchant critiques of European society starring distinguished French actors – the performance registers across both periods remain the same. Such strategies are fundamental for Haneke, for they are indicative of a director who refuses to pander to audience expectations. Alongside his provocative visual style, his sustained critique of a duplicitous mass media, and what he perceives as the frustrating and alienating effects of contemporary existence, Haneke also critiques and defamiliarises our common notions of 'stardom', with its attendant forms of identification and sympathy. Rather than foregrounding his stars, or at the very least privileging them as the key players in the narrative, Haneke 'tempers the audience's ability to project anything onto a figure laden with so many associations' (Frey 2003). Yet, if his Austrian films employed performance registers that were appropriate to his own formal experiments in modernism and reminiscent of Bresson's filmic language (refuting pleasure, distancing the spectator from the cinematic image, forcing a direct engagement with the film's content), it might initially seem inevitable that Haneke's post-2000 career would employ stars in quite different ways. After all, along with their more complex subject-matter – immigration, multiculturalism, post-colonialism and the implications of post-apocalyptic breakdown reframed as 'nationally-specific concerns within a transnational enquiry' (Saxton 2008: 85) – the films were generously financed through co-productions with French backing, were successfully marketed to an international audience and starred such high-profile French actors such as Daniel Auteuil, Juliette Binoche, Annie Girardot, Isabelle Huppert and Benoît Magimel.[7] Whereas the earlier films negotiate the tensions between narrative and performance by relying on actors that are not immediately recognisable to a non-Austrian or non-German viewer, Haneke's accomplishment with his recent films has been to remain consistent to his aesthetic and philosophical impulses without necessarily diluting them for the sake of placating audiences accustomed to seeing particular actors successfully negotiating particular narrative trajectories. Most notably, film stars bring with them both star quality (charisma and unique personal characteristics that create a strong on- and offscreen presence which is often embraced by audiences as a separate, mythic persona) and craft (the ability to embody distinctly different characters through the use of strong acting techniques), two properties to which Bresson remained resolutely indifferent, and to which Haneke also has remained impassive.[8]

So an inevitable tension permeates Haneke's later work: how to employ stars without allowing the star to assume a greater role than the one planned? The economic importance of stars to the success of a film has been a long-standing one, for, as a valuable commodity, they play a crucial role in the marketing, promotion and exhibition of a film. Consequently, the pairing of Auteuil and Binoche in *Hidden* becomes an integral component of the film's investment strategy. Their presence, as much as Haneke's 'name-above-the-title', coupled with the Paris setting, the international film festival exposure, the widespread critical acclaim and the enigmatic narrative, mark the film out as a sophisticated blend of star appeal and art-house credentials. Furthermore, Haneke's move towards a pan-European star system has gone hand in hand with his appropriation of a carefully modulated genre cinema. Reviews of Haneke's recent films attempt to categorise them into genres: *La Pianiste* (*The Piano Teacher*, 2001) has been categorised as melodrama, 'cinema of excess' and 'the free-fall movie'[9], *The Time of the Wolf* as a disaster and science-fiction film, while *Hidden* and *Funny Games U.S.* (2007) explicitly draw on the thriller format and the 'domestic invasion' genre respectively.

Yet any appropriation of genre by Haneke would run counter to the aesthetic and ethical principles he holds dear, and would repudiate his oft-cited remark that his films are 'an appeal for a cinema of insistent questions instead of false (because too quick) answers, for clarifying distance in place of violating closeness, for provocation and dialogue instead of consumption and consensus' (1992: 89). Haneke is not adopting a generic approach to filmmaking, nor is he comfortable working within the limiting conceptual thresholds of genre. Instead, he is mobilising and subverting the narrow properties of genre by employing a star and immediately engaging the audience's attention in order to short-circuit the need for narrative exposition or an all-too-easy rationalisation of events. Stars for Haneke do not signpost traditional generic attributes but instead rather they condense the emotional effects of genre, which leaves Haneke free to draw on generic structures without making the presence of such structures overly explicit. In *The Time of the Wolf*, for example, as well as Isabelle Huppert, there are a number of other recognisable faces from French arthouse productions, such as Maurice Bénichou, Patrice Chéreau, Béatrice Dalle, Daniel Duval and Olivier Gourmet. Their presence in a narrative overwhelmed by muted iconography and catastrophic resonances removes any vestiges of residual stardom. Stars are of no importance in *The Time of the Wolf*; in opposition to the triumphalism and collective spirit of the will that characterises humanity's responses to disaster and destruction in mainstream American cinema, the presence of Huppert and Dalle and our attendant identification with them is subverted by a *mise-en-scène* of abjection that suggests that the film's unidentified apocalypse is 'beyond the control of the human beings who are its victims, a fate too immense to be altered by one figure on-screen' (Orr 2004: 106).[10] Close-ups are minimised, dialogue is excised or eliminated, and Jürgen Jürges's cinematography makes use only of available natural light, reducing movements and gestures to flickering shadows. Just as in *Benny's Video* (1992) and *Funny Games*, where Haneke challenged audience preconceptions about genre filmmaking and their expectations of specific narratives, *The Time of the Wolf* destabilises the recognisable generic topography of the disaster genre and 'cuts straight through it to the dirty, complex human reality at its core' (Bingham 2004). Thus, Haneke is making genre films with star actors, but entirely on his own terms. With its formal rigour, its thematic austerity and its wallowing in an anti-stardom inconsistent with the co-ordinates of the 'disaster film', Haneke shares Bresson's disinterest in the rigid parameters of genre. Writing about *A Man Escaped*, André Bazin argues that the film's inherent lack of 'dramatic geometry' and a 'systematic indifference to time and space' (1997: 31) undermines the very feelings of suspense that a 'prison break' genre film should generate. For both Bazin and Bingham, these films are examples of anti-genre cinema of the most exacting kind.

As the nominal star of *Code Unknown* and *Hidden*, Binoche is the ideal paradigm of a newly-emergent European star system. She has 'succeeded in going international while remaining identified as an auteur cinema star' (Vincendeau 2000: 241) and, by dint of collaborations with non-French auteurs like Krzysztof Kieślowski, Abbas Kiarostami and Hou Hsiao-Hsien, epitomises the dynamic transnational flexibility of current filmmaking practice. Yet for all this emphasis on Binoche in the promotional material of both films, and despite Haneke's own appreciation of Binoche as an actress (he has stated that her roles in both films were written specifically for her), Haneke shares Bresson's own disdain for conventional screen acting. He is influenced by a performance convention that originates in *Notes on Cinematography*: 'Star System: Makes nothing of the immense power of attraction which belongs to the new and unforeseen. Film after film, subject after subject, confronting the same faces that one cannot believe in' (Bresson 1977: 54). Accordingly, in both of Binoche's films for Haneke, the combination of that 'cool exterior [and] intensity of passion' (Vincendeau 2000: 242) upon which her stardom has consistently been predicated is undermined by Haneke's editing and staging practices. In *Hidden*, for example, she is frequently filmed in an unflattering way, with little or no make-up, distressed hair and wearing dresses that frequently seem several sizes too large for her. Whereas previous directors like Léos Carax and Kieślowski conveyed Binoche's beauty through the sustained use of the close-up, Haneke rejects lingering close-ups, framing her instead in medium-close or medium-long shot, and often at awkward angles to other characters around her.

Two images used for the publicity poster and DVD cover jacket of *Code Unknown* also subvert expectations of Binoche's luminosity. Although her face features prominently on both poster and cover, the former captures Binoche's face severely out-of-focus, as if being viewed through frosted glass. It is clearly Binoche (those sculpted cheekbones give her away), but this divested representation of her radiance and recognisable femininity interpolates allegorical resonances of opacity and the manipulability of seductive images that reverberate throughout Haneke's work. Likewise, the DVD cover shows an image of her in the swimming pool, looking at the boy about to fall from the roof. Her mouth is frozen, gaping wide, emitting a silent scream. Whereas a close-up of Binoche's face would traditionally lure spectators into consuming a particular film, Haneke subverts its appeal by instead representing the face as a site of indeterminacy and ambiguity.

This is not to deny the impressive acting accomplishments of Binoche in both films. As befits an actress trained in the traditions of European theatre and art-house cinema, Binoche is adept at the 'underplaying of emotion in order, paradoxically, to get a real sense of it' (Macallan & Plain 2007). In *Code Unknown*, when Georges' father picks at specks of dust and rearranges breadcrumbs on the tablecloth, Binoche reaches towards the older man, takes his arm, and holds his hand. The sequence hints that meaningful human interaction can be initiated through tiny signals of rapprochement and offers a glimmer of hope within the dominant emotional austerity of the rest of the film. Instead, Binoche's display of tentative empathy here typifies her own acting style; one of 'extreme mobility and extreme stillness' (Vincendeau 2000: 249) that Haneke exploits and subverts.

In contrast to Binoche's divested stardom in *Code Unknown* and *Hidden*, Huppert's star persona is foregrounded in *The Piano Teacher* through her acting ability and the marshalling of almost imperceptible micro-movements. Her acting style – a mixture of distance and emotion – is an important part of her allure, and had already been impressively showcased in richly modulated performances in *La Dentellière* (*The Lace-maker*, 1975), *Heaven's Gate* (1980) and *Madame Bovary* (1991); and the unusualness of her physicality – red hair, freckles, pale skin, upturned upper lip – coalesce to form 'a cryptic face, one that seem[s] to be absent as it [is] present, as coolly distant as it [is] burningly intimate' (Turk 2007: 161). Her acting instincts rely on strategies of subtraction rather than addition, for the blankness of her face means that it can be transformed endlessly. Two statements in particular reveal a kinship with Haneke: Huppert has stated, 'I never feel I am playing characters … I play certain states, certain ranges of emotions, certain feelings. The contours of a character are something very vague' (quoted in Rose 2006) and 'The essential rule for me is the director … I tend to be guided. I don't mind at all being an instrument' (quoted in Vincendeau 2006: 39). In both instances, Huppert's favoured performative registers converge with the techniques employed by Haneke, which in turn links back to Bresson's strategies with his 'models'. There is a fearlessness and a risk-taking impulse in Huppert's approach to acting that is aligned with Haneke's own explorations of the abject so that, far from using Huppert in a bid to encourage emotional engagement, Haneke colludes with Huppert's illegibility, divesting her star persona and clinching the emotional exigencies of the narrative.[11]

Although much of the complexity of Huppert's performance in *The Piano Teacher* comes from Haneke's choice of shots and his compositional framing, she brings a range of expressive gestures and body language to the role. As Richard Combs writes:

> Isabelle Huppert, in probably Haneke's first star performance (Juliette Binoche in *Code Unknown* [2000] only partially excepted), now commands an extraor-dinary expressive range through features that seem as placid (passive?) as ever. In barely perceptibly but frightening ways, they will tighten into a rictus, whether to dole out punishment to her pupils at the piano or vent her ulti-mate anger on herself. (2002: 27)

In *The Piano Teacher*, Haneke's sustained use of medium- and close-up shots serve to frame her within the diegesis and create a correlative between the claustrophobia of the Viennese salons and her domestic life and the frigidity of her personality. Yet the close-up – that most constricting and controlling of cinematic devices – also func-tions subversively. Far from colluding with spectatorial expectations to present unme-diated access to Huppert's star persona, Haneke frustrates audience identification with the star's image by employing repeated close-ups of the back of Huppert's head. As Libby Saxton argues, these compositional strategies accord with Haneke's continuing thematic and formal preoccupations, 'frustrating our desire for psychological insights [and] impeding visual contact with the bodies on the screen' (2008: 100).

To conclude, let us recall Haneke's admiration for *Au hasard Balthazar*: 'the donkey does not pretend to be sad or to suffer when life is hard on him – he does not cry, we cry for an icon of imposed forbearance, precisely because he is not like an actor peddling his ability to exteriorize emotion' (1998b: 554). Like Bresson before him, Haneke rejects

'Your models must not feel they are dramatic': the face and anti-stardom in Haneke

the emotional untruthfulness of 'Acting', seeking instead to foreground a performance praxis that prioritises almost invisible shifts in body language and what Gilles Deleuze calls 'all kinds of tiny local movements' (1986: 87). Yet, as Naomi Watts makes clear, the benefits of these minimalist procedures integrated into Haneke's working methods are not wholly unequivocal, not least because his attempts to generate an unembellished, unself-conscious acting style problematise the status of performance. Watts's experiences demonstrate how inevitable tensions arise when the austerity of a high-end European art-house gestural rhetoric collides with the psychologically-inflected, intuitive acting technique that has characterised American film acting for half a century, not least when the film in question is a shot-for-shot remake of the director's own film. Unlike Huppert, content to be the director's 'instrument' and prepared for a ceaseless deconstruction of her identity, or Binoche, skilled at negotiating both Hollywood genre and European art-house dynamics, Watts appears less attuned to the performative rigour Haneke demands of his actors. Moreover, in an era where stars are ever mindful of creating, refining and perpetuating their own image both off- and onscreen, Watts is understandably cautious about destabilising audience expectations of her, not least because her recent roles in *The Ring* (2002), *The Ring 2* (2005) and *King Kong* (2005) have each configured her as the 'Final Girl' confronting and overcoming the horrific and the abject.[12] Perhaps more pertinently, and in keeping with the Bresson/Haneke consonances, Watts's comments recall similar protestations made by the renowned stage actress Maria Casarès, who played Hélène in Bresson's *Les dames du Bois de Boulogne* (*The Ladies of the Bois de Boulogne*, 1945). In a television interview in 1958, she criticised Bresson: 'On the set he was a genuine tyrant ... He murdered us so sweetly, so politely ... When we entered the studio we abandoned everything that could resemble a life of our own, a personal will, in order to drag before our sweet tyrant ... a body, hands, and a voice that he had chosen' (quoted in Cunneen 2003: 41). Ultimately, for Haneke, like Bresson, the specificities and nuances of individual performance style matter little in a shared worldview that privileges the austere and the alienated. His frequent reluctance to explicate either his protagonists or his motivations is mapped onto the gestures and movements of his actors, so that the suppression of psychological realism and the adoption of an opaque aesthetic are mirrored in the tightly-controlled performances. Actors in Haneke's work, then, are required to negotiate complex trajectories; to essentially de-dramatise themselves, to work in unfamiliar or punishing ways and correct their own instinctive or intuitive sensibilities while simultaneously serving the demands of fragmentary and de-psychologised narratives, adhering finally to a suitably Bressonian invocation: 'YOUR MODELS MUST NOT FEEL THEY ARE DRAMATIC' (1977: 44).

Notes

1   'Watts' tough time with taskmaster Haneke', posted by Jess on 14 January 2008, http://www.naomiwatts.org/archives.php?subaction=showfull&id=1200313454 &archive=1201845891&start_from=&ucat=4& (accessed 30 September 2008)

2   I am thinking of the likes of Mike Leigh, whose actors improvise their performances through pre-production workshop rehearsals, Woody Allen, who only ever gives his actors their own lines, and never the full script, and Stanley Kubrick, who asked Shelley Duvall for 127 takes of a single scene in *The Shining* (1980).

3   In his 1998 Bresson retrospective essay, Haneke recalled the first time he saw *Au hasard Balthazar* (1966) at university: 'The film crashed into our seminar like a UFO fallen from a distant planet, and divided us up into fanatic supporters and fierce opponents' (1998b: 553).

4   The other films were Tarkovsky's *Mirror* (*Zerkalo*, 1975), Pier Paolo Pasolini's *Salò o le 120 giornate di Sodoma* (*Salò, or the 120 Days of Sodom*, 1975), Luis Buñuel's *El ángel exterminador* (*The Exterminating Angel*, 1962), Charles Chaplin's *The Gold Rush* (1925), Alfred Hitchcock's *Psycho* (1960), John Cassavetes' *A Woman Under the Influence* (1974), Roberto Rossellini's *Germania anno zero* (*Germany Year Zero*, 1948) and Antonioni's *L'eclisse* (*The Eclipse*, 1962).

5   Of the 45 scenes in *Code Unknown*, Binoche appears in only 14.

6   Binoche has recently exhibited a series of 34 sets of paintings at the BFI South-
    bank in London depicting a director that she has worked with and a self-portrait
    of a character that she played in that director's film. Her self-portrait as Anne in
    Hidden 'shows the eyes lowered, perhaps deeply hurt, ashamed by the lies and
    evasions of her character's husband' (Bradshaw 2008b).

7   According to Haneke, 'I think that the co-production represents the only chance
    that Europe has in film. Beyond the diversity and specificity of each country and
    film production, it offers the possibility of working together to create films and to
    oppose the American cultural imperialism' (2005).

8   Daniel Auteuil's role in *Hidden* came at a time when he was primarily known to
    international audiences as a comedic actor in films such as *Après vous* (*After You*,
    2003), *La Doublure* (*The Valet*, 2006), *Mon meilleur ami* (*My Best Friend*, 2006)
    and *L'Invité* (*The Dinner Guest*, 2007).

9   See Wheatley (2006c), Grønstad (2008) and Orr (2004). For John Orr, the 'free-
    fall movie' is a form of narrative that 'stresses ontological descent and nausea'
    (2004: 103).

10 The appearance of Dalle in particular is startling, not least because it reminds
    audiences of her unbridled depiction of female sexuality in *37°2 le matin* (*Betty
    Blue*, 1986), a 'star-making' role that simultaneously defined and destroyed her.

11 Huppert admitted in an interview with *Cahiers du cinéma* that Haneke often required
    her to do 45 takes for one scene. Huppert concludes the interview by stating that she
    turned down the role of Anna in the original *Funny Games* because she thought the
    script too manipulative. Haneke 'pushed the exercise so far that the characters exit
    the fiction and enter into an experimental process, which was extremely demanding
    to watch as well as to act' (Huppert in Frodon 2005: 30).

12 This is not to question, of course, Watts's impressive acting abilities. Her repertoire
    covers 'women in terror' roles (*The Ring*, *King Kong*), prestige auteur-driven work
    (*21 Grams* (2004), *Eastern Promises* (2007)) and, most memorably, as Betty in
    Mulholland Dr. (2001), whose audition for the film-within-a-film has become the
    'Rosetta Stone for the mysteries of star acting in Hollywood' (Toles 2004: 13).

References

Bazin, A. (1997) '*Un condamné à mort s'est échappé*', in *Robert Bresson: Eloge*. Milan and
    Paris: Mazzotta and Cinémathèque Française, 30–2.
Bingham, A. (2004) 'Life, or something like it: Michael Haneke's *Der siebente Konti-
    nent* (*The Seventh Continent*, 1989)', *Kinoeye*, 4, 1. On-line. Available at: http://
    www.kinoeye.org/04/01/bingham01_no2.php (accessed 17 January 2008).
Bradshaw, P. (2008b) 'Portraits of Binoche', *Guardian*, 5 September. On-line.
    Available at: http://www.guardian.co.uk/film/filmblog/2008/sep/05/
    binochepaintingsatbfisouth (accessed 11 November 2008).
Bresson, R. (1977) *Notes on Cinemtatography*. Trans. J. Griffin. New York: Urizon
    Books.
Combs, R. (2002) 'Living in Never-Never Land', *Film Comment*, 38, 2, 26–8.

Cunneen, J. (2003) *Robert Bresson: A Spiritual Style in Film*. New York and London: Continuum.

Deleuze, G. (1986) *Cinema 1: The Movement Image*. Trans. H. Tomlinson and B. Hebberjam. London: Athlone Press.

Donner, W. (1993) 'Das Gegenteil von Hollywood', *Tip*, 3 June, 34–9.

Eisenman, P. (2008) 'The Eisenman-Haneke Tapes', *Iconeye*, 55, January. On-line. Available at: http://www.iconeye.com/index.php?option=com_content&view=article&id=3062:the-eisenman-haneke-tapes (accessed 19 September 2008).

Engelberg, A. (1999) 'Nine Fragments about the films of Michael Haneke', *Filmwaves*, 6, 4, 32–4.

French, P. (2006) '*Hidden*', *Observer*, 29 January. On-line. Available at: http://www.guardian.co.uk/film/2006/jan/29/philipfrench1 (accessed 11 November 2008).

Frey, M. (2003) 'Michael Haneke', *Senses of Cinema*. On-line. Available at: http://www.sensesofcinema.com/contents/directors/03/haneke.html (accessed 11 November 2008).

Frodon, J.-M. (2005) 'Un pacte de croyance', *Cahiers du cinéma*, 603, 28–30.

Grønstad, A. (2008) 'Downcast Eyes: Michael Haneke and the Cinema of Intrusion', *Nordicom Review*, 29, 1, 133–44.

Haneke, M. (1992) 'Film als Katharsis', in F. Bono (ed.) *Austria (in)felix: Zum österreichischen Film der 80er Jahre*. Graz: Edition Blimp, 89.

_____ (1998b) 'Terror and Utopia of Form, Addicted to Truth: A Film Story about Robert Bresson's *Au Hasard Balthasar*', in J. Quandt (ed.) *Robert Bresson*. Ontario: Wilfred Laurier Press, 551–9.

_____ (2005) 'Family is Hell and So is the World', *Bright Lights Film Journal*. On-line. Available at: http://www.brightlightsfilm.com/50/hanekeiv.htm (accessed 11 November 2008).

Lane, A. (1999) 'Robert Bresson: A Man Entranced', *The New Yorker*, 25 January, 82–6.

Macallan, H. and A. Plain (2007) '*Hidden*'s Disinherited Children', *Senses of Cinema*. On-line. Available at: http://www.sensesofcinema.com/contents/07/42/hidden.html (accessed 11 November 2008).

Matthews, P. (2003) '*The Time of the Wolf*', *Sight & sound*, 13, 11, 64–5.

Nevers, C. (1993) 'L'oeil de Benny', *Cahiers du cinéma*, 466, 66–8.

Orr, J. (2004) 'Stranded: stardom and the free-fall movie in French cinema, 1985–2003', *Studies in French Cinema*, 4, 2, 103–11.

Reader, K. (2000) *Robert Bresson*. Manchester and New York: Manchester University Press.

Rose, S. (2006) 'Unspeakable acts', *Guardian*, 16 November. On-line. Available at: http://www.guardian.co.uk/film/2006/nov/16/1 (accessed 8 June 2010).

Roud, R. (1980) *Cinema: A Critical Dictionary*. London: Secker & Warburg.

Saxton, L. (2008) 'Close Encounters with Distant Suffering: Michael Haneke's Disarming Visions', in K. Ince (ed.) *Five Directors: Auteurism from Assayas to Ozon*. Manchester: Manchester University Press, 84–111.

Sontag, S. (1967 [1964]) 'Spiritual Style in the films of Robert Bresson', in *Against Interpretation, and other essays*. London: Eyre and Spottiswoode, 177–95.

Thompson, R. J. (1998) *'Pickpocket'*, *Senses of Cinema*. On-line. Available at: http://www.sensesofcinema.com/contents/cteq/00/7/pickpocket.html (accessed 11 November 2008).

Toles, G. (2004) 'Auditioning Betty in *Mulholland Drive'*, *Film Quarterly*, 58, 1, 2–13.

Truffaut, F. (1978) *The Films in My Life*. New York: Simon and Schuster.

Turk, E. B. (2007) 'Isabelle Huppert; or, The Gallic Valkyrie Who Bewitched Brooklyn', *Camera Obscura*, 65, 22, 2, 158–63.

Vicari, J. (2006) 'Films of Michael Haneke: Utopia of fear', *Jump Cut*. On-line. Available at: http://www.ejumpcut.org/archive/jc48.2006/Haneke/index.html (accessed 11 November 2008).

Vincendeau, G. (2000) *Stars and Stardom in French Cinema*. London and New York: Continuum.

_____ (2006) 'Isabelle Huppert: The Big Chill', *Sight & Sound*, 16, 12, 36–9.

Wheatley, C. (2006c) 'The masochistic fantasy made flesh: Michael Haneke's *La Pianiste* as melodrama', *Studies in French Cinema*, 6, 2, 117–27.

CHAPTER THREE

Ethical Violence: Suicide as Authentic Act in the Films of Michael Haneke

Lisa Coulthard

Known for the brutal psychological and physical violence of films such as *Benny's Video* (1992) and the two versions of *Funny Games* (1997, 2007), Michael Haneke offers viewers critical and ironic documents of social disaffection, alienation and interpersonal abuse that resist easy absorption or consumption. Yet, although addressing the murder of children, bodily dismemberment, graphic suicide, rape, sadism and brutality, Haneke's films eschew the direct representation of explicit violence in favour of more subtle, minimalist and complex depictions. Manipulating sound, offscreen space and the long take, his films explore rather than expose and thus offer an analysis of violence that interrogates its complexity: violence in Haneke has many forms, functions and incarnations, and films such as *Der siebente Kontinent* (*The Seventh Continent*, 1989), *La Pianiste* (*The Piano Teacher*, 2001), *Caché* (*Hidden*, 2005) and *Benny's Video* are as much about questioning what constitutes violence as they are investigations into its manifestations, attractions or mediations. While violence shocks and erupts as a climactic event in Haneke films (the father's death at the beginning of *Le temps du loup* (*The Time of the Wolf*, 2003), the murder of the young girl in *Benny's Video* or the child in *Funny Games*, the suicide of Majid in *Hidden* or the murder/suicide in *71 Fragmente einer Chronologie des Zufalls* (*71 Fragments of a Chronology of Chance*, 1994)), it is never depicted as an isolated incident but is yoked to larger social, political and ethical issues. The estrangement of filmed or televised culture, the alienated nature and communication failures of late capitalist society, the mechanical and emotionally vacant functioning of the family unit or the hidden violence and paranoia of sexual and romantic relationships: these are the true concerns of Haneke's film violence.

As an integral component of this interrogation of violence, his films demand audience contemplation and active engagement as they manipulate generic referencing, narrational and formal structure and spectatorial positioning to both draw the audience in and alienate them from a position of full comprehension, sympathetic identification or unencumbered cinematic pleasure. Representing cruelty in its agonistic complexity and framing interpersonal abuse within the failures of capitalist, romantic or familial formations, Haneke's films thus foreground the connection of physical violence to ethical, political and philosophical concepts and debates. This ethical interrogation of violence is especially significant in his treatment of acts of self-abuse and suicide. To be more precise, I will argue that in the suicidal gestures or acts in films such as *The Seventh Continent*, *71 Fragments of a Chronology of Chance*, *Hidden*, *The Time of the Wolf* and *The Piano Teacher*, Haneke condenses his concerns regarding postmodern, late capitalist alienation and brutality into the singularly shattering act of self-destruction; further, when considered together, these depictions offer an ethics of suicide that can be aligned with the kind of revolutionary potential conceptualised by psychoanalyst Jacques Lacan as constitutive of what he terms the authentic 'Act'.

Developed most explicitly in his work on tragedy in *The Ethics of Psychoanalysis* (1986), Lacan's concept of the authentic act relies upon a theorisation of its potential for revolutionary or radical consequence. For Lacan, the ethical act is distinguished from ordinary violent action by its shattering impact: as 'Act', such a gesture is differentiated from the mere violence of a *passage à l'acte* insofar as it restructures the frameworks of the symbolic networks that organise subjectivity and, in so doing, ensures that the individual is forever changed in the act. For example, theorised with reference to *Antigone*, Lacan's notion of the act posits the significance of Antigone's monstrous, inexplicable and radical self-imposed social disengagement and suicide as a fundamentally ethical gesture. Antigone's actions lack rational sense in terms of either self-preservation or the well-being of the community: indeed, her insistence on the burial of her brother, regardless of consequence, shatters these terms of social conformity and cohesion. Instead, her act follows its own ruthless logic to a final conclusion that cannot be shifted or diverted: Antigone quite simply *must* bury her brother, there is no thought of punishment or outcomes, only a resolute, unyielding and almost mechanistic determination.

Further, although Lacan develops this idea apropos of Antigone and mentions Medea only in passing, it is clear that Euripides' tragic heroine is an equally illustrative model of the Lacanian authentic act, a detail that shifts its register into the explicitly violent. As an act, though, Medea's murder of her own children goes beyond mere homicide as she aims to eradicate not only what is most precious to Jason, but that which is most precious and essential to Medea herself. Echoing Medea's final words in Pier Paolo Pasolini's 1969 film version of the play, 'nothing is possible anymore', Jacques-Alain Miller notes that after this moment of murder, 'all words are useless, and she exits once and for all from the register, or the reign, of the signifier' (2000: 19). An ethical act intervening in and suspending the symbolic network of superegoistic forced choice (you are free to choose as long as it is the right choice), Medea's act restructures and reorients the possible. Moreover, because radical acts cannot be separated from subjectivity, Medea's act is one of self-erasure and subjective reorientation as well: as Miller notes, her 'whole self is in the act' (ibid.).

Thus, whether suicidal, murderous or simply extreme, the ethical act as such falls outside the realms of forced choice and instead intervenes in the symbolic order in a way that asserts the impossible, that forces the reorganisation and reconsideration of what is recognised as possible. Disjoined from the symbolic network of the big Other and exemplified by uncompromised desires, the authentic ethical act is thus both defiant and (self) destructive; it is by its nature outrageous and in it, the parameters of the ethical are reorganised.

But it is equally important to remember that authentic acts are non-pathological and non-psychologised; rather, as theorist Slavoj Žižek notes, in confronting the abyss of absolute freedom, these acts are carried out as obligations, they are rational acts, without passion or reflection: 'an act is not irrational; rather it creates its own (new) rationality. This is what Antigone accomplishes; this is the true consequence of her act. And this cannot be planned in advance – we have to take a risk, a step into the open, with no big Other to return our true message to us' (2004: 243). The authentic act is not an attempt to communicate – as Lacan and Žižek stress, it is not directed at an Other – but a rejection of the symbolic system that structures communication itself. This is why it is so radical and risky: it moves beyond the limit of what is achievable within the intersubjective, social world into an area of radical alterity (Medea, for example, is not merely letting Jason know she is upset, but is rather rendering all interaction unthinkable).

It is in this radical, unpathological and risky nature of the act that we can draw parallels to Haneke's depiction of violence generally and suicide in particular. Haneke insists on the anti-psychological nature of his films, a feature as evident in the objectified, distanced framing, lack of dialogue or introspection, as it is in the absent or at least unsettlingly muted emotionalism. Although dealing with intense psychological states (Erika Kohut's self-mutilation in *The Piano Teacher*, the family's decision to commit suicide in *The Seventh Continent*, the disavowed guilt of *Hidden* or the absolute and murderous frustration of *71 Fragments of a Chronology of Chance*), these films do not attempt explication or psychological insight. Haneke's films are about externalised depictions, the actions and consequences of violence, not psychological motivations. Indeed, overt emotional engagement is something to be questioned in his films. In *Benny's Video*, for example, Benny's murder of the girl and his final rejection of his parents' complicity are presented as dispassionate, detached and radically ambiguous acts – we are given no psychological insight, no remorse and no movement towards a recognition of guilt. In contrast, his father's dismemberment and disposal of the body is fraught with emotions, yet seems to be all the more morally suspect and perverse for this.

This coldness of emotionality is intimately tied to the investigation of communication and its failures in Haneke's films. In a brief film on the making of *The Time of the Wolf*, Haneke claims that refusing to communicate is a kind of terrorist gesture that activates violence, a hypothesis illustrated by the failures of intersubjectivity evident in his films. This breakdown of communication is most manifest in his 'glaciation trilogy' of *The Seventh Continent*, *Benny's Video* and *71 Fragments of a Chronology of Chance* (where the deadlocks of communication and violence are murderously coextensive), but it is equally apparent in the failures of familial, romantic or social communication that we note in *Hidden*, *The Time of the Wolf*, *The Piano Teacher*, *Code inconnu: Récit incomplet de divers voyages* (*Code Unknown: Incomplete Tales of Several Journeys*, 2000) and *Funny Games*.

But rather than considering these silences and communicative failures in light of the usual discourse of postmodern alienation, I would argue that in Haneke the question is one of a more fundamentally philosophical nature, especially as these breakdowns relate to the acts of terrorism and violence upon which he comments. In *Benny's Video*, for instance, although Benny's murder of the girl is inseparable from a discourse of the alienating effects of the video age, the critique is a much larger one: for Haneke, the world of late capitalism, its emphasis on accumulation, its mechanistic functioning and crushing bourgeois conformity are central to the failures of communication and he clearly establishes the isolating effects of this world narrationally, stylistically and thematically (the repeated motifs of capitalist exchange, for example). However, it is equally evident that the violence that results is not merely contained or explicated by these circumstances alone. In *Benny's Video*, as well as other Haneke films, the family, couple and other social groupings are not only inseparable from these forces but contain their own failures that persist even when these social structures are removed, as is evidenced in *The Time of the Wolf*. In this film, the Western, developed world is stripped of the wealth and goods that define and separate it and, as Haneke notes in interviews, that is the point: the film asks the question, what happens when the late capitalist, developed world is drained of the capital that allows it to maintain its distance from the so-called third world? The answer in this film is ambiguous at best as suicide, persistence of racial and class divisions and murder coexist with humane, collective acts of sacrifice, sharing or selflessness. It seems that in *The Time of the Wolf* removing capital or privilege changes very little; on its own, this excision is insufficient in reshaping the subjectivity and social formations that have been determined by Western capitalism.

But this is not to suggest, as many do, that Haneke's films are pessimistic. Rather, it is in negative potentiality that we see the utopic ethical force: in Haneke's film violence, each act is a result of small decisions, each changeable at every step and at every point there is a suggestion of the changes that could have resulted in a different outcome. For instance, taking true stories and working backwards from brutal end points, as Haneke does in *71 Fragments of a Chronology of Chance* and *The Seventh Continent*, does not explain or seek to gain full knowledge of motivations, but rather offers an examination of the minute details, the measured signs of the breakdown of social structures and the slow dawning of the lack of personal fulfilment. Although acts of brutal self-destruction occur in both films, these are not presented as inevitable outcomes. In Haneke, conclusions are never certain: *Hidden*, for example, addresses guilt but significantly the film does not dwell on the culpability of past actions or events but rather on their present manifestations. The traumatic event that returns is less important than the way in which the characters confront, cope with or fail to correct past wrongs today.

It is significant that this possibility for correction always relates back to the issue of communication. In *71 Fragments of a Chronology of Chance, The Piano Teacher* or *Hidden*, for example, the violence that erupts is at core a kind of failed communication; in each film, the mounting frustration of this failure is palpable as suspicion, aggression and secrecy dominate all human interactions. Seemingly polite exchanges mask perceptible tensions and hostilities, and pleas for understanding or help go unheeded. This stress on the failures of interlocution or communication is echoed in the formal and spatial properties of the films: claustrophobic and fortress-like domestic spaces, a prominence of silence and muteness, the emphasis on mediated images and an infrequency of facial close-ups define Haneke's cinematic style. Most prominently, however, communicative failure is reflected in the isolating suicidal gestures that pervade many of the films. Suicides of both minor and main characters occur in films such as *The Piano Teacher, The Seventh Continent, Hidden* and *71 Fragments of a Chronology of Chance*, as well as in television works such as *Lemminge* (1979). In addition to these explicit acts of self-violence, in many of Haneke's films there are acts of destruction that can be viewed as suicidal gestures, even when death does not result: Erika's self-stabbing at the end of *The Piano Teacher*, Ben's attempt to leap into the fire in *The Time of the Wolf*, Benny's murder of the girl and subsequent two confessions in *Benny's Video*.

The film that addresses suicide most directly and intensively of course is *The Seventh Continent*, Haneke's first feature film release, and a film that many critics and scholars still consider his strongest. Taking its cue from a true story of a seemingly content and upwardly mobile bourgeois Austrian family's decision to kill themselves and their child, *The Seventh Continent* documents the three years leading up to the event as well as the deaths themselves. Divided into three parts marked by dates, the film uses parallel structure to depict the routinisation, isolation and lack of communication that characterise the family's existence: formally then, the film ensures that viewers not merely witness but experience the boring repetitiveness of the family's quotidian existence. This parallelism is emphasised by the structural precision of the film: each of the three segments is marked by an extended blackout (there are briefer blackouts used throughout the film to divide scenes) and a title card (Part 1: 1987; Part 2: 1988; Part 3: 1989). The temporal certainty of these title cards is, however, misleading: the titles suggest a traceable progression whereas this is exactly what the film refuses, as there are no teleological or causal relations evident across the segments. Other than a shift in what constitutes the routine as they move towards suicide, each of the parts offers parallel rather than progressive relations. There is no point of decision, no cause and effect or climactic moment that leads to the suicides; indeed, the opposite is true, insofar as we see increasing prosperity, upward social mobility and stability.

Minimising narrational causality and muting emotional tonalities, the film proceeds along these lines of repetition rather than climactic progression. The structural pattern of similarly orchestrated segmented parts works to emphasise sameness

The Seventh Continent (1989): the deadly routines of late capitalism

rather than plot development driven by crisis, character desire or even episodic variation. This is not to suggest, however, that there are no modifications or dissimilarities across the segments; but, these differences are evident only against overwhelming, oppressive and claustrophobic uniformity. Any development occurs gradually, as the spectator slowly and almost unconsciously becomes aware of the characters' decision to commit suicide. For instance, in the third sequence there is a sense of subtle variation: in this section, we open with a shot of Georg's parents in the country rather than the usual morning routine and we hear the letter to the parents written and narrated by their son Georg rather than their daughter-in-law Anna (a letter to the parents marks each of the three segments). Although the shifts that occur are small, it is significant that in the third part the film moves out of the spaces of home, work, supermarket and highway that have so far dominated it, and there are more facial shots than in the previous segments. Moreover, after it has become perceptible, even if not obvious, to the viewer that the family has made a decision to kill themselves, we actually see slight signs of familial interaction and communication (for example, a small smile passes among Georg, Anna and Eva as they eat their last supper, the first smiles of the film).

These minor variations are barely perceptible, however, and the dominant mode is one of an almost forensic documentation of seemingly insignificant acts, gestures, movements and interactions. In emphasising habitual and mundane similarity, the move towards suicide appears to be driven by the routine itself rather than as a climactic or traumatic deviation. This stylistic mode of objective scrutiny is evident from the beginning of the film, the first shot of which isolates in close-up not a human (the usual agent of visual cinematic identification), but a car. By opening with a shot of a vehicle licence plate being hosed down before going into a car wash, *The Seventh Continent* exemplifies Haneke's concentration on what I would describe as cinematic de-subjectivisation, a stylistic muting of character centrality, psychology or insight and a concomitant de-emphasising of the processes of audience identification.

This de-subjectivisation continues across the credits (an extended sequence of four minutes, during which we do not hear anything except the sounds of the car wash and do not see the characters except in outline, shot from behind and partially obscured by darkness) and the following opening scenes. For example, after the credit sequence and a blackout, the next scene introduces the characters in more detail, yet reveals only voice and partial body shots. Indeed, the first words of the film come not from a human but from an onscreen radio, followed by offscreen voices saying single word morning greetings as they awake. We view the family's morning routine in fractional close-up shots of body parts but never faces: hands make coffee, tie shoes, reach for toast. Even here, there is very little dialogue and indeed, it is almost twelve minutes before there is a shot of a character's face as she speaks. Further, it is significant that when this de-acousmatisation of the human figure occurs, it involves not the main adult characters (Georg or Anna), arguably the identificatory and narrational centre of the film, but their child Eva, who is pretending to be blind. Thus the suspense of visual discovery built up by the obscured views offered in this opening twelve minutes achieves only partial satisfaction as a somewhat secondary character, who ostensibly cannot see, is the first human face to be simultaneously heard and seen. The postponed disclosure consequently turns into a kind of ruse as what we are shown is an image of duplicity and pretence (the feigned blindness but also the emphatic presentation of Eva as the first speaking character, a point indicative of a more significant narrational moment that remains unfulfilled), a circumstance that seems to suggest a kind of ambiguity in the revelatory capacities of the visual field itself.

The film proceeds in this de-subjectivised, partial and fragmented way: all the main characters of the family (Georg, Anna and Eva) are revealed to the audience bit by bit and in isolation from each other. As already noted, each of the characters is initially acousmatic – only voice, not body – and when their faces are finally shown onscreen, they do not immediately acquire voices. In fact, the first facial shots of both Georg and Anna are presented as interpreted or dominated by the voices of others: Anna's voice narrating a letter to her parents-in-law governs the scene of Georg entering his work place and the introduction of Anna is acoustically dominated by the patient's storytelling (which is paralleled visually by the masked iris close-up shots of the patient's pupil intercut with Anna's reaction shots). Indeed, it is over twenty minutes before Anna is fully de-acousmatised (that is, before her face is shown while she speaks synchronised and simultaneous dialogue) and even then it is on the phone; it is several minutes later before Georg is given an onscreen voice.

In combination with the total lack of non-diegetic music, sparseness of dialogue and refusal of facial close-ups or even medium close-ups for the introductory minutes of a film, this acousmatisation creates not only a distanciation from the characters but an intense de-personalisation and objectivisation: these characters are their outer appearance and actions, the film suggests, as it invites us to observe rather than empathise or identify. Within the first thirty minutes, the film ensures that it positions the viewer at a distance from the characters. Any attempt to approach them psychologically, personally or in a more direct identificatory fashion is thwarted, and this impenetrability is echoed in their relations to each other. Stylistically and thematically then, the characters are isolated both from each other (and when we see interaction, it is rarely positive – for example, the second visible exchange between mother and daughter involves a slap and a broken promise) and the viewer.

Further, by focusing on Eva the child first, Haneke de-hierarchises the familial structure: rather than a single protagonist driving the narrational impulse and operating as focaliser, all members of this family get approximately equal screen time and attention (a feature that continues until the end of the film when the father, Georg, receives more visual attention as he is the last family member to die). The suicides are thus not pathologised or individualised through a single protagonist but are presented as a more collective event. More importantly, this egalitarianism in representation suggests an impartiality associated with objective documentation, a feature reinforced by the title cards and temporal and spatial locatedness of the action. By basing the film on a true story and beginning with film titles that indicate a linear and temporally definite trajectory, there is an extent to which the suicides at the end of the film have already occurred at its beginning; in this way the film can be seen as a retroactive forensic documentation, but a documentation that does not even attempt to search for causes. There is no real sense of suspense in the film's development but rather a pervasive sense of imminence, dread and morbid certainty.

This objectivity, narrational repetition and de-psychologisation work with the austere minimalism of Haneke's cinematic style to de-subjectify and de-personalise the suicides and frame them instead within the larger field of ethics. Suicide in this context becomes a pointed and severe critique of the routinised, empty and glacial existence of contemporary global capitalism. *The Seventh Continent* does not present the suicides as eruptive, as mere escapism or even the result of escalating events, but rather as a perverse end point to prosperous and stable family life. In this film, then, extreme (self) violence is not depicted as disturbing the status quo, but pursuing it to its end, a much more radical critique. The suffocating insulation of the family structure and the narcotising nature of bourgeois existence are thus rendered quite literal in *The Seventh Continent*'s depiction of a family's decision to shut out society and kill themselves with legally acquired drugs prescribed for the mass anxiety usually associated with late capitalism.

In fact, where a reversal or traumatic rupture of the status quo or social stability is most notable is not in the suicide itself but in its preparation, more specifically in the shift from capitalist accumulation to destruction as Georg, Anna and Eva set about destroying every trace of their wealth and comfortable existence (family photos, furniture, fish and money are all destroyed). As Haneke notes in interviews, his experience with audiences of the film indicates that the most disturbing element for many viewers is the image of money being ripped up and flushed down a toilet. This is perhaps not surprising as this is where the film takes aim at the system of capitalist wealth, happiness and prosperity most intensely and aggressively. Yet despite its apparent radicalism, this subversive destruction of capitalist wealth is as methodical and efficient as the other aspects of the family's daily routine. Indeed, Georg even states that the best way to approach the domestic demolition is systematically, and this dispassion is one of the most peculiar and disturbing elements of the film. In a film that critiques bourgeois conformism, this destruction of the accoutrements of capitalist accumulation ought to feel freeing, explosive or carnivalesque in its oppositional force. At the very least, it should be annihilating in its devastating power. But instead, there is an absolute lack of revolutionary release in the destruction of capitalism's goods and materials as this destruction is carried out (and filmed) with the same mechanistic objectivity as the mundane, quotidian acts that have led up to this point. Not only do we see the organisation and structure that are fundamental to this act (they put on gloves, divide the tasks among themselves and pursue the action individually within a predetermined time frame), but the sequence is stylistically parallel to earlier shots of the family waking and preparing coffee (in isolated shots we see a portion of the action, hands tearing family photos or smashing a fish tank, for example). In this obvious visual parallel, Haneke suggests that destroying your home and ripping up all your money and flushing it down the toilet in preparation for mass suicide is, within this film and for these characters at least, no more radical than making your morning coffee. The banality of devastation thus indicates that conformist societal structure pervades all actions, even those conceived of as potentially absolute, world-shattering or deviant. Georg, Anna and Eva have not broken out of their routine but are continuing it – self-eradicating suicide is in this way no more revolutionary than dull persistence. Moreover, if we pursue this parallelism, the message seems to suggest that suicide is not merely a part of their quotidian existence, but the natural corollary, the result of, this daily life.

But does this parallel suggest that Haneke does not make room for revolutionary or radical action (a reading that would suggest the impossibility of breaking out of capitalism's double binds and bourgeois conformity)? Or, is it rather that the film offers a much more extreme stance in suggesting that suicide is not a perversion, is not the result of a specific pathology or particular familial dysfunction or dissatisfaction, but the potential end point to daily life as we know it? In order to address this question I think it is important to go back to the concept of choice and its relation to the notion of the authentic act with which I began. Indeed, the family's suicide seems in many ways to lack the radicality of the act as Lacan conceives it: it appears to not intervene in social or subjective orientation but merely further its patterns. However, this is where the significance of the act as a movement towards death drive – its conscious embracing of that unconscious impulse – lay. It is in Haneke's emphasis on the eschewal of pathology and on the absolute certainty of pursuing a choice to its end (Georg notes in his letter to his parents that they taught him that you must stick to something once you have decided to do it) that we can see the film's radical stance. The suicides are presented as a clear, rational and logical choice, but one that cannot be perceived as such by those outside of the action. To underscore this, Haneke ends the film with a note regarding Georg's parents' refusal to accept the deaths as suicides; there is still a perseverance of the values of prosperity that make the family's suicidal acts inconceivable, literally *impossible*, to an outside observer. This is what pushes the act towards the ethical: its impact does not necessarily register with others nor is that its intention. Rather, the act is the impossible choice, the one not understood or absorbed by the symbolic network of explanation; for example, Medea could have left, killed herself or killed Jason – all possible choices – but instead she pursues the impossibly absolute choice of murdering her own children.

This impossible nature of the radical act arguably pervades all the suicidal gestures in Haneke's films. All fail to communicate even when staged as aggressive attacks on the double binds of existence. For instance, if we consider Majid's suicide in *Hidden* or Erika's self-obliteration (whether suicidal or merely self-mutilating) in *The Piano Teacher*, what we note is the failure of their acts to register on those around them: these suicides do not communicate a message, are not received or understood. In both instances we are given no isolatable moment of decision and the suicide itself is staged in a shockingly and excruciatingly objective fashion: Erika disappears into isolating darkness and the camera lingers on Majid's bleeding corpse far beyond what is necessary for narrative information or even emotional impact. In each of these examples, the effect is one of visual surplus, but a surplus that reveals the fundamental shortcomings of knowledge or comprehension. These long takes and sequences are not explanatory or orchestrated for emotional impact alone but are emphatic indications of intersubjective failure: we are faced with the results, the consequences, not with the motivations or causes. Their acts do not therefore communicate but effect: like Medea's murder of her own children, they put us in a place where it is impossible to respond within the parameters of familiar symbolic exchange. There is no 'proper' response immediately at hand.

This is where the uninvested nature of the family's self destruction in *The Seventh Continent* or the suddenness of Majid's suicide in *Hidden* become significant in an ethical context. The mechanistic, impenetrable and inexorable nature of these acts becomes essential to the anti-pathological structure of their presentation. In this way, the suicides are statements but not communications: there is no frame, no psychological trauma, existential angst or address to a big Other, but instead a radically ambiguous depiction of an extreme and irreversible action. It is therefore significant that in each instance, the act of self-destruction arises when there is no more choice to be made. As already noted, I contend that Haneke's ethical optimism lay in exposing the relatively minor choices that result in massive devastation, a feature evidenced by the fact that in all of these films, the ordinariness of error is rendered central through the stylistic attention to banality, detail and small actions. The violent outcomes are not, therefore, inevitable, but a clear result of a series of seemingly insignificant or innocent mistakes or actions. The final acts of destruction occur only after a point of accumulation, saturation or disavowal of minor errors based in personal choice: brutality, cruelty or self-destruction are not isolated, extreme moments but the cumulative effects of failed communication and alienation from oneself and others.

It is in this attention to the ambiguities of choice and consequence that Haneke presents the authentic act of self-erasure as beyond choice, as what happens when the world of choice no longer exists and we are faced with only consequence. The question then becomes how do we respond: how, when faced with eradicating power, does one continue? Rather than being an attempt at communication, these suicidal gestures are the end point of communication's failures and, as such, are parallel to Antigone's refusal to discuss or change her decision or Medea's destruction of the realm of the possible: the limit has been passed and, once passed, the move towards destruction is beyond desire and the effects are final and decisive.

But the crucial point to understanding Haneke's ethical position here is that, even when decisive, the consequences are not conclusive insofar as the act opens new territory. As Lacan notes, the act restructures and in Haneke's films, this is the significant detail. This potentiality is the decisive aspect of the narrative ambiguity that ends films like *The Piano Teacher*, *Hidden*, *The Time of the Wolf* and *71 Fragments of a Chronology of Chance*. Each of these films ends mid-action, in process, with an exceedingly ambiguous image: the moving train in *The Time of the Wolf*, the long shot of the school in *Hidden*, Erika walking into the night in *The Piano Teacher*, and the repeated newscast at the end of *71 Fragments of a Chronology of Chance*. A persistence of movement and time, suggestive of narrative openness and ambiguity, becomes in the end the ethical force of the films, as the importance of consequences and effects is stressed and reiterated.

Further, in encouraging audience reflection and engagement through minimalism and fragmented narration, Haneke formally confronts the viewer with the very problematics of choice, intersubjectivity and impossible communication that the films address diegetically. The audience's alienation from the films thus operates as spectatorial analogue for the impossibility of full comprehension of the solitary, subjective and aporetic dimensions of self-violence, while simultaneously working to draw the audience into the ethics of choice and consequence addressed in the films. The audience is left at the end of the films with the question of what happens next, as these open, ambiguous conclusions emphasise continuous, ongoing interrogation rather than closure or certainty.

Both formally and thematically then, these films suggest that suicidal gestures may be radical in their shattering impact but that this devastation should not attain the dubious elevation, closure and certainty so often associated with the cinematic representation of such acts of extreme and destructive violence. Rather, for Haneke, the significance of these acts is in their ethical force, the potentialities for change and transformation. Illustrated by *Hidden*'s examination of guilt that focuses not on the past but on the ability (or rather inability) of the present to address past errors and move forward, Haneke's ethical violence stresses effects, not causes, and asks how we respond to the territories and consequences opened up by extreme acts. In films like *The Seventh Continent*, *71 Fragments of a Chronology of Chance*, *The Piano Teacher*, *Hidden* or *The Time of the Wolf*, then, the suicidal gesture as such, although momentous, is only the beginning: as an authentic act, suicide in Haneke occupies an ethical force as it encourages the audience to confront the more difficult and significant questions of the ambiguities of choice and consequence and this is where the real interrogation and engagement begins.

References

Lacan, J. (1986) *The Ethics of Psychoanalysis*, 1959–1960: Book VII. Ed. J.-A. Miller, trans. D. Porter. New York: W. W. Norton and Company.
Miller, J.-A. (2000) 'On the Semblances in the Relation Between the Sexes', in R. Salecl (ed.) *Sexuation*. Durham, NC: Duke University Press, 13–27.
Žižek, S. (2004) *Revolution at the Gates: Žižek on Lenin, the 1917 Writings*. London: Verso.

CHAPTER FOUR

Thinking the Event:
The Virtual in Michael Haneke's Films

Oliver C. Speck

Michael Haneke's films clearly bear the marks of creation by a classic auteur: the recurring use of names (Georges and Anne), stories (the breaking down of the basic family unit), plot devices (real or imagined traumata, an open ending), motifs (the droning noise of television, sudden violence without justification or explanation) and signature shots, such as the extreme close-up on objects of ritualised actions (preparing breakfast) and on objects of exchange (the often equally ritualised actions of shopping or buying drugs). Critics see his films as a trenchant critique of our society and its postmodern relativism. One leitmotif in particular has earned Haneke the reputation of being 'the last moralist of cinema': in practically all of Haneke's films the images of civil wars that happen in other parts of the globe appear flashing on television screens, apparently unnoticed by the characters. This instant mediatisation of any event into a medial double, generally understood as simulacrum, instantiates a 'virtual reality' that takes over the real world, thus eroding all moral values. Critics who seek to preserve certain moral values perceive this as a clear sign of Haneke's lamenting the erosion of the values they hold so dear. While it might be true that Haneke's critique pertains to the erosion of the sense of the real, his stance – especially as far as the role of the virtual is concerned – is more subtle and complex, and deserves a closer look.

Apart from the aforementioned characteristics, all of Haneke's films are also self-referential, ranging from frame-within-the-frame-shots – the video monitor on which we barely see the horrible action in *Benny's Video* (1992) comes to mind – to the direct address of the spectator in *Funny Games* (1997). However, the most openly authorial and authoritarian gesture is not the alienation effect of breaking the fourth wall, but the subtle device that brings about the shock of realising that we are not gazing *at* something, but *with* something: at the beginning of *Caché* (*Hidden*, 2005), for example, a perfectly innocent shot of a tranquil urban neighbourhood is suddenly revealed to be a surveillance video by a fast-forwarding of the tape and by voices that comment on what can be seen on the tape. Here the gazes of audience, surveillance- and film camera, characters and unknown agent find themselves suddenly aligned – except that, of course, each of them sees something different. This difference is significant and, as I argue, it takes place on the level of the virtual, allowing us paradoxically to see what did *not* happen. As I will show, Haneke's cinema does not seek to represent the 'truth of events', such as that which is commonly proffered by the media. Instead, it thinks events as *aporias*, as paradoxical and irreducible to one point of view, that is, one explanation. It thinks them as fragmented, multiple accretions of different perspectives with a temporality of their own, rather than as unitary, eternally fixed facts in a sequence. Seeing events as aporetic effects a confrontation with them on the level of ethics that does not simply relegate them to the past, but 'actualises' them in the present, ethical consequences and all. Indeed, the films of Michael Haneke make a similar attempt with aesthetic means as the philosophy of Gilles Deleuze does through concepts to sensitise us to our relationship to the past, be it recent or historical. This attempt can be described as the thinking of a possible alternative to the global culture of what we commonly call postmodernity where the past is increasingly obliterated by the eternal present of pervasive mediatisation, apathy of the *polis* and general deracination.

Let us for a moment return to Haneke's purported defence of values in the mode of a critique of ideology. As was pointed out above, there is certainly a substantial amount of critique of ideology in Haneke's cinema. Certain moments in his early films – the ubiquitous television images in the 'glaciation trilogy' (*Der siebente Kontinent* (*The Seventh Continent*, 1989), *71 Fragmente einer Chronologie des Zufalls* (*71 Fragments of a Chronology of Chance*, 1994) and *Benny's Video*) and in the thematically related *Code inconnu: Récit incomplet de divers voyages* (*Code Unknown: Incomplete Tales of Several Journeys*, 2000) – appear to be perfect illustrations of Guy Debord's now-classic theses, published as *The Society of the Spectacle* in 1967. An often-repeated stylistic device in Haneke's trilogy, the extreme close-up on objects at the moment of their exchange – the hands of the choir boys in *Benny's Video* handing over money come to mind – suggests that the image of the limitless exchange of commodities has already become the phenomenal form of capital, and that life and image are one and the same. In short, it could be said that these close-ups perfectly illustrate the scathing analysis of Thesis 49:

> The spectacle is the flip side of money. It, too, is an abstract general equivalent of all commodities. But whereas money has dominated society as the representation of universal equivalence – the exchangeability of different goods whose uses remain uncomparable – the spectacle is the modern complement of money: a representation of the commodity world as a whole which serves

as a general equivalent for what the entire society can be and can do. The spectacle is money one can only look at, because in it all use has already been exchanged for the totality of abstract representation. The spectacle is not just a servant of pseudo-use, it is already in itself a pseudo-use of life. (Debord 2002)

The 'pseudo-use of life' also explains why the potlatch in *Der siebente Kontinent* (*The Seventh Continent*, 1989) must be suicidal. Once all moveable goods have been converted back into money, the paper money as material form of capital has been treated as excrement and flushed down the toilet and every remaining object of use value has been destroyed, the life that remains after this subtraction must necessarily also be voided, because it is already void of any substance. The film ends with the nightmarish image of the dead eyes of the family staring at the non-image of the television's white noise, their life-as-spectacle come to an end.

Another prime example of a society where the spectacle has mediated all social interaction into a spectacular 'virtual reality' can be found in the guise of the seemingly-average bourgeois family in *Benny's Video*. Benny himself lives a monadic life, where even the view from his window is replaced by the live video-capture of the busy intersection. His family seems to have internalised bourgeois values completely, and like all the bourgeois families in Haneke's cinema, Benny's seems cold and sterile to the point of being dysfunctional, communicating only by notes or sarcastic, that is, coded, remarks. As human beings, they are bankrupt consumers who have completely bought into capitalism. Such is the conclusion reached by many critics. And it is exactly the conclusion that Maximilian Le Cain (2003), Gail K. Hart (2006) and Brigitte Peucker (2007), draw in their readings of Haneke's cinema, finding an implied conservative message that weakens or even belies the critical import of his films. However, we must consider whether Haneke shows us human beings who have become not only willingly dehumanised points in the exchange of capital, but also thoroughly mediatised – or 'spectacularised' to use Debord's language – members of a society. Notably, there is no promise of a return to wholeness ever held out by Haneke. If Haneke is said to ultimately fail because he leaves a backdoor in the form of a 'return-to' – a return to values, substance, meaningful communication, in one word, wholeness – then we must pose the question of whether Haneke does not attempt a critique subtly different from the one observed by his critics, one that successfully avoids precisely the position these critics attribute to him. His critique of a thoroughly mediatised society of postmodernity is not simply relayed as a moralising message, but rather is produced by means of sophisticated cinematic techniques and filmic forms in careful relation to one another that have yet to be examined and explicated. As I will show later, Gilles Deleuze echoes Haneke's critique of the simplistic distinction between the real and mediatised 'virtual reality' by contrasting the pairs of the real and the possible and the virtual and the actual. To do so, we must first engage Haneke's critics more closely on their terrain.

Looking at the dysfunctional families in the 'glaciation trilogy', Peucker observes rightfully that form and content mirror each other, that is, that the characters' attempts to cope with their fragmented lives is itself narrated in a fragmented style.

From this, Peucker deducts that the family serves as an emblem for the society as a whole, summing up the film's underlying message as: 'The wholeness of the bourgeois family as a guarantee for the wholeness of society' (2007: 187). Peucker concludes that 'Haneke's films are multiply-anchored in notions of organicism after all' (ibid.). Comparing *Funny Games* to Oliver Stone's *Natural Born Killers* (1994) Hart recognises that in the Hollywood version of the senseless killings the perpetrators' actions 'are mired in the muck of explanation' (2006: 67) while Haneke's film refuses any explanation of what motivates these two natural born killers by constantly shifting their identities. Referring to Haneke's own statements regarding the intention behind his project, Hart then compares this refusal convincingly to Friedrich Schiller's and Bertolt Brecht's programme for an aesthetic education. This stance expresses for Hart the typical disdain and arrogance of 'old European high culture' for less sophisticated forms of entertainment (2006: 70). In the final paragraphs of her article Hart basically accuses Haneke of beating a dead horse since the audience can very well distinguish between fact and fiction and no scientific evidence exists that violent films cause violence. Le Cain, in his overview of Haneke's films, arrives at similar conclusions. While he generally praises the visual sophistication of these films, which according to his reading serve to 're-humanise' the fragmented parts of society, Le Cain counts *Funny Games* as Haneke's only failure. With *Funny Games*, Haneke's intentions – 'doubtlessly honourably moralistic', as Le Cain puts it – were to create a film that pits a 'heroic, beleaguered family battling for their lives and property against an unspeakable, child-killing other'.[1] The film, by Le Cain's account, suffers from a reductive and caricatural representation and, again, defence of bourgeois values.

What is interesting here is that these critics, after a thorough analysis of the aesthetic devices used, see the strengths of Haneke's project, but arrive at a troubling conclusion, namely, that Haneke is a renegade 'organicist' who appears to seek to bring us back to the fold of sound bourgeois values, only to hold them out as unattainable for us. Even Robin Wood's highly personal, enthusiastic and, at times, even gushing praise of *Code Unknown* concludes with a note of puzzlement about an ending that suggests that 'communication is impossible, the "unknown code" that might save us will never be found' (2003: 48). Indeed, these readings must necessarily arrive at this conclusion because of their underlying assumption that Haneke pursues a basic humanism, with a message in the mode of the above-mentioned 'return-to', or at least a recollection of, values that will help to heal – make 'whole' – the broken society at its very core, the basic family unit.

There are, of course, good reasons to take Haneke as a 'physician of culture', what Gilles Deleuze calls a 'clinician of civilisation, somebody who diagnoses the disease in society' (2001: 237), as I have shown elsewhere.[2] However, while Haneke certainly provides a diagnosis, he is far from suggesting a cure that works only within the limits of the already-moribund system. Furthermore, his diagnoses do not hold out the hope-against-hope that life and spectacle could ever be separated again, as some critics mistakenly conclude. They are already and indissociably one. In this Haneke concurs with Debord, who states in Thesis 6 that the spectacle 'is not a mere decoration added to the real world. It is the very heart of this real society's unreality. In all of its particular manifestations – news, propaganda, advertising, entertainment – the spectacle represents the dominant model of life' (Debord 2002). To assume that Haneke propagates humanistic values is tantamount to holding out a hope that Haneke has long abandoned.

Looking closely at Haneke's cinematic techniques and film style in the 'Flight into Egypt' sequence in *Benny's Video*, in relation to theories of the point-of-view shot, can provide some clues as to what is at stake in the insistence upon Haneke's critique being more subtle than critics' readings of it. The week that mother and son spend in a holiday resort in Egypt is important, because the audience must retroactively locate Benny's change of mind in this short vacation that primarily serves to give the father enough time to accomplish the gruesome task of cutting up the victim's body into small enough pieces to flush them down the toilet. The obvious irony here is, of course, that the Biblical holy family flees into Egypt to avoid Herod's murdering troops, while Benny's 'Flight in(to) Egypt' happens after an innocent has been massacred and appears to trigger Benny's flight from his 'un-holy' family.

The roughly twenty minutes of screen time are filled with a repetition of all stylistic devices that we encounter in this film and, indeed, in all other films by Haneke. Rather than the extreme close-up on hands exchanging goods for money, Haneke's signature shot here is the video image framed by a monitor or a television set, as well as people framed by doors and windows.[3] The significance of these frames, sometimes overlapping, warrants a short taxonomy: the basic distinction in *Benny's Video* is of course that between video and film. The video image is also the object of the film camera and appears sometimes framed by a television set and sometimes unmediated, but narrowed by the film's aspect ratio of 1:1.66. In either case, it is clear that only the grainy video image can render a moment from the past. For example, the moment when Benny literally flies and cries out 'Mama, I am flying!' is shown on the small television screen in the hotel room. However, this scene is preceded by a shot of Benny filming another tourist who has just opened his parachute. Due to the abrupt transition and the grainy image, the audience must assume in the first seconds of the video that it is this tourist that they are seeing on the screen. Only the ecstatic cry identifies the flying figure as Benny, and his mother as the camera operator. This transition is mirrored a short time later: once, when the intra-diegetic sound – a Bach organ concerto on television – becomes extra-diegetic by being carried over into the next

Flight in(to) Egypt: *Benny's Video* (1992)

video; then again when the shaky, hand-held video that Benny shoots is replaced by a calm pan across the landscape. Again, Benny wearing a cap and sunglasses is difficult to recognise, only his and his mother's voices identify him as the person in the picture and her as the camera operator.

This crucial sequence functions on four distinctive levels. First, it repeats the basic distinction in *Benny's Video* between video and film image, thereby stressing the importance of the basic cinematic distinction between the *hors champs* – for example, what happens outside of the field of vision of Benny's video camera – and the *hors cadre*, pointing to the image the director allows us to see and its constructedness. Drawing attention to the materiality of the film reveals the image as image in its manipulative power.[4] Second, only the video provides the functional equivalent of flashbacks – something that happens throughout the film but might have passed unnoticed by most viewers; this points to the paradox that the video capture of the present instantly passes into the past, thus creating difference in itself, the present's non-identity with itself. Third, the different film styles underline that Benny is, at first, not interested in a future audience. As opposed to the more touristy pictures his mother takes, Benny treats his video camera up to then solely as a device to capture and mediate reality. Even his video-diary on the hotel terrace seems to be more an externalisation of his own thoughts and doubts than a message to another person. Not only does he expose his naked chest in a narcissistic gesture but he is also wearing a T-shirt with a picture of his own face on it. Significantly, it shows him with his full-length hair, that is, before he became a murderer. Fourth, Benny for the first time uses the implicit threat of sharing with others his video as a means to an end. In a short scene, he films his mother, who sits down on the toilet with the bathroom door open. Benny would probably not show this video to anybody, but makes the point that he is emancipated and not a child anymore.

Most importantly, however, the 'Flight into Egypt' sequence works on a meta-level, combining all other functions to foreshadow the major *mise-en-abyme* of the film where all these levels or frames, if we want to extend the metaphor of the frame to the multiple frames of reference, are realigned. The repetition of a prior scene the audience witnessed earlier brings up the memory of the original circumstance. The recognition, then, that the director did not show Benny taping his parents and that Benny is now screening this segment for the authorities happens in a flash. Sharing his video with the police will, of course, emancipate Benny completely, cutting all ties to his family, but also make him a director who makes images *for* somebody. This shock of realisation, an abrupt adjustment of the frame of reference, was already rehearsed in the above-mentioned video of Benny's parachuting and, before, in the repetition of the girl's killing that Benny shows to his parents. The construction of these devices can serve as perfect examples of what Michel Chion famously calls an 'acousmêtre', a person who is not visible but whose voice is heard, 'a kind of acting and talking shadow', as Chion puts it (1999: 21). The voice of the young man who assaults Anne in *Code Unknown*, for example, is even more threatening and powerful when it suddenly comes from the *hors champs*. But maybe even more important for the cinema of Haneke than the 'acousmatic voice', the voice whose source is not seen onscreen but which is implied, is the opposite operation, when the audience has to assign an onscreen body to the voice they are hearing, as in Benny's ecstatic cry, mentioned above. Chion calls this 'a voice that seeks a body' (see 1999: 127–36). In any case, a voice without a body or a voice that seeks a body, the shock of recognition, when voice and body are associated, could be described as a reframing: the frame of reference that assured the spectator of a stable meaning is suddenly revoked. Indeed, the last sequence of *Benny's Video* features two instances of acousmatic reframing: at first, the audience needs to remember the key sentences of the cover-up ('The pieces must be small or they'll block the drains') concerning the disposal of the corpse, and recognise the parents' voices in order to understand that they are witnessing a recording of something that they experienced from another perspective. Then, while the screen still shows the bedroom door, an unknown male voice from the *hors champs* asks Benny a question, and, after a cut, a hand touching a video recorder is shown in close-up. Again, the shock of recognition stems from the necessary reframing – voice and hand must belong to a police officer, whose face the audience never gets to see. Instead, the video monitor shows a glimpse of Benny ready to take off with his parachute, again demanding a remembering of the first reframing, but also pointing to the possibility that Benny handed over the incriminating video because of this flight in(to) Egypt.

Before drawing conclusions from Haneke's multiple frames and their alignment, let us consider his use of the point-of-view shot. Indeed, critics have noticed the curious incidence of the traditional point-of-view shot in Haneke's oeuvre. Insofar as these point-of-view shots are used sparingly, they are either reserved for the rare instances when we should identify with a character, for example for Eva in *The Seventh Continent* who will be murdered by her parents (see Bingham 2004), for the young boy in both versions of *Funny Games*, or for a direct reference to the conventions of Hollywood cinema. In *Code Unknown*, an action sequence – a child is falling from a roof – is later revealed to be a clip from a film in which one of the main characters has a role (see Wood 2003: 42). In any case, if a point-of-view shot occurs, it is already framed in multiple ways. The point-of-view shot of Eva looking at the boat is, as Jörg Metelmann recognises, an intertext to Michaelangelo Antonioni's *Il deserto rosso* (*Red Desert*, 1964) where a ship appears in a similar shot and where the reality of the vision is equally enig-matic: it could be a real ship but the shot also gains a metaphoric quality in relation to the journey on which the parents will later take Eva. As Metelmann points out, this is one of the few instances where Haneke uses extra-diegetic music, in this case Alban Berg's violin concerto 'To the memory of an angel', in order to contrast the poverty of the parents' life with Eva's vision (see 2003: 76–8). The obvious irony in this choice is of course counterbalanced, or rather countered, by the mournfulness of the music itself and, again, disturbs the spatial and temporal continuum by foreshadowing Eva's death. The surprising action sequence in *Code Unknown* is also framed, drawing the viewer in with typical means – action, fast cuts, point-of-view shots – even though Anne's sudden change from struggling actress to member of an upper-class couple should alert the audience that this cannot be part of the diegetic reality. Significantly, we find again acousmatic voices at work, insofar as the action sequence is just being dubbed by the actors. Here, a new frame of reference retroactively discloses the prior sequence as fake, or rather, fictional in the framework of the diegetic reality. Haneke's point-of-view shot thus becomes something else, no longer a simple point-of-view shot but a multilayered frame of intertextual references.

Just how Haneke's point-of-view shot differs from the traditional point-of-view shot can best be shown by looking again at *Benny's Video* and *Hidden*, thereby also showing that the sudden ontological adjustment effected by Haneke's use of point-of-view shots emphasises the artificial character of the film itself in a complex form of self-referentiality. The aesthetic shock in *Benny's Video* of a shot that is suddenly revealed to be surveillance video clearly anticipates the above-mentioned beginning of *Hidden*. There, as here, the bodiless acousmatic voices commenting on the events the audience witnesses abruptly adjust the frame of reference. In *Hidden*, we find again the manipulation of the tape that we encounter in the sequence that begins *Benny's Video*, the slaughter of the pig. In the latter, the rewinding and slowing down immediately introduces the device of adjusting the frames of reference: we are watching Benny's video in a film called *Benny's Video*. As was pointed out above, all possible gazes overlap in moments like this – audience, characters, unknown agent, surveillance- and film camera all look at the same images. The crucial difference from a traditional point-of-view shot becomes immediately clear. In the traditional point-of-view shot 'the camera assumes the spatial of a character in order to show us what the character sees, the camera lens, so to speak, becomes the eye of the character (hence also the metaphor "camera eye"), with the result that our sensory perception is restricted to that of the character' (Branigan 1984: 6). However, in Haneke's films and here especially in the surveillance sequence in *Hidden*, the shot rendered in a seemingly impersonal point of view that happens in the 'past' to the diegetic present and is taped in a locale different from that diegetic present, suddenly is revealed as not only not impersonal, but as 'part' of the diegetic present, that is, as surveillance. It is not only that the point of view of the surveillance causes the diegetic fictional reality to be split from within by a threatening element, whose provenance is unknown – the spatial and temporal continuum in the surveillance sequence as such is always already split. This amounts to an ontological and epistemological split that cannot be overcome by any kind of 'return' to a stable identification of subject and object of the gaze, not being predicated on such easy distinctions but instead calling them radically into question.

Having considered Haneke's nuanced use of the point-of-view shot, we can finally pinpoint the difference in his aesthetic. I would argue that Haneke deliberately transforms the classic point-of-view subsequence into these framed shots of and through another medium – an intertext under the guise of video or a Hollywood-style action film – in order to draw attention to the mediality and the temporality of all images. Indeed, every image in these films – the news specials on the war in Bosnia, the trivial daily news ('a tramway accident in Stockholm'), the slaughter of the pig, the film itself – is always mediated, that is, framed. In a more traditional film that follows the convention of classic realist Hollywood cinema, a point-of-view shot is nothing but a supplement to a recording of events that is supposed to be basically objective. However, as several film theorists have pointed out, the shot/counter-shot mechanism of Hollywood cinema, with its classic realist narration, 'sutures' the viewer with the filmic text. According to this model, the viewer interprets the glance of the 'absent' person as source of a first shot and in a second step reads the counter-shot as the look of a diegetic person, shot one becomes signified for the signifier '*l'absent*'. The second shot is in its turn defined by the point of view of the first shot – the 'other field' as Daniel Dayan calls it – and is therefore the signified of the first shot. It is exactly through this tautological short-circuit, this displacement of meaning from one shot to the other, that the subject of enunciation shifts or inserts itself into the fiction. The image is taken as a 'true' representation: 'By means of the suture, the film-discourse presents itself as a product without a producer, a discourse without an origin' (Dayan 1976: 451). The position of the subject of enunciation is, however, a phallic and therefore impossible position. The permanently threatening castration stems from the real inability of the viewing subject to influence the picture, and this threat is sublated through a fetishistic disavowal, as Kaja Silverman formulates following Laura Mulvey (see Silverman 1988: 30–1). Such sublation, however, is not the goal of Haneke's cinema. The ontological and epistemological split that develops in Haneke's films through his own use of point-of-view technique cannot in the end be sublated or sutured into an organic whole in the manner allowed by the traditional point-of-view shot of Hollywood cinema.

In his book on Krzysztof Kieślowski, Slavoj Žižek mentions two ways of refusing a suture with simple cinematic means: one is to set up a point-of-view shot, only to reveal the character through whose eyes we are supposed to see as located within the frame; the other option is to include the face of another person as a reflection in a window within the same shot. Žižek describes this as 'the shift from the objective "God's-view shot" into its uncanny subjectivisation' (2001: 38). In early Haneke films, this threat of castration is anticipated and underlined by the insertion of black film, a strategy that he later abandoned. Bert Rebhandl describes the effect of these inserts as destruction of the 'conventional knowledge of the sequencing in storytelling and narrative causality' (2005: 80–1). Beginning with *Benny's Video*, Haneke opts for the mediatised point-of-view shot discussed above, the uncanny subjectivisation of the video image with its threatening castration in the form of the disturbed space-time continuum.

Let us return to the question of how we might interpret Haneke's multiple frames and their alignment. In trying to assess the different devices he uses, we can see not only a systematic and radical refusal of any closure, either in form or content, but, indeed, the systematic destruction of any possibility for a reconciliation of these fragments on any level. No frame, to stay with the metaphor, is entirely closed: the rules of the genre are established, then suddenly broken, images change their ontological status, suture is promised, then permanently refused, and so on. It is important to recognise the temporal aspect behind this strategy, whereby a possible closure is announced, but then destroyed. The most infamous example here is, of course, the rewinding of the film *Funny Games* itself by one of the young killers, just after the audience has had a brief moment of hope for a narrative closure in the form of the genre-typical catharsis. This punitive impetus might be misunderstood as moralistic, as some critics have done, but the very possibility of a position on which to ground a moral judgement is also denied. What prevents Haneke's cinema from falling into nihilism is, however, the insistence on the difference that is already in the image, and the repetition that forces the audience to remember and readjust the frame of reference for this image. This readjustment, as I will argue below, can only be understood as an actualisation in the sense that Deleuze uses this concept.[5]

In the case of *Hidden*, Haneke finally articulates in a pure form the *aporia* that is already implicit in all of his films by concentrating all devices that were mentioned earlier – the overlapping gaze, the frame-within-the-frame, the acousmatic voice that reframes the image, the refusal of suture – in one sequence, consisting of one long take in a long shot. As was pointed out above, the ontological and epistemological split inherent in the sequence cannot be overcome by any kind of stabilising – hence reassuring – attribution to a subject and an object of this gaze. Indeed, this split is the very expression of this crisis. Significantly, the film is shot on digital video, thus also folding the difference of film and video into one image. Consequently, the tracking lines of the video appear from an outside, the impossible realm of the *hors cadre*, the space where the surveillance camera also seems to be located – Georges would have found it otherwise, since he walks towards it in one scene, and the curious viewer will in vain rewind the film and freeze the frame in order to search for the video camera in the bookshelf of Majid's apartment.[6]

The first sequence of *Hidden* sets the stage for an exploration into the nature of surveillance by showing surveillance at work. The act of surveillance, in a continuous arc, becomes both an event and a staged performance – a surveillance is taking place whose only object or purpose is indeed the surveillance that took place. The implied audience of this circle is split into (i) the audience in the cinema looking at this spectacle which is, in the diegetic frame of reference, 'real', yet, in extra-diegetic terms, staged entirely in order to point to its own mediality, and (ii) the audience's point of reference, the fictional addressees of the tape. This dizzying circle of self-referentiality could be seen as signs of a Brechtian programme, as Metelmann has done (see 2003: 151–79), but the truly new dimension of filming that Haneke's *aporia* opens up is that the camera, as agent of the mediality, actually *performs* the difference in the repetition. By repeating the frame, the difference emerges as a kind of performance. It could be said that surveillance paradoxically happens and is impossible at the same time. However, it is only impossible when we refuse to acknowledge that the opposition is not between reality and virtual reality, but between the pairs possible/real and virtual/ actual, that is, if we stay within the metaphysical view of a timeline where certain possible outcomes become reality.

It is at this point that the projects of Haneke and Deleuze overlap. Indeed, the nature of the difference that appears in the repetition should not be confused with the so-called 'virtual reality' that seems to provide such an easily-identifiable target for Haneke's filmic critique. While the instant mediatisation of any event is certainly a prevailing theme in the cinema of Michael Haneke, it mirrors Deleuze's scheme by differentiating the pairs of the real and the possible and the virtual and the actual. For Deleuze the virtual is linked to memory, or 'pure recollection': 'What Bergson calls "pure recollection" has no psychological existence. This is why it is called *virtual*' (1988: 55; emphasis in original). Instead of being a point on the chronological timeline, the present must paradoxically be grasped as coexisting with and independent from the past, which we have to actualise in order to have access to it, but should be careful not to think of as a subjective memory *in us*, but on the contrary as radically exterior: 'Only the present is "psychological", but the past is pure ontology; pure recollection has only ontological significance' (Deleuze 1988: 56). Ontological here means precisely not psychological, internalised and subjective – a thinking that would be grounded in a model that imagines the future event as a realisation of one of many possible outcomes. Instead, the virtual is as real as the actualised present.

At the moment of a perception, time 'splits', as Deleuze puts it, and the actual perception-image gains its virtual image (Deleuze 1989: 81). It is precisely from this point of view that Deleuze can claim that the present is a function of the past, a contraction of the past. From this perspective, it is the psychological present that 'passes', while what is normally understood as the past has an existence of its own that is independent from the chronological time-line and where everything is preserved more or less contracted, but without hierarchy: 'The whole of our past is played, restarts, repeats itself, *at the same time*, on all the levels that it sketches out' (Deleuze 1988: 61; emphasis in original). In *Hidden*, the video images of the surveillance camera provide this virtual archive, while the images of the young Majid are always marked as dream- and memory-images which are presently actualised in Georges' mind. Notably, the scenes when the young Majid kills the chicken and when he is forcibly removed by the authorities are clearly focused by and through the narrative presence of Georges. They are filmed from a low angle that suggests Georges' point of view and exaggerate the menacing appearance of the young Algerian boy.

Since the virtual has its own existence, the act of recollection asks for nothing less than a leap of faith: 'The appeal to recollection is this jump by which I place myself in the virtual, in the past, in a particular region of the past, at a particular level of contraction' (Deleuze 1988: 63). This is exactly the jump required by the audience when an acousmatic voice requires the actualisation of a prior image, that is, transposes it to the present of the mind. An act of recollection can thus be compared to remembering the original circumstance of the frame. Again, it should be underlined that this is not a step back in time, but rather a search in a virtual archive for places where this text also appears. The past, as Deleuze explains, 'is the virtual element into which we penetrate to look for the "pure recollection" which will become actual in a "recollection image"' (1989: 98). Arguably, these are images that are not visible on the screen, because this recollection image appears in the mind of the spectator.

Underlying the couple virtual/actual is the distinction between possible and real, as commonsensical as it is dangerous. The reconstruction of a 'possible' is deceptively easy, since it is made in the resemblance of the real. Deleuze writes in *Difference and Repetition*: 'Such is the defect of the possible: a defect which serves to condemn it as produced after the fact, as retroactively fabricated in the image of what resembles it ... Actualisation breaks with resemblance as a process no less than it does with identity as a principle' (1994: 212). In the case of Haneke's project, this means a 'return to' older values is not only not possible, but the attempt is outright dangerous, since it introduces a teleology. Instead, Haneke's films as well as Deleuze's philosophy ask for a completely different concept of history that seems to be inspired by Walter Benjamin. In Thesis VI of the *Theses on the Philosophy of History*, Benjamin famously warns about the reconstruction of history and instead postulates an alternative to this historicism:

> To articulate the past historically ... means to seize hold of a memory as it flashes up at a moment of danger ... The danger affects both the content of the tradition and its receivers ... Only that historian will have the gift of fanning the spark of hope in the past who is firmly convinced that *even the dead* will not be safe from the enemy if he wins. (2003: 392; emphasis in original)

Written under the fascist threat of a teleological rewriting of history by appropriating the dead as 'martyrs for the cause', Benjamin's messianic strategy instead retains this 'moment of danger' – the moment when events took the wrong path – as a virtual image. The seizing of this moment means that we should remember what did *not* happen, or, in Deleuzian terms, actualise the virtual. Looking at Haneke's films, we can see that his entire oeuvre – and this includes his work for television – demands from the spectator this act of recalling what did not happen, instead of harking on what should have happened.

With the actualisation of the virtual, a virtual event comes into existence because the act of remembering is, in the words of Deleuze, always a 'genuine creation' (1994: 212). The virtual is therefore something that will always be new and does not resemble the real at all, while the possible is only a reconstruction, a mere 'virtual reality'. Whence the importance of the 'pyramid scheme' in *Benny's Video*, a perfect illustration of acting in bad faith as opposed to the leap of faith required by Benny at the end of the film. This 'virtual reality' of capitalism imagines time as a forking tree and the observers of the possible outcome – everybody's wealth will grow exponentially – as watching from an ahistorical, omniscient point of view. However, it can, of course, be proven mathematically that only the initial 'players' will become rich (see Valentine 1998). Significantly, the scenes from the two pyramid parties show fights in the background, stressing that the virtual reality of the game is already coming apart at the seams.

It is important to be precise about Haneke's and Deleuze's diagnoses: the characters in Haneke's films do not confuse the virtual and reality, that is, succumb to a false consciousness, but rather are cut off from the past in the form of the virtual and can therefore not remember what did *not* happen, instead, projecting a possible, a virtual reality into the past and the future.[7] To stay with the example of *Hidden*, we can quickly see that the traumatic event of the massacre of Algerians by the French police could have been dealt with in the typical form of a virtual reality based 'on a true story', which, in turn, can easily be judged in terms of how 'well' it represents the past (for example, *Nuit noire, 17 octobre 1961* (*October 17, 1961*) by Alain Tasma, incidentally released in the same year as *Hidden*).[8] However, Haneke introduces the event of the massacre of Algerians only indirectly, almost as an original sin that reverberates through the lives of the characters, thus preventing a historicist appropriation. We should not forget that the main character of *Hidden* cannot possibly be found guilty since he was six years old at the time of the event and not able to foresee the consequences of his jealous actions. And he certainly had no influence on the abuse the Algerian victim possibly received in a French orphanage. If anybody is to blame, it is the parents who all too readily believed their son and did not enquire about the disappearance of Majid's parents. However, it seems strange that Georges barely reacts to *the* traumatic event of the film, the sudden suicide of Majid. In the scene immediately preceding Majid's suicide, we see Georges acting in bad faith, manipulating images, in a shot that mirrors the surveillance shot at the beginning of the film. But instead of recognising that he had failed to help the grown-up Majid, Georges afterwards still acts on his main fear, namely that of losing his public image, something that connects him to Benny's father, who also immediately thinks about the possible loss of his status. Even though shaken by the event he witnessed, Georges' primary concern seems to be whether his wife kept up appearances when she sent their friends away. And the next day, he assures Majid's son that he does not feel guilty at all. Indeed, Debord's sixth thesis, quoted above, holds true for Georges: 'the spectacle represents the dominant model of life' (2002).

Furthermore, deprived of any identification with the main character, we find here again the systematic and radical refusal of any closure that was addressed above. The *topos* of self-aggression that pervades Haneke's oeuvre, for example the murder-suicides in *The Seventh Continent* and *71 Fragments of a Chronology of Chance*, the attempted self-sacrifice of the young boy in *The Time of the Wolf* or Erika's self-mutilation in *The Piano Teacher*, is remarkable insofar as none of these gestures carry any meaning. The destruction of any possibility for a reconciliation of the fragments exposes suicide and self-mutilation as completely nihilistic gestures that have no redemptive value.

There is, however, one more perspective that can help us to seize a moment and remember what did not happen: in most of Haneke's films – as was pointed out above – a television set displays news from an armed conflict around the world. In *Hidden*, for example, the television set, which is ironically built into the bookshelves, is clearly centred in the frame, while Georges and Anne talk in the foreground, not paying attention to the routine display of violence. Indeed, the suffering person on the news is virtually always already all other victims. Again, we can formulate an affinity to Debord, who points out in his Thesis 61: 'The agent of the spectacle who is put on stage as a star is the opposite of an individual; he is as clearly the enemy of his own individuality as of the individuality of others' (Debord 2002). It is this individuality that needs to be seized, and this through the act of actualisation of a virtual. We could say, then, that Haneke's cinema combines the radicality of a Debordian take on the mediatisation of events with the Deleuzian response to the postmodern condition.

In other words, to actualise the virtual means to think each event as aporetic and not as a metaphysical example for the nature of man and the typical horrors of war. Every actualisation carries therefore an ethical demand, in this case, to actualise the virtual of the victim. When we remember Benny's enthusiastic response to his flight as the only time he shows any emotion, for example, we need to resist the temptation to read a 'deeper', that is, psychological meaning into this event, but should instead attempt to seize the purely ethical dimension of his action. The famous last scene in

Hidden – Majid's son talks to Georges' son while they might be under the gaze of the surveillance camera, an event that allows several, mutually exclusive readings – is thus not only the consequent refusal of closure, but also the actualisation of the virtual of the entire film.

Notes

Unless otherwise stated, all translations are by the author.

1   Le Cain underlines his position in a response to a letter to the editors, posted on the *Senses of Cinema* website, that perfectly sums up his position: 'He [Haneke] is not simplistically preaching a message, but creating cinematic constructs that cause us, the viewers, to think and to analyse along with him. Therefore if the film should fail on a formal level – as, it seems to me, *Funny Games* does – there is the possibility of ideological distortion, something less gifted and courageous directors, content with mere didacticism, do not risk.'

2   See Speck 2008.

3   The penchant for frame-in-frame composition is something that Haneke shares with Rainer Werner Fassbinder: the tightly framed shots through doors and windows in *Benny's Video* or, for example, *La Pianiste* (*The Piano Teacher*, 2001), bear a strong resemblance to Fassbinder's famous *Angst essen Seele auf* (*Fear Eats the Soul*, 1974). While the cinematography for *Benny's Video*, *71 Fragmente einer Chronologie des Zufalls* (*71 Fragments of a Chronology of Chance*, 1994), *The Piano Teacher* and *Hidden* was done by Christian Berger, Haneke chose to work with the cinematographer Jürgen Jürges, who shot *Ali: Fear Eats the Soul*, for *Funny Games*, as well as *Code Unknown* and *Le temps du loup* (*The Time of the Wolf*, 2003). For the American remake of *Funny Games*, *Funny Games U.S.* (2007), Haneke worked with Darius Khondji who could be called a veritable specialist of threatening interiors. He is responsible for the cinematography of *Se7en* (1995), *Panic Room* (2002) and *The Interpreter* (2005), among others. Khondji is also a favourite cinematographer of Jean-Pierre Jeunet and Marc Caro: *Delicatessen* (1991) and *La cité des enfants perdus* (*The City of Lost Children*, 1995). Jeunet used Khondji again for *Alien: Resurrection* (1997).

4   In narratological terms, this is clearly a metalepsis in the sense of Gérard Genette (2004), insofar as this move between narrated world (*histoire*) and the world of narration (*discours*) is aimed at exploring the implicit rules of representation itself (see Pier & Schaeffer 2005).

5   Michael Hardt points out in his excellent introduction to Deleuze that the concept of actualisation 'relies heavily on the primary French meaning of *actuel* as "contemporary"' (1993: 16).

6   However, the shadow of the surveillance camera is clearly visible in the second tape, when the lights of a passing car briefly illuminate the scene. That Georges rewinds this tape, showing the shadow again, could indicate that Haneke included this silhouette on purpose, again an indication for a metalepsis.

7   Martine Beugnet therefore misses the point entirely, when she states: 'As the actual and the virtual become enmeshed, it is not, in the more poetic Deleuzian fashion, the past that comes to haunt the present but, rather, almost simultaneously presents that overlap in an uncanny fashion' (2007: 230). Mathias Frey seems to argue along similar lines when he confuses the virtual and virtual reality: 'This conflation of the actual and the virtual (Deleuze) and the role of information providers and transmitters (Baudrillard) in the loss of this distinction is clearly one of the central problematics that Haneke seeks to address in the film' (2002: 6).

8   The difference between the two films cannot be stressed too much: Tasma's film, produced by the French television channel Canal+, is a gripping film, consequently using all available cinematic means to give the rendering of the events the strongest emotional impact possible, also introducing several protagonists with whom the viewer can identify. The fierce intensity of the climactic massacre is certainly worthy of the beach assault in Steven Spielberg's *Saving Private Ryan* (1998).

References

Benjamin, W. (2003 [1940]) 'On the Concept of History', in *Selected Writings*, Vol. 4. Ed. H. Eiland and M. W. Jennings, trans. H. Zohn. Cambridge: Harvard University Press, 389–400.

Beugnet, M. (2007) 'Blind Spot', *Screen*, 48, 2, 227–31.

Bingham, A. (2004) 'Life, or something like it: Michael Haneke's *Der siebente Kontinent* (*The Seventh Continent*, 1989)', *Kinoeye*, 4, 1. On-line. Available at: http://www.kinoeye.org/04/01/bingham01_no2.php (accessed 17 January 2008).

Branigan, E. (1984) *Point of View in the Cinema: A Theory of Narration and Subjectivity in Classical Film*. Berlin: Mouton De Gruyter.

Chion, M. (1999) *The Voice in Cinema*. New York: Columbia University Press.

Dayan, D. (1976) 'The Tutor Code of Classical Cinema', in B. Nichols (ed.) *Movies and Methods: I*. Berkeley: University of California Press, 483–51.

Debord, G. (2002 [1967]) *The Society of the Spectacle*. On-line. Available at: http://situationist.cjb.net (accessed 17 January 2008).

Deleuze, G. (1988) *Bergsonism*. New York: Zone Books.

____ (1989) *Cinema 2: The Time Image*. Trans. H. Tomlinson and B. Hebberjam. London: Athlone Press.

____ (1994) *Difference and Repetition*. New York: Columbia University Press.

____ (2001) *Logic of Sense*. London: Athlone Press.

Frey, M. (2002) 'Supermodernity, Capital, and Narcissus: The French Connection to Michael Haneke's *Benny's Video*', *Cinetext*. On-line. Available at: http://cinetext.philo.at/magazine/frey/bennys_video.pdf (accessed 10 October 2008).

Genette, G. (2004) *Métalepse: De la figure à la fiction*. Paris: Edition du Seuil.

Hardt, M. (1993) *Gilles Deleuze: An Apprenticeship in Philosophy*. Minneapolis: University of Minnesota Press.

Hart, G. K. (2006) 'Michael Haneke's *Funny Games* and Schiller's Coercive Classicism', *Modern Austrian Literature*, 39, 2, 63–75.

Le Cain, M. (2003) 'Do the Right Thing: The Films of Michael Haneke', *Senses of Cinema*. On-line. Available at: http://www.sensesofcinema.com/contents/03/26/haneke.html (accessed 17 January 2008).

Metelmann, J. (2003) *Zur Kritik der Kino-Gewalt: Die Filme von Michael Haneke*. Munich: Wilhelm Fink.

Peucker, B. (2007) *The Material Image: Art and the Real in Film*. Stanford, CA: Stanford University Press.

Pier, J. and J.-M. Schaeffer (2005) 'La métalepse, aujourdhui', *Vox Poetica*. On-line. Available at: http://www.vox-poetica.org/t/metalepses.html (accessed 16 June 2008).

Rebhandl, B. (2005) 'Kleine Mythologie des Schwarzfilms', in C. Wessely, G. Larcher and F. Garber (eds) *Michael Haneke und seine Filme: Eine Pathologie der Konsumgesellschaft*. Marburg: Schüren, 79–86.

Silverman, K. (1988) *The Acoustic Mirror: The Female Voice in Psychoanalysis and Cinema and Literature*. Bloomington: Indiana University Press.

Speck, O. (2008) 'The New Order: The Method of Madness in the Cinema of Michael Haneke', in R. Thomas (ed.) *Crime and Madness in Modern Austria: Myth, Metaphor and Cultural Realities*. Cambridge: Cambridge Scholars Press, 462–76.

Valentine, D. A. (1998) 'Prepared statement of Debra A. Valentine, General Counsel for the U.S. Federal Trade Commission on "Pyramid Schemes"', presented at the International Monetary Fund's seminar on current legal issues affecting central banks, Washington, D.C. May 13, 1998'. On-line. Available at: http://www.ftc.gov/speeches/other/dvimf16.shtm (accessed 15 October 2007).

Wood, R. (2003) 'In Search of the *Code Inconnu*', *CineAction*, 62, 41–9.

Žižek, S. (2001) *The Fright of Real Tears: Krzysztof Kieślowski between Theory and Post Theory*. London: British Film Institute.

CHAPTER FIVE

Michael Haneke and the Politics of Film Form

Temenuga Trifonova

'Insofar as truth is always obscene, I hope that all of my films have at least an element of obscenity.' (Haneke quoted in Sharrett 2004b)

Michael Haneke's films belong to a philosophical/theoretical/cinematic tradition that encompasses anti-systematic philosophy (Friedrich Nietzsche), sociological theories of modernity (Georg Simmel, Walter Benjamin, Siegfried Kracauer), the Frankfurt School's critique of the culture industries (Theodor Adorno), and modernist European cinema.[1] Nietzsche dismissed systematic philosophers like G. W. F. Hegel and Immanuel Kant as 'philosophical labourers' whose main contribution consisted in *collecting* all past valuations and *abbreviating* them into formulas: 'It is the duty of these scholars to take everything that has hitherto happened and been valued, and make it clear, distinct, intelligible and manageable, to abbreviate everything long, even "time" itself, and to subdue the entire past' (1973: 142). In his critique of systematic/dogmatic philosophy Nietzsche privileged the fragment, which, like existence itself, does not have a beginning or an end but begins or returns eternally: 'Existence begins in every instant; the ball There rolls around every Here. The middle is everywhere. The path of eternity is crooked' (1961: 234). The fragment was particularly suited to Nietzsche's genealogical project, whose purpose was to challenge the false belief in the eternal, essential nature of values and to demonstrate instead how and why particular values are constructed and privileged over others. Nietzsche's critique of systematic philosophy's reliance on the 'collection' and 'abbreviation' of past valuations anticipated not only the emergence of a new understanding of philosophy as the invention of new concepts (Gilles Deleuze) but also a similar shift from representational literature, whose realism was predicated precisely on amassing an exhaustive amount of 'evidence', to modernist literature – influenced by, and in turn influencing, cinema – whose political potential lay, as Tom Conley has argued, in the privileging of visuality over narrativity. The increased awareness of the graphic or visual aspect of language in modernist (cinematic) literature meant that 'any word or sentence can be used to construct the meaning of any life whatsoever … [attesting] to an ultimate and ubiquitous democratisation [and, we might add, globalisation] of experience' (Conley 2008: 141).

Nietzsche's philosophy of the fragment, his dismissal of totalising, exhaustive, evidentiary accounts of reality, along with modernist literature's emphasis on the graphic aspect of language – an emphasis on the rootlessness or groundlessness of the signifier, on its democratisation and deterritorialisation – reverberate in contemporary cinema's tendency to privilege visuality over narrativity and multiple, intersecting, fragmentary narratives over singular, linear ones. This is not surprising after all: with the idea of a closed, homogeneous society becoming increasingly untenable, the classical film narrative has proven equally obsolete. Fragmentary narratives register more truthfully the complexities of life in the age of globalisation, drawing connections between seemingly disparate phenomena while, at the same time, exploring local resistances to the homogenising forces of globalisation, which often threaten to obscure social, cultural and national differences.

Structured around the principles of fragmentation, indeterminacy, chance and multiplicity, Haneke's aesthetics reveals his indebtedness to theories of modernity, especially those of Simmel, Kracauer and Benjamin. The core principle of Simmel's sociological criticism, on which Kracauer would model his own investigations of cultural ephemera, and which anticipated the transformations in narrative structure brought about by globalisation – most visible in migrant and diasporic cinema, cross-border films and hyperlink films – was the belief that all 'expressions of spiritual/intellectual life are interrelated in countless ways. No single one can be extricated from this web of relations, since each is enmeshed in the web with all other such expressions' (Kracauer 1995: 232). Kracauer's explorations, like Simmel's, were guided by the search for relationships of analogy or essential congruence between the most disparate phenomena. Haneke's emphasis on the social, ethical and political significance of the trivial, the accidental and the everyday, along with his predilection for fragmented and digressive narratives, revives Kracauer's fascination with the ephemeral, the habitual and the banal. Although Haneke's films belong to the moment of globalisation, not to the moment of modernity, the principles of fragmentation, indeterminacy, multiplicity and fortuitousness have not lost their significance, regardless of whether they are posited as basic affinities of the film medium (Kracauer) or as characteristics of an increasingly transnational, deterritorialised, fragmented, global reality (Haneke). The basic affinities of film for 'the fortuitous', 'the indeterminate', 'the flow of life' and 'endlessness' are no longer elements of an ontological *theory of film* but aspects of a concrete *historical reality* shaped by the forces of globalisation. In other words, Kracauer's recommendation that the impression of 'endlessness', for instance, can be suggested by recording a plethora of sense data with no consideration for how it all fits together narratively, is no longer a *stylistic point* (how best to achieve the impression of endlessness or indeterminacy in cinema) but a *description of an objectively existing reality* composed of elements the relationships between which are continually shifting, deferred or occluded.

Haneke views film as an alternative public sphere with a demythologising and democratising potential which he – following Nietzsche, Kracauer, Benjamin and Adorno – locates in the fragment. Benjamin's critique of systematic explorations of culture and his preference for montage and collage eventually led him to abandon the conventional book form in favour of the essay:

> incomplete, digressive, without proof or conclusion, in which could be juxta-posed fragments, minute details ('close-ups') drawn from every level of the contemporary world … The style of the essay was to be an 'art of interrup-tion' … Benjamin's procedure was 'to collect and reproduce in quotation the contradictions of the present without resolution' … This collage strategy was itself an image of the 'break-up', the 'disintegration' of civilisation in the modern world, relevant to one of Benjamin's most famous formulas: 'Allego-ries are, in the realm of thoughts, what ruins are in the realm of things' (*Tragic Drama* 178), the premise being that something becomes an object of knowl-edge only as it 'decays' or is made to disintegrate. (Ulmer 1983: 97)

Fragmentation foregrounds the loss of coherent meaning but, at the same time, it has an emancipating potential since, as Kracauer asserts in *Theory of Film*, 'only once the current state of things is revealed as provisional [that is, incomplete, fragmented] can the question of their proper order arise' (1978: 22). Narrative fragmentation, which, according to Kracauer, conveys a sense of the endlessness and indeterminacy of reality, is central to Haneke's conception of film form. By fragmenting the narrative – for instance, consistently leaving out the beginnings and endings of scenes, or using 'cut cuts', which draw attention to the audiovisual *découpage* – Haneke demands that we stay alert and react spontaneously – emotionally, rather than intellectually – to the events represented on the screen. Challenging the idea of the art work as internally coherent, unified and self-sufficient, and the false notion of 'Truth' derived from this idea, Haneke insists that only fragments can reveal momentarily, perhaps even unin-tentionally, something truthful without ever revealing 'the Truth'.[2]

Haneke's belief in the emancipating potential of an aesthetic of fragmentation, dissonance and displeasure places him, as well, in the tradition of the Frankfurt School's critique of mass culture. For Adorno the fragment was the last vestige of truthfulness in a mass society ruled by the culture industries: 'The highest products of art are caught up in fragmentariness, which is their way of confessing that even they do not have what the immanence of their form claims they have … The enigma of art works is the fact of their having been broken off. If transcendence were really present in them, they would be mysteries rather than riddles. They are not. They are riddles precisely because they are fragments disclaiming to be wholes, even though wholes is what they really want to be' (1984: 133, 184). Adorno insisted that aesthetic experience ought to overcome the attitude of tasting and savouring, for in a false world all pleasure is false, including aesthetic pleasure. However, rather than encouraging art to simply negate this false world, Adorno foregrounded the critical and demythologising potential of mimesis. The modernity of art, he maintained, lies in its mimetic relation to a petrified and alienated reality, not in the direct negation of that reality, which would produce merely a 'jargon of authenticity'.[3]

While Haneke's films are a product of the historical moment in which he works – the 'moment' of globalisation – they also belong to a European tradition of modernist filmmaking that includes directors such as Robert Bresson, Michaelangelo Antonioni and Andrei Tarkovsky.[4] In the interviews included on the DVD releases of *The Seventh Continent* and *Hidden*, Haneke acknowledges his interest in characters whose motives cannot be explained, and in situations or conflicts that cannot be resolved. He professes no interest in exploring causes and reasons and instead focuses on consequences and effects, on that which is readily observable, the inconspicuous surface-expressions of the age. The majority of critics attribute the 'lack of emotion' in Haneke's films to his preoccupation with form and structure, rather than with psychological analysis. The general agreement seems to be that Haneke's 'beautifully controlled' films force viewers to *think* (and generally to 'feel bad') but rarely *move* them. However, I would argue that Haneke's 'cold' films produce a far more intense sort of viewer identification than most mainstream films. Providing the viewer with the reasons and motivations of a character increases the distance between the viewer and the character: the viewer understands the character objectively. Conversely, the less we know about a character's psychology, the stronger our identification with him as we strive to 'fill in' the frustrating psychological gap we sense by projecting onto the character our own desires, fears and frustrations.[5] Paradoxically, it is precisely by withholding the psychological analysis of characters (showing the effects but not the causes of their actions), and by fragmenting the narrative – both modernist techniques of *distanciation* – that Haneke intensifies viewer identification. It is harder for us to become emotionally invested in a full-blown, self-sufficient story than in fragments of a story: we cannot integrate the complete story into our psychic life; we cannot experience it as something happening to us. The complete story, like the motivated character, appears frozen, objectified – both appeal to our understanding and to our judgement rather than to our emotions.

Although Haneke's fragmentary, minimalist aesthetics seems to embody a quintessentially postmodern affectlessness or moral indifference – for instance, the fragmentary narratives of *The Seventh Continent*, *71 Fragmente einer Chronologie des Zufalls* (*71 Fragments of a Chronology of Chance*, 1994) and *Code inconnu: Récit incomplet de divers voyages* (*Code Unknown: Incomplete Tales of Several Journeys*, 2000) do not distinguish between significant and insignificant events and do not analyse characters' desires or motives, as if to suggest that these are inherently unknowable – Haneke does not brush aside the problem of guilt and moral responsibility. Precisely by treating any-moment-whatever or any-action-whatever as a potential catalyst for a dramatic, irreversible sequence of events, Haneke creates the impression that all events are always already over-determined, that is, destined. Both *The Seventh Continent* and *71 Fragments of a Chronology of Chance* are based on true stories involving what appear to be unmotivated suicide and murder, although unmotivated does not necessarily mean unpremeditated. How does one explain the meticulously premeditated yet unmotivated suicide in *The Seventh Continent*, or the chronologically escalating network of chance events that lead up to, without necessarily 'causing', the senseless mass murder at the end of *71 Fragments of a Chronology of Chance*? Although Haneke denies that we can pinpoint the exact causes that led a perfectly normal middle-class Austrian family to commit suicide, or an average looking student to shoot a dozen strangers in a Viennese bank, the disciplined obsession with which he amasses the unnoticeable details that make up our daily lives, down to the most banal gesture, the most offhand comment, the most insignificant action – putting on one's socks in the morning, washing the car, or trying to arrange, in less than sixty seconds, a few pieces of paper in the shape of a cross – or the most automated action (children jumping over a pommel horse in physical education class, in *The Seventh Continent*, or Max playing an interminable game against a table tennis robot in *71 Fragments of a Chronology of Chance*) – suggests *not* that each of these details might have been 'the' clue, the piece of the puzzle that can finally demystify the reasons for the gruesome line of events to follow, but rather that there are aspects of our existence so inexplicably banal and over-familiar that they inexorably dictate the course of our life in an almost magical way. As we watch Haneke's films, we have the uncanny feeling that the events we see are absolutely accidental, unmotivated and senseless but at the same time – or precisely *because* of that – inevitable.

The Seventh Continent is divided into three parts, 1987, 1988 and 1989. Since 1989 is the fatal year in which the family commits suicide, we naturally look for possible reasons amidst the fragments of the family's life we see in the two years preceding the suicide. However, Haneke does not give us anything to 'work with'. The only traumatic event that could potentially serve as an explanation – the death of Anna's mother – is a red herring: the death takes its toll on Anna's brother, who sinks into depression as a result of it, but Anna herself appears unaffected. It is not her own mother's death but the accidental death of a couple of strangers in a car accident on a rainy night, as Anna and Georg are driving back from a visit to Georg's parents, that brings Anna to tears as she becomes suddenly and violently aware of the sheer insupportability of existence. Throughout the film Haneke's narrative economy repeatedly clashes with the unabashedly transparent symbolism of certain scenes. As Anna and Georg leave the car wash in the first scene of the film, the camera focuses on a poster advertising Australia as a tourist destination. The car wash scene is repeated again later in the film – right after the family drives past the car accident – and so are the travel poster (which gradually comes to signify 'death' rather than 'vacation'), the trip to the supermarket, the family's morning routine (Haneke foregrounds the sheer automatism of these routine actions by 'inverting' the classical *plan américain* and showing us only the lower part of the characters' bodies rather than their faces), and the television news coverage: these trivial events become suffused with symbolism simply by virtue of being repeated. The most striking instance of this transparent symbolism is the motif of obstructed vision developed through the car wash scenes, Eva's imaginary blindness, Anna's professional career (optometry), and the story one of her customers tells of a girl casting a spell on her classmates for making fun of her glasses.[6]

For all its formal inventiveness *The Seventh Continent* presents the meaningless-ness of middle-class existence simply as a fact rather than a problem: Georg and Anna decide to commit suicide because they cannot find a good enough reason not to. In a letter to his parents Georg writes: 'I believe if one looks at the life one has lived straight in the eye, it's easy to accept the notion of the end ... This is not a critique, but a statement of fact.'[7] *71 Fragments of a Chronology of Chance*, on the other hand, suggests that existence does not consist of 'basic facts' but of choices actively pursued or rejected, that not choosing is also a choice.[8] In one scene a friend explains to Max that one cannot 'not bet' on God's existence, because not betting presupposes that one does not believe in God: one cannot simply claim indifference for indifference, too, is a moral and political choice. Thus, while in *The Seventh Continent* Haneke explores an abstract existential crisis unfolding in an isolated, private drama, in *71 Fragments of a Chronology of Chance* he is more interested in the larger – social, political and media – context within which events take place. Throughout the film Haneke cuts violently – in the middle of a line of dialogue or in the middle of an action – from one narrative strand to another; however, the abrupt cutting points up the interconnection of events and characters rather than their isolation or independence from one another. Although Max's particular motive for going on a killing rampage is left as unclear as that of the family in *The Seventh Continent*, placing his story in the context of other similar stories drives home the point that the general deterioration of human (specifically parent-children) relationships – the old man and his estranged daughter, the married couple driven apart by their shared sense of powerlessness in the face of their baby's sickness, the orphaned Romanian boy who crosses illegally into Austria because someone told him 'in Austria they treat children well', the alienated orphaned girl and the Austrian family trying to adopt her – lies at the heart of Max's impulsive, senseless crime.

Insofar as it explores the subjects of alienation and globalisation in a deliberately fragmented, multiple narrative, *Code Unknown* could be seen as a sequel to *71 Frag-ments of a Chronology of Chance*. The film opens with a characteristically Hanekean juxtaposition of art cinema elements – whose effect we expect to be obfuscation rather than clarification – with an unabashedly transparent aesthetic of coding/decoding. Although on one level the opening – a variation on charades in which a group of deaf children try to guess what kind of emotion one of them is 'acting out' – can be easily seen as a piece from art cinema's 'distanciation techniques kit', on another level it func-tions as a straightforward summary of the film's 'theme' already announced in its title, 'Code Unknown'. In fact, the deaf children's various interpretations of the girl's behav-iour read like a synopsis of recurrent themes in Haneke's oeuvre: loneliness, alienation, failure to communicate, bad conscience and entrapment. Although the girl dismisses all of these interpretations as incorrect, the film eventually makes it clear that the 'correct' interpretation is not one of these but all of the above. Paradoxically, then, the opening *stages* – in the literal sense of the word – *the absence of a code*, but it does so in such a straightforward, transparent, almost allegorical way, that we immediately *decode* the meaning of the sequence. The effect of 'book-ending' the film with an explicit reiteration of the film's 'theme – Haneke repeats this sequence, though with a different child, at the end of the film – is to conflate distance (art cinema's distanciation) with proximity (mainstream cinema's immediacy and narrative transparency).

Among the most readily observable effects of the dialectic of globalisation/expansion/dispersal/inclusion, on the one hand, and localisation/contraction/collapse/exclusion, on the other hand, is the increased significance of the accidental, the random and the potential.[9] Haneke's films reflect the 'intensification' or 'potentialisation' of time and space brought about by globalisation, an acute awareness that every 'moment' and every 'place' are potential sites of conflict with an indeterminate number of potential ramifications. In *Code Unknown* a teenager's trivial, thoughtless gesture – Jean throws his croissant wrapper in Maria's lap thereby provoking Amadou's indignation – sets in motion a series of random encounters between strangers that dramatise a range of personal, social, class, racial and ethical conflicts. Haneke's interest in any-moment-whatever and any-place-whatever, to use Deleuze's terminology, in arbitrary moments and accidental encounters, is not only aesthetic but ultimately ethical and political. His films do not gravitate towards metaphysical reflections on destiny, fate and coincidence; instead, they explore the indefinite potential for conflict that each moment holds within itself. The fragmentary structure of Haneke's films does not, however, merely dramatise or enact the failure of communication that often constitutes the films' subject matter.[10] Such a reading would cast Haneke in the role of a romantic pessimist who longs for an ideal community he knows perfectly well is unattainable. On the contrary, the fragmentary structure of his films undermines the utopian idea of a community premised on a vague notion of the 'common'; in this respect, his films should be read in the context of recent theoretical debates on the idea of a 'European identity', specifically Étienne Balibar's attempt to conceive a 'community without community' and his call to 'deterritorialise' citizenship, to establish a 'citizenship in Europe' (based on human and civil rights) rather than a 'European citizenship' (based on nationality and ethnicity) (2003: page numbers if these are direct quotes]. In a 'community without community' the principles of democracy are tested on a daily basis rather than taken for granted. From this point of view, the conflicts Haneke's characters struggle with should be seen not as 'proof' of the failure of the conventional idea of 'community', based on the principles of belonging and exclusion, but as absolutely essential to the establishment of a democratic order precisely by virtue of contesting these principles on a daily basis, transforming them from abstract principles into immediate, everyday problems that demand an immediate individual response.

The structure of *Code Unknown* dramatises the dialectic between the global and the local: the story unfolds by means of dispersal and expansion, bringing together characters from diverse racial, social and national backgrounds but refraining from privileging a single, regulating point of view. Like all of Haneke's films *Code Unknown* explores the victim/victimiser dialectic that was also a major concern of *enfant terrible* of New German Cinema, Rainer Werner Fassbinder. Both Haneke and Fassbinder (in films such as *Katzelmacher* (1969), *Die bitteren Tränen der Petra von Kant* (*The Bitter Tears of Petra von Kant*, 1972) and *Angst essen Seele auf* (*Fear Eats the Soul*, 1974)) reject the simplistic, binary view of oppression that automatically assigns the blame to empowered characters thereby ruling out any chance for subjective agency among the disempowered. In *Code Unknown* everyone is both guilty and wronged. For instance, while the likable and fragile Anne easily wins our sympathy, it is not entirely clear that she is free of racial biases. While riding the Métro Anne is accosted by two Arab teenagers who accuse her of being a beautiful, arrogant woman who does not want to mix with commoners, let alone Arabs like them. As in an earlier scene, in which Anne hears her next-door neighbours abusing their daughter but does not interfere (although she is visibly disturbed by it), she once again fails to act and simply moves to another seat, though we cannot tell if she is really guilty of the arrogance the two Arabs attribute to her or if she is merely trying to avoid any complications (a 'defensive' attitude that could be seen as racist in itself). Conversely, the scene can be read as an instance of reverse racism, with the two Arabs assuming that Anne is a racist simply *because* she is white.

Haneke seeks to expose and condemn the principles of exclusion underlying various forms of oppression and victimisation without however automatically blaming those occupying privileged positions of power and supposedly most likely to perpetuate established strategies of exclusion; instead, he reminds us that the principles of exclusion and marginalisation are universal, that they exist among both the powerful and the disenfranchised. Two scenes draw attention to the fact that marginalisation or the failure of communication happen not only in the space separating the 'centre' from the 'margins' but *within the margins* as well. The opening scene, as we saw, features a group of deaf children, whose 'deafness' is usually constructed as 'marginal' from the perspective of those with a functioning sense of hearing. However, as the scene makes painfully clear, even those who are supposed to possess the specific 'technical competence' required for decoding the messages of other members of their 'community' (the 'community of the deaf') prove incapable of decoding the messages they receive. Later in the film, the French authorities establish Maria's illegal status – Maria managed to 'smuggle' herself on a German truck, along with other East Europeans, into France – and extradite her back to her native Romania. One night, surrounded by family and friends, she breaks down in front of a friend and confesses that while she was still in Paris she once gave money to a gypsy beggar, but when she saw how dirty he was she ran to wash her hands. She then recalls another, painfully similar situation when a well-dressed French man on St. Germain threw money in her lap, as disgusted with her as she had been with the gypsy beggar. In the space of a few lines of dialogue, Haneke shifts gears, transporting the viewer from the level of the personal to the level of the national and the transnational: in relation to West Europeans, Maria suddenly realises, East Europeans occupy the same subservient position that gypsies occupy in relation not only to the 'community' of Europeans (both West and East Europeans) but, more generally, to the 'community of humanity' from which they are excluded.

Although one cannot doubt the sincerity of Haneke's critique of the practices of exclusion and marginalisation in Europe, *Code Unknown* is not entirely free of the West European's stereotypical image of Eastern Europe. When Maria is extradited back to Romania, we see her dancing with her family and neighbours at her daughter's wedding: the scene reproduces the stereotypical image of the Balkans as a predominantly agrarian, pre-modern part of Europe.[11] During a dinner conversation with friends Georges repeats another familiar stereotype concerning the difference between life in the West and in the East: in the Balkans life is simple, he says, since people worry only about their survival; it is here, in the West, that we complicate life needlessly, torturing ourselves with moral questions. It is not surprising that West Europeans are the most complex characters in *Code Unknown*, whereas the 'complexity' of Maria's character is derived entirely from the double life she leads: an illegal worker in France, a mother and wife in Romania. Although Haneke appeals to our sympathy and understanding by presenting 'both sides of her story', it is significant that he never puts Maria in a situation where she has to make a difficult moral choice for example. On the other hand, what makes Anne's character complex and, ultimately, more interesting and believable, is her personal struggle with moral issues, such as trying to determine the limits of her moral responsibility (whether or not she should do something about her neighbours' abuse of their daughter).

Haneke is committed to presenting local injustices and inequalities as particular manifestations of universal problems that transcend national borders. The opposite, however, is equally true: history on a grand scale (the war in Kosovo) is just an extension, or a more visible version, of small, everyday conflicts, which demand an equally urgent response. Thus, the philosophical discussion of the ethics of media coverage of the war in Kosovo ('Do I need to see starving children in order to know what hunger is?') is inseparable from everyday, concrete situations that appeal to our moral and civil duty (Anne's knowledge of her neighbours' abusive behaviour and her failure to intervene). While transnational political problems are treated on the same level as smaller, domestic problems of miscommunication and racism, characters move abruptly from highly-charged dialogue – 'Have you ever made someone happy?' Anne asks Georges in the supermarket – to something as banal as 'Didn't you want rice?' The parallel Haneke draws between two sets of photographs Georges takes (both represented by means of montage sequences) further underscores the interdependence of 'History' and 'histories'. The first sequence of photographs we see consists of images Georges has taken in Kosovo. The second one appears towards the end of the film and consists of snapshots of people riding the Paris Métro (Georges takes these photographs secretly). The second montage sequence is accompanied by Georges' voice-over as he reminisces about his experience in Kosovo rather than commenting on the photographs we see. He recalls a time when he was mistakenly taken hostage. His original Taliban guard was eventually replaced by an American guard, who, in answer to all of Georges' questions, would ask him again and again: 'What can I do for you?' This question, repeated several times over the blank faces of Métro passengers, implicates them visually and morally in the Kosovo atrocities, regardless of their actual knowledge of, or participation in, them.

Rather than viewing ethics as an abstract philosophical question, Haneke assigns moral responsibility to everyone. No one is guilt-free. During the above-mentioned montage sequence Georges reflects: 'It's easy to talk about "the ecology of the image" and "the value of the non-transmitted image". But what really matters are the end results.' The media are bound to present a skewed image of other people's suffering, and often use it to bolster up their own image as a vehicle of democracy. However, defending the 'ecology' of the image, insisting on its undecipherability – on the absence or unknowability of a code – can be just as easily exploited as a justification for moral and political apathy. To question, as Francine does, the ethics of media coverage of human suffering in Kosovo might be necessary, but to claim that media coverage does not tell us – or cannot tell us – anything about what is going on in Kosovo, that the media only mediates a reality that continually recedes from us, is to wash our hands of this reality and perhaps even to justify forgetting it. Haneke continually walks the line between refusing to interpret images for us and foregrounding their undecodability while, at the same time, remaining aware of the political risks inherent in this insistence on the lack of a code. Even as he refuses to interpret events and characters explicitly – on the level of 'story', for example – he insists on the importance of interpretation on the level of form and structure. Indeed, in an interview included on the DVD release of *The Seventh Continent* he argues that since all stories have already been told, the only way a film can convey meaning, tone or attitude is through its form and structure.[12] Thus, the 'code' in the film's title refers to two different codes: the code of social communication, which Haneke sees as broken, and, on the other hand, the cinematic code which offers greater hopes of being decoded, possibly breaking the code to social communication as well.

Haneke is often compared to Alfred Hitchcock: the DVD release of *Hidden*, for instance, features the following critical praise, 'Like Hitchcock, only creepier' (Rea 2006). The comparison is usually justified in terms of genre: Hitchcock is, of course, known as the master of the thriller, while Haneke is often praised for his revision (critique) of the genre, particularly in *Funny Games*, *Benny's Video* (1992) and *Hidden*, all of which can be described as 'thrilling' in a kind of chilling rather than suspenseful and playful (Hitchcockian) way. Hitchcock's films often explore the interpenetration of reality and fantasy, the real and the imaginary;[13] however, whereas Hitchcock tends to emphasise the playful or ironic implications of the conflation of the two realms, Haneke tends towards the serious and the moralistic, engaging in 'games' rather than in 'play'. His films are often structured like Hitchcock's, with fantasy and reality feeding into each other in a sort of infinite loop. Nevertheless, rather than problematising the relationship between reality and fantasy *within* the film diegesis, as Hitchcock does, Haneke, who is much more interested in the media's social and political role, in the film as a medium rather than as a means for telling stories, prefers to disturb the distinction between the diegetic and the non-diegetic. In *Code Unknown*, *Hidden* and *Funny Games* he underscores the ambiguity of the image by continually undermining the viewer's assumed distance or proximity to it: in *Code Unknown* certain scenes are revealed to be part of the film-within-the-film, in which Anne stars; in *Hidden* particular scenes are shown to be pre-recorded on a tape the film's protagonists are watching. Like Jean-Luc Godard, who often provides a commentary on the film-within-the-film (in *À bout de souffle* (*Breathless*, 1960), Michel tells Patricia a story about a gangster and his faithful girlfriend, which foreshadows Patricia's eventual betrayal), Haneke plays with the diegetic/non-diegetic distinction as a way of addressing the audience or even suggesting how he wants us to respond to the film we are watching.

For instance, at one point in *Code Unknown* we see Anne rehearsing a scene for a thriller in which she plays an upper-middle-class woman looking for a new house (following an incident in which her son almost falls from a high-rise apartment). She is shown into a large house whose major selling point is its insulation/isolation: it is fenced in with bushes and shrubs and the windows in the music room have been walled up so that the 'noise' of the outside world does not penetrate it. As Anne prepares for the first take she exchanges a few words with the film director who remains offscreen. Anne addresses him, looking straight into the camera, and in that moment the camera acquires a ghostly, double existence, both shooting the film *Code Unknown* and shooting the thriller within the film. The director offscreen tells Anne she is locked in the room and will die there. She begins to cry, pleading with the invisible director, who tells her that the only reason she is there is because she fell into his trap, not because he wants anything from her; in fact, he admits, he quite likes her. The scene is clearly meant to dramatise, and thus make us aware of, our own vulnerability and acquiescence to the shocking, violent images typical of thrillers, but also, increasingly, of other Hollywood genre films as well. Yet, even as the scene forces us into an awareness of our unforgivable passivity as film viewers, it also spells out what our engagement with a film ought to be: 'Show me your true face; react spontaneously to what you see.' This scene (along with others) exemplifies the sense of 'game' or 'hyper-play' peculiar to Haneke, who consistently manages to drain any lightheartedness we might have associated with 'playfulness' and to infuse it instead with unmistakable gravity. We are left to wonder whether what we see is an actress delivering a convincing performance of her role in a thriller, an actress on whom the director within the film is playing a nasty practical joke, or a woman threatened by a psychopath. The game Haneke plays has nothing to do with the hyperself-conscious, self-referential tricks of postmodernists like Quentin Tarantino;[14] it is a calculated game of strategy challenging our implicit assumptions about the immediacy and transparency of the image.

While in some scenes in the film – scenes coded as 'real' within the film diegesis – characters act inconsistently or do not act at all, making it difficult to attribute to them a specific motivation, other scenes, like the one just cited, blur the distinction between acting and not acting. As a result, the emotions expressed during a scene when a character is supposed to be acting (as we discover after the scene is over) often appear as exaggerated versions of the emotions that remain unspoken in the 'real scenes' where Haneke's cold formalism reigns supreme. For instance, Anne's anxiety over her relationship with Georges, who seems incapable of intimacy, is expressed in, or displaced onto, the scenes in which she is acting. In one scene she performs a monologue from *Romeo and Juliet* and in the middle of it breaks into hysterical laughter. It remains unclear, however, whether the scene expresses in an exaggerated, theatricalised manner what remains unsaid in her real romantic life, whether the hysteria is part of the performance, or a displaced expression of her real feelings for Georges. In another scene she cannot stop laughing at the sequence she is supposed to dub until the director asks her if it is too difficult to say 'I love you' to the actor dubbing the male character in the film. In a scene to which I have already referred a few times, Anne overhears her neighbours abusing their daughter and later receives an anonymous note (we do not know if the note is real or if it is some kind of prank) in which the girl asks Anne for help. Anne does nothing about it and blames Georges for not wanting to help her make a decision. Her failure to make a decision – that is, her decision to ignore the note – is displaced onto a scene in the thriller she is shooting. In that scene we see her swimming in the pool with her husband, while their son starts climbing over the balcony railing; he almost falls off the balcony but his father manages to get to him in time. Anne's character is in shock: she slaps her son and falls into her husband's arms crying, pleading with him that they move out of the apartment. She completely forgets about the child who walks away from the couple, once again unprotected. The scene functions as a sort of displaced call of conscience, the return of repressed feelings of guilt over Anne's failure to react spontaneously to the cry for help she receives 'offstage'.

The motif of responding to a missive whose author remains anonymous or inconclusively established is repeated in *Hidden* whose middle-class protagonists receive anonymous recordings of their own home which has apparently been under surveillance. In both cases, the author of the warning (the note, the tape) is not identified even though we are given some likely possibilities (the neighbours' daughter, Majid or Majid's son). These missives function as a call of conscience, of which the characters are painfully aware but nevertheless fail to answer. The problem these messages raise is summarised by Anne in the supermarket scene in *Code Unknown*. Frustrated with Georges' unwillingness to help her decide what to do about the note, Anne asks him how he would react if she told him she were pregnant. Georges wants to know if she is joking or serious but Anne demands that he must decide whether he can trust her or not just as he had advised her to decide whether she should believe the note or dismiss it as a prank. *Hidden* rests on the same hypothetical situation: is Majid trying to get revenge on Georges, which is why he sent him the tapes, or is Georges' guilt independent of the identity and motivation of the author of the tapes? How does one hear the call of conscience? Does one wait for the wronged party to claim retribution? As Jean-François Lyotard asks in *The Differend* (1989), how can one be the addressee of a question whose answer depends on one's very ability to be the addressee of the question?

The repression of guilt and the moral and social consequences of living in 'bad faith' (Jean-Paul Sartre) are recurring themes in Haneke's films. However, on more than one occasion, Haneke has professed his reluctance to limiting the interpretation of his films to a particular historical period, nation or political problem. In an interview included on the *Hidden* DVD, he emphasises the fact that although the film is set in France and makes specific references to the Algerian War and the 1961 FLN (Front de Libération Nationale/National Liberation Front) revolt, the events in the film could take place in any country. He does not seek to represent or comment on a particular political problem but rather to draw attention to the inevitably political nature of the personal. Although the film does not try to suggest a one-to-one correspondence between the political and the personal – after all, Georges was six when he lied to his parents to prevent them from adopting Majid – it does suggest that political conflicts have their roots in family conflicts insofar as both the family and the nation perpetuate, and operate according to, a similar politics of inclusion and exclusion, belonging and not belonging.

The defining characteristic of European cinema, according to Ian Ang, that which makes it 'European', is Europe's refusal to recognise its own colonial guilt, which comes back to haunt it in the form of a self-indulgent, quasi-existential feeling of loss, whose real historical causes remain conveniently disguised: 'For the white European ... it is all too easy to be overwhelmed by a redemptive but unproductive sense of loss, to cling to a residual identity and be stuck in it because it is so comforting ... [It] is precisely a celebration of such a sense of loss, stripped of its historical particularity and universal-ised in terms of the predicament of the modern human condition, which we encounter all too often in European audiovisual culture' (1992: 26). From this point of view, the 'existential angst' that has become almost interchangeable with 'European cinema' is merely a cover-up for the historical guilt white Europeans desperately try to suppress. Too often European films (Antonioni's films, for instance) distract our attention from Europe's historical guilt by universalising it as a 'predicament of the modern human condition' and even reversing its meaning: they refigure guilt as existential melancholy, which redeems the guilty party instead of forcing on them an uncompromising self-examination. While the white European cinema Ang criticises disguises pressing social and political problems as existential angst, by insisting on the political nature of the personal Haneke demands that everyone consider their life as an act of bad faith. In another interview, included on the DVD of *The Seventh Continent*, Haneke recalls a Q & A session, following a screening of the film, in the course of which an audience member asked him if life in Austria was really as bleak as it was represented in the film. This kind of response is indicative of the viewer's unconscious repression of the problems raised in the film and of their convenient displacement onto a different national context. For Haneke, guilt is an objective rather than a subjective category: Georges' guilt, for instance, is independent from Majid's, that is, it does not ultimately matter whether or not Majid is telling the truth when he denies sending the tapes.

Despite the commonalities between Haneke's and Adorno's views on the status of the aesthetic under the conditions of mass culture, the *earnestness* with which Haneke revives familiar strategies and techniques we had assumed had lost their original subversive potential, his transparent – rather than self-conscious – modernist aesthetics, signals a new 'moment' or 'turn' in the critique of modernity and postmodernity. In the early 1980s Hal Foster declared the imminent obsolescence of Critical Theory's concept of the aesthetic as a 'negative category':

> The adventures of the aesthetic make up one of the great narratives of moder-nity: from the time of its autonomy through art-for-art's sake to its status as a necessary negative category, a critique of the world as it is. It is this last moment (figured brilliantly in the writings of Theodor Adorno) that is hard to relinquish: the notion of the aesthetic as subversive, a critical interstice in an otherwise instrumental world. Now, however, we have to consider that this aesthetic space too is eclipsed – or rather, that its criticality is now largely illusory (and so instrumental). In such an event, the strategy of an Adorno,

of 'negative commitment', might have to be revised or rejected, and a new strategy of interference ... devised. (1983: xv–xvi)

Haneke's films offer a glimpse of this new strategy of interference. Whatever his 'cold', unsentimental or 'super-intellectual' critique of middle-class complacency owes to Critical Theory (three of his earlier films – *The Seventh Continent, Benny's Video* and *71 Fragments of a Chronology of Chance* – have been appropriately called 'Vergletscherungs-Trilogie' or 'glaciation trilogy'), ultimately what distinguishes Haneke's films is their *untimeliness* (*Unzeitgemässheit*), which emerges most strongly in the juxtaposition with Adorno's critique of pathos, seriousness and responsibility in art. The more art tries to be dignified, Adorno argued, the more ideological it becomes: the dignity of art demands that it give up the pretension of dignity. Haneke's films, however, are pervaded by an unmistakable sense of gravity – ethical, existential, political and aesthetic – that no amount of wit or irony can quite dissipate. There is a certain uncompromising, almost punitive moralism and earnestness that strike us as surprisingly untimely or perhaps even slightly embarrassing – the way the discovery of naivety in the midst of cynicism might appear 'embarrassing' – especially when we consider them against the background of the 'affected affectlessness' that constitutes the privileged postmodern stance. According to Christopher Sharrett (2004b), however, Haneke is anything but anachronistic: '[Haneke] rigorously eschews the snide humour, affectlessness, preoccupation with pop culture, movie allusions, and moral blankness of postmodern art. Yet nothing about Haneke's work seems anachronistic, precisely because he recognises that the crises that affected twentieth-century humanity, in particular alienation and repression, continue in the new millennium even if they are simply embraced as features of contemporary life in much postmodern artistic expression.'[15]

If there is one other filmmaker whose work conveys a similar sense of passionate detachment, in an unlikely combination with uncompromising moralism, it is David Lynch. Haneke and Lynch are masters of the uncanny – particularly the uncanniness of the banal and the everyday when it is decomposed, taken out of context, deprived of motivation, purpose or function – although Lynch develops the uncanny in the direction of the surreal while Haneke takes it in the direction of the super-ordinary. As Jeff Johnson argues in *Pervert in the Pulpit: Morality in the Works of David Lynch* (2004) next to postmodernist filmmakers like Tarantino, for example, Lynch is a 'Po Mo Puritan', a director whose cool 'postmodern' visuals and convoluted narratives conceal an untimely, Old Testament-like vision of the world divided between the 'Forces of Evil' and the 'Forces of Good'. While Lynch's films combine a Po Mo coolness with an untimely, and from a certain perspective obsolete, puritanism, Haneke's reinvention of the type of realism promoted by Kracauer and André Bazin – the episodic slice-of-life narrative that brings together random and disparate events and phenomena – takes realism one step further by suggesting that when random events are considered together they are bound to produce certain results; that there are, in fact, no accidents for every event is from the very beginning ethically and politically implicated in every other event, just as every person is implicated in – and ultimately responsible for – the life of every other person. In other words, events whose causes remain occluded – suicide (*The Seventh*

Continent) or murder (*71 Fragments of a Chronology of Chance*), for example – are not accidental at all. The more one scratches the surface, the more one examines the superficial, the ordinary and the routine, rather than sounding the depths of existence for possible hidden causes and motives, the closer one gets to the truth of the matter, until the most random events appear nothing less than inevitable or destined.

Notes

1   Other theoretical frameworks within which Haneke's films have been discussed include Guy Debord's *Society of the Spectacle*, Paul Virilio's media theories, Jean Baudrillard and Gilles Deleuze (see Frey 2003).

2   Thus *Caché* (*Hidden*, 2005) reveals something truthful about its characters without however disclosing the 'hidden (caché) Truth' around which the entire film is structured: it remains unclear, and ultimately irrelevant, whether Majid is telling the truth or lying.

3   In *Der siebente Kontinent* (*The Seventh Continent*, 1989), for instance, Haneke deliberately uses close-ups of objects and enlarged faces that resemble television advertising in order to 'convey not just images of objects but the objectification of life' (see Sharrett 2004b).

4   Alternatively, for a discussion of Michael Haneke in the context of Austrian cinema see Dassanowsky (2007: 253–63).

5   'I try to make anti-psychological films with characters who are less characters than projection surfaces for the sensibilities of the viewer; blank spaces force the spectator to bring his own thoughts and feelings to the film. Because that is what makes the viewer open for the sensitivity of the character' (Haneke quoted in Frey 2003). Haneke's slow pacing of certain scenes or sequences, his use of long takes rather than montage, is dictated by the same desire to transfer the responsibility to the viewer: 'The faster something is shown, the less able you are to perceive it as an object occupying a space in physical reality, and the more it becomes something seductive' (Haneke quoted in Sharrett 2004b).

6   Several times we see Anna standing by the window, looking out, although there is nothing to see but an empty street. In moments like these, we are reminded of another European director 'specialising' in middle-class existential angst and maladjustment: in Antonioni's *Il deserto rosso* (*Red Desert*, 1964) Giuliana looks at the industrial wasteland around her and asks anxiously, 'What am I supposed to look at now?'

7   And yet the systematic way in which the family goes about the destruction of their material possessions matches the systematic obliviousness or automatism with which they were using them up until then. As Haneke notes, the sequence is 'portrayed as work' rather than as liberation (quoted in Sharrett 2004b). Although the couple decide to kill themselves because life is meaningless, they cannot help but turn their own death into a kind of secret project no one else is to know about: it is not enough for them to simply die for they insist on not leaving behind any

of their possessions, and they clearly need the cathartic experience of destroying everything that used to be of value – emotional or material – to them. In other words, even though Georg claims that their suicide is merely a statement of fact, the elaborate preparation and execution of the suicide suggests that they want it to be a *significant*, even if unmotivated, act.

8   Hence Mattias Frey (2003) divides Haneke's career into two phases: 'his initial feature films in the period 1988–1997, devastating critiques of Austrian society, funded predominantly by public Austrian funds, and … his last three efforts, investigations of broader European problems, financed in co-productions with largely French monies, starring high-profile French actors.'

9   The dialectic of globalisation and localisation informs Haneke's semiotics of space, particularly the polarity in his films between 'inside' and 'outside', 'private space' and 'public space'. Public spaces – the city street, the subway, the supermarket – are usually constructed, and privileged, as *sites of overexposure*: insofar as they openly stage a variety of ethnic, racial, social and political conflicts, such spaces function as potential sites of truthfulness. On the other hand, private spaces, usually identified with the domestic/family arena (in particular middle-class domestic space) are criticised as *sites of underexposure* or repression/bad conscience (*La Pianiste* (*The Piano Teacher*, 2001), *Hidden*, *The Seventh Continent*). See Mattias Frey (2003) for a discussion of Haneke's semiotics of space with reference to social theorist Marc Augé's notion of *surmodernité* ('supermodernity' or 'hypermodernity').

10 'I am trying as best I can to describe a situation as I see it without bullshitting or disingenuousness, but by doing so I subscribe to the notion that communication is still possible, otherwise I wouldn't be doing this' (Haneke quoted in Sharrett 2004b).

11 This flaw is partially redeemed by Haneke's skills in bringing into the open the usually hidden symbiotic relationship between the West and the East by means of a simple travelling shot taken from a car driving through a Romanian village: the shot shows a long series of houses under construction, all built with the money Romanians earn by working illegally in wealthy West European countries (France, Ireland and Italy).

12 'All important artworks, especially those concerned with the darker side of experience, despite whatever despair conveyed, transcend the discomfort of the content in the realisation of their form' (Haneke quoted in Sharrett 2004b).

13 See Hitchcock's *Vertigo* (1958), for example.

14 As Mattias Frey (2003) argues, 'Haneke had always sought to position himself as the opposite of Tarantino, as the "last Modernist" whose bare, deliberate cinema treated violence and media with a non-titillating distance without the illusionist chicanery of Tarantino's multilayered association project.'

15 Although Haneke's films are a provocation against 'the moral blankness of postmodern art' they are still postmodern. The very structure of his films 'demonstrate[s] his postmodern transnational hybridity as a German-born filmmaker in Austria who utilises French casts' (Dassanowsky 2007: 254).

References

Adorno, T. (1984) *Aesthetic Theory*. Trans. C. Lenhardt. London: Routledge & Kegan Paul.

Ang, I. (1992) 'Hegemony-in-Trouble: Nostalgia and the Ideology of the Impossible in European Cinema', in D. Petrie (ed.) *Screening Europe: Imaging and Identity in Contemporary European Cinema*. London: British Film Institute, 21–31.

Balibar, E. (2003) *We, the People of Europe?: Reflections on Transnational Citizenship*. Princeton: Princeton University Press.

Conley, T. (2008) 'Fabulation and Contradiction: Jacques Rancière on Cinema', in T. Trifonova (ed.) *European Film Theory*. New York: Routledge, 137–50.

Dassanowsky, R. (2007) *Austrian Cinema: A History*. Jefferson, NC and London: McFarland, 253–63.

Foster, H. (1983) 'Postmodernism: A Preface', in *The Anti-Aesthetic: Essays on Postmodern Culture*. Port Townsend, WA: Bay Press, ix–xvi.

Frey, M. (2003) 'Michael Haneke', *Senses of Cinema*. On-line. Available at: http://www.sensesofcinema.com/contents/directors/03/haneke.html (accessed 10 October 2008).

Johnson, J. (2004) *Pervert in the Pulpit: Morality in the Works of David Lynch*. Jefferson, NC: McFarland.

Kracauer, S. (1978) *Theory of Film: The Redemption of Physical Reality*. Oxford: Oxford University Press.

_____ (1995) 'Georg Simmel', in *The Mass Ornament: Weimar Essays*. Ed. T. Y. Levin. Cambridge, MA: Harvard University Press, 225–57.

Lyotard, J.-F. (1989) *The Differend: Phrases in Dispute*. Trans. G. Van Den Abbeele. Minneapolis: University of Minnesota Press.

Nietzsche, F. (1961) *Thus Spoke Zarathustra*. Trans. R. J. Hollingdale. London: Penguin.

_____ (1973) *Beyond Good and Evil*. Trans. R. J. Hollingdale. London: Penguin.

Rea, S. (2006) 'A chilling spin on guilt, lies and videotape', *Philadelphia Inquirer*. On-line. Available at: http://www.philly.com/philly/entertainment/movies/16112872.html (accessed 29 September 2008).

Sharrett, C. (2004b) 'The World that is Known: Michael Haneke Interviewed', *Kinoeye*, 4, 1. On-Line. Available at: http://www.kinoeye.org/04/01/interview01.php (accessed 19 April 2008).

Ulmer, G. (1983) 'The Object of Post-Criticism', in H. Foster (ed.) *The Anti-Aesthetic: Essays on Postmodern Culture*. Port Townsend, WA: Bay Press, 83–100.

Space

CHAPTER SIX

Glocal Gloom: Existential Space in Haneke's French-Language Films

Kate Ince

As Janet Harbord remarks at the start of her article for *Vertigo* on Haneke's *Code inconnu: Récit incomplet de divers voyages* (*Code Unknown: Incomplete Tales of Several Journeys*, 2000) and Alejandro González Iñárritu's *Amores perros* (*Love's a Bitch*, 2000), recent interest in and debate about space and cinema 'has everything to do with the current context, an age of globalisation, which has radically reconditioned our relationship to space' (2004: 3). Uncertainty about local life, decreased contact in local communities, the encroachment of electronic communications upon a large proportion of Western households and the 'shrinking' of space brought about by ever-increasing air travel are some of the social trends of globalisation Harbord considers, which with the release of films like Iñárritu's more recent *Babel* (2006), show no signs of disappearing from our cinema screens. *Code Unknown* is probably the film in which Haneke tackles the theme of the global city most directly, but running rapidly through his German- then French-language filmography, it is immediately obvious that he has always been a film-maker of space *rather* than place, in the sense that 'local' phenomena defined as events, customs or practices particular to one city, region or even nation, seem of little interest to him. Haneke's eye is detained less by the quirky, the idiomatic or the quaint than by the flat, the anonymous and the expressionless: as Paul Arthur observes, 'the treatment of urban exteriors in *Hidden* and *Code Unknown* recalls the huge architectural photostudies of Thomas Struth and Andreas Gursky' (2005: 28).

The aspect of this aloofness from locale Haneke has been most articulate about is the *in*difference to his films of their national setting – and perhaps therefore also their language(s). *Code Unknown* gained its title because of the long-standing use in France of a 'digicode' that has to be punched into a keypad to admit apartment-dwellers to their apartment blocks, but Haneke's reason for setting the film in Paris was just that he

> can only see two multicultural cities in Europe: Paris and London, two capitals of countries with a colonial past ... This is obvious just from sitting in the underground/métro. Vienna was also the capital of an empire, and if you pick up the phone directory, you see more than 50 per cent Yugoslav- or Czech-sounding names, but in the underground, it's not as visible. (Guilloux 2000: 2)

Multiculturalism – either as failed project or utopian ideal – is clearly one of Haneke's chief preoccupations, but as a filmmaker he is concerned more with the visibility of a city's social fabric than with the political history that brought it about. In his adoptive Austria, the generation born of parents who emigrated from Hungary, Yugoslavia or Czechoslovakia 'has forgotten [its origins] to the point where it sees itself as more strictly and radically Austrian than those descended from Austrians' (Guilloux 2000: 3). But, Vienna could not have played the global city Paris acts as so effectively in *Code Unknown* and *Caché* (*Hidden*, 2005) – and that the city has become a character in these two films is highly revealing – only because the physiognomy of its inhabitants does not visually signify their provenance.

Haneke, then, is a leading example of transnational filmmaking, a dimension of his cinema literalised – since it already had supranational concerns – by the move from Austria to Paris and shift from German into French that took place with *Code Unknown* in 2000. However, it is another – and, I shall argue, the second major – aspect of his cinema of space rather than place I shall dwell on here: his use and realisation of existential or lived space, the type of space transformed by the movement within it of human subjects. Existential space as theorised by phenomenology is the very opposite of unowned, neutral, untouched space; the raw materiality of untilled ground, unexplored forest or abandoned, unsold manufactured objects. Animated by the lived bodies that move through it, existential space has 'atmosphere', resonates with past happenings, and thrills with the possibility of future ones. A number of scenes and moments from Haneke's four French-language films, *Code Unknown*, *La Pianiste* (*The Piano Teacher*, 2001), *Le temps du loup* (*The Time of the Wolf*, 2003) and *Hidden*, will serve to demonstrate how existential space is crucial to the atmosphere of anxiety and tension generated throughout his cinema – the pervasive questioning, uncertainty and fear that have become his trademark. First, though, to illustrate this drama inherent to Haneke's *mise-en-scène*, the writings on cinematic space of an architect-turned-critic will help to show the interest – and indeed, contemporary currency – of a phenomenological approach to film. Juhani Pallasmaa's *The Architecture of Image: existential space in cinema* (2001) consists mainly of essays on Alfred Hitchcock's *Rope* (1948) and *Rear*

Window (1954), Michaelangelo Antonioni's *Professione: reporter* (*The Passenger*, 1975), Stanley Kubrick's *The Shining* (1980) and Andrei Tarkovsky's *Nostalghia* (*Nostalgia*, 1983),[1] but the introduction to his book treats diverse issues that pertain to cinematic lived space, including poetry, the architecture of imagery, emotion, light and matter.

Unsurprisingly, the main argument of Pallasmaa's introduction, 'Lived Space in Architecture and Cinema', is that cinema is closer to architecture than any other art form, because both arts articulate lived space and 'create experiential scenes of life situations' (2001: 13). Lived space may be defined (although Pallasmaa offers several mutually enhancing explanations rather than one definition) as 'space that is inseparably integrated with the subject's concurrent life situation' (2001: 18), an integration that takes place through the mental or psychical internalisation of our perceptions of the spaces we move in. As conscious, embodied and mobile beings, our experience of space is 'a kind of exchange – I place myself in the space and the space settles in me' (2001: 22).[2] Central to this understanding of the experience of space is a phenomenological understanding of consciousness as embodied, the obverse of the Cartesian 'mind/body split': the mental cannot exist independently of the physical, or as Pallasmaa puts it, 'We do not live separately in material and mental worlds; these experiential domains are fully intertwined' (2001: 18). Through explaining that lived space 'is always a combination of external space and inner mental space, actuality and mental projection' (ibid.), Pallasmaa is able to claim convincingly that this 'identification' of physical and mental space is 'intuitively grasped' (2001: 22) by film directors and architects: real architecture, like the space of filmic projection, 'is an exchange of experiential feelings and meanings between the space constructed of matter and the mental space of the subject' (2001: 35).

The Hitchcock, Antonioni, Kubrick and Tarkovsky films discussed in *The Architecture of Image* probably contain an above-average proportion of 'architectural' images created by the filming of complex or grandly designed sets and locations. But although Pallasmaa's book addresses mainly the look of the films he analyses, his conviction about the intimate relationship of cinema to architecture (and vice versa) concerns not only architectural imagery but the articulation of space *per se*. Between them, architectural imagery and the articulation of space 'create the basic dramatic and choreographic rhythm of any film' (2001: 32): when one runs Haneke's French-language films through the projector of the mind, there are not many imposing or painterly images to linger over, but one is (I certainly am) immediately struck by the unusually choreographic approach he takes to directing. In the 'Filming the Boulevard sequences' extra included on the Artificial Eye DVD release of *Code Unknown*, Haneke talks non-stop for a full eleven minutes about how he planned the film's rather virtuoso eight-minute sequence shot 'Boulevard 1 – Ball of Paper', whose entire look *and movements* were sketched out mentally and on storyboards before filming began. As he confirms in another interview about *Code Unknown*, 'I write my ideas down on little pieces of paper, then assemble these on a big board. This is the longest and the most necessary part of the work … Constructing the overall picture [*l'ensemble*] is much more complicated [than writing dialogue] and takes time. Anyway, I never start writing if I haven't got the entire structure in my head' (in Cieutat 2000: 25). Calling

Haneke's working method 'architectural' is no exaggeration: the identification of a Parisian boulevard appropriate for the filming of this early scene of *Code Unknown* was determined entirely by its having a suitable spatial configuration.

The already much-commented-upon first image of *Hidden* is almost a textbook demonstration of how to film lived space. Although emptiness is the dominant impression made by the fixed shot of Georges' (Daniel Auteuil) and Anne's (Juliette Binoche) Fdiscreetly situated and ivy-clad Parisian home, this nothingness (Anne's reply to Georges' 'Well?', the first word on the soundtrack and the moment at which we realise we are watching a tape with them, is 'Nothing') is carefully punctuated by several human presences: first, a pedestrian wearing a satchel who walks down the Rue d'Iris (the street in which the couple's house is situated); second, Anne herself exiting from the house; and third, a cyclist who speeds down the street that leads off the Rue d'Iris just opposite Anne's and Georges' property, the street in which the camera is situated. At this point, as the soundtrack cuts in bringing to the spectator's consciousness the important realisation that s/he is watching a recording – a realisation requiring articulation, albeit not aloud – a sudden flurry of activity occurs in the scene: a red car passes in the Rue d'Iris, a female pedestrian emerges from behind the camera into the field of vision, and another woman walks across the T-junction formed by the two streets, moving in the same direction as the first. This pretty but rather claustrophobic corner of Paris's 13th *arrondissement* is populated, despite the verdict of non-activity passed by Anne's 'Nothing'. Haneke's delayed revelation to the spectator that in filmic space s/he is situated in front of Anne's and Georges' television screen (probably on one of their cool cream sofas), rather than experiencing the comforting rhythm of street activity, is powerfully jolting because public space becomes private: the spectator is teleported (as it were) into the anxious, threatened interior of the couple's spacious living and dining area. It is, I would argue, only by so effectively setting up the exterior of this opening scene as lived, existential space that Haneke is able to make the spectator feel the fear that Anne and Georges experience when they receive the videotapes and drawings, which come out of nowhere (their origins remain unknown and unidentified). The interior of the couple's home begins as and remains a cold, uneasy space, divided up rather than shared: as Catherine Wheatley observes, its colour scheme of greys, browns and beiges 'indicates a climate of disaffection and alienation as powerfully as Douglas Sirk's Technicolor spectacles convey his characters' emotional excess', and 'Haneke's framing of the Laurents, who rarely face each other or the camera, reaffirms this atmosphere. At dinner parties the two adults talk at cross-purposes, neither looking at nor listening to the other' (2006d: 32). The couple's lack of comfortable familiarity with their own domestic space is illustrated again when their son Pierrot (Lester Makedonsky) goes missing, and is absent for several hours before they realise he is not in the house: characteristically, Georges has been working (at home), while Anne has been out for dinner with Pierre (Daniel Duval), the family friend who may be her lover.

In Haneke's films, private and public space, like interior, mental and exterior, 'real' space, refuse to remain in the clearly delimited, self-identical categories that would ensure the spectator's peace of mind. Jean-Philippe Gravel finds another striking instance of this instability in *Hidden*:

This slippage sometimes operates in an extremely subtle, almost subliminal fashion: during a shot filmed by one of the TV cameras in the studio Georges works in, a strange pan takes us from the set where Georges is finishing shooting his programme into the wings, where Georges is summoned to take a phone call. In this way the camera, with a rarely used sliding movement, transports us seamlessly from the public into the private sphere, from an 'official and authorised' point of view to one that is indiscreet and potentially intrusive. (2006: 9)

There are in fact very few scenes in *Hidden* where Georges is seen in public space, two of them being this brief signing-off statement of an episode of his literary show and the awkward interview with his boss in which he has to 'go public' about receipt of the threatening tapes and drawings. Georges is filmed almost entirely in domestic and family spaces, as a private individual, which of course corresponds to the psychological domain in which the fiercely resented and unavowed guilt from his childhood lies. Correspondingly, it is of more than symbolic significance that his lie to Anne about his first visit to Majid's (Maurice Bénichou) flat – he says that the apartment was unoccupied – takes the form of a denial of Majid's lived, domestic space. After Majid's suicide, Georges wanders through Paris for several hours, during which we see him only briefly, emerging from a cinema (a very ambiguously 'public' space, given the privacy film screens allow). When he finally returns home, he climbs a previously unfilmed staircase to the couple's bedroom. Both stairs and bedroom are in darkness, and when Anne arrives after being summoned, he requests that she leave the lights off. The bedroom is cut off from the rest of the house, a spacious but sombre loft to which Georges retreats again at the end of the film. He returns home early from work, claiming to have caught some kind of virus but in all probability just unable to face the world after the reassuring security of his professional environment has been comprehensively threatened by Majid's son, in a confrontation that finally takes place in the men's lavatory (since the offices are open plan, with huge glass windows and partitions, this is the only place at the television station not overheard or exposed to public view). The bedroom's private darkness and the oblivion it offers speak volumes about Georges' experience of space at this point in his life: haunted by nightmares that throw him back into childhood, his interior life has taken him over, leaving him neither the energy nor the attention to actively inhabit the world in which his family and colleagues move.

Strong associations of individual characters with the spaces they move in are a sure indication of the prevalence of existential space, and although one such association emerges with Georges at the end of *Hidden*, they are much more marked throughout *Code Unknown* and *The Piano Teacher*. Three of the four principal characters of *Code Unknown* are defined by the regular journeys they make between Paris and territories strikingly 'other' to the crowded, moneyed activity of the global city: Maria (Luminita Gheorghia) is deported back to Romania then returns; Georges (Thierry Neuvic) shuttles back and forth between Kosovo and Paris in his work as a war photographer; and Amadou's (Ona Lu Yenke) family lives between Paris and Mali, culturally but also literally (his father returns to Africa early in the film, leaving Amadou's younger Paris-based brothers and sisters uncertain about what is going on). Only Anne (Juliette Binoche) dwells in Paris in a way that makes it, and it alone, her lived space, an association I would argue is striking in 'Boulevard 1 – Ball of Paper', where the breezy, urbanite manner of her conversation with Georges' temporarily homeless brother Jean (Alexandre Hamidi) harmonises perfectly with the boulevard's constant traffic, human and motorised.

In *The Piano Teacher*, private spaces – particularly the apartment Professor of Music Erika Kohut (Isabelle Huppert) shares with her dominating, possessive, intrusive elderly mother (Annie Girardot) – abound with meanings and with the feelings of the characters who inhabit them. While the studio where middle-aged Erika teaches the piano is her fiefdom, and the scene of much bullying disciplining of her pupils, the apartment is her mother's. In the opening scene of the film we see Erika trying to cross the hall of the apartment to her own room (a very dubiously 'private' space given the non-availability of a key, and not the room she sleeps in, since she and her mother share a bedroom), only to find entry to it physically barred by her mother, who insists on knowing where she has spent the three hours since her last pupil left the conservatory. Her mother's territorial attitude manifests itself most dramatically when Erika is followed home by Walter (Benoît Magimel), the handsome young pupil romancing her, desperate to find a private space for the two of them to share. Her mother's ever-vigilant guard over the apartment is such that Erika has to ask permission for the privacy Walter is so urgently seeking: in the time it takes her mother to get over the surprise of this spontaneous (and unprecedented?) visit by a male friend, she and Walter have barred the door to her room from the inside with a heavy wardrobe.

Erika's battle for privacy at home is of course inseparable from the years of stiflingly close and disciplinarian contact with her mother that seem to be responsible for the repressed, perverse and above all masochistic sexuality she has developed: practices we witness include voyeurism and self-harming that takes the form of the cutting of her labia, while she indulges in fantasies of full-blown sadomasochism that disgust Walter and lead to retribution that sets off a downward spiral of self-hatred. As the film's narrative reaches this sombre conclusion, however, space becomes more and more meaningful: where Walter was formerly desperate to share privacy with Erika, she now seeks it out with him at the club where he plays ice hockey. Persuaded into having intercourse but disgusted again by her inability to go through with it, Walter then turns up at the apartment in the middle of the following night. It is entirely fitting that the revenge he takes upon Erika – violent blows, a kicking, and intercourse it is difficult to describe as rape, since she offers no resistance and displays not a flicker of either pain or pleasure – takes place in the windowless, oppressively claustrophobic hallway of her mother's fiefdom. More than just material space, the hallway, heavily coded 'interior' and 'female' like the whole apartment, is a space into which Erika's psychological confinement to her mother's sphere of influence is projected, an existential space of anguish, conflict and ultimately defeat. Walter will never enter it again, and since she can no longer play the piano in the public spaces of performance where Walter moves without guilt or shame, Erika has nowhere left to go.

In *The Time of the Wolf*, the filming of which Haneke brought forward after the events of 11 September 2001 in the United States (see Cieutat & Rouyer 2005: 21), existential space is as important as it is to *Code Unknown*, *The Piano Teacher* and *Hidden*, but through its absence rather than its presence. Most striking in this regard is the film's final shot, where a look out onto a landscape from a moving train is not attributed to any of the characters with whom we have become familiar – principally Anne (Isabelle Huppert), her daughter Eva (Anaïs Demoustier) and her son Ben (Lucas Biscombe). In the opening scene of the film, as the family arrive at their holiday home in a subdued atmosphere indicating extraordinary circumstances (the unspecified catastrophe that has caused society to regress to a condition as ungoverned as in the *Wolfzeit*, a German term describing something very like 'the Dark Ages') Anne's husband Georges (Daniel Duval) is shot down by an intruder in cold blood. They take flight, and eventually find refuge with an assorted group of strangers based next to a railway. The dystopic narrative of *The Time of the Wolf* envisions a borderless Europe whose spaces can only be measured and known by the movement of the few trains that still pass through them: as one would expect in the circumstances, the characters are preoccupied by locomotion and regaining their lost mobility, and react with desperate – though repeatedly disappointed – excitement whenever a train passes inexplicably by without stopping. Trains function symbolically in the film, standing in for the movement and modernity the characters have lost, but the spectator cannot help also being reminded of the overdetermined symbolism of trains in European history – that is, of the trains of the Holocaust, whose cargos were destined for extermination. At a moment in history when everyday living is a struggle morally as well as materially, a situation best illustrated by Anne's obligation to cohabit with her husband's murderer (since there is no judicial system that can establish his guilt), the future is entirely uncertain.

The drama of *The Time of the Wolf* ends with an ominous scene in which Ben, almost mute throughout the action, approaches a bonfire built at a distance from the settlement and takes off all his clothes, apparently under the influence of the obscure and primitive belief-system circulating among adults in the settlement who are regarded by his educated, bourgeois mother as slightly crazed. Since most of the film is comprised of extremely long takes, the abrupt cut to the final shot that occurs at this point comes as a shock which reinforces the vigour of the question it puts to Haneke's audience: *who* is in the train? Who has regained mobility? Who has broken away from the settlement in the name of modernity, history and progress? And will s/he arrive at a better place than the one s/he has left? As others have noted, *The Time of the Wolf* is a kind of inverted image (a photographic negative, perhaps) of most of Haneke's other films: it has a forward-looking narrative, however thwarted, and invites identification with characters where *Code Unknown*, *The Piano Teacher* and *Hidden* repeatedly impede it.[3] In Haneke's other French-language films, the key players are firmly linked to the spaces within (or between) which they move – that is, the films depend upon existential space for their drama. In *The Time of the Wolf*, on the other hand, there are no spaces inhabited by bodies/people who are either content to be alone or can cohabit peacefully with their fellow humans, male and female. Spaces are unpopulated, threatening and dangerous, then conflict-riven and entirely lacking in privacy and the mark of individuals: their emptiness sucks the visitor in rather than welcoming him/her, and there is no safe place in which to reside. The film is a drama of negative existential space, a cumulative experience of tension and discomfort that makes its final shot all the more memorable, because the atmosphere suddenly becomes dreamy and contented. The questions Haneke is putting to the spectator may be 'who do *you* identify with? Which member of the fatherless Laurent family do *you* want to survive? Will s/he play an instrumental role in rebuilding society, and will the society that results be similar or radically different from the late modern (or postmodern) patriarchal capitalist one that has been inexplicably wiped out?'

Despite being much less engaging than Haneke's other French-language films (it received generally poor reviews), *The Time of the Wolf*, then, is particularly interesting to consider for its *mise-en-scène*, and in relation to Haneke's status as a quintessentially 'European' filmmaker with an articulated anti-Hollywood stance. Transnational space is one of its themes: its displaced characters no longer have national borders or other administratively delimited zones by which to orient themselves, but the film's landscapes and geography are (arguably) recognisably European, suggesting that its collapsed modernity may be viewed as so marked. On the other hand, its unspecific verisimilitude may be the best example of a glocalising *mise-en-scène* in Haneke's French-language films, one compromised by the Parisian setting of *Code Unknown* and *Hidden*, even if Haneke makes light of the Frenchness of the multiculturalism and 'national' guilt the two films examine. If globalisation is reconditioning our relationship to space in as thoroughgoing a fashion as many writers and commentators surmise, Haneke is surely one of the best contemporary observers and recorders of this historic shift, a dramatiser of glocal discomfort and unease.

Notes

Unless otherwise stated, all translations are by the author.

1   Tellingly, Pallasmaa confirms the preference for an auteur cinema such as Haneke's indicated by the directors discussed in his book when he states 'Regardless of their unavoidable nature as the products of collective effort, both film and architecture are arts of the *auteur*, of the individual artistic creator' (2001: 14).

2   As well as 'exchange', Pallasmaa uses the word 'dialogue' to describe this reciprocity in our experience of space, despite having previously specified that he does not think that the meaning of images is necessarily 'tied to verbalised meaning ... Only a fraction of images received by our nervous system and having an influence on our behaviour and emotional states find a verbal correspondence in our consciousness. We react to images before we understand them' (2001: 9, n. 3). Pallasmaa's use of the word 'dialogue' is casual, however (a 'mention' rather than a 'use', in the language of speech act theory), and has no significant impact on his conceptualisation of our reciprocal experience of existential space.

3   Haneke himself has said that in *The Time of the Wolf* he wanted his fiction to have 'identificatory potential', something he was aware of resisting when making *Code Unknown* (quoted in Anon. 2003: 51).

References

Anon. (2003) '*Le Temps du Loup*', *Positif,* 512, 51.

Arthur, P. (2005) 'Endgame', *Film Comment,* 51, 6, 24–8.

Cieutat, M. (2000) 'Entretien avec Michael Haneke: La fragmentation du regard', *Positif,* 478, 25–9.

Cieutat, M. and P. Rouyer (2005) 'Entretien avec Michael Haneke: On ne montre pas la réalité, juste son image manipulée', *Positif,* 536, 21–5.

Gravel, J.-P. (2006) 'Le cinéma du soupçon', *Cinébulles,* 24, 2, 6–13.

Harbord, J. (2004) 'The Poetry of Space: The Geography of Uncertainty: Thoughts on Cities and Cinema', *Vertigo,* 2, 6, 3–4.

Pallasmaa, J. (2001) *The Architecture of Image: existential space in cinema.* Helsinki: Building Information, Rakennustieto Oy.

Wheatley, C. (2006d) 'Secrets, lies & videotape', *Sight & Sound,* 16, 2, 32–6.

CHAPTER SEVEN

The Vacant Vacationer: Travel as Symptom and Antidote in Michael Haneke

Christopher Justice

Provocative motifs in Haneke's films are plentiful. Scholars have documented the popularity of the names Georges and Anna; the damaging effects of postmodern media culture; the impersonal topography of interpersonal communication prevalent in urban environments; the antagonistic role of the family in psychological develop-ment; the recurrence of suicide; the rebelliousness of children; and Haneke's theories of spectatorship, to name a few. However, one pervasive motif that warrants more scrutiny is Haneke's notion of travel as escape. Maximilian Le Cain notes that the families in *Der siebente Kontinent* (*The Seventh Continent*, 1989) and *Benny's Video* (1992) for example, 'have in their own ways attempted withdrawal from or evasion of reality' (2003); vacationing facilitates withdrawals in both films. Although escape and travel are most poignantly delivered in *The Seventh Continent*, *Benny's Video* and *Funny Games* (1997), escapes are not limited to those early Haneke films, and reality is too ambiguous a catalyst for evasion. One must ask, then, what specifically are Haneke's characters evading? What are they escaping to? And why is travel such an appealing antidote for their afflictions?

In *The Seventh Continent*, Georg (Dieter Berner) and Anna (Birgit Doll) acutely recognise the horror of modern existence, which Haneke represents through excessive close-ups that reveal the ubiquity and intimacy of consumer culture's mundane objects. Through group suicide, the family seeks, as LeCain writes, 'to purge themselves utterly of matter' (2003) and reclaim their identities, which the materialism surrounding them has diluted and consumed. In *Benny's Video*, the failure of personal empathy and dread of bourgeois normalcy govern a family that accepts objectified realities defined by video, television and film culture. Those realities virtually normalise young Benny's (Arno Frisch) heinous act, which then prompts an unusual escape, veiled as a 'getaway vacation' with his mother (Angela Winkler) to Egypt. Since *Funny Games* and *Le temps du loup* (*The Time of the Wolf*, 2003) open with family vacations that quickly turn deadly, the justification for each family's escape is rendered impotent: Haneke refuses to provide information that elucidates each family's reasons for vacationing; rather, their decisions must be assumed to suggest that vacationing in rural locations and, by default, escaping to locations reflecting the opposite of one's urban or suburban existence, are expected behaviours of modern bourgeois life. Paul Arthur writes, 'the traditional Romantic remedy for estrangements of urban society, the pastoral sojourn, has long ceased to be an option' in Haneke's films (2005). Furthermore, the murderous acts traumatise our memory and force us to scrutinise the characters' present and future conditions because their pasts are narratively neutered. But why is Arthur's 'pastoral sojourn' no longer viable? Either implicitly or explicitly, travel as escape is fundamental to Haneke's aesthetic mythos.

In *The Seventh Continent*, *Benny's Video*, *Funny Games* and *The Time of the Wolf*, escape manifests itself metaphysically as family vacation, which is why Haneke's characters do not travel alone; they travel with members of their nuclear family. They do not always travel for reasons of leisure; instead, they travel to escape some form of familial or personal drama. Thus, travel in Haneke's films is represented as an escape from domestic traumas or problems, but paradoxically, since his travellers often vacation with the people they are evading and the problems they represent, their ability to recreate themselves, the essence of all travel experience, is rendered impotent. The concepts of 'travel' and 'vacation' carry complex meanings and should be explored in more detail to understand Haneke's treatments of them.

Funny Games and *The Time of the Wolf* both begin with family vacations, but viewers are provided with limited explanations about each family's past. We must assume that vacationing is normal behaviour for these bourgeois families; Haneke adeptly negates the suppositions we harbour about each family's travel motivations. However, the relationships between what these travellers are escaping and what they are fleeing to and the motivations behind those behaviours are fundamentally paradoxical. Although in *Funny Games* and *The Time of the Wolf* such an analysis places interpretive burdens on spectators, one of Haneke's aesthetic aims has been to rattle viewers from their passive stances and encourage analysis because it will provide important insights about personal subjects, something the director demands of his audiences.

Travel invites indifference and irresponsibility because tourists do not make long-term commitments to affect change or impact their destination; their travel experience is relegated to the unidentifiable, ambiguous space of memory, and tourists are rarely held responsible for negatively impacting a destination. Such non-committal experiences allow tourists to recreate their identities through temporal and impersonal travel commodities such as hotel reservations, photographs or rental car contracts, while avoiding the consequences new identities summon. This experience is one form of pleasure vacations provide. However, Haneke challenges this state of avoidance, which grows proportionately to the tourism industry's growth, because it deludes us from our problems, offering only temporary solutions to long-term challenges that foster a chilling aloofness to moral, familial and societal obligations. When tourists are aware of this state of avoidance, travel produces negative results because their memory of the travel experience is embedded in identity. Since the travel experience was prompted by a psychological need linked to one's identity, problems are not recreated or replaced, but displaced, thus further alienating travellers from themselves. When tourists are aware that their escapes exacerbate their problems, and when their solutions prompt additional angst, another layer of confusion and tension emerges that demands a release no vacation can provide.

Benny uses his travel experience to erase the memory of murder (and its associated guilt) and replace it with the memory he now has of himself in Egypt and another important but vulnerable female in his life, his mother. But as *Benny's Video* concludes, the true culprits of this heinous act, according to Benny, are visually indicted by a surveillance camera; Benny's parents are most culpable as they are summoned into a police interrogation room, which forces one to question how effectively Benny's vacation helped him erase or, in his video-saturated mind, delete his memory of murder. He has not erased it; instead, he has cognitively rewound it and displaced blame onto his parents, and his trip to Egypt helped him to formulate, confront and redirect the accusations. Also, 'another aim [of Benny's] is the control of narrative flow and time: he manipulates this footage in order – half-seriously – to interfere with the inevitability of its narrative and to reverse "reality"' (Peucker 2004). Although his parents may be guilty of horrendous parenting, Benny is guilty of murder, but his vacation offers re-creation that fosters a betrayal of his parents that borders upon virtual matricide and patricide.

Travel as a panacea does not always fix one's problems, and in fact, it may exacerbate them. Modern travel is a perfect metaphor for what Christopher Sharrett describes as the 'death of affect' (2005) that habitually preoccupies Haneke. The director strives to jolt viewers into action by depicting strikingly passive characters, or, as Peucker writes in the case of *Benny's Video*, 'Benny, like many other Haneke characters, projects an opacity that renders individual motivation inaccessible' (2004). Travel in Haneke's films is often represented in affective ways, as if travel can alter or erase the alienation, anonymity and displacement his characters feel while in their homes and native cities. But the converse is too often what unfolds: travel recursively amplifies Haneke's characters' angst. Travel redefines and expands our sense of space and forces us to appreciate its multi-dimensionality while helping us to understand the contracting nature of personal space. Travel also expands and contracts our personal identities; our selves expand through the travel experience, yet they do so in limiting, impersonal and often inconsequential ways. The paradoxical and contradictory nature that haunts many Haneke films is captured presciently in his treatment of modern travel.

In *The Seventh Continent*, we watch Georg and Anna and their adolescent daughter Eva (Leni Tanzer), a middle-class family with a seemingly normal lifestyle, drive through a car wash. The excessive close-ups of the car's parts reveal how material

In *Benny's Video* (1992), Benny is Haneke's most opaque character, and although naked and seeking re-creation, he cannot shed media technology

objects have produced a mind-numbing, overbearing state of boredom, routine and materialism. The car wash carries a ritualistic tone of indifferent solemnity and graveness that, from the start, undermines the superficial normalcy haunting the family. Interestingly, their real cleansing appears when the wash is completed, as they pass a large poster promoting tourism in Australia. The poster reads, 'Welcome to Australia' and 'Sponsored by the Australian Travel Agency'. Since the family later considers emigrating to Australia to escape their dissatisfaction, this poster is the first sign that the seductive refuge tourism promotes may itself be illusory. Since this sign appears in Haneke's first scene and several times throughout the film, most notably as the film's final image, it reveals how important the image of tourism is in Haneke's aesthetic universe.

Although the poster states Australia twice, nothing in the landscape uniquely suggests Australia; in fact, the landscape's features are so generic they could represent any continent. The anonymity inherent in the poster's subject matter, like the ambiguity of the film's title, are exactly what Georg and Anna want; however, the ambiguity and anonymity they currently experience are traumatising them and initiating their need for escape and travel. They are strangers to each other and Eva, yet they are seduced by the allure of leaving one's home and establishing themselves as strangers in another land. The recursive and problematic nature of travel as escape surfaces. The next time the poster appears the print has disappeared, the sound of waves emerges, and the waves are moving, suggesting this image of Australia, packaged and commodified by a national tourist agency, has come alive for the couple, prompting their decision to emigrate there as permanent tourists.

During another scene, Anna's brother, Alex (Udo Samel), cries while eating dinner with her family, but they are uncomfortable with Alex's emotional display because they feel obligated to react to his raw emotions. However, only Anna does; Georg responds coolly, and Eva does not know how to respond. We learn that Alex suffers from depression, and what helps him, according to a letter Anna writes to her in-laws, is travel. She writes, Alex 'took a cruise to Scandinavia in the summer, and it did him a world of good'. After this dinner scene, we learn Alex is not living in a 'world of good' and that travel did not cure him, but somehow the seduction of travel as antidote persuaded them otherwise. Le Cain (2003) suggests that Alex's grief alienates him from the scene's festive atmosphere, and that the opposite also resonates: this pure display of emotion alienates the family members from their own 'malaise' because at least Alex is managing his. Since we learn Alex was apparently cured and that his travel served a remedial purpose, Georg and Anna consider Australia as their potential antidote and transcendent hope. However, it is the failure of travel as antidote, as Alex's tears remind us, which forces Georg and Anna to question and later reject travel to Australia that ultimately helps them understand their own problems.

Several important insights about travel occur during this scene. Alex uses this travel experience as an antidote to the depression he is suffering, but what is remarkable about his travel experience is that he does not visit a country, but a region (in Anna's description), which is more difficult to define. In fact, Alex's travel experience may better reflect Anna's needs because she is projecting her own motivations for travel upon Alex. The more anonymous the travel experience, the more fulfilling it becomes and the better it reflects the travellers' psychological emptiness. Anna's phrase 'world of good' reveals her penchant for recreating her bleak existence into a paradise. Similarly, as Georg sells his car in a junkyard, Eva watches a boat pass by (possibly a cruise ship, another symbol of tourism). Sharrett writes, 'The Berg piece briefly accompanies Eva's observation of the boat. Like a recurring image of an ad for Australian tourism that becomes the film's emblem, the Berg/passing boat moment suggests the impossibility of utopia, or of the construction of an alternative society under the current order of things' (2005). Anna wants the same for Alex but is fooled into believing his Scandinavian excursion was utopian. The dinner scene forces Georg and Anna to question whether Australia is a viable alternative. Travel serves a similar purpose in *Benny's Video* when Benny and his mother travel to Egypt: 'when Benny attempts a "flight into Egypt" with his mother – while his father remains behind to dispose of the corpse – their trip, despite its macabre motivation, takes on some of the qualities of a utopian space and time' (Peucker 2004). Thus, travel and its re-creational activities become an opportunity to experience utopia and rid one's world of past transgressions. However, when that opportunity for utopia vanishes, more drastic decisions are needed.

Although Georg and Anna want to emigrate to Australia and escape their mundane existence in Europe, they dramatically change their minds and succumb to the freedom that a family suicide, in their eyes, offers. Determining what caused this decision, beyond Alex's breakdown, is difficult, but two possible answers emerge. Georg and Anna discuss how this move might affect Eva, and they conclude Australia will be a difficult transition for the young girl. Secondly, after a short ski trip and visit to Georg's parents' house, they decide; their fate is sealed and a remedy identified after a mini-vacation. Although travel is not ultimately the cure, it is for Georg and Anna part of the healing process.

Benny's Video also begins within the context of a family vacation. Benny watches video footage of a pig led to slaughter, and this sadistic scene occurs during a getaway at a farm where his parents routinely vacation; in fact, his parents are in the video watching the pig's death, and Benny is videotaping the action. Later, after Benny kills the girl, he does so while his parents, once again, are away for the weekend. However, the dramatic locus of *Benny's Video*, the murder of an unnamed girl, occurs not only during but also because of a vacation. Benny's parents are on vacation as authority figures: they have no idea Benny has stolen the weapon used to kill the pig; although

Benny's room is swamped with surveillance equipment, his parents are ironically incapable of surveying or monitoring him (a reality his father (Ulrich Mühe) quickly recognises when considering their culpability in Benny's crime); and they are impotent in administering any structure or punishment for their children. Peucker writes, 'The teenager finds replacements for his absent parents … in the eyes of the video camera and the movement of video images' (2004).

Given his parents' frequent weekend getaways and decision to 'vacate' to facilitate the murder's cover-up, one can conclude that these parents vacation often. Since the photograph specifically and visual images in general are important parts of the commodification of vacationing, his parents' appreciation for visual culture contributed to his obsession with film, video and television. That both parents are transfixed by the video footage of Benny's murder, that the mother is an art dealer and there is an Andy Warhol picture looming over their dinner table all remind us of this appreciation. Benny's unstructured, undisciplined lifestyle has led to an addiction with visual culture, and since this culture is often predicated on the passive-aggressive experience of watching, Benny recreates his parents' behaviour with the assistance of video: he too kills an innocent victim, but relives the experience by watching the murder scene, and replaying it at various speeds, on video. Ironically, the murder transpires while his parents are away: if they are on vacation to escape their domestic lives, Benny is essentially on vacation to escape them, which fuels his need for re-creation. One of Benny's transformations occurs when he disrobes and smears blood on his stomach and chest, as if to paint, conceal and replace his skin. However, we witness this transformation through the mediated confines of his image trapped in the virtual stasis of a mirror: nothing about Benny is real.

Irresponsibility and displacement pervade *Benny's Video*. The parents and Benny do not feel responsible for Benny's murderous act; Benny is never held accountable for cheating in his computer studies class; and Benny's sister (character/actor's name) is never held accountable for hosting a party in her parents' home. News reports of Croatian and Bosnian refugees occupy television screens; videos are never owned but rented; Benny's adolescent victim is removed from the narrative like the pig itself; and the film's only restorative act is triggered by Benny's displacement – visiting an alien location, Egypt, and videotaping the experience. Subsequently, vacation, an impersonal act of evacuation, is the elixir that destroys the family's passive-aggressive, irresponsible treatment of murder.

Benny and his mother's week-long vacation in Egypt is perhaps the most revealing example of travel in Haneke's films. The trip serves two purposes: psychologically, it offers an escape for young Benny and his mother; practically, it allows Benny's father to clean up the mess and dispose of the body. In general, the vacation demonstrates the recursive nature of travel; vacations return people to what they are escaping. For example, LeCain suggests that when Benny and his mother are in Egypt, and she begins crying, Benny essentially re-experiences his criminal act, as represented by the spectacle of a woman in 'uncontrollable distress' (2003). While one may argue the vacation facilitates Benny's transformation, it does nothing similar for his mother. In her eyes, their vacation is a replica of their lives in Austria: they do not talk much during meals, Benny continues to videotape most of his reality, they remain isolated and swim alone on the beach, he cannot sleep and she is still restless. Even more ironic and revealing is that the parents suggested earlier that the victim's body parts be taken to the farm, which is the place that initiated this mess. When symptoms of a disease become its antidotes, cures are impossible.

The choice of Egypt is a provocative one. Full of allusions to exile, the fact that a young male named Benny travels to Egypt is reminiscent of the Biblical Benjamin, the youngest son of Rachel and Jacob, who travelled to Egypt to help his eleven brothers harvest corn. Benjamin and his father eventually moved to Egypt, and the Benjaminites were a tribe of warriors known for vicious behaviours. Like Benny, the Benjaminites were known to attack their victims unawares. Egypt is a land of complex histories, occupying volumes of history representing ancient, classical, medieval and modern epochs and many cultures, religions and political structures. When Benny and his mother explore a Christian church, 'their lives have become a holiday from the reality of their situation' (Le Cain 2003). Holiday is an appropriate word because something religious and ritualistic about this vacation resonates, and in some cultures holiday and vacation are synonymous. The ritualistic overtones of their vacation in Egypt reveal their desire to seek spiritual transcendence. Meals punctuate their days, and board games inundated with rules fill their hours. They visit popular tourist destinations while following prototypical travel agendas on tour buses with guides. Nothing spontaneous occurs for them during this holiday. As Peucker suggests, Benny 'is using video technology to examine the process of dying' (2004) and he may be experiencing a metaphorical death himself. The old Benny fades as the new Benny surfaces; like Christ himself, Benny is trying to resurrect his image along the Red Sea in the deserts of the Middle East. His time in Egypt launches new behaviours, which represent his desire for redemption and salvation. He sleeps alongside his mother, videotapes himself, reveals modest signs of affection for his parents and proactively engages in a physical (and not virtual) activity, parasailing. However, old habits die hard, especially when trapped in the confining expectations and protocol of the tourism experience, which is why Benny and his mother visited a tourism shop to arrange their vacation. This is why Benny's footage of a church contains the same chamber music he heard while channel surfing and settling on television footage of a church service. Video will always be his reality; however, in Egypt, this footage assumes a different purpose: it is defined by the illusion, or image, of spiritual conversion. Similar to Georg and Anna in *The Seventh Continent*, travel offers opportunities for metamorphosis, but they are polluted and corrupted when wrapped in the packaging of tourism.

Since Benny and his mother's behaviours in Egypt are similar to their behaviours at home, both seem reticent to change. They succumb to the illusion vacations present: that a short, one-week hiatus from one's normal routines will magically transform the soul. They seek a cheap, quick transformation without responsibility or obligation. Mattias Frey writes, 'When he and his mother go to Egypt, this too is a sprawl of non-places: hotel, tour guide, video camera, and back ... Benny could be anywhere; most important is the dialectic between anonymity and identity. And this is how Benny perceives the world: as an "anonymous user", watching a filtered "virtual reality" without being seen himself' (2002). However, although nothing uniquely Egyptian is experienced during their vacation, something distinctly Middle Eastern and, by default, non-European occurs. Benny and his mother assume that performing similar activities in a different location will somehow produce unique, transformative results, which is why they vacation in a radically different space than Austria. The more exotic and different the destination, the more likely and profound the transformation will be. Egypt is different from Austria in every possible way: it is located on a different continent; composed of mostly Muslims; boasts a much hotter and arid climate, a point that Benny emphasises more than once; and possesses a rural, desert geography that is the antithesis of Benny and his mother's urban, European, Christian home. Also, according to Benny, there are mostly old people in Egypt, suggesting Egypt is ancient and generationally unique. All this suggests that they want a spiritual and psychological transformation, but they do not know how to attain it. Adopting a tourism-based, as opposed to a spiritually-based, travel experience does not serve their needs. Subsequently, they fall victim to the capitalistic allure that vacationing presents. Perhaps this is why his mother states, after viewing various photographic images of potential destinations, 'We'll settle on Egypt.' The word settle, with its implications to real estate, suggests they will purchase this time and space in Egypt, as if the purchase itself, and not the psychological or spiritual experience of being in Egypt, will alleviate their trauma.

Le Cain (2003) suggests that Benny's Egyptian holiday provides morality to the film; by finally dealing with his reality and handing his parents to the police, he is asserting his own innocence and pursuing justice. Peucker sees the film's conclusion differently: 'In keeping with the film's trenchant critique of contemporary mores, it remains unclear whether Benny's act is a moral one – a Bressonian assumption of guilt, with religious overtones – or merely an act of violence against his parents, the flipside of the utopian space suggested in Egypt' (2004). When Benny returns from Egypt, his father rearranges his room, which is now full of light. This change upsets Benny, and shortly thereafter he betrays his parents. While in Egypt, Benny does not transform; he returns to his indifferent and immoral ways, further confirming the recursive nature of travel. When his mother tries to videotape him at Egyptian landmarks, Benny rebels and quickly exits the picture, but when he videotapes himself, he is comfortable and wears a T-shirt with his old face on it, one full of hair. Benny's desire to control and mediate his reality through video is his tragic flaw, but since he perpetuates this behaviour while on vacation, he has not been transformed. He cannot live with the guilt of his actions, so he transfers it upon his parents, an immoral act that is more haunting than his original murder: he uses his video as capital to assure his innocence and guarantee his parents' guilt. His sojourn in Egypt provided him with the opportunity to frame his parents.

In Haneke's *Funny Games*, nothing remedial occurs during this family vacation: the entire family is murdered. In essence, nothing and nobody are re-created; the opposite is true – the family is negated, transforming the vacation into an antithetical experience. Furthermore, Jürgen Felix and Marcus Stiglegger (2003) argue that horror in *Funny Games* emerges directly from the senseless absurdity of Peter (Frank Giering)

The family vacation is transformed into a fatherless nightmare in *Funny Games* (1997)

and Paul's (Arno Frisch) violence, and Tarja Laine (2004) suggests that this contradiction (why should such abnormal acts be committed against such normal characters?) invites empathy from the viewer. Extending this idea further, viewers may also empathise with the family because they are tortured in a space (a holiday residence) during a time (a family vacation) that represents the antithesis of pain. However, their vacation is also an extension of their lifestyle, and although we may feel empathy for them, it is quickly neutralised by the cavalier way they mismanage these absurd intruders.

With *Funny Games*, we come full circle in experiencing what vacations and their existential trappings bring in Haneke's mythos: death, tragedy and torture. His earlier films suggest the more idealistic the family vacation is, the more nightmarish it will become, and the more bourgeois the family, the greater the tragedy. In *Funny Games*, the family circle extends to the professional and personal relationships the family has with fellow vacationers, and from within this friendly circle the thugs, who are labelled as 'friends of a business partner', appear. Vacations offer the illusion of experiencing an extended family circle, but, as *Funny Games* makes clear, families are rarely what they appear. As Haneke states in an interview, 'in the end they are trapped in a sense by their bourgeois notions and accoutrements, not just by the killers alone' (in Sharrett 2004b).

Funny Games coalesces much of Haneke's art: not only does he indict the packaging of violence as a consumer good, but also film itself and vacations as consumer goods. Like violence and films, vacations have been corrupted by the tourism industry because they celebrate consumption, consensus and closeness instead of dialogue, provocation and distance. What is damaging about the depiction of violence in the media is also troubling about how vacations function in contemporary society: they are often inconsequential and restricted to experience only; their purposes are confused and deluding; their popularity is pervasive; their meanings are mediated by others. However, Haneke reminds us that we should be deprived of entertainment and return to a more intelligent, humanistic dialogue about our needs, motivations and curiosities. Instead of being passively entertained, perhaps we should more proactively entertain our own questions and answers.

The Time of the Wolf culminates Haneke's notions about travel and vacation. A nuclear family journeys to a vacation residence and immediately encounters violence precipitated by a father's act: in *Funny Games*, the father (Ulrich Mühe) strikes Peter; in *The Time of the Wolf*, the father (Patrice Chéreau) is shot while proposing a compromise with his executioner. Bourgeois commodities insulate both families; each family owns a weekend home, suggesting their wealth has provided them with the superfluity of a second residence. As in *Benny's Video*, we again have violence that triggers a mother and her children engaged in a fatherless odyssey. And like many Haneke films, the violence seems senseless and representative of the most uncivil of behaviours. Haneke's intentions for *The Time of the Wolf* were to expand the limiting confines of mainstream genres, in this instance disaster films, and make the reality of catastrophe more personal. Instead of packaging disasters into adventuresome, and therefore lucrative, thrill rides, Haneke wanted to reveal all catastrophes for what they are: horrific tragedies that profoundly impact upon real human beings.

Since much of the film transpires in a railway station and along railroad tracks, Haneke again places his characters in another anonymous 'non-place' of modern urban space. However, this urban space is not urban, nor is it sub-urban; the action in *The Time of the Wolf* occurs in rural spaces, but those tracks link rural fields with cities, and the inhabitants of those fields are city residents. Travel and vacation offer no escape whatsoever; they extend our identities but do not erase or re-create them. Travel can never be an impersonal experience in a distant land; travel always is a personal experience in a land made familiar by our presence.

If *The Time of the Wolf* is read as a vacation turned upside down, an experience where survival supercedes entertainment, where pain displaces pleasure, where introspection overcomes socialising, where questions trump answers, and where discovery defeats escape, the darkness that pervades the film is the nihilist's blank slate, one that offers a more accurate opportunity to re-create, not an ominous front. Haneke's darkness paradoxically resonates with beauty, opportunity and hope. It is fitting that the film's final scene offers a point-of-view shot from a moving train travelling through lush countryside. Haneke rewards us with this important maxim: hope is our natural state, and our natural state is to hope.

The complex vision inherent in Haneke's films can be better understood by analysing his treatment of vacations and travel. Never satisfied with the status quo, Haneke questions the capitalist impulses of the tourism industry and the way in which they have diluted the spiritual and psychological aspects of travel. Haneke's characters force us to question our own travel experiences and transform them from quick excursions devoid of ramification to thoughtful, consequential explorations of identity, culture and spirituality. Instead of travelling to escape, Haneke inspires viewers to travel, discover and question their motivations, inspiring them to ask important questions such as 'Why do we travel?', 'What are we seeking?' and 'What are we escaping?'

In *The Time of the Wolf* (2003), railroad tracks symbolise travel's recursive spirit: we often return to what we escape

Understanding how our instincts for travel reflect our relationships with cities, homes and cultures, and most importantly our identities, will help us better understand others. If we can understand the recursive nature of travel and realise that vacations are often reduced to reiterations of our own angst displaced in another state, culture or nation, we may begin to penetrate the troubling 'death of affect' that haunts Haneke's films. But we cannot begin this affection without a more aggressive interrogation of our own motivations for travel.

References

Arthur, P. (2005) 'Endgame', *Film Comment*, 51, 6, 24–8, also available at http:// filmlinc.com/fcm/ND05/hidden2.htm (accessed 10 October 2008).

Felix, J. and M. Stiglegger (2003) 'Austrian psycho killers & home invaders: the horror-thrillers *Angst* & *Funny Games*', in S. J. Schneider (ed.) *Fear Without Frontiers: Horror Cinema Across the Globe*. Surrey: FAB Press, 175–84.

Frey, M. (2002) 'Supermodernity, Capital, and Narcissus: The French Connection to Michael Haneke's *Benny's Video*', *Cinetext*. On-line. Available at: http://cinetext. philo.at/magazine/frey/bennys_video.pdf (accessed 10 October 2008).

Laine, T. (2004) '"What are you looking at and why?" – Michael Haneke's *Funny Games* (1997) with his audience', *Kinoeye*, 4, 1. On-line. Available at: http://www. kinoeye.org/04/01/laine01.php (accessed 28 March 2009).

Le Cain, M. (2003) 'Do the Right Thing: The Films of Michael Haneke', *Senses of Cinema*. On-line. Available at: http://www.sensesofcinema.com/contents/03/26/ haneke.html (accessed 17 January 2008).

Peucker, B. (2004) 'Effects of the Real', *Kinoeye*, 4, 1. On-line. Available at: http:// www.kinoeye.org/04/01/peucker01.php (accessed 19 April 2008).

Sharrett, C. (2004b) 'The World that is Known: Michael Haneke Interviewed', *Kinoeye*, 4, 1. On-line. Available at: http://www.kinoeye.org/04/01/interview01. php (accessed 19 April 2008).

_____ (2005) '*The Seventh Continent*', *Senses of Cinema*. On-line. Available at: http://www.sensesofcinema.com/contents/cteq/05/34/seventh_continent.html (accessed 10 October 2008).

CHAPTER EIGHT

Cosmopolitan Exteriors and Cosmopolitan Interiors: The City and Hospitality in Haneke's Code Unknown

Paula E. Geyh

> Hospitality is culture itself and not simply one ethic amongst others. Insofar as it has to do with the *ethos*, that is ... one's home ... inasmuch as it is a manner of being there, the manner in which we relate to ourselves and to others, to others as our own or as foreigners, *ethics is hospitality*. (Derrida 2001: 17; emphasis added)

In 1996, Jacques Derrida addressed the International Parliament of Writers in Strasbourg on the issue of 'cosmopolitan rights' for refugees, asylum seekers and immigrants.[1] In that address, later published under the title 'On Cosmopolitanism', he raised the possibility of a new instantiation of the historical 'cities of refuge', an 'open city' emerging out of and requiring a new cosmo*politics* that encompasses both the duty of and the right to hospitality. Within the context of global cities and globalisation, such a cosmopolitics would require us to think about hospitality, democracy and justice beyond the borders of the nation-state; it would, in effect, require the creation of a new political imaginary. To speak of cosmopolitanism and hospitality, I will argue here, is inevitably to speak of what is simultaneously a politics and ethics of exteriority and interiority, of otherness both without and within. A cosmopolitics and ethics of hospitality, then, would need to operate not just on local, national and global levels, but also, critically, on the personal level. It would need to be consciously and sometimes unconsciously lived, both externally and internally. I will also argue that, as it mediates between us as postmodern subjects and the geopolitical landscapes of postmodernity, the contemporary global city is always already, as Derrida would have it, a city of refuge. It mediates these relationships between exterior and interior hospitality through its inside and outside spaces and also through our experience and conceptualisation of these spaces. These are then my two interconnected subjects here: the relationships between an exterior and interior hospitality, and the cosmopolitan city as the primary space, the primary interior/exterior, in which these relationships are mediated.

Michael Haneke's film *Code inconnu: Récit incomplet de divers voyages* (*Code Unknown: Incomplete Tales of Several Journeys*, 2000) is a powerful depiction of the complexities of these forms of hospitality, and it offers a way to think through a city-mediated cosmopolitics – what it might involve, the difficulties we would have to overcome in order to bring it about, and how we might begin. These issues are not new to Haneke's 'cinema of insistent questions': his first theatrically-released feature film, *Der siebente Kontinent* (*The Seventh Continent*, 1989) explores one bourgeois family's ultimately fatal experience of urban alienation and anomie.[2] *71 Fragmente einer Chronologie des Zufalls* (*71 Fragments of a Chronology of Chance*, 1994) and *Caché* (*Hidden*, 2005), like *Code Unknown*, feature portraits of citydwellers (many of them anonymous) whose seemingly disparate lives intersect and collide amid a steady background beat of news reports of civil wars and genocides. *Le temps du loup* (*The Time of the Wolf*, 2003) examines the plight of refugees in a post-apocalyptic Europe; *Hidden* depicts the return of the colonial repressed into the lives of a Parisian family.

Composed, like *71 Fragments of a Chronology of Chance*, of a series of fragmented, interlocking storylines, *Code Unknown* opens with a brief, silent scene sandwiched amid the opening credits. In the scene, a young girl slowly shrinks against a wall and crouches for a moment. Then, she stands up. The camera cuts from her to the face of another child who, in sign language, asks, 'Alone?' The girl shakes her head. Another child signs, 'Hiding place?' And she shakes her head again. We are, we realise, watching a game of charades played by children who are deaf. None of the guesses – 'Gangster?' 'Bad conscience?' 'Sad?' 'Imprisoned?' – elicits a nod. The screen reverts to the opening titles.

As we discover, this strange prologue telegraphs some of the key questions posed by the film. There is, first and most obviously, the eponymous unknown code, often linked to an indecipherable message, which is central to many of the situations depicted in the film. Much of the film's action takes place in Paris, depicted as a global, heterogeneous city, where the many languages of its inhabitants (in addition to the children's sign language, the film includes dialogue in French, German, English, Malinka, Romanian and Arabic) routinely appear as unknown codes for one another, as do their customs, values and intentions. The characters of *Code Unknown* face one another across a series of cultural divides that separate them from each other and fragment the city – divisions that are formally emphasised by the brief cuts to black that separate one scene from another throughout the film (a technique similarly deployed in *71 Fragments of a Chronology of Chance*). Placing us within this divided city, the film repeatedly suggests the question, what do we owe to others? To our relatives and friends and neighbours? To passersby and foreigners in our midst? To our former colonial subjects? To those who seek refuge among us?

The first scene, after the opening credits, is of a chance encounter at a busy Paris intersection that brings together Anne (Juliette Binoche), a Parisian actress; Jean (Alexandre Hamidi), a young French man from the provinces; Marie (Luminita Gheorghiu), an illegal immigrant from Romania; and Amadou (Ona Lu Yenke), a young teacher who is the son of Malian immigrants. Entitled 'Ball of Paper', the scene begins with Anne coming out of the door of her apartment building onto a busy street. Jean, the younger brother of Anne's boyfriend Georges (Thierry Neuvic), is waiting for her outside.[3] He has run away from his father and the farm, he explains, and he needs a place to stay. He would have come upstairs, but the code to the electronic lock on the door has been changed, and he did not know the new one – yet another 'unknown code' in the film. He tried to call, but Anne was in the bath and did not hear the phone, so he got the answering machine. His brother Georges is away, Anne tells him, photographing the war in Kosovo, and she is on her way to a meeting. She and Jean have a quick conversation as they walk, and, after buying him a pastry and reminding him that 'there isn't room for three' in her apartment, she gives him the code and the keys.

On his way back, Jean passes Marie, who is sitting against a wall just inside an alley, begging. He tosses the empty, crumpled-up pastry bag into her lap and keeps going. But Amadou sees this and decides to intervene. He confronts Jean, asking him, 'Was that a good thing to do? Do you feel that was right?' and demands that he apologise to the woman. They scuffle, Anne returns and demands to know why Amadou is beating up on Jean, and the police arrive. They ask for everyone's papers, they arrest Amadou, and the next time we see Marie, she is being escorted, in handcuffs, onto a flight back to Romania.

On multiple levels, this scene might be understood as a series of failures of hospitality: Jean's failure to offer hospitality to Marie (which is then made 'official' by the police), but also Anne's failure to offer hospitality to Jean (which might be part of what triggers Jean's subsequent mistreatment of Marie) and, finally, the failure of Amadou's attempt to correct the situation with Marie by forcing Jean to apologise and acknowledge her right to be treated with dignity, and thus to reinstate hospitality. We may understand these failures and the nature of hospitality itself with the help of Derrida's analysis of the subject, which I would like to enter by way of Sigmund Freud's comment on altruism.

In *Civilization and Its Discontents* (1961), originally published in 1930, Freud argues that no ideal runs so counter to our original natures as altruism – the command that we love one another as ourselves – and that we are therefore not naturally inclined to offer much hospitality, let alone love, to our neighbours, much less strangers. *Homo homini lupus* [Man is wolf to man]. Although not in disagreement with Freud's argument, Derrida, following Immanuel Kant and Emmanuel Levinas, nevertheless believes in the possibility of hospitality, at least in principle or at least as a principle, even towards an absolute stranger.[4] According to Derrida, hospitality is 'an unconditional injunction – I have to welcome the Other whoever he or she is unconditionally, without asking for a document, a name, a context, or a passport. That is the very first opening of my relation to the Other: to open my space, my home – my house, my language, my culture, my nation, my state, and myself' (1997).

Derrida's invocation of hospitality as 'an unconditional injunction' here contains echoes of Kant's 'categorical imperative' – the 'unconditional moral imperative', dictated by reason, that instructs us to 'So act that you use humanity, whether in your own person or in the person of any other, always at the same time as an end, never merely as a means' (1998: 38). This imperative and its corollaries create a foundation for Kant's political and legal cosmopolitanism, including the right to hospitality which comprises the third (and final) 'Definitive Article for a Perpetual Peace' in his essay 'Perpetual Peace'. Kant asserts that 'hospitality is not a question of philanthropy but of right', a right that all men have 'by virtue of their common possession of the surface of the earth' (1963: 103). According to Kant, the right to hospitality entails 'the right of a stranger not to be treated as an enemy when he arrives in the land of another' (ibid.).

As Derrida points out, however, in practice, hospitality of this type is not possible without further conditions, which are not sufficiently examined by Kant. First, in order to offer hospitality, one must be the 'master' of the house or nation – one must in some sense control it, have sovereignty over it – in order to be able to 'host' at all. But the control does not stop there, for the host must have some degree of control over his guests, as well. If they take over the house, he is no longer the host. Extending hospitality might, given a bad guest, result in the displacement, undermining or destruction of everything – and everyone – in the house, in the space of hospitality. The host, therefore, has the duty, Derrida argues, 'of choosing, electing, filtering, selecting [his] invitees, visitors, or guests, those to whom [he] decide[s] to grant asylum, the right of visiting, or hospitality' (Derrida & DuFourmantelle 2000: 55).

Embedded in hospitality, then, there are several impasses or, in Derrida's terms, 'aporias' defined by the conflicts between the (unconditional) principles of hospitality and the conditions, ultimately irreducible (as against what the principles in question would require), under which these principles must be implemented. Thus, while the moral injunction to hospitality might be 'unconditional' in principle, in practice it does involve conditions, and these conditions are not without their troubling implications. There is, Derrida says, 'no hospitality, in the classic[al] sense, without sovereignty over one's home, but since there is also no hospitality without finitude, sovereignty can only be exercised by filtering, choosing and thus by excluding and doing violence. Injustice, a certain injustice ... begins right away, from the very threshold of the right to hospitality' (ibid.). Accordingly, the ethical imperative to offer unconditional hospitality is inevitably bound up with political considerations of property, sovereignty and control. Thus, as against Levinas's more strictly ethical view, but closer to Kant's, Derrida's vision of hospitality necessarily encompasses both the ethical and the political domains, which we must always negotiate. Derrida argues that 'We will always be threatened by this dilemma between, on the one hand, unconditional [ethical] hospitality that dispenses with law, duty, or even politics, and, on the other, [political] hospitality circumscribed by law and duty. One of them can always corrupt the other, and this capacity for perversion remains irreducible' (Derrida & Dufourmantelle 2000: 135).

Even leaving aside psychological or psychoanalytic, for example, Freudian, complexities (on which I shall comment below), Derrida's analysis directs us towards the apparently irreducible ethical-political complexity, almost impossibility, of hospitality, while still insisting on the necessity, the imperative, of practising it. For Derrida, hospitality is both necessary *and* impossible. There is no formula, no decidable or decipherable algorithm for hospitality, which would establish or guarantee it once and for all. This does not mean, however, that we should not institute or practise certain general ethical, political or legal laws of hospitality. Quite the contrary: such laws are *necessary*, including and in particular those that guarantee all our rights, such as the right to political asylum, which is also one of Derrida's points. Laws, however, are *never sufficient*, for each situation is ultimately singular, unique, and what worked in one case might fail in another, even very similar, situation.

Thus, in *Code Unknown*, we might see Amadou as caught within some of the impasses, the conflicting demands, of hospitality, including those of a psychological nature, between which we all must navigate, and with a much greater chance to fail than to succeed. First, though, it is necessary to acknowledge that Amadou's own aims are divided and therefore already problematic. He sees that an injury (itself arguably a gesture of inhospitality or at least a failure of hospitality) has been done to Marie. In what might be construed as a gesture of hospitality, he seeks to remedy it, to affirm her dignity as a person. But he also wants to teach Jean a lesson: he wants him to apologise, to admit that he was wrong. He wants Jean to acknowledge Marie's humanity, in a sense, to make the gesture of hospitality *for him*. But Amadou cannot offer her someone else's hospitality; he cannot host what he does not control. He could, of course, have simply directed his attention, extended his hospitality, to Marie from the very beginning. He might have asked her, for example, what she needed, and then helped her as much as he could. But while Amadou is seizing the moral high ground, feeling righteous (and most of us are probably cheering for him), he has also brought Marie to the attention of the police, who will ensure her deportation. The involvement of the police reminds him (and us) that issues of law – not just ethical but also juridical law – are implicated in hospitality, and that hospitality has its unhappy exclusionary aspects, its inevitable violence. The police's handling of the situation raises other questions as well. Since they do not arrest Jean or even take him in for questioning, they have apparently decided, despite the conflicting accounts, that Amadou, who is polite, reasonable and articulate, but, nonetheless, black, must be at fault. (We later learn that he is beaten by the police, who also ransack his family's apartment.)

The scene is also an object lesson in the perils of unintended consequences – we can never be absolutely certain, when we try to help, whether we might instead be doing harm. Yet the film is hardly an apology for non-involvement. In several scenes, Haneke shows us the consequences of not intervening, of standing back, of thinking some failures of hospitality are none of our business. In the film, the most grievous, large-scale failure of hospitality is that of the recent Balkan wars, invoked by Georges' photographs. The mutilated and murdered Muslim citizens of Kosovo might be seen as victims of the Serb's brutal failure of hospitality to, as Derrida puts it, 'Others as our own', as fellow citizens of Yugoslavia, whatever their religion or ethnicity or simply as fellow human beings. Georges' photographs of the slaughter also offer compelling witness to the international community's failure to intervene in a timely manner, and to the costs of this political and ethical neglect.

The category of the 'stranger', the Other, is of course not limited to those from other countries or ethnicities or races or religions whom we might encounter in foreign lands or in those places we consider ours: our countries, cities and towns, however much we might consider them to be 'our homes'.[5] The stranger seeking welcome might come to us as a neighbour, one whom we believe we know. Even among neighbours, however, where close proximity would seem to lend a particular urgency, we do not always intervene. One night Anne's ironing is interrupted by the screams of a child down the hall. She stops, mutes the television, listens, but then, after a moment, she starts to iron again. A note asking for help appears under her door, but she cannot 'decode' it, she cannot decide whether it is really a plea for help or a joke. Nor is she certain of the identity of its sender. The woman across the hall refuses to look at it, but assures Anne that she did not write it. Anne doubts that a ten-year-old girl would sign herself 'a defenceless child'. She is reluctant to act without being sure. And not long after, she is standing mute over the child's grave.

Kant's right to hospitality encompasses both 'a right to associate' and a 'right to establish communication', and surely the willingness to engage in conversation with the Other would be part of most definitions of cosmopolitanism. But Anne's inability to correctly decipher the child's plea for help reminds us that these conversations with Others are likely to involve problems of both context and content. Here the problem arises out of a lack of certainty about the identity and motivations of the message's sender. Yet even when these seem to be clear (though we can likely never be certain about another's identity or motivations) and we believe we share a common language, we are likely to encounter difficulties, especially in the heterogeneous landscapes, city-scapes and households of postmodernity. But then, as Jean-François Lyotard likes to say, the postmodern precedes (logically, not ontologically) the modern, and perhaps the human as well, and hence he defines all hospitality or at least justice by the hetero-geneity of the postmodern. In the postmodern world we move, deliberately or not, among a heterogeneous array of what Lyotard in *The Postmodern Condition* (1984), following Ludwig Wittgenstein, terms 'language games' – different discourses (for example, political, economic, scientific, philosophical) that deploy different vocabu-laries (or 'technical jargons') and types of statements (denotative, prescriptive, and so on). Each language game also has different 'rules' for what can be said and how the validity of those pronouncements is determined.[6] Communication between different language games, therefore, can be difficult, and it is not always easy to understand, or be understood, when one enters a different game. As Lyotard points out, 'the social bond is linguistic, but is not woven with a single thread. It is a fabric formed by the intersection of at least two (and in reality an indeterminate number) of language games, obeying different rules' (1984: 40). These 'language games are heteromorphous, subject to heterogeneous sets of pragmatic rules', so they can neither be reduced to one another nor subsumed beneath some universal metalanguage (1984: 65). How to negotiate these different language games and the gaps among them, then, poses one of the primary challenges to our hospitality. Haneke's film makes the contempo-rary (global) city, its interiors and exteriors (both need codes thus far unknown), the primary site of the negotiations among heterogeneous language games, and through them, heterogeneous hospitalities, including interior and exterior, local and global, and ethical and political hospitalities.

Most importantly, however, a cosmopolitan openness must be defined by an essential willingness to engage with and, beyond that, to extend hospitality to the Other. This 'categorical imperative' of cosmopolitan hospitality turns out to be a complex matter as well since, as Derrida points out in 'Politics and Friendship', 'the Other is not simply the Other as coming from the outside ... the Other is already inside, and has to be sheltered and welcomed in a certain way' (1997). There are always at least two 'Others' at any given moment – the Other without and within – and they are inseparable.

Though we are not always aware of it, all of us contain, within ourselves, several forms of internal 'otherness'. In our own minds, all of us engage in heterogeneous language games as well, and they, too, must be negotiated. Thus, even within ourselves, language games are always, to use Mikhail Bakhtin's term, dialogic. When we attempt to reduce this dialogism to a monologism, and these internal or external dialogues to monologues, hospitality becomes more difficult. We must, then, acknowledge and learn to be open to and negotiate this dialogism.

As the film demonstrates, these negotiations encounter many other barriers (beyond, but often linked to those of language), psychological as well as practical, that cause our hospitality to fail, or us to fail in our hospitality. We see this, for example, in the story that Marie relates to a friend, after she returns to Paris. 'One day, in Certeze', she begins, 'I gave some money to a gypsy beggar. She was so dirty, I ran to wash my hands to avoid catching a disease. She simply disgusted me.' She pauses for a moment and then continues. 'Last winter, on Boulevard St. Germain, a well-dressed man was about to give me twenty francs ... But when he saw my outstretched hand, he threw the bill into my lap as if I nauseated him. I rushed back here and hid myself in the attic. I cried my eyes out all day. It was so embarrassing. Do you see'? In Paris, she is the abject one, a realisation that is made all the more painful because she knows, since she once experienced it herself, how a gesture of hospitality might be aborted by disgust. And we realise, also, that these two incidents echo the opening scene in which Jean tosses his empty pastry bag into her lap – a gesture of inhospitality which these two gestures involving Marie invert, since they at least originated in a kind of hospitality. The film makes us travel between the places, within and outside Paris or even within and outside ourselves, where the characters, and sometimes we ourselves, appear, sometimes simultaneously (Anne often does) at different ends of the host-guest economy of hospitality that is both ethical and political.

To illustrate this aspect of the film, I want to explore a bit further the psychological mechanism, beyond an aversion to dirt, that might have produced Marie's and the well-dressed man's failures of hospitality. Marie's account of these two incidents might also, I think, be understood as an inverted allegory of the encounter with one's own, internal otherness, though a somewhat different form of internal otherness than the one discussed previously. Marie is first in the position of rejecting the abject Other, whose 'dirt' threatens to be contagious and must be washed off. Marie's disgust, however excusable, might be a sign of something deeper; that in some sense the gypsy beggar was also already experienced (perhaps unconsciously) as a reflection of herself, specifically of her own repressed fears or desires. The second incident she describes is a mirror of the first; now the debased, abject Other is revealed to be herself. She has, then, occupied both positions (of the ambivalent charity-giver and of the abject Other) in what is essentially the same, twice-told narrative. While the reversal in these two instances of failed or aborted hospitality is ironic, the lesson we might draw from it might have more to do with the necessity of negotiating the hospitality within ourselves in order to be able to extend it to others.

The form of internal otherness in question here is, I believe, that of the unconscious and all its repressed, unacceptable and unacknowledged fears and desires. Expelled from the conscious self in order to defend it, these repressed parts of ourselves tend, nonetheless, to return as projections onto a host of Others, including racial, ethnic and religious Others. Refusing to see them in ourselves, we instead see them in (or as) Others. The external Other's perceived alterity is, then, also and perhaps primarily a reflection, a return, of our own unperceived, internal otherness – of all those things we refuse either to *recognise* in ourselves or to *be* in ourselves.

Thus, the roots of our fear and hatred of Others lie not just in the fear of the unknown stranger who might harm us, but also in this dialectic of our own repression and projection. Those who cannot reconcile or at least tolerate the Other within will project both that otherness and their fear and aggression towards it outward, onto the exterior Other. Our internal repressions are, accordingly, strongly linked to the oppression of various racial, ethnic or religious Others who are the objects of our projections. As Derrida observes, in order to be hospitable to the Other, it is first necessary 'to negotiate this hospitality within ourselves', to welcome what is 'already a society' within oneself, 'a multiplicity of heterogeneous singularities' (1997).

Our failures of hospitality are, thus, in various ways fated to return to haunt us. The return of the repressed, particularly in the form of the colonial oppressed, is itself one of Haneke's favourite themes. The entire plot of *Hidden* revolves around the devastating consequences of the actual event of such a violent return: the betrayed childhood friend of a French Algerian literally appears in Paris years later to seek vengeance for the betrayal. In *Code Unknown*, too, there is a scene in a crowded Métro carriage in which Anne is forced to confront an emissary from France's colonialist past.

In the scene entitled 'Life Underground', which also contains the only wholly positive intervention in the film, Anne is harassed by a young Arab (he terms himself 'un petit Arabe'). Standing in front of Anne, he first attempts to engage her in conversation using the rather antiquated 'Aren't you a top model?' line. When Anne refuses to respond, he becomes more aggressive, asking her, 'Don't talk to commoners? I wonder if you're one of these rich, beautiful people from high society? No? A shy little typist, then, waiting for Prince Charming to race up in his Ferrari? How can you be so beautiful and so arrogant?' At that, Anne gets up and moves to the front of the car. 'Maybe I'm not good enough for her', the young man continues. He follows her and stands in front of her. 'Now what will you do?' he asks. 'Stand me up again? Hop off into the next car? ... Why? Do I smell? Is that it? I'm just a little Arab looking for a little affection, like everybody else. Nothing doing?' he asks. 'Too bad.' He sits down next to her and, as the train pulls into the station, spits in her face. An older man, described in the credits as 'the old Arab', intervenes and chastises the young man saying, 'Shame on you!' When the young man challenges him physically, the old man silently hands his eyeglasses across the aisle to Anne and stands up to face him. The young man steps out of the car, saying, 'I'll see you around. Don't worry.' Just as the door is about to close he leans back in and shouts, startling them. In a city riven by ethnic boundaries, the old man crosses them and asserts the primacy of a basic decency, though he never says a word to Anne. At the same time, the young man's promise to 'see you around' lingers in the air as a reminder that the boundaries of the inhospitable will return to reassert themselves in our facing each other, our facing the faces of each other, the defining event of hospitality according to Levinas.

There is very little to alleviate the darkness of Haneke's vision of the global city in *Code Unknown*. As the film comes to a conclusion, it cycles back through a variation of the opening scenes – Marie returns to find someone else has taken up her place in the alley; she finds another place but is threatened and chased away, and, then, ominously, followed. Georges returns home and finds the code to the front door has been changed and Anne, again, does not hear the phone ringing. A child performs an elaborate, indecipherable pantomime. Whatever spaces of hospitality might have emerged appear to be dissolved now.

Most of the failures of hospitality in *Code Unknown* may well be failures of ethical rather than political hospitality, but if we are to make our heterogeneous, globalised cities work, if we are to make them hospitable, we will need both, and a balance of both. The practice of ethical-political hospitality is difficult, nearly impossible, but it is also absolutely necessary. If we could speak in terms of codes here, the codes of this hospitality are unknown, which may be the ultimate meaning of Haneke's title. It appears, however, that in order to improve the inhospitable world of the new cosmopolis, we must work with unknown codes or even with codes that may never become known. For, as Derrida *argues* and as Haneke's *Code Unknown shows*, hospitality is always singular, a matter of an act or event or decision without a code to underlie or guarantee it. We need to find new types of solidarity, new ways of imagining and practising hospitality among our cities and ourselves, as we encounter one another on our journeys, of which we can only give each other incomplete tales.

Notes

1   The International Parliament of Writers was founded by Salman Rushdie and Wole Soyinka in 1994. The IPW's Cities of Asylum Network included more than 35 cities, most of them in Europe, and offered residencies and stipends to refugee writers.

2   In 'Film als Katharsis', Haneke argues that his films 'are an appeal for a cinema of insistent questions instead of false (because too quick) answers, for clarifying distance in place of violating closeness, for provocation and dialogue instead of consumption and consensus' (Haneke 1992: 89).

3   Haneke uses the names 'Anne' and 'Georges' for characters in several of his films, thus suggesting that they might be seen, at least to some extent, as 'Everywoman' or 'Everyman' figures.

4   See, in particular, Kant's 'Perpetual Peace' (1963) and Levinas's *Totality and Infinity* (1969).

5   The question of hospitality towards an absolute stranger is an important and even defining part of Levinas's and Derrida's analysis, and their critique of Kant. The question is beyond my scope here, but it must be mentioned.

6   Lyotard differentiates, for example, among the 'denotative' game (whose statements have 'cognitive value' and emphasise the truth or falsity of empirical fact (see 1984: 36, 40, 46)), the 'technical' game (which emphasises efficiency or inefficiency, a distinction that combines fact and, usually, values (1984: 44)), and the 'prescriptive' game (which emphasises moral/ethical considerations of the just and unjust, right and wrong, good and evil (see 1984: 36, 40)). Different communities use different versions and combinations of these to constitute their own games, so, for instance, scientists might work mostly within the provinces of the denotative (ascertained via 'the scientific method'), politicians within the technical and prescriptive, and so on.

References

Derrida, J. (1997) 'Politics and Friendship: A Discussion with Jacques Derrida'. Centre for Modern French Thought, University of Sussex, 1 December. On-line. Available at: http://www.hydra.umn.edu/derrida/pol+fr.html (accessed 10 July 2007).

_____ (2001) 'On Cosmopolitanism', in *On Cosmopolitanism and Forgiveness*. Trans. M.Dooley and M. Hughes. London and New York: Routledge, 3–24.

Derrida, J. and A. Dufourmantelle (2000) *Of Hospitality: Anne Dufourmantelle Invites Jacques Derrida to Respond*. Trans. R. Bowlby. Stanford: Stanford University Press.

Freud, S. (1961) *Civilization and Its Discontents*. Ed. and trans. J. Strachey. New York: W. W. Norton.

Haneke, M. (1992) 'Film als Katharsis', in F. Bono (ed.) *Austria (in)felix: Zum österreichischen Film der 80er Jahre*. Graz: Edition Blimp, 89.

Kant, I. (1963 [1795]) 'Perpetual Peace', in *On History*. Ed. L. W. Beck, trans. L. W. Beck, R. E. Anchor and E. L. Fackenheim. New York: Bobbs-Merrill, 85–132.

_____ (1998) *Groundwork of the Metaphysics of Morals*. Ed. and trans. M. Gregor. Cambridge: Cambridge University Press.

Levinas, E. (1969) *Totality and Infinity: An Essay on Exteriority*. Trans. A. Lingis. Pittsburgh: Duquesne University Press.

Lyotard, J.-F. (1984) *The Postmodern Condition: A Report on Knowledge*. Trans. G. Bennington and B. Massumi. *Theory and History of Literature 10*. Minnesota: University of Minnesota Press.

Unseen Haneke

CHAPTER NINE

The Early Haneke:
Austrian Literature on Austrian Television

Deborah Holmes

Michael Haneke's international success, in particular with the French casts of *Code inconnu: Récit incomplet de divers voyages* (*Code Unknown: Incomplete Tales of Several Journeys*, 2000) and *Caché* (*Hidden*, 2005), not to mention the 2007 Hollywood remake of *Funny Games* (1997), has confirmed the universality of his concerns with multi-cultural tension, social responsibility and media manipulation. In retrospect, it seems almost inevitable that he should have moved away from Austria, not only because of the wide resonance of his works, but also for cultural-political and practical reasons. National film funding in Austria leaves much to be desired, and the political climate has not always been favourable to uncompromising artists, in particular under the coalition government of the conservative Austrian People's Party and the right-wing Freedom Party 2002–2006.[1] Nevertheless, Haneke developed his art during the 1970s and 1980s within the horizons of South German and Austrian broadcasting, and four of his early films were literature adaptations of Austrian authors for television. When these lesser-known early films are compared with his later works for cinema, many thematic and aesthetic parallels become apparent. Interestingly, the similarities are more striking between the literature adaptations for television and the feature films written by Haneke himself rather than between the early literature films and his later cinema adaptation of Elfriede Jelinek's 1983 novel *Die Klavierspielerin*, *La Pianiste* (*The Piano Teacher*, 2001).

Conversely, there are also many ways in which these early works show him in an unfamiliar light. In a 1995 interview, Haneke said of his literary adaptations for television: 'as films they are failed projects in the final instance. The question is of course on what level they fail. It is possible to fail in a primitive or in a relatively intelligent way' (in Diethardt 1995: 11–12). As they were being made, Haneke was keen to stress the contrasts between the media of film and literature, insisting that the two are ultimately incompatible. At the same time, however, he also highlighted the creative input given to his work by the writers he had chosen. This chapter will explore these aspects of his television work concentrating in particular on the first adaptation, made in 1976, of Ingeborg Bachmann's 1972 short story, *Drei Wege zum See* (*Three Paths to the Lake*).

The consensus amongst Austrian film critics was that it was a relief for all concerned when Haneke was finally able to turn away from television to cinema, throwing off the limitations of the smaller, less innovative medium. Referring to Haneke's beginnings as a theatre director and script developer for television, Alexander Horwath, for example, writes, 'It seems paradoxical that the two "arch-enemies" of Austrian film should have determined the prehistory of the genuine *film* director Haneke ... All too often, Austrian film has lived as a parasite off these two genres, which – financially and as far as cultural acceptance is concerned – constitute better developed genres' (1991a: 17; emphasis in original). Horwath sees Haneke as an exception to this rule – rather than carrying mannerisms from television and theatre over into his feature films, he began in television with an essentially cinematic approach. His early works therefore deserve to be seen as part of his development as a whole, 'as personally, historically, aesthetically and culturally significant constructions' (ibid.). Horwath goes on to analyse all of Haneke's television films up to the epiphany of his first theatrically-released feature film *Der siebente Kontinent* (*The Seventh Continent*, 1989) as a 'Gesamtwerk' in the making (1991a: 18).[2] At the time Horwath was writing, Haneke had only produced two of his four literary adaptations for television – *Three Paths to the Lake* and *Wer war Edgar Allan?* (*Who was Edgar Allan?*, 1984), from the novella by Peter Rosei. In the 1990s, these were followed by *Die Rebellion* (*The Rebellion*, 1993), based on a Joseph Roth novel, and *Das Schloß* (*The Castle*, 1997), a film of the prose fragment by Franz Kafka. Haneke not only directed but also wrote the screenplays for *Three Paths to the Lake*, *The Rebellion* and *The Castle*.[3] These three films can be seen as a distinct corpus, not only within Haneke's television works, but within his oeuvre as a whole, especially as he has always been adamant that television adaptations of literature fulfil a different purpose from cinematic adaptations.

Haneke's interview comments reveal a respect for literature which at times, at least rhetorically, gives it precedence over his chosen metier of film. He often compares the moving image unfavourably to the written word, defining his own aesthetic in relationship to the latter rather than the former: 'Our eyes have been over-stimulated by all the images which beat down on us daily. That's why I prefer to leave so many things in my films to the imagination of the viewers, who paint their own picture, rather than showing everything explicitly. The reader of the written word has to let the pictures form in his own head. In film, the screen robs the viewer of his own pictures. I try to compensate aesthetically for this drawback' (in Greuling 2003: 12).[4] Haneke's television adaptations have been both praised and criticised for their overtly 'literary' style, above all for their slow-paced editing and deadpan narrative voice-overs taken verbatim from the original texts.[5] The question of fidelity to the original, for better or worse, seems to have distracted reviewers not only from the means, but also from the purpose of Haneke's adaptations.[6] In a 2001 interview, the director claimed that 'After *The Seventh Continent* I carried on making television films but they were only literary adaptations because that was the only ghetto left ... to do critical stuff' (in Holmes 2005: 97). Elsewhere, he has described these films not as independent artefacts, but as a form of 'adult education', a way of fulfilling state-funded television's obligation to the public (in Diethardt 1995: 11). In this he is, ostensibly at least, out of step with the trend in the critical literature from the 1990s on of seeing adaptations as works in their own right.[7] He has stated in no uncertain terms that there are fundamental differences between his earlier literary adaptations and the feature film of *The Piano Teacher*, as the former use the medium of television primarily to support, indeed, to advertise the medium of literature: 'I would draw a definite line between *The Castle* and *The Piano Teacher*, because *The Castle* was made for television ... Films for TV have to be much closer to the book, mainly because the objective with a TV movie that translates literature is to get the audience, after seeing this version, to pick up the book and read it themselves. My attitude is that TV can never really be any form of art, because it serves audience expectations. I would not have dared to turn *The Castle* into a movie for the big screen; on TV, it's OK, because it has different objectives. But with *The Piano Teacher*, if you compare the structure of the novel to the structure of the film, it's really quite different, and I feel I've been dealing very freely with the novel and the way it was written' (in Foundas 2001). Although Haneke protests too much here as far as television conventions are concerned – ever media-critical and avant-garde, he often frustrates audience expectations in his television work – nevertheless, the combination of text and visual medium in his case does seem to result in films that overtly defer to their literary source. For Haneke, television is not a cultural instance, but a mediator of culture, and literary adaptation is a hybrid that must bear the marks of its origins (see Haneke 1998a: 44–5). He adheres to this even in the face of what he sees, with characteristic radicalism, as the inevitable failure of his television adaptations.

His first full-length literature adaptation, *Three Paths to the Lake*, can be seen as paradigmatic in this respect. The short story was published in 1972, one year before Bachmann's tragic early death. It tells of the photographer Elisabeth Matrei, on a visit to her widowed father in her childhood home of Klagenfurt, a town on the border between Austria, Croatia and Italy. The protagonist escaped her provincial origins as a young woman, and is now a successful professional who works all around the world and lives in Paris with a succession of unsatisfactory partners. Bachmann intersperses her account of Elisabeth's annual return with flashbacks to the immediate past – Elisabeth comes to Klagenfurt from her brother's wedding in London – and to more distant events, often from the stormy relationship with the man described as the love of her life, Franz Josef Trotta. Trotta committed suicide twenty years previously. As his imperial forenames suggest, he stands in the story for Austria's multinational past, and the fragile and unconvincing nature of its continuing existence as, as Trotta himself puts it, 'an amputated state' (Bachmann 1978: 427). His surname is one of many references in the story to *Radetzkymarsch* (1932), Josef Roth's elegiac novel on the collapse of Habsburg Austria. Bachmann makes her Trotta a distant relative of the character Roth invents as the hero of Solferino, a battle lost by Austria against Italy in 1859. Already in Roth's novel, set primarily during World War One, this Trotta has become an almost legendary figure; he is even further obscured by the mists of time and intertextuality in Bachmann's short story.

When visiting her father, Elisabeth spends her days walking in the woods, looking out over the borders to lands that used to belong to the empire. The hiking map she follows claims that there are three trails that lead to the lake (Klagenfurt lies directly on the 'Wörthersee'), the 'drei Wege' (three trails) of the title. Each time she tries to reach the lake, however, the paths end in a building site, as they are being dug up to make room for a new motorway. Disheartened by this, and upset by the news that an acquaintance has been shot by her millionaire husband in a nearby hunting lodge, Elisabeth pretends she has been called back to Paris for work reasons, and breaks off her holiday. The story ends in Paris, as yet another partner leaves her. Elisabeth goes to bed, having decided to leave the next day to take on an offer of work at the front in Vietnam. In her hand, she crumples a piece of paper given to her at Vienna airport by a cousin of Trotta's she happens to meet: 'I love you. I will always love you.' The story's conclusion is characterised by an ambivalence typical of Bachmann, in which the reader is left in suspense as to whether actual violence has been done to the protagonist and by whom: 'Before she dropped off, already on the edge of sleep, struck by a dream, and grabbed at her head and her heart, because she couldn't work out where all the blood was coming from. She still carried on thinking though: it's nothing, it's nothing, nothing more at all can happen to me now. Something can still happen to me, but nothing has to happen to me' (1978: 486). The surface realism of the rest of the story is also permanently under threat from the flashbacks to the past, and the references to Josef Roth's fictions of the Austrian empire's demise. These two features create a network of resonances undermining the 'facts' of Elisabeth's present. The symbolism of her ceaseless travelling, her walks and the lake shifts and changes – the lake, for example, is not in fact completely unattainable, like Kakfa's castle. Although she never manages to reach it on foot, Elisabeth and her father go there together by bus one rainy day to swim in the cold yet 'glorious' water, 'Neither he nor she wanted to go back and go home ... they met together in the lake at a tree trunk, which rolled like a buoy in the water. Daddy I love you [English in the original], she shouted to him, and he called: What did you say? She shouted: Nothing. I'm cold' (Bachmann 1978: 465).

The challenge posed to a filmmaker is how to convey the story's mixture of surface narrative realism with its many chronological strata and intertextual symbolism. As in all three of the literary adaptations to be discussed here, Haneke achieves this while making minimal changes to the text he appropriates from the originals, both in the narrative voice-overs and the characters' dialogue. He makes no substantial textual additions to any of his three adaptations for television; *The Rebellion* and *Three Paths to the Lake* feature at most snatches of background conversation not to be found in the originals, and there are no additions at all to the texts taken from *The Castle*. Here,

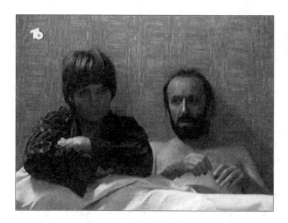

Three Paths to the Lake (1976): pillow talk on the horrors of war photography

we suspect, Haneke's deference and diffidence was probably greatest in the face of Kafka's influential novel fragment. In *Three Paths to the Lake*, he does however change the order of two key passages. In many of the flashbacks, Trotta and Elisabeth argue heatedly about her job as (war) photographer, in scenes that foreshadow the tension between Anne and Georges in his later film *Code Unknown*. Trotta's line of argument is pure Haneke: 'It's an imposition, it's humiliating, it's despicable on top of everything else to go and show people how others are suffering. Because of course it's different in reality. So you're doing it just so that someone will look up from his coffee for a moment and murmur, oh, how horrible!' (Bachmann 1978: 419).

This disagreement between the lovers is exacerbated by Trotta's nihilism, his inability to find a place for himself in the modern world, which to him means post-1914. When Elisabeth accuses him of not living in the same era as she does, he retorts 'I don't live at all, I've never known what it means' (Bachmann 1978: 420). This exchange is repeated word for word in two different scenes in the film, a repetition not in the literary original. The first time, the argument is filmed in one take, and set in bed, where Elisabeth (Ursula Schult) and Trotta (Walter Schmidinger) sit beside each other facing the camera. She leans forward slightly, staring ahead, whilst he, bare-chested, looks forward and sidewards at the back of her head, amused, if cynical. The second time, later in the film, the couple are fully-dressed and shouting at each other across and around a sparsely furnished hotel room, filmed with frequent cuts and rarely in the same shot together. Thus Haneke is able to suggest both the deterioration of their relationship and the repetitive nature of their disagreements.

With his other major textual shift, Haneke changes the causality of the story in a way that actually renders it more conventional as regards sexual mores, ironing out the uncompromising disillusionment of Bachmann's Elisabeth. He takes a passage from the story's middle section, long before there is any suggestion that Elisabeth's current partner Philippe will leave her, and builds it into the narrative voice-over at the very end, just before Elisabeth begins to dream: 'There was one hope which she shouldn't and couldn't leave open, for if she had not yet met a man in over thirty years, not one single one ... who was strong, and brought her the mystery that she had been waiting for, not one who was really a man and not a crank, a lost soul, a weakling ... then this man just didn't exist ... and all that one could do was to be friendly and nice to each other, for a while...' (Bachmann 1978: 449–50). In the film, this passage is set immediately after Philippe's (Yves Beneyton) departure from her apartment, and seems directly motivated by his defection to a younger, pregnant partner. In the literary original, Elisabeth is already wondering how she can get rid of Philippe during her holiday in Austria. Combined with Haneke's decision to cast Philippe and include flashbacks with him and not necessarily with the series of Elisabeth's other partners mentioned by Bachmann, this constitutes a reduction of her character, or at best, an interpretation that the original story does not dictate. A brief, visual addition further underlines Haneke's interpretation – as she is tinkering with her camera, Elisabeth does not even try to catch the bouquet thrown in her direction by her brother's bride. A close-up of the fallen flowers fluttering forlornly on a grey London pavement places considerable emphasis on a detail that is nowhere to be found in the literary original.

There are, however, other visual additions that are both more effective and more revealing of Haneke's subsequent development as a filmmaker. Four minutes into *Three Paths to the Lake*, Elisabeth is driving home from the train station with her father (Guido Wieland): we see alternate shots of the view from the taxi window and father and daughter sitting next to each other on the back seat. This logical progression is interrupted by a jump cut to a naked black man, covered with soap, standing at a washbasin. The viewer sees him from the perspective of someone who, we suppose, has just opened a bathroom door by mistake and surprised him. The bathroom is big, the distance and lighting make the details unclear (is he naked, or at least wearing dark trousers?), and the echo almost certainly makes his irate 'Get the hell out!' (English in the original) incomprehensible to an Austrian television audience. Elisabeth's father has just asked her why she flew via Vienna – we do not yet know that she has come from London, where she had to wait a week alone in a hotel before getting a flight. Over the next few minutes, the context of this cut is gradually explained, and the scene itself is eventually repeated in a sequence of scenes from Elisabeth's tedious wait in London. However, its original eruption into the action of the film constitutes a reality break of a kind that was to become typical of Haneke, an irritation to the viewer seldom seen in conventional television drama. He develops this technique further in *The Rebellion* and *The Castle*, using not only jump cuts (particularly in the former), but also the blackouts later to become such a distinctive feature of his cinema work (see Holmes 2007: 117–18). Although many of the other flashbacks in *Three Paths to the Lake* are abrupt, this is not only the first, but also the most obscure, as it does not feature any of the characters the viewer has already been introduced to. Elisabeth's uneasy interaction with the multinational personnel of the hotel in London can also be seen as a foreshadowing of the social and ethnic tensions apparent in *Code Unknown* and *Hidden*.[8] The jump cut to the man in the bathroom seems threatening, not only because it is initially inexplicable, but also as it comes immediately after a gradual close-up (through the taxi window) of the fangs of the Klagenfurt 'Lindwurm' monument. At first it seems as if the black man has erupted into (Elisabeth's?) consciousness as a result not of her father's question, but of this ferocious dragon. The impression of a potential or perceived threat is strengthened by the apparent idyll of the images that follow: Elisabeth affectionately taking her elderly father's hand in the taxi, and their arrival at the Matreis' picturesque wooden house, surrounded by flowers, and typical of southern Austria.

A further visual addition frames the whole film. Before the first narrative voice-over and the opening credits, Haneke fills the screen with a close-up of the waters of the lake, rippled and reflecting the sunset. This, accompanied by diegetic sounds of birds and the wind in the rushes, constitutes a meditative introit, over which the story's opening motto is read. At the end of the film, Elisabeth lies curled up on her bed in a flowing white bathrobe; her recumbent form dissolves into the waters of the lake, once again in rippled close-up, but without the warming golden streak of the sunset. Night has fallen. Apart from providing a satisfying visual representation of the story's development and Elisabeth's twilight state of mind, this imagery also constitutes a subtle and concentrated reference to the bleak Habsburg nostalgia of *Three Paths to the Lake*. The cliché of the Austrian empire as a realm upon which the sun would never set supposedly dates from the reign of Charles V (1519–56). In *Radetzkymarsch*, Josef Roth takes it up to describe the empire's gradual disintegration. He describes the ageing Emperor Franz Josef inspecting his troops: 'For a moment, he felt proud of his army and for a moment he also felt regret for their loss. For he already saw them defeated and scattered, divided up between the many peoples of his vast empire. He saw the great, golden sun of the Habsburgs set … saw it fall into many little sun orbs … They just don't want to be ruled by me anymore! the old man thought. There's nothing to be done! he added with resignation. For he was an Austrian…' (1956: 210–11). Haneke's water close-ups capture this elegiac mood perfectly: although their natural imagery is verging on the abstract and proffers no overt political or social comment, the symbolism is clear without imposing itself on the viewer. This is in keeping with Bachmann, at least as far as *Three Paths to the Lake* is concerned – her representation of Austria's history in this particular work is more atmospheric than analytical.

The opening shot of *Three Paths to the Lake* also sets the scene for a film that, along with *The Rebellion*, ranks as one of Haneke's most picturesque. Elisabeth's walks through the woods are worthy of a 'Heimatfilm', the escapist genre which dominated Austrian film from the late 1930s to the early 1960s, glorifying the country's land-scapes and rural life. The scene in which Elisabeth reaches a clearing and looks out over the Karavanke mountains to Yugoslavia is breathtakingly beautiful – dwelt on

Three Paths to the Lake: problematic nostalgia on Austria's southern borders

almost lovingly by a slow panning shot along the alpine range. The narrative voice-over names the setting and tells of how Elisabeth feels she would like to live in rural solitude somewhere near the border. Birgit Flos, in one of the few published analyses of the film, claims that both woods and water are kept carefully anonymous, indeterminate (see 1991: 168). This is patently not true, and seems to me to demonstrate the continuing uneasiness of Austrian cultural critics with depictions of idyllic alpine settings, in particular when combined with references either to the National Socialist past, or to former imperial territories. The idyll is of course exploded when Elisabeth comes upon the diggers carving away the hillside for the motorway. The familiar strains of the adagio of Mozart's clarinet concerto in A major accompany the preceding scene, as Elisabeth bathes her feet in a ferny pool. With rather heavy-handed irony, Haneke allows the music to continue, overlaid with the sound of the building site, just as it was overlaid with the sound of birdsong previously. The woods here are a far cry from the genuinely anonymous and threatening woods of *Funny Games* and *Le temps du loup* (*The Time of the Wolf*, 2003), but however beautiful, they are themselves under threat and offer Elisabeth no refuge in the final instance. The sections of Jelinek's *Die Klavierspielerin* which tell of the protagonist's summer holidays as a girl in a similarly idyllic alpine setting are without exception omitted from Haneke's film version of *The Piano Teacher*. Apart from the narrative cohesion which the film's exclusively urban setting imparts, could it be that Haneke was loath to evoke parallels with the 'Heimat-film' on the big screen?

The Rebellion also has uncharacteristically picturesque touches; this is the nearest Haneke gets to costume drama in his early works. For instance, he uses a wealth of archive footage to establish time and setting: the opening credits roll over images of Emperor Franz Josef's funeral in 1916, accompanied by the measured strains of Haydn's 'Kaiserquartet'. The dignity of the music and poignant images are given very short shrift, however. Almost immediately, a military band takes over the melody, and it is combined with a cacophony of other national anthems over footage of trench warfare, cut frequently to make the running, firing and dying seem completely aimless. A lengthy lap dissolve further combines this front footage with the first tracking shot of the film along a row of invalids standing to attention by their hospital beds, the last of whom is the protagonist Andreas (Branko Samarovski). The novel's opening sentence, 'The barracks of the war hospital number XXIV were situated on the edge of town' (Roth 1956: 289) is read by Udo Samel over the last archive image to be shown before the lap dissolve, a field gun firing repeatedly. This is a good example of a technique Haneke uses throughout his literary adaptations for television. Voice-over and images are not synchronised, one often anticipates the other, creating a tension which attracts the audience's attention to exactly which shots are juxtaposed and how. Similarly, at the beginning of *Three Trails to the Lake*, we see Elisabeth's father from a distance fidgeting on the station platform, but the narrator does not tell us who he is and what he is doing until the film has cut to Elisabeth sitting smoking in the approaching train. As Haneke himself has said, 'Coordinating literature and film is difficult. In literature I can think up a sentence that unites three different times and locations. In film I have one image, I am here and now. Then the next image comes – and I am somewhere completely different. In film, there is an immediate contrast, whereas in a book I can create simultaneity' (in Diethardt 1995: 18).

These attempts to recreate the simultaneity of literary narrative add texture to the three films, which are optically mostly extremely understated. Haneke's comment on *The Rebellion* would apply to *Three Paths to the Lake* and *The Castle* as well: 'We have been jaded by the flood of images the visual media saturates us with. I made the Roth film optically as unremarkable and modest as possible. The aim of having a permanent parallel of image and sound was to use both elements in counterpoint to create a new state of being in the viewer' (in Diethardt 1995: 19). *The Rebellion* is mostly in black- and-white, and the colours of *The Castle* and *Three Paths to the Lake* are extremely muted. The slow pace of all three comes to a standstill at several decisive junctures, where photographs, paintings or other static images are shown. These paradoxically often have the effect of propelling the narrative forward whilst stopping the visual action. In *Three Paths to the Lake*, for example, a series of black-and-white photographs 'summarises' Elisabeth's childhood and youth, her early career as a photographer and the famous contacts she has made. The juxtaposition of private family shots with pictures of the pyramids, Winston Churchill and Pablo Picasso also gives the viewer a taste of the almost grotesquely wide spectrum covered by Elisabeth's chosen medium. They provide Haneke with a neutral, documentary-style technique for covering a necessary minimum of her backstory.

Backstory is something Haneke tends to avoid in his screenplays as much as possible: 'Backstory doesn't interest me, the viewers should make it up for themselves. In real life there is no backstory; you meet someone, but you only get to know a tiny excerpt of their life. Genre cinema always pretends that everyone's entire behaviour is explicable. It delivers short-circuit biographies, which explain everything, and the viewer can then go home reassured. The worrying thing about everyday life is that we don't know anything. If you are trying to show reality, this is something you have to deal with' (in Greuling 2003: 11). It therefore comes as no surprise that most of the omissions in Haneke's literary adaptations concern details from the characters' previous lives. These are often peripheral anyway, but occasionally, notwithstanding his defer-ence to the original texts, he makes omissions that give a strikingly interpretative twist to the film. In *Three Paths to the Lake*, he chooses to omit the murder of Elisabeth's Viennese acquaintance by her husband. In Bachmann's story, the millionaire husband owns most of the woods around Klagenfurt, the last straw for Elisabeth and her fruit-less walks to the lake. Haneke replaces this as her final motivation for leaving early with a comparatively harmless scene with a former schoolfriend. She has also suffered at the hands of her husband, but has become a plump middle-age gossip rather than a murder victim and sensational headline. Once again, Haneke's Elisabeth is subject to more localised, less systemic disillusionment than Bachmann's protagonist. It is almost as if Haneke wants the literary original to retain its superiority over his film in terms of stylistic ambiguity and the radicalism of its social criticism.

At their most effective, Haneke's adaptations combine all these methods of omis-sion, narrative concentration/stasis and understatement to convince us of his interpre-tation of the literary original. In *The Castle*, Haneke makes a fundamental textual cut, omitting all but the first sentence of the opening paragraph. Here Kafka establishes not only that the castle exists, but that the protagonist K. is already aware of it: 'It was late in the evening when K. arrived. The village lay in deep snow. Nothing could be seen of the castle hill. Mist and darkness covered it, not even the weakest ray of light indicated where the big castle was. K. stood for a long time on the wooden bridge which connected the highway to the village and looked up into the seeming emptiness' (1983: 7). Haneke's only visual representation of the castle is a picture of a medieval walled town and fortress stuck on the inside of the door of the inn which K. (Ulrich Mühe) enters at the beginning of the film. This paper rendering of the text's totemic topos means that Haneke does not need to open up his claustrophobic village set with landscape shots showing K. looking for the castle in the distance. Nevertheless, Haneke still achieves an equivalent of the obscuring effects of distance and weather; first the picture is hidden by the opening credits, then by K. opening the door, causing a chart of statistics hung above the castle picture to waft down over it, leaving only its outlines visible.[9] More significantly, the paper castle and its positioning illustrate the effect of Haneke's omission. As the paper castle hangs on the inside of the door, we must assume that K., the outsider, has not seen it, and nothing else in the voice-over or setting suggests that he has. Haneke's K. seems much more ingenuous than Kafka's, hapless rather than manipulative: we can take him at his word moments later when he says to Schwarzer, 'What, is there a castle here?' (Kafka 1983: 8).

Although Haneke has claimed that his television adaptations were first and foremost a means for promoting the works of literature in question, analysis of his methods shows that many of the devices he uses under the guise of producing a 'literary' film are ones that he uses anyway. He is a 'literary' director when filming his own screenplays, and a cinematic director when working for television. When asked, he has attributed his choice of authors to pragmatic reasons: Austrian state television's insistence on Austrian works of literature. Nevertheless, his comments on the subject – that it is better to stick to things 'which one at least thinks one knows' – are an acknowledgement, however grudging, of the importance of the cultural traditions of Austrian modernism to his works.

Author's note:
I would like to thank Thomas Ballhausen from the Austrian Film Archive for helping me gather material for this article.

Notes
Unless otherwise stated, all translations are by the author.

1   On national funding for Austrian film, see the 2006 statement by the Association of Austrian film directors at http://www.austrian-directors.com/jart/prj3/regieverband/data/uploads/Regieverband_Situation_Film.pdf (accessed 16 May 2008).
2   Horwath outlines how each film mirrors the intellectual trends of its time, listing them as follows: 'the self-reflexive experiment *After Liverpool* (1974); the spare, aloof literary adaptation *Drei Wege zum See* (1976); the very personal generational

epic *Lemminge* (1979); the urban "fast comedy" *Variation* (1983); a luxurious game with reality and identity – *Wer war Edgar Allan* (1984); the "demythologised" 50s melodrama *Fraulein* (1986)' (1991a: 18).

3   *Who was Edgar Allan?* was adapted by Peter Rosei himself together with Haneke, under the pseudonym 'Hans Broczyner' (see Horwath 1991b: 181).

4   See also Haneke's comment in an interview on *Code Unknown*: 'Modern literature would never dare to claim that it explained the world, whereas genre cinema does just that but with the participation of the audience' (Holmes 2005: 104).

5   On *The Rebellion*, see Bert Rebhandl (1993: 10); on *The Castle*, see Rebhandl (1997: 10); the only feature of *Three Paths to the Lake* that Alexander Horwath really criticises is the choice of Axel Corti as voice-over narrator, as he was very well-known to an Austrian audience and therefore inappropriately reassuring. Horwath is also dissatisfied with the fact that a male voice narrates a text written by a woman about a woman here (see 1991a: 22).

6   For a more detailed discussion of this point, see Deborah Holmes (2007: 107–22).

7   See, for example, Deborah Cartmell (1999: 23–8).

8   For Haneke's view of the social energies inherent in global migration and how they are perceived as a threat by the West (and how he chose to portray them in *Code Unknown*) see Holmes (2005: 101–2).

9   One of the only two sequences Haneke adds to Kafka's *The Castle* is a brief scene that seems to be designed to remind the viewer of the picture. K. returns from visiting the 'Gemeindevorsteher', revealing the castle in a blast of wind and snow which blows up the statistical chart briefly as he opens the door.

References

Bachmann, I. (1978 [1972]) '*Drei Wege zum See*', in *Ingeborg Bachmann. Werke* (vol. 2). Eds C. Koschel, I. von Weidenbaum and C. Münster. Munich: Piper, 394–486.

Cartmell, D. (1999) 'Introduction', in D. Cartmell and I. Whelehan (eds) *Adaptations. From Text to Screen, Screen to Text*. London and New York: Routledge, 23–8.

Diethardt, U. (1995) 'Literatur folgt einer anderen Struktur als Film', in U. Diethardt, E. Polt-Heinzl and C. Schmidjell (eds) *Fern-Sicht auf Bücher. Materialienband zu Verfilmungen österreichischer Literatur*. Vienna: Dokumentationsstelle für Neuere Österreichische Literatur, 11–22.

Flos, B. (1991) 'Ortsbeschreibungen', in A. Horwath (ed.) *Der siebente Kontinent. Michael Haneke und seine Filme*. Vienna: Europaverlag, 165–9.

Foundas, S. (2001) 'Michael Haneke: The Bearded Prophet of *Code Inconnu* and *The Piano Teacher*', *indiewire*. On-line. Available at: http//www.indiewire.com/people/int_Haneke_Michael_011204.html (accessed 14 September 2004).

Greuling, M. (2003) 'Michael Haneke. Der Ohrenmensch', *Celluloid. Die Österreichische Filmzeitschrift*, January/February, 10–13.

Haneke, M. (1998a) 'La negazione è l'unica forma d'arte che si possa prendere sul serio', in A. Horwath and G. Spagnoletti (eds) *Michael Haneke*. Turin: Lindau, 44–5.

Holmes, D. (2005) '*Code Unknown*', in Kevin Conroy Scott (ed.) *Screenwriters' Master Class: Screenwriters Discuss Their Greatest Works*. London: Faber, 91–107.

_____ (2007) 'Literature on the Small Screen. Michael Haneke's Adaptations of Josef Roth's *Die Rebellion* and Kafka's *Das Schloß*, in J.Preece, F. Finlay and R. Owen (eds) *New German Literature. Life-Writing and Dialogue with the Arts*. Oxford and Bern: Peter Lang, 107–22.

Horwath, A. (1991a) 'Die ungeheuerliche Kränkung, die das Leben ist. Zu den Filmen von Michael Haneke', in A. Horwath (ed.) *Der siebente Kontinent. Michael Haneke und seine Filme*. Vienna: Europaverlag, 11–39.

_____ (1991b) 'Wer war Edgar Allan?', in A. Horwath (ed.) *Der siebente Kontinent. Michael Haneke und seine Filme*. Vienna: Europaverlag, 181.

Kafka, F. (1983 [1926]) *Das Schloß*, in *Franz Kafka. Kritische Ausgabe* (vol. 1). Eds J. Born, G. Neumann and M. Pasley. Frankfurt am Main: Fischer, 7–495.

Rebhandl, B. (1993) 'Bilder aus dem beschädigten Leben', *Der Standard*, 25/26 October, 10.

_____ (1997) 'Fluchtbewegungen am Gartenzaun', *Der Standard*, 2 April, 10.

Roth, J. (1956 [1932]) *Radetzkymarsch*, in *Joseph Roth. Werke* (vol. 1). Ed. H. Kesten. Cologne and Berlin: Kiepenheuer & Witsch, 1–311.

_____ (1956 [1924]) *Die Rebellion*, in *Joseph Roth. Werke* (vol. 2). Ed. H. Kesten. Cologne and Berlin: Kiepenheuer & Witsch, 287–374.

CHAPTER TEN

Tracing K: Michael Haneke's Film Adaptation of Kafka's Das Schloß

Willy Riemer

Originally published in *The Journal of the Kafka Society of America* (1997), 21, 47–55

Franz Kafka's *Schloß*, it seems, is everybody's enchanted castle, and an enigma that awaits explanation. What of the castle and K.'s obsession with it: why doesn't this would-be surveyor simply leave the dreadful village? Interpretations of *Das Schloß* (1926) tend to pin down its undetermined details, once and for all putting forth its meaning in terms of social, political or religious allegories. Kafka's textually dense narrative and ambiguous scenarios are difficult candidates for film adaptation; nonetheless they continue to challenge filmmakers, most recently Michael Haneke.[1]

The feature films of Austria's most distinguished auteur have met with great acclaim at major international film festivals, but Haneke also directs film adaptations for television. His adaptation of Kafka's *Das Schloß* was produced for television, but after its successful premiere at the Berlin Film Festival it was given a theatrical release. The reviews refer to the excellent cinematography and meticulous directing, they note the impressive performances of Ulrich Mühe as K. and Susanne Lothar as Frieda, but they have some difficulty in engaging the substance of the adaptation and fail to mention the striking features that give Haneke's work its creative authenticity. Most often the atmosphere of the film is interpreted in terms of Haneke's published observations on the 'emotionale Vergletscherung' (emotional glaciation) of the contemporary world.[2] Josef Lederle perceives K. as 'a bureaucrat without a heart' (1997: 11) whose inner permafrost prevents his acceptance in the village. Almost without exception the reviews note that the film closely follows the text. While the spoken text in the film is indeed taken from the novel and its overall structure is retained, Haneke in fact makes changes and significant deletions that necessarily skew possible interpretations.

In the film the narrative line is tightened, dialogue is shortened, the character structure is simplified and symbolic references are thinned out to narrow interpretative options. For example, in the novel K. often sees the castle, if only at a distance. He steps out into the wintery morning, the castle up above is just as he had expected it to be; he compares its tower and ramshackle buildings to those of his home town. In the film the tower is not shown, and the church is not mentioned. The castle appears only as a simulacrum, not revered, grandly framed or with pride of place, but as indistinct detail in a landscape etching fastened to the back of the entrance door at an inn. Amalia's story is shortened and told by Olga, rather than shown as an extended flashback. In Haneke's film she appears in one enigmatic close-up and in a short exchange with K., but her story receives very little screen time and her parents hardly matter. Castle officials are given less prominence: the elaborate scene on the distribution of files, for example, is deleted, as are some encounters with Artur and Jeremias, and with Gerstäcker. Leaving out the lengthy conversation with the innkeeper's wife makes Klamm less of a sexual predator and more of a key contact for gaining entry into the castle. The connection with the castle is further depersonalised by avoiding all mention of Count Westwest by name. In the novel Schwarzer points out to K. that the village is the property of the castle; in the film this comment is deleted.

In the absence of the castle there is no conspicuous signification or direct exercise of power. By abstracting from the person Klamm, but also by deleting almost all references to the Count, the castle itself assumes an even more anonymous structure of fascination and oppression. Notable, on the other hand, is the endless ringing of the telephone in the scene with Bürgel, and the meeting with the village official, who explains the workings of the telephone system. The castle thus connotes a baffling rationality. Presence or absence in film, whether an image appears on the screen or not, greatly affects its perceived importance. In Haneke's film the focus is distinctly shifted from the castle to the village.

The film reveals even less about K.'s origin and motives than does the novel. The self-possessed surveyor K. has neither theodolite nor assistants; he does not ever demonstrate any knowledge of surveying. With a sly glance he receives the announcement that indeed he has been engaged as a surveyor by the castle. Though K. appears to be an imposter, Haneke's K. retains at least a degree of credibility: neither wife nor child are mentioned. That is, he is not made out to be a liar or bigamist. K.'s sadistic trait is mellowed, Jeremias is spared the whipping. K.'s reminiscences about his childhood experiences and some long passages of his reflections are passed over; his manipulative bent is thus less evident. Though the audience sees what K. looks like and what he does, it knows much less about K. than do readers of the novel. To use Walter Benjamin's metaphor, K. is stripped of his aura (see Benjamin 1963).

K.'s characterisation and the visual prominence of the village are the result of film adaptation as interpretation. The first paragraph of the novel immediately poses a dilemma: how are references to absence and the unrepresentable to be shown in film? In the novel K. hesitates on a wooden bridge before deciding to continue to the village.

In the film an equivalent sense of transition is conveyed by K.'s entrance through the door at the inn. On the bridge K. gazes into the emptiness in the direction of the castle; he sees no evidence of it, not even a shimmer of light. The novel can mention what is not seen; film can only allude to what is absent. Haneke's film therefore begins with an etching of a rural landscape that fills most of the frame – rounded hills, woods and some buildings. The background music of a village band picks up in mid-phrase and at full volume; it turns out to be diegetic, from a 1960s-style radio in the inn. Thus the first image and the music on the soundtrack, both of them fragments, allude to a reality that includes village and castle, without directly showing either.

After the titles and the credits for author and director, the image pivots towards the spectator and with a smooth cut to a medium shot the film now has K. make his entrance. It becomes evident that the landscape etching is attached to the back of a door, with part of its framed image covered by a torn sheet of newspaper tacked to the door being opened by K. Thus the opening shots render the central elements of the novel: K. and the village juxtaposed with data that has the appearance of order, and expression of authority presumably linked with the castle. Their weights, however, have been redistributed: in the film the village with its contentious atmosphere has much greater prominence than in the book, it is shown in concrete terms. As the sequence unfolds and K. attempts to arrange for lodging at the inn, this impression is enhanced by Haneke's use of soundtrack, lighting and proxemics.

In Kafka's novel there is conspicuously little that belongs to the modern world: a photograph, electric lights, the telephone at the inn; Haneke adds a radio from which can be heard music and the voice of an announcer. That is, technologies are represented that separate production from perception, that are technically functional but not personally intimate. K. has hardly oriented himself, when the soundtrack falls silent, as if to deny him admission to the community of villagers. This motif is repeated a number of times: at K.'s approach, the innkeeper turns off the radio. As the radio with its folksy music is associated with the village, the castle is represented by a telephone, which in this context can be taken as an instrument for asserting order. K.'s makeshift bedding is in the foreground; behind an expanse of empty chairs and tables the villagers are huddled around a table at the far end of the room, with the lighting of the telephone intruding into the villager's space. The *mise-en-scène*, soundtrack and lighting thus all suggest the opposition between K., the villagers and the castle, with the tension between K. and the villagers especially evident. With this change in emphasis the question of adaptation is raised.

In the discourse that has developed around film adaptation, fidelity in letter and spirit continues to have high priority, even though the notion of singular meaning has long ceased to be part of literary studies. The key events and characters are expected to be retained, as well as the right kind of meaning, with the assumption that in the reading process meaning is evident and details are clear in their function. In effect, the film adaptation is regarded as a somewhat deficient copy of a literary work in another medium, and as for any copy, the original, the more highly esteemed literary work, provides the standard and base for evaluation. It seems to me, however, that the question of fidelity is not particularly illuminating for writings rich in interpretative ambiguity. While Kafka's *Das Schloß* challenges the reader for interpretation, it also obstructs any approach to ready meanings. The ambiguity of this novel thus opens the possibility of adaptation without the benchmark of fidelity and with more weight given to the film as an autonomous work of art. Andrei Tarkovsky, whom Haneke mentions in interviews, speaks for film artists when he maintains that literary texts and even film scripts themselves are there to be freely quarried and shaped in the creative conception of the auteur filmmaker (see 1996: 21).

Analyses of film adaptation distinguish aspects of the source text that are readily transferred from those that are problematic. The chief events of a story, for example, do not depend on the signifying system and thus find an adequate equivalent in film. In this regard Haneke follows Kafka's novel quite closely. Characterisation, the underlying mood and range of implied meanings, however, bear the signature of the auteur in terms of framing, *mise-en-scène*, editing and use of soundtrack. Rather than checking film against novel for matching details and with fidelity as a measure, an appropriate metaphor is provided by the idea of diffraction. A light beam that passes through a structured medium produces a pattern that is determined both by source and diffractive device. By analogy, film adaptation derives from the auteur's reading of the source text, but also reflects his use of the cinematographic apparatus. With this approach, film adaptation and source text can be taken on equal terms. I will in particular consider Haneke's use of voice-over and tracking shot, as well as his creative agenda regarding the position of the spectator and the representation of reality.

In a letter written near the end of his work on *Das Schloß*, Kafka muses: 'If we were on the right road, such a defeat would be boundlessly depressing, but we are only on some road or other, which must first lead to a second and this to a third and so on, and even after a long while we may not reach the right one, perhaps may never reach it, so we are exposed entirely to uncertainty but also to inconceivably beautiful diversity. So the fulfilment of hopes and especially of such hopes remains the ever-unexpected but ever-possible miracle' (1978: 344–5). In the complexity of the real world, the quest is filled with uncertainty, each path is provisional and merely a stretch along the way. Kafka is sceptical of linear continuity, of universals and comprehensive world views that Jean-François Lyotard later would call grand narratives. The branchings and itera-tions from path to path, the provisional and fragmentary perception of reality and the attraction of an elusive fulfilment in their imagery anticipate the paradigm provided by the theory of deterministic chaos.

Chaos theory was developed to explain the seemingly unpredictable behaviour of nonlinear systems; since the processes of reality are nonlinear to various degrees, this paradigm soon took its place as one of the normal modes of channelling inquiry. In this approach, recursive procedures incrementally track systems to reveal regularities in their behavioural orbit or path. In systems that are characterised by deterministic chaos such orbits are indeterminate as a whole, yet constrained within regions governed by so-called 'strange attractors'. The algorithms employed in generating the fragments or iterations of chaos theory require no interpretation, they are precisely defined proce-dures that remain stable between iterations. To be sure, Paul Wühr has shown with his poetry that twists and curls, tangled layers and braids can be created by submitting the processes of deterministic chaos. But in general, literary texts and film depend on signi-fication, they thrive on ambiguity and they are open to intertextuality at every level. They have few iterative cycles compared to the normal practice of chaos theory, and even these are blurred by competing stylistic devices. On the level of analogy, however, some concepts of chaos theory may be useful in the interpretation of texts based on iterative development or, to use a phrase that is more familiar, in which theme and variation structured by central motifs play an important role. In Haneke's adaptation K. is obsessed with the castle, a strange attractor for his every waking thought. K.'s origins are obscured; he repeatedly sets out on a path to the castle; these are repeated attempts at gaining access on the basis of partial views and fragmentary information.

In the undated introductory notes to his film *71 Fragmente einer Chronologie des Zufalls* (*71 Fragments of a Chronology of Chance*, 1994), Haneke observes: 'Kafka formulated ... the fragmentary as the inevitable basic condition of reality and of basic knowledge acquisition'. The adaptation of *Das Schloß* shows how fragmentation can serve as structural principal and as condition of perception.

The film begins without explanation and ends without closure: K. enters the inn out of nowhere and disappears into the snowstorm of the night. The numerous encounters in the village are episodic, held together by K.'s consuming fascination with the castle. Each character contributes some insight that is limited by an indi-vidual perspective. The framing of persons and objects favours the fragment as well: the viewer is amply confronted with unusual close-ups of body parts and point-of-view shots of details. In the opening shot, for example, the landscape appears torn, but in a later sequence the intact picture is shown. Reduced fields of view often draw atten-tion to the space offscreen. As K. arranges his bedding, for example, the viewer sees in succession an empty corner bench, K.'s bottom and the back of his head, all the while being acutely aware of activities offscreen. Music plays an important role in all of Haneke's films; in *The Castle* it provides an additional channel for commenting on the screen action. Just before K. meets with his assistants in the inn, two musicians practise some music. They play badly, out of tune and with little sense of rhythm. After a few bars their efforts disintegrate into a jumble of sounds. But they persist; again and again they start the same piece. In its variations the fragment thus provides the counterpoint to K.'s quest, but it also disturbs the viewing habits of the mainstream spectator.

The public expects art museums to provide high culture; television and main-stream cinema stand for entertainment. Indeed, the history of film art can be read as an account of its struggle against the aesthetic of commercialism. The opening sequence of Haneke's *The Castle* makes some concessions to television: the takes are short, the cuts are crisp; music, gestures and lighting all arouse the interest of the viewer. The compo-sition of these shots, however, invites a reflective reception; the viewer is challenged to more than diversion. In an interview published in *Der Spiegel* Haneke explains, 'I want the audience as a serious partner' (1997: 147). In order to leave an appropriate role for the viewer, Haneke withholds explanation and psychological realism even more reso-lutely than does Kafka. The spectator is left in the unaccustomed position of having to make sense of the fragments and tantalising details of the film.[3] For example, as K. waits to meet with Erlanger (Hans Diehl) in the hallway of the *Herrenhof*, there is an interminable ringing of telephones and the kind of sawing buzz heard at construction sites. The telephone is the conspicuous link with the castle; the buzzing sound is not explained and can perhaps be taken as a reminder that this is the constructed set of a film in progress. In other words, the cinematographic apparatus and the fictional world of the film is revealed as a construct. While mainstream film hides the apparatus so that the spectator can surrender to the flow of images, Haneke's camerawork, *mise-en-scène* and editing are designed to foreground the production of the film and to provoke critical distance.

In his essay on Robert Bresson's *Au Hasard Balthazar* (1966) published in the *Frankfurter Allgemeine Zeitung*, Haneke makes a comment that could be applied to his own films as well: 'Instead of "beauty", accuracy – every picture shows only the minimum, each sequence is presented in its most compressed form' (1995: 6). In *The Castle* there are some exquisite images, but not simply for the sake of appearing 'beautiful'. Framing and camera angles generally rebuff the spectator's gaze; the predominant bluish-grey does not connote warmth and compassion. There are no heroic scenes; a very ordinary reality is reduced to a sparse composition of shapes and movements. K.'s even voice and impassive expression discourage identification. His anxieties and little victories are not acted out, he is not presented ready for consumption: the spectator has to work at finding a place in the film.

Mainstream films are edited to produce the illusion of continuity in which each image smoothly emerges from its predecessor. Haneke breaks conventions in this regard as well. There are no establishing shots to ease the spectator into a sequence. For some dialogue and set-ups the takes seem unendurably long, so that the circumstances of the image are not merely registered, but felt: the spectator feels the frustration of K., his exhaustion as he confronts officials from the castle. When the camera is redirected, the changes are not always synchronised with speech. A number of sequences end with an abrupt cut on the terse reply 'Klamm', leaving questions dangling and curiosity piqued. Haneke further undermines the illusion of continuity by inserting black film between sequences, thereby giving the spectator space for reflection.

Mainstream films position the spectator as a voyeur who in the anonymity of darkness can observe the enactment of intimate emotions, illicit fantasies and violated taboos. Haneke works against this practice. The love scenes with K. and Frieda have none of the usual close-ups caressing body parts, the long or medium shots of a drab *mise-en-scène* are better suited for analysis than for eroticism. The novel describes K. looking at Klamm through a hole in the door; in the film the spectator sees K. looking through the hole at Klamm, but the camera does not follow his gaze. The spectator does not get to see Klamm and is thus explicitly confronted with voyeuristic practices. The film denies voyeurism. As a result, the spectator generally knows less than does K. Amos Vogel, the co-founder of the New York Film Festival, discusses the editing and camerawork of *Der siebente Kontinent* (*The Seventh Continent*, 1989) and concludes: 'This style and cinematic approach lead to a kind of transcendence, a heightened sense of engagement on the part of the spectator' (1996: 74). But such an agreement too is channelled, in *The Castle*, ostensibly by the voice-over narrator.

In the opening sequence an anticipatory camera guides the spectator along K.'s entry into the inn; it records his glance at some hats and coats on a rack, and a hand turning off the radio. What seems to be a point-of-view shot taken from the outside of the building through the window now shows a table with beer mugs, shoulders and arms. The image seems oddly out of place; it is not immediately clear how it can be attributed. In reply to K.'s question about lodging, the innkeeper, filmed in a frontal shot, claims that there is no vacancy; however, his synchronous explanation is not heard, but rather a voice-over in the past tense faithfully reciting the second passage from the novel. This non-diegetic voice-over narrator is heard intermittently throughout the film. He seems to be reduced to providing continuity and locating action, sometimes expressing feelings and on a few occasions doubling the voice of a character or describing an action as it takes place in the image. Located offscreen, speaking with the kind of even voice familiar from documentaries, this voice-over narrator appears to assume the authoritative position held by the omniscient narrator of the novel.

Narrative films attempt to mask the heterogeneity of the cinematic apparatus; synchronous sound and background music are therefore designed to smoothly complement the image. Although voice-over occasionally appears in interior monologue or in flashbacks, it is only sparsely used in mainstream films. Quite apart from signalling fidelity to Kafka's novel, the voice-over narrator thus serves as a frequent reminder that the film is a construction; but as we shall see, the interplay of sound and image as independent channels also exposes the fragmentary nature of experienced reality, or rather the fragmentary view of reality that seems to depend on point of view.

Seymour Chatman has suggested the notion of an impersonal cinematic narrator who serves as a 'transmitting agent of narratives' (1999: 480). Such an abstract narrator tells the story by arranging, for example, the *mise-en-scène*, camerawork and editing. In each frame the cinematic narrator draws complex conventions of the apparatus to guide the gaze of the viewer. Anticipatory set-ups in *The Castle*, for example, have the spectator puzzle over the significance of an etching until K. appears nicely centered in the frame; they are made to look at a slab of wall or the back of K. until he actually lies down. The cinematic narrator inserts many narrative devices, such as the doubling of voices, characters and action. The visual component of the presentation normally dominates the soundtrack. But since the voice-over narrator in *The Castle* recites from Kafka's canonical novel, both impersonal narrators command authority and suggest reliability. What the voice-over narrator says, however, does not always accord with the image presented by the cinematic narrator. The best example of this dissonance is provided by a sequence at the end of the film.

Just as K. is beginning to weaken under Pepi's (Birgit Linauer) entreaties to come and live with her, with evident sexual connotation, Gerstäcker (Wolfram Berger) blusters in and cajoles K. to come along; he offers the alternative of an untroubled, if not comfortable life, working for him in the stables. K. protests that he knows nothing of stable skills or horses. No matter. He did not, in the entire narrative, give the least indication that he knew anything about surveying either. The voice-over narrator embellishes this offer by reading the last paragraph of the novel to the point where it breaks off in mid-sentence. But by the sheer power of the image, this narrator is discredited, since the cinematic narrator in a tracking shot has K. and Gerstäcker not in a cosy cottage, as the novel indicates, but struggling through a blinding snowstorm in the dark of night, on and on.

Kafka's strategy of ambiguity and sceptical irony involves the subtle manipulation of narrative perspective; the voice-over and cinematic narrators provide two distinct channels for ironic interplay, with the spatiality of the image giving further range of ironic comment to the cinematic narrator. Haneke structures his adaptation around two quite different spatial arrangements that are often used alternately: deep-focus shots and tracking shots.

The deep-focus shots almost without exception are set indoors, with bluish-grey and yellowish warm lighting on multiple planes suggesting village and castle; the scenes usually include women. The opposition of K. and the castle is frequently expressed in deep-focus shots of concurrent actions in the foreground and background set at the inns, the school or at the home of Barnabas (André Eisermann). When K. meets Frieda at the inn, Haneke takes some liberties with the dialogue in order to bring together different parts of the encounter. In the foreground K. makes his advances to Frieda, professing his affection, imploring her to become his lover. In the background all the while and in plain view the coarse and raucous servants of the castle officials engage in their sexual adventure with Olga (Dörte Lyssewski). The scene seems grotesque in the juxtaposition of its two components.

The opening sequence provides another example of such use of space. K. has arrived at the inn, the innkeeper has agreed to let him sleep on a bench. This area and also the tables at which some peasants have gathered are in subdued bluish-grey lighting. At the far end of the room is the telephone, the link with the castle. It is illuminated with a yellowish halo of light, lighting that is frequently used later in the film to evoke the castle. The tension between K. and the castle is thus suggested both spatially and by the lighting. Arrangements and movements associated with the castle tend to be circular. The servants dance a lascivious round with Olga; Jeremias (Felix Eitner) and Artur (Frank Giering) wantonly hop around K. at their praise in Klamm's letter; K. and Frieda roll on the floor in desire supposedly motivated by Klamm. K.'s resolutely linear project, however, finds its expression in the tracking shot, the central device of the film.

Haneke uses very little camera movement in *The Castle*; the numerous tracking shots of K. therefore stand out all the more. The tracking shots often come after a meeting that seems to hold promise for K. They are set outdoors, yet their structure gives them a peculiar flatness: in medium to long shot K. trudges along a single plane between an empty snowy foreground and bleak wall or the woods on the outskirts of the village. It is as if K. is trapped between oppressive walls or the expanse of the trees and the hostile coldness offscreen in the foreground. The deep snow makes every step cumbersome. Unlike the deep-focus shots, where the spectator becomes a participatory interpreter, the shots tracking K. are devoid of ambiguity. The abrupt beginning and ending of the shot, with the camera moving from right to left, leave a discomforting feeling that puts into question any prior signs of hope for K. The tracking shots thus appear to be the cinematic narrator's ironic commentaries on K.'s stubborn quest. As in deterministic chaos, orbits are retained in the proximity of 'strange attractors', so K.'s path is headed towards the castle without ever reaching it.

Haneke's film is as much of an enigma as Kafka's novel, even though some of the details, such as the asymmetry of the tracking shots, seem to invite a simple explanation. Whenever the camera tracks from left to right, K. is about to have an encounter with inhabitants of the village or representatives of the castle. He meets the teacher, he hurries to Klamm's sleigh, he paces along the hallway to Bürgel and then Erlanger. But these opportunities never work out. Far more common are long tracking shots from right to left. They usually show K. alone, self-absorbed, outdoors in the night and blowing snow. In the wonderful final shot, K. and Gerstäcker are tracked into the stormy night as the voice-over narrator reads the final paragraph of the novel. This may be the implied end of K.'s endeavours, but the cinematic narrator gives a different reading: the tracking shot promises more alienation for K.

Kafka ends the novel in mid-sentence; with his last sequence Haneke would seem to suggest that this occurred not for want of vigour or opportunity. While Chatman suggests that an 'implied author' (1999: 479) intrinsic to the story yet another layer of narration, be used as an agent to account for discrepancies between narrators, it seems to me that such a model is not really needed: the dissonance in the ending, just as much as the dissonance in the music scene, suggests that reality can only be understood in local bits and pieces that make sense within a particular local point of view oriented by the respective 'strange attractor'. In other words, Haneke is not offering a solution to Kafka's novel, even though he is introducing his own views in the making of the film. In his analysis of Jean-Luc Godard's tracking shots in *Weekend* (1967), Brian Henderson (1999) argues that their flatness metaphorically expresses the condition of the bourgeois world. With the inexorable tracking shots and the shift from the castle to the village, Haneke seems to suggest not a quest for absolutes and myths, but rather that the modern condition of eroded identity amidst indifferent relationships and dysfunctional communication form the underlying problem of *Das Schloß*, a condition that he also engages in his feature films.[4]

Notes

Unless otherwise stated, all translations are by David Sorfa.

1   *Das Schloß* (*The Castle*, 1997) produced by Veit Heidushka, Wega Film. There have been two adaptations for television: one directed by Sylvain Dhomme in 1962 for NDR (Germany), and the other directed by Colin Nears for the BBC in 1974. In 1968 Rudolf Noelte directed a feature film based on the narrative. See Diethardt *et al.* (1995).

2   See, for example, Anon. (1997: 118). In his undated 'Notes to *The Seventh Continent*' Haneke refers to a central theme in his work: 'The cold. That is what we all create; this indifference with which we ourselves and others are permanently faced.'

3   Tarkovsky similarly demands a creative participation by presenting fragments
     which the spectator then combines into an overall sense for the film (see 1996:
     23).
4   See Haneke's undated 'Notes to *71 Fragmente einer Chronologie des Zufalls*'.

References

Anon. (1997) 'Michael Haneke verfilmt Franz Kafka', *Skip*, 4/97, 118.

Benjamin, W. (1963) *Das Kunstwerk im Zeitalter seiner technischen Reproduzierbarkeit*.
     Frankfurt: Suhrkamp.

Chatman, S. (1999) 'The Cinematic Narrator', in Leo Braudy and Marshall Cohen
     (eds) *Film Theory and Criticism*, Fifth Edition. New York and Oxford: Oxford
     University Press, 473–86.

Diethardt, U., E. Polt-Heinzl and C. Schmidjell (eds) (1995) *FERN-SICHT auf
     Bücher: Materialienband zu Verfilmungen österreichische Literatur. Filmographie
     1945–1994*. Vienna: Dokumentationsstelle für neuere österreichische Literatur.

Haneke, M. (n.d.) 'Notes to *Der siebente Kontinent*', Vienna, Wega Film.

____ (n.d.) 'Notes to *71 Fragmente einer Chronologie des Zufalls*', Vienna, Wega Film.

____ (1995) 'Schrecken und Utopie der Form', *Frankfurter Allgemeine Zeitung*, 6.

Henderson, B. (1999) 'Towards a Non-Bourgeois Camera Style', in Leo Braudy and
     Marshall Cohen (eds) *Film Theory and Criticism*, Fifth Edition. New York and
     Oxford: Oxford University Press, 57–67.

Jenny, U. and S. Weingarten (1997) '"Kino is immer Vergewaltigung": Regisseur
     Michael Haneke über Zuschauer als Opfer, die Obszönität brutaler Bilder und
     seinen neuen Thriller *Funny Games*', *Der Spiegel*, 38, 15 September, 146–7.

Kafka, F. (1978) 'To Robert Klopstock', 24 July 1922. *Letters to Friends, Family, and
     Editors*. Trans. R. Winston and C. Winston. London: John Calder, 344–5.

Lederle, J. (1997) 'Mit Kafka im Kino', *film-dienst*, 6/97, 11.

Tarkowskij, A. (1996) *Die versiegelte Zeit: Gedanken zur Kunst, zur Ästhetik und Poetik
     des Films*. Frankfurt/M: Ullstein.

Vogel, A. (1996) 'Of Nonexisting Continents: The Cinema of Michael Haneke', *Film
     Comment*, 32, 4, 73–5.

Glaciation

CHAPTER ELEVEN

Attenuating Austria: The Construction of Bourgeois Space in The Seventh Continent

Benjamin Noys

We can say of the fate of the family in Michael Haneke's first film *Der siebente Kontinent* (*The Seventh Continent*, 1989) what Theodor Adorno said of Little Nell in Charles Dickens' *The Old Curiosity Shop*: 'Because she is not able to take hold of the object-world of the bourgeois sphere, the object-world seizes hold of her, and she is sacrificed' (1992: 177). Tracing the life of husband Georg (Dieter Berner), wife Anna (Birgit Doll) and daughter Eva (Leni Tanzer), Haneke presents a world in which this outwardly successful family in fact function as mere appendages to the objects around them. This is made evident in the opening scenes of the first part of the film in which Haneke systematically deprives the viewer of facial close-ups for over ten minutes, drawing our attention instead to a range of quintessentially 'bourgeois' objects: the alarm clock, the fish tank, the coffee maker and the car. He allegorises the fact that it is the inability of the family to truly take hold of the space of the object-world that leads to them being seized by that world and (self-) sacrificed to it. Their final self-destruction is no act of wild revolt or nihilistic protest against the inertia of this world but the slow, mechanical, repetition of that world in negative form.[1] We see how the father and mother first accumulate further objects (hammers, saws and other tools) to take apart the objects that surround them. The methodical and largely lifeless destruction of these objects and, almost unbearably, the mechanical act of suicide signify not the freedom of the family but their final capitulation to the dead state of being objects amongst objects.

In a filmed interview with Serge Toubiana on this film Haneke recalls an audience response during public discussions at the Cannes Film Festival: a woman in the audience stood up and said, 'Is Austria really so depressing?' Laughing, Haneke explains that this reaction is a flight from the subject matter of the film and a way of saying this has nothing to do with me. Although derived from an Austrian newspaper story Haneke is insistent that the film should not be mistaken for an Austrian story. As he goes on to state in the interview, *The Seventh Continent* 'isn't a portrait of Austria' but 'a portrait of rich countries'. Therefore, to construct this portrait of the 'glaciation' of capitalist culture Haneke tries to attenuate any reference to a supposedly 'pathological' Austrian national space. It is this methodical removal of any reference to Austria that permits the construction of the film as having a universal address, whether that is taken philosophically (such as in terms of existentialism or nihilism), or politically (in terms of alienation or *Kultur critique*).

Adam Bingham makes exactly this kind of interpretation when he argues that *The Seventh Continent* is an example of the 'cinema of existentialism': 'the focus on the actions and morality of individuals in a seemingly empty universe found in the work of filmmakers like Chantal Akerman, Gaspar Noé and the Krzysztof Kieślowski of *Dekalog* (*Decalogue*, 1988)' (2004). In this way Haneke is joined to the pantheon of both contemporary and past European filmmakers. He is also marked out by his development of 'an entirely original narrative syntax to convey directly the experiences of his characters as their souls are ground down in the crushing vacuum of modern existence' (ibid.). Such a mode of address serves to reinforce the ambiguity that Haneke prizes, and opposes to mainstream or genre cinema, by detaching the film from any explanation in terms of place. Haneke mentions that the number plate on the car allows the film to be identified as being set in Linz (it is seen in close-up at the beginning of the film as the car enters the car wash), but that he avoided any typically Viennese sights so that the film would 'remain completely neutral'. As he says his aim is to achieve something specific 'without being local'. In this case it is the presentation of the bourgeois world – for Haneke the world he knows best and one that can be found in *any* Western capitalist society (he mentions Japan, France and the United States as examples). Therefore, Haneke's strategy as a 'European filmmaker' is to present what is not so much a 'European' space but an international or 'universal' space of bourgeois culture.

Is the question of the audience member really as naïve as Haneke supposes? I want to suggest not. First, there are several elements in the film, in addition to the number plate, which allow us to identify the Austrian setting. These are no mere minor points but, as we will see, connected to the central themes of the film. Second, we might then pose the question of the possible costs of the filmmaking strategy Haneke adopts. While it allows him to construct a 'universal' space of alienation it ignores the specific *national* elements of the articulation of that alienation. There is no doubt concerning the disturbing qualities of this film, precisely, as Bingham notes, in terms of the calmness with which it traces this mundane narrative of catastrophe. What concerns me here is a suspicion of what is being avoided in this narrative, and, in a related fashion, the accessibility of this narrative of general alienation to a specific audience – to put it bluntly, Western intellectuals. This will lead me, finally, to the vexed question of the mode of response Haneke demands for his films. Despite all his professed desire for, and insistence on, 'ambiguity' Haneke is remarkably doctrinaire in terms of his positioning of his films. In this way Haneke himself provides a convenient framing narrative for critics, one I wish to suggest we treat with at least a little suspicion.

What, then, are the 'Austrian' elements of the film? The first element is the question of language. For the non-German speaker this might not be thought enough to identify the film as specifically Austrian. There is a scene, however, where this difference is highlighted. After a scene at the school where Eva has pretended to be blind, we cut to a scene in which Anna is working with her brother (Udo Samel) in their jointly-owned opticians. Anna is conducting an eye examination of a patient who tells a story of a childhood friend who hid her short-sightedness. Then the girl, already regarded as ugly, appeared at school with thick-framed glasses and was mocked by her putative friend and classmates. With 'that German accent nobody liked' she 'curses' them, saying she hopes that one day they will all have to wear glasses – then she wets herself. And, in fact, the 'curse' comes true: by the time they have graduated everybody in the class wears glasses. Although told as an amusing story, and repeated as such by Anna and her brother later when having a family dinner, the viewer is aware of Eva's own pretence to blindness and the sense of violence and even horror underlying this story of everyday humiliation.

Part of this humiliation turns on an 'internal' linguistic difference. Considering that many of Haneke's films, including this one, are concerned with the failure of communication – self-evidently in the later *Code inconnu: Récit incomplet de divers voyages* (*Code Unknown: Incomplete Tales of Several Journeys*, 2000) – then the problem of linguistic difference might not be so easily brushed over. This is especially the case, as here, where the difference lies in the pronunciation or accent of a 'shared' language. The more minor points of difference *within* a language form, especially to a non-speaker, are here used to mark someone as Other – as 'disgusting'. This draws a contrast with Haneke's use of 'major' failures of communication in his other films, such as deafness in *Code Unknown* or the failure of the illegal immigrant boy in *71 Fragmente einer Chronologie des Zufalls* (*71 Fragments of a Chronology of Chance*, 1994) to speak German. Here the Otherness or alterity of communication is presented in a more subtle manner, one which is not so immediately obvious. We can see it as also linked to Eva's own act of dissimulation, first from her teacher and then her mother, concerning her 'feigned' blindness. The film intimates, through a newspaper story kept by Eva headlined 'Blind but no longer lonely', that Eva is trying to escape some invisible existential loneliness. Communication has failed her. When Eva does confess that she lied her mother slaps her despite her earlier promise to not punish her. In a similar fashion to the girl from the earlier story this failure is internal to a linguistic and social code; an enforced failure, enforced through this social and cultural stratification of communication.

A second unacknowledged point of specificity is the use of the Austrian schilling in the film (the Euro was first officially 'introduced' in Austria in 1999, but this was solely as 'bank money' or 'book money'. The Euro as a form of payment in daily life only came into existence in Austria on 1 January 2002). What is noticeable to the British viewer of the film are the high sums of this currency required by the family for the purchase of the various tools by which they are to carry out their final destruction. In part three of the film – 1989 – the decision is made to 'leave', first signalled by the cancellation of the newspaper subscription. Georg writes a letter to his parents, itself unusual as it is usually Anna that writes, to tell them of their decision. While Anna buys luxury food for their final meals Georg purchases the necessary tools which we see the cost of totalled on the cash register as 10510.00 schilling. In the next scene Georg picks up Anna from work and they both go to the bank to withdraw their savings – 478,000.60 schillings according to the bank teller.

Of course money is being used here in a traditional fashion as the symbol of bourgeois alienation. Haneke demonstrates this effect of alienation by taking care to always focus on the mechanical process of ringing-up purchases and avoiding showing the faces of those involved. Money quite literally alienates and removes the social relation between human subjects. Money is also the key to one of the most shocking scenes in the film. As Haneke remarks in the interview he told the producer two scenes would particularly shock the audience: the smashing of the aquarium and so the death of the fish, and the scene where the couple flush their money down the toilet (which actually happened in the original story the film is based on). The producer could accept the first scene would be shocking but not the second; he was proven wrong by the audience reaction. What this scene does is to render strange our usual relation to money. Slavoj Žižek notes that while people recognise that money is merely a pure signifier, that its value is the result of a social convention, 'the problem is that in their social activity itself, in what they are *doing*, they are *acting* as if money, in its material reality, is the immediate embodiment of wealth as such' (Žižek 1989: 31; emphasis in original). Therefore we consciously believe one thing – money is a mere convention – but act another – money really is wealth.

What Georg and Anna do is realise the Freudian fantasy of money as voidable excrement. They traverse our materially and socially embodied belief in money as wealth (simply recall the feeling of distress when one has, or simply believes one has, lost money – even comparatively minor amounts); as with language though, we find the same issue of a generic form given a specific national articulation – and the trace of this articulation, this alterity, that remains within the construction of the supposedly neutral space of alienation. It is not just 'money' that Georg and Anna dispose off but

The Seventh Continent (1989): Money as voidable excrement, and the signifier of Austria

a particular national form of money, and obviously part of the impact of this scene depends on our knowledge of how much this money is worth, of our translating back into our own national currency. Earlier in the film Haneke makes clear, through one of Anna's letters, that the family is well off to partially avoid this problem.

If these two remnants refer to the space of alienation we might hazard that one final remnant (there may be others I have not detected) signifies more to a utopian trace resistant to glaciation. During the title sequence of the film we see the family in their car pass through a car wash. As they leave we see a poster with the title 'Welcome to Australia' showing a slightly strange deserted beach scattered with rocks, a blue sea and mountains in the distance. Later, at the end of part one, we will see the same poster, but this time the sea is lapping the shore and we can hear the waves. This image will recur just before the family hold their final party before the destruction begins, after the death of Eva, and at the end of the film as one of Georg's dying memories. Bingham argues:

> The context for these appearances, then, is that of dreaming and death: the only two viable, even possible escapes for the characters from the drudgery of their existence. The fact of its association with the prayer, with meeting the Lord in Heaven, neatly encapsulates both death (meeting God in the after-life) and dreaming (Eva is going to sleep), whilst the image before the suicide hints that the family may find in death what they so clearly could not in life. (2004)

I would not deny the allure of this interpretation, but simply point to the ambiguity of dreaming and death. At the same time I want to take more precise stock of this image in the local context of Austria, rather than inserting into a 'universal' narrative of death and dreaming as escape.

This recurrent image of Australia, which Haneke insists should remain ambiguous, is also where Anna claims the family is leaving to when they withdraw their money from the bank. When she does so she has to correct a possible error by the bank clerk by stating she means emigrating to 'Australia' because of a possible linguistic confusion with Austria. The ambiguity here is the confusion between Austria and Australia, which further exacerbates this possibly utopian image of escape or death.

There are no kangaroos in Austria:
The Seventh Continent

In fact, this is a well-known tourist confusion, reputedly most common among North Americans. It is so familiar that a T-shirt is available with the slogan 'There are No Kangaroos in Austria'. What I want to suggest is that Haneke's film is again putting to use a particular 'national' element within the deployment of this ambiguous image. The ambiguity of this image of 'escape' is that it has as its obverse Austria. This slippage speaks to the nature of this ambiguity, poised between an image of hope and an image of the crushing of hope – that, in Philip K. Dick's phrase, 'the exit door leads in'.

I want to suggest that we can understand this essential ambiguity, poised between Australia and Austria, as a utopian image or trace (*Spuren*) in the sense given by Ernst Bloch. What Bloch argues is that ideology is not simply a complete image of repression but that it also contains latencies and tendencies that indicate a utopian space of hope (a procedure also followed by Adorno and Walter Benjamin). 'Critique of ideology, Bloch argues, is not merely unmasking (*Entlarvung*) or demystification, but is also uncovering and discovery: revelations of unrealised dreams, lost possibilities, abortive hopes – that can be resurrected and enlivened and realised in our current situation' (Kellner & O'Hara 1976: 15). In this case the image, a travel poster, has its latent utopian potential revealed in its *movement* – when it shifts from poster to dream image. Bloch writes of the human ability to create 'utopian projections, mirrored ideals, dream-manufactures, and travel-pictures' (quoted in Kellner & O'Hara 1976: 25). Therefore, contra Bingham, I want to suggest that dreaming and even death are not as unequivocal as he supposes. They each contain, via this image, a utopian trace of hope. Within the crushing finality of the object-world we are not completely debarred from transcendence, but that transcendence is materialised as a utopian promise held within that world – in this case a tourist poster. We should not mistake the utopian trace as some simple moment or trace free of ideology, rather as the fractured promise held within ideology.

We might speculate, however, in a more pessimistic register that this promise is cancelled by the final image of the 'snow' on the television screen. As Brigitte Peucker remarks, 'signalling the materiality of the video image and of the screen itself, the absent images for which the snow stands are reflected in their spectators' unseeing eyes, while the noise that substitutes for sound falls on deaf ears' (2004). This would seem to conform to the general critical movement of Haneke's early films, in which the media image obliterates and alienates seemingly without the possibility of recovering any utopian trace. Again, this is also a rupture of communication. The ambiguity of the image of Australia is increased, in its play against this other image, but also threatened with containment or recuperation by the reign of what Guy Debord (1990) called the 'integrated spectacle' – the point at which the social is saturated by the alienating effects of the image. This ambiguity is made evident in Haneke's argument, concerning *The Seventh Continent*, that 'much of the film could be said to resemble television advertising' (Haneke in Sharrett 2004b). Here this aesthetic is turned against itself to render the object-world of bourgeois alienation. This, negatively we might say and in a more Adornonian register, signals the retention of hope only in its loss. Against this threat of complete obliteration, figured in the transition from the images that convey Georg's dying thoughts to the random white noise of the television screen, the disappearing image of utopian hope is thrown into relief.

In each case we have come up against the deliberately produced ambiguity of Haneke's film. The difficulty is how that ambiguity is itself managed and staged not only within the film but also by Haneke's own commentaries on his films. When he remarks that 'I have no interest in self-interpretation. It is the purpose of my films to pose certain questions, and it would be counter-productive if I were to answer all these questions myself' (in Sharrett 2004b), it comes as a surprise. Haneke certainly always insists on this ambiguity, but despite caveats he displays quite a commitment to self-interpretation, and often around questions of national space. While he is keen to refute any specific Austrian element for *The Seventh Continent* he makes exactly the opposite argument in relation to *Benny's Video* (1992). Now Haneke remarks, again in an interview with Serge Toubiana, on the obtuseness of the film's Austrian viewers for failing to understand the film as a reflection on their own national history. The fact that this film displays the 'normalisation' of a crime is seen as an allegorical reflection on Austria's own refusal to come to terms with its wartime past. In claiming 'first victim' status Austria moved from cooperation with the Nazis to victims of the Nazis and so avoided coming to terms with both its past and the continuing careers of those involved in Nazi politics during the war.

Of course, another film may well demand another mode of response but the viewer is entitled to a certain perplexity in the face of these different demands by the filmmaker. For all the supposed 'freedom' licensed by the use of ambiguity in both films, we are placed back in quite a traditional mode of authority in terms of Haneke's own demands. This tendency towards insistence on localisation is even more evident with *Caché* (*Hidden*, 2005), which he remarks 'is about the French occupation of Algeria on a broad level, but more personally a story of guilt and the denial of guilt' (in Sharrett 2004b). Again, we have an under-determined act of suicide, but this time the act is placed far more securely within a particular national context of guilt. Perhaps this suggests something of the ambiguity of capitalism itself, if we consider this as the 'subject' of *The Seventh Continent*. Rather than particular war crimes the 'crimes' of capitalism (if we consider them as such) remain anonymous. Alain Badiou points out: 'Let's agree – so that we may then seek an explanation – that this century [the twentieth] has served as the occasion for vast crimes. But let's immediately add that it's not over, now that criminals with names have been replaced by criminals as anonymous as joint-stock companies' (2007: 10).

Therefore, *The Seventh Continent* concerns one of these crimes committed by criminals with no names: the object-world. This then conditions the particular framing of the film and its own 'anonymity'. It also constrains the viewing of the film through the very figure of 'universality' – implying, like Haneke, that the viewer will find themselves interpellated as a member of the bourgeois world which the film portrays. This puts a limit on the claims made by the film; in the words of Bingham, Haneke 'seeks audience activity both by leaving the ultimate meaning of the film up to us, and by facilitating (by shaking us from our apathy) a sense where we might relate the very everyday reality presented for much of the film to our own lives' (2004). Of course this relies on the viewer sharing this common identification of that everyday reality as their own, which is itself constructed in the film through the elimination of local particularity. In addition to this difficulty in terms of the assumption of audience, we could also note how this 'everyday reality' itself conforms to one of the self-images of capitalist ideology (and which is also mirrored amongst anti-capitalists); that of capitalism as a 'smooth', 'frictionless' or deterritorialised space that has successfully achieved detachment from what Karl Marx and Friedrich Engels called 'all fixed, fast-frozen relations, with their train of ancient and venerable prejudices and opinions' (2005). Such a totalising reading is implied, for example, by Michael Hardt and Antonio Negri's work *Empire*. They state that 'Empire', as the form of capitalist power, 'is a *decentred* and *deterritorialising* apparatus of rule that progressively incorporates the entire global realm within its open, expanding frontiers' (2000: 12; emphasis in original). From a similar critical perspective Haneke also is at risk of producing a totalising vision of capital that, ironically, flatters the powers of capital.

This portrait of a self-contained global capitalist image space may well, as Bingham argues, be intended to provoke critical activity in the audience. It goads us to recognise that what might appear a space of affluence is, fundamentally, a space of alienation and misery. The political thinker and activist Raoul Vangeim put it well when he wrote 'who wants a world in which the guarantee that we shall not die of starvation entails the risk of dying of boredom?' (1983: 8; see also Noys 2008). This is conveyed in Georg's final letter to his parents which insists, against what we have seen, on the fundamental horror of the life of the family which makes suicide preferable. The difficulty is that as equally as it may function as a spur to activity we could argue that the portrait of the creeping horror of bourgeois alienation may function to induce passivity in the audience. The seeming lack of any possible critical purchase, except for the nihilistic repetition of the object-world in the act of suicide, leaves us with nowhere to go. It was exactly this kind of problem that Massimo De Angelis (2007) has pointed out in regard to Negri and Hardt's *Empire* – that their image of a seamless deterritorialised capital poses not so much a new ground of struggle as the elimination of any alternative realm to capitalist value-production. Therefore, I am suggesting that Haneke's film relies on a certain audience class position and fraction – the intellectual alienated from alienation. Also, that its ambiguity extends to producing an image of capitalism that is all too consonant both with capitalism's own ideological self-image and the images of those opposed to it, which suggests the limits of anti-capitalism.

Certainly, I do not want to argue that this exhausts the interpretation of the film. I do think, however, it is worth raising these critical questions in light of the broad acceptance of Haneke as a member of the canon of 'European filmmakers', especially filmmakers of alienation. In a way here I am reconstructing some of the specific, local, traces of both capitalist valorisation *and* of the utopian traces that signal, however weakly, an outside. This is by no means to deny the power of the film in its current form, or, I hope, of falling into the critical trap of supposing another 'better' film that should have been made. The power of the film rests, quite precisely, on this construction of a 'neutral' space as a space of horror and terror. It would be almost possible to read the film as a horror film, in this case a horror at capitalism that never materialises itself into a simple 'monstrous' form, but which provides a form of monstrosity 'framing' social and psychic space.

Although I have been caught in the no doubt unavoidable trap of offering further interpretations for these ambiguities I am suggesting that putting Austria back into the filmic space does not 'ground' the ambiguity, but only further exacerbates it. In fact, the very neutrality of the image of bourgeois space itself creates a rather safe and secure image (and interpretation) for the viewer, especially the viewer familiar with and sympathetic to such codes. What I have been tracking here is another 'fold' of the image that traces the edges of 'Austria' as it touches upon this ungrounded 'object-world'. In this way I want to draw attention to the risk that a 'pure' or 'neutral' modernism is, at once, never 'pure' and risks reproducing an ideological image of capitalism as detached from national or local places. Haneke as 'European filmmaker' is a reading that may present a falsely unified image of European space, even if in the negative of the bourgeois object-world. I want to insist on a further political (in the Left sense) ambiguity in the trace of Austria that leaves itself on the film.[2]

Notes

1   As Haneke states: 'They carry out the destruction with the same constricted narrowness with which they lived their lives, with the same meticulousness as life was lived, so I see this as the opposite of the vision of total destruction in *Zabriskie Point*. The sequence is portrayed as work. I have tried to portray it as something unbearable. As the wife says, "my hands really hurt from all that arbeit", so all this hard work of destruction merely precedes the self-destruction' (quoted in Sharrett 2004b).

2   I would like to thank Barbara Rassi for her willingness to share with me her local and specific knowledge of the 'Austrian'.

References

Adorno, T. (1992) 'On Dickens' *The Old Curiosity Shop*', in *Notes to Literature vol. 2*. Ed. R. Tiedemann, trans. S. W. Nicholsen. New York: Columbia University Press, 171–7.

Badiou, A. (2007) *The Century*. Trans., commentary and notes Alberto Toscano. Cambridge and Malden: Polity Press.

Bingham, A. (2004) 'Life, or something like it: Michael Haneke's *Der siebente Kontinent* (*The Seventh Continent*, 1989)', *Kinoeye*, 4, 1. On-line. Available at: http://www.kinoeye.org/04/01/bingham01_no2.php (accessed 19 April 2008).

De Angelis, M. (2007) *The Beginning of History*. London: Pluto.

Debord, G. (1990) *Comments on the Society of the Spectacle*. Trans. M. Imrie. London and New York: Verso.

Dick, P. K. (1984 [1979]) 'The Exit Door Leads In', in *Robots, Androids, and Mechanical Oddities: The Science Fiction of Philip K. Dick*. Eds P. S. Warrick and M. H. Greenberg. Carbondale, IL: Southern Illinois University Press.

Hardt, M. and A. Negri (2000) *Empire*. Cambridge, MA: Harvard University Press.

Kellner, D. and H. O'Hara (1976) 'Utopia and Marxism in Ernst Bloch', *New German Critique*, 9, 11–34.

Marx, K. and F. Engels (2005 [1848]) 'Manifesto of the Communist Party', *Marxists Internet Archive*. On-line. Available at: http://www.marxists.org/archive/marx/works/download/manifest.pdf (accessed 19 April 2008).

Noys, B. (2008) 'Is Boredom Always Counter-revolutionary? On Michael Haneke's *The Seventh Continent* (1989)', *Kinofist: Boredom*. On-Line. Available at: http://kinofist.blogspot.com/2008/03/is-boredom-always-counter-revolutionary.html (accessed 19 April 2008).

Peucker, B. (2004) 'Effects of the Real', *Kinoeye*, 4, 1. On-Line. Available at: http://www.kinoeye.org/04/01/peucker01.php (accessed 19 April 2008).

Sharrett, C. (2004b) 'The World that is Known: Michael Haneke Interviewed', *Kinoeye*, 4, 1. On-Line. Available at: http://www.kinoeye.org/04/01/interview01.php (accessed 19 April 2008).

Vangeim, R. (1983) *The Revolution of Everyday Life*. London: Left Bank Books and Rebel Press.

Žižek, S. (1989) *The Sublime Object of Ideology*. London and New York: Verso.

CHAPTER TWELVE

Supermodernity, Sick Eros and the Video Narcissus: Benny's Video in the Course of Theory and Time

Mattias Frey

A Preview of Coming Attractions

A shaky video camera films a dark corridor with a door open to the outside: a man leads a pig out of a barn and the camcorder follows. Pan to a man standing nearby, pan back to the pig. Two hands appear in the frame and press a gun to the pig's head. Zoom-in. The gun fires and the pig falls to the ground; the camera closely follows the pig's convulsing body. Pause. Rewind. Repeat in slow-motion. The pig dies again. Stop. The screen flickers with snow and the title of Michael Haneke's 1992 feature appears in red: *Benny's Video*.

The second instalment of Haneke's 'glaciation trilogy'[1] immediately places the spectator into a voyeuristic perspective and fetishistically re-views the slaughter of a pig on home video. The plot which follows is bare. In Vienna, the middle-class teen Benny (Arno Frisch) meets a girl, kills her and records the act with his video camera. His parents Georg (Ulrich Mühe) and Anna (Angela Winkler) discover the deed and attempt to cover it up. Georg dismembers the girl's corpse and disposes of it while Benny and his mother vacation in Egypt. When they return, Benny brings a video of his parents discussing the cover-up to the police.

Haneke's film garnered a maelstrom of controversy on its initial release. Nevertheless, graphic portrayals of gun violence did not constitute the force of this shock: surveying a room outfitted with every imaginable piece of video, television, stereo and surveillance equipment, the camera's position and the editing deny visual access to the girl's killing. Only the pig dies on-camera. The truly disturbing aspect of what a Swiss newspaper called 'the most disgusting film of the year' (quoted in Falcon 1998: 12) was not the images represented on the screen, but how these sequences are perceived and processed.

Re-viewing *Benny's Video* more than 15 years after its initial release is a strange exercise. The film's address and stance – indeed, the very aesthetic and moral questions it raises – seem to come from an uncannily distant past. In order to understand its creative energies, *Benny's Video* needs to be read against contemporary social and cultural theory and the anxieties these theorists address. In the 1980s and 1990s, Marc Augé, Jean Baudrillard and Gilles Deleuze were scrutinising the very perceptual systems (and the environment and conditions fostering them) that Haneke took to task in *Benny's Video*. Indeed, in a larger sense, Haneke and these thinkers shared a common perspective: they sought to revive moribund fields with a respective cinematic/theoretical shock therapy. Michael Haneke has often insisted that he creates a 'non-psychological' cinema. In contrast to what he claims takes place in American films, Haneke's cinema is inhabited by characters whose behaviour is not easily explicable in sociological or psychological terms (see Falcon 1998: 12). These are figures 'who are less characters than projection-surfaces for the perceptions of the spectator' (Haneke quoted in Donner 1993: 35). The aforementioned French theorists correspondingly rejected psychoanalysis and structural semiotics in their investigations of culture and society. *Benny's Video* not only actualises, reflects on or modifies forms of these thinkers' theories, however. The impetus behind Haneke's cinematic programme is analogous to the way these media and social critics see society and culture.

Supermodernity

Marc Augé's anthropology of everyday life sets the theoretical scene for Benny's world. In his book *Non-places: Introduction to an Anthropology of Supermodernity*, Augé investigates the transit points at which we spend an increasing proportion of our lives: airport lounges, hotel rooms, ATM machines, supermarkets and highways. For Augé, 'the word "non-place" designates two complementary but distinct realities: spaces formed in relation to certain ends (transport, transit, commerce, leisure), and the relations that individuals have with these spaces ... As anthropological places create the organically social, so non-places create solitary contractuality' (1995: 94). Although we pass through these spaces rather than reside in them, Augé argues, we enter into a contractual relation with 'non-places'. Tickets, tollbooth transponders and supermarket trolleys are all reminders of this contract (1995: 102). Augé calls the condition behind these spaces 'supermodernity':

> If a place can be defined as relational, historical and concerned with identity, then a space which cannot be defined as relational, or historical, or concerned with identity will be a non-place. Supermodernity produces non-places, meaning spaces which are not themselves anthropological places and which, unlike Baudelairean modernity, do not integrate the earlier places: instead these are listed, classified, promoted to the status of 'places of memory', and assigned to a circumscribed and specific position. (1995: 77–8)

Supermodernity is a paradoxical condition. On the one hand it implies a proliferation of events, a surfeit of history and, above all, an abundance of news and information describing these occurrences. At the same time, this excess means that 'there is no room for history unless it has been transformed into an element of spectacle, usually in allusive texts. What reigns there is actuality, the urgency of the present moment' (Augé 1995: 104). Supermodernity generates a paradoxical excess and dearth of identity. ATM cards, PIN codes, e-mail addresses, Social Security cards, drivers' licences and national identity cards with biometric data function to differentiate between individuals. At the same time, this proliferation has made personal identity more rigid and formally interchangeable: everyone can be identified by a 'number' and one's 'identity' can be 'stolen'.

Benny, it would seem, dwells in supermodernity. He wanders aimlessly and seemingly without motivation between Augé's anonymous transit points and temporary abodes. Benny might be a regular at McDonald's and the video store, but this hardly means the employees there know his name. Haneke telegraphs these interactions in close-ups of hands, money, cash register LED panels, hand-stamp club 'tickets' and video identification numbers. The service personnel, when shown at all, never feature in two-shots with Benny. These are contractual transactions rather than personal encounters. When Benny and his acquaintance discuss the upcoming AC/DC concert, they are less concerned with the music or even the experience; *possessing* the tickets is most important.

In shots from Benny's window, masses of cars drone along a clogged six-lane *Autobahn*. The highway is one of Augé's key transit points: 'Motorway travel is thus doubly remarkable: it avoids, for functional reasons, all the principle places to which it takes us; and it makes comments on them' (1995: 97). The surrounding architectures of high-rise condominiums and office buildings are anonymous and menacing. We are a felt universe away from the horse-drawn carriages and narrow alleys of Vienna's cosy first district. Even Benny's school is a site of consumer exchange: he sells drugs in the boys' choir.

The scene at the travel agency is revealing. An employee offers mother and son four postcard images: a sandy beach backed by palm trees, a fleet of sail boats before an impressive but unrecognisable bridge, a camel and 'native' in the background of a massive desert and a view of New York at night. The photographs are generic, picture-book imaginaries in keeping with the service they advertise. The last-minute travel

Benny's Video (1992): A supermodern transaction at the boys' choir

package – and certainly in the case of the family's wish to disappear from Vienna – yields not, as traditionally the aim of travel has been, a 'destination' with absolute value, but rather an interchangeable 'anywhere but here'. Travel, according to Augé, 'constructs a fictional relationship between gaze and landscape. And while we use the word "space" to describe the frequentation of *places* which specifically defines the journey, we should still remember that there are spaces in which the individual feels himself to be a spectator without paying much attention to the spectacle' (1995: 86; emphasis in original). When Benny and his mother sojourn in Egypt, this too is a sprawl of non-places: hotels, guided bus tours and marketplace encounters with the 'natives', all documented with the video camera. They could be anywhere. Exotic Egypt is a scene similar to Benny's room: the teen perceives as an anonymous user, watching a filtered virtual reality without being seen himself. In the hotel in Cairo he channel surfs through the Egyptian programmes and then stops at the familiarity of the church music: an organ playing Bach's 'Liebster Jesu, wir sind hier'. (At the school concert Benny sings the Bach motet 'Jesu, meine Freude'.) At stake here, as Augé theorises, is the dialectic between anonymity and identity.

Simulation

If Augé sets the anthropological scene and situates us in supermodernity, Jean Baudrillard explains the rules of representation. Baudrillard's theory of simulation announces the death of representation: 'All of Western faith and good faith was engaged in this wager on representation: that a sign could refer to the depth of meaning, that a sign could *exchange* for meaning and that something could guarantee this exchange' (1983: 10; emphasis in original). According to Baudrillard, this wager has been irrevocably lost: our situation today is simulation and signs have become pure simulacra. In simulation,

> The real is produced from miniaturised units, from matrices, memory banks and command models – and with these it can be reproduced an indefinite number of times. It no longer has to be rational, since it is no longer measured against some ideal or negative instance. It is nothing more than operational. In fact, since it is no longer enveloped by an imaginary, it is no longer real at all. It is a hyperreal, the product of an irradiating synthesis of combinatory models in a hyperspace without atmosphere. (1983: 3)

The loss of the distinction between original and copy in the age of digital media disturbs Baudrillard. This loss, according to the theorist, also signals the end of rationality: the *Abbild* (copy) now needs no *Urbild* (prototype). Thus, for Baudrillard, to simulate is not just to fake or feign something, but to make something more real than real.

> To dissimulate is to feign not to have what one has. To simulate is to feign to have what one hasn't. One implies a presence, the other an absence. But the matter is more complicated, since to simulate is not simply to feign: 'Someone who feigns an illness can simply go to bed and make believe he is ill. Someone

who simulates an illness produces in himself some of the symptoms.' (Littre) Thus, feigning or dissimulating leaves the reality principle intact: the difference is always clear, it is only masked; whereas simulation threatens the difference between 'true' and 'false', between 'real' and 'imaginary'. Since the simulator produces 'true' symptoms, is he ill or not? He cannot be treated objectively either as ill, or as not-ill. (1983: 5)

Because of the processes and logic of simulation, according to Baudrillard, it becomes increasingly difficult or impossible to distinguish between true and false, appearance and reality. Haneke subscribes to this vision of the world. As he warns in an interview, 'through the permanent falsifying of the world in the media, leading us only to perceive the world in terms of images, a dangerous situation is being created … a Coca-Cola advertisement takes on the same level of reality as news footage' (in Falcon 1998: 12).

Benny is a video freak accustomed to experiencing life through a viewfinder. He dwells in a dim room with the shades permanently drawn, while his video camera gazes onto the street and transmits the signal to a monitor. The actual reality on the street below is rendered into a consumable and controllable virtual reality. Only experiences translated through videotape are palatable. (Michel Foucault designates this voyeur's gaze 'a superb formula: power exercised continuously for what turns out to be minimal cost' (quoted in Denzin 1995: 1)). Benny thereby replicates the conflation of actual and virtual he receives from television transmissions. He watches a news report on neo-Nazis in Greifswald before a splatter film before a documentary on the Bosnian conflict. Zap, zap, zap: seamless channel surfing.[2] Benny is not the film's only amoral character. Georg and Anna command a creative regime of truth and lie. While interrogating Benny after the murder, Georg sternly warns his son not to lie; Benny should reveal precisely with whom he spoke about the murder. This commandment, however, is rehearsed in service of a greater deception, that is, Georg's gruesome disposal of the girl's body and concealment of the crime. Anna, similarly, feigns her mother's death in order to receive the school director's permission to take Benny to Egypt.

This lack of distinction is reproduced in Benny's videos, those privileged items conflated in the title's singular referent. Is 'Benny's Video' his footage of the pig slaughter, the recording of the girl's murder or the document of his parents' conspiracy that he delivers to the police in the final scene? In some sense, the title implies that all of these videos are in fact just one. They are all precisely as real, actual or virtual to Benny. In fact, because of his inability to distinguish between the real and the mediated, it is not possible for Benny to comprehend the consequences of his action; only at the end of the film does he realise that there is no rewind button in life. But for as much as Benny is unable to distinguish between the actual and the virtual and the extent to which the distinction is, according to Baudrillard, irrelevant in the supermodern moment, Benny does have a desire for some experiential sense of the real. After all, his stated reason for killing the girl in the first place is 'to see how it is'. In Egypt, furthermore, the otherwise taciturn teen parachutes and gleefully shouts, 'Mommy, I can fly!'[3]

More real than reel: Benny's TV

Baudrillard addresses this nostalgia for the real. In our age a paradoxical fixation on authenticity has developed, an 'escalation of the true, of the lived experience ... a panic-stricken production of the real and the referential' (1983: 12–13). This fascination with lived experience constitutes, however, a symptom of its loss. Benny hardly seeks a modernist form of authenticity. His desire for the real is in fact already a mediated version, which he betrays in his formulation that wants to 'see' how it is. Benny wants to be the agent in a killing, but, more importantly, he wants to see himself on his monitor killing and to be able to rewind, slow down and edit the act on his console. For Benny, the experience of this after-the-fact virtual reality is even more dramatic than the actual deed itself – it is more important and somehow more real to him. He spends much more time viewing and re-viewing the video than cleaning up the body.

Eros is Sick: Communication and Capital

The subtitle of *Benny's Video* in the scheme of Haneke's comments on the 'glaciation trilogy' is 'the glaciation of feelings'. In works such as *Anti-Oedipus: Capitalism and Schizophrenia*, Gilles Deleuze diagnoses the contemporary age as one in which emotions are dulled, communication dissolves and relationships are eroding and losing connectivity. He examines the postwar disillusionment and breakdown in interpersonal bonds and concludes that Eros is sick, a metaphor he extends to the cinema in the form of intra- and inter-shot relations (that is, composition and editing) of the postwar national cinemas. This dissolution of communal, sexual and image relations occurs, in Peter Canning's lucid summary of Deleuze,

> because relations (sexual, social, affective, episto-phenomenological) mediated by a signifier that keeps us unconscious of their erotic-aggressive condition have broken down and only money-power differentials link one 'character' to another, one movement or gesture to another, in a chain of erotic-aggressive attitudes. Money, the diffuse conspiracy of capital, is the immanent symptom of our 'universal schizophrenia'. (2000: 343–4)

In *Benny's Video*, the breakdown of communication and relationships in the bourgeois family yields to a power structure defined, organised and enervated by capital. The apartment is divided into plots of land marked by an unspoken respect of private ownership. Georg treats the doorway to Benny's room as a border that he cannot step over; capitalism triumphs over parenting. Haneke constructs the parents' lack of moral distinction in a set design dominated by a pick-and-mix art collection. In the dining room, the prevalence of still life paintings and a series of preserved butterflies convey the home's emotional lifelessness. The diverse collection of prints ranging from Leonardo da Vinci's 'Mona Lisa' and Claude Monet's 'Houses of Parliament, London' to a poster of Andy Warhol's Marilyn prints indicate, on the one hand, Georg and Anna's middlebrow bourgeois status and, on the other, implicate the parents and their so-called higher forms of art on the same moral level as Benny's comic books, slasher flicks and video games. The appearance of Warhol's works in the set design is particularly revealing. Baudrillard deploys the pop artist as his paradigm for the principle of art as 'absolute commodity'. When Warhol painted his 'Campbell's Soup Cans' in the 1960s, according to Baudrillard, he set the 'drumbeat of simulation' and of the entire modern art. When the artist painted the 'Soup Cans' in 1986, he fell victim to the stereotype of simulation (see Baudrillard 1990: 121). In the system of Georg and Anna's living room, Warhol's original purpose is completely lost. Warhol's attacks on *l'art pour l'art* are deflated – in the context of poster-prints by iconic artists from various periods – to yet another poster-cised decoration intended to be 'beautiful' or at least 'recognised'.

Benny's parents subscribe to a form of *Zettelerziehung*: they parent with notes and bills. Benny wakes up to notes that say that the money on the table is to buy lunch or 'x'; capitalism becomes parenting.[4] Ironically (or not, when perceived through Deleuze), communication between father and son fails to change after Benny's murder comes to light. Benny makes no attempt to speak to his father, who must conduct an interrogation to ascertain a sketch of the crime. Georg, for his part, keeps his distance, and seems more annoyed than shocked about Benny's deed. This is a fitting reaction for someone more concerned with a potential loss of social standing than with the moral ramifications of his son's act. Anna is an emotional wreck, vacillating from silence to outbursts of tears. There is never a coming to terms with the murder, nor any moral lesson drawn. Anna, in the same way as her husband, never mourns for the girl. She merely regrets an unfortunate situation that might damage Benny's future career.

If capitalism causes schizophrenia, then the symptoms are surely legible in Benny's situation. Benny has no friends. Indeed, he tells his victim that the boy he hangs out with is 'just a guy [he knows] from school'. Taciturn at home, Benny is a drug dealer at choir practice, a brute in computer class and a murderer when his parents are on holiday. If one considers Benny's murder of the girl to be a call for help or at least attention, then one arrives at a chilling balance. This would imply that Benny is the sole character in the film who tries to communicate and that violence is the only remaining absolute capital and option for communication.

The Video Narcissus

Commentators on *Benny's Video* nearly unanimously cite Benny's murder of the nameless girl he meets at the video store to be the key scene in the film. Like the two other panels in Haneke's triptych (the family's suicide at the conclusion of *Der siebente*

Kontinent (*The Seventh Continent*, 1989) and when the student runs amok at the end of *71 Fragmente einer Chronologie des Zufalls* (*71 Fragments of a Chronology of Chance*, 1994)), a murder serves as the focal point of *Benny's Video*. This moment is the nexus for the critics' respective agendas, whether moral/theological issues or formal concerns (that is, Haneke's denial of unmediated visual access to the murder). As important as this scene is, what the scene *is not* could be perhaps more revealing. Of the three films in the trilogy, *Benny's Video* is most aesthetically and formally mainstream (see Vogel 1996: 74). Therefore, for example, when Benny brings the girl back to his place after meeting her at the video store, the spectator expects – both by conditioning via traditional cinematic narratives as well as through the way Haneke conventionally stages the meeting – a sexual encounter: boy meets girl, girl meets boy, boy kisses girl.

Instead, in this film, boy meets girl, boy kills girl. What should be Benny's first sexual experience becomes a violent act which he records and ritually rehashes. A sexual act comes only *after* the violent one. In an auto-erotic spectacle, Benny strips naked and observes himself in the mirror, smearing himself with the girl's blood.[5] Benny even rearranges the girl's shirt so that she is 'properly' covered, a lack of curiosity that further distances him from normative heterosexuality. This scene points to Baudrillard's comments on the Narcissus myth:

> The digital Narcissus replaces the triangular Oedipus … the clone will be your guardian angel … Your 'neighbour' will be this deceptively similar clone, so that you will never be alone again and never again have a secret. 'Love thy neighbour as thyself': this old scriptural problem is solved – your neighbour, *you are him*. The love will thus be absolute. Absolute self-seduction. (1979: 233; emphasis in original)

In the postmodern moment, according to Baudrillard, the myth of Narcissus has now become the guiding paradigm that structures experience and narrative, rather than the Oedipus initiation story. If the Oedipal myth entertains the idea that human subjectivity is sexually realised in the bonded, love relationship, then the Baudrillardian Narcissus myth choreographed in *Benny's Video* reveals that video violence is the 'authentic' experience in a 'me' world without connections. Benny comes of age not through sexual conquest and replacing a mother figure,[6] but rather by eliminating the potential object of desire and distancing himself into a Plato's cave of video equipment, over which he commands absolute control.[7]

Credits

Control for Benny means, above all, the mediating act of filming. Benny is a collector, an anthropologist of supermodernity, albeit one who draws no conclusions and derives little morality from his field research. Benny's objective ends with possession. He aims to *own* specific pieces of the experienced world: the pig's death, his sister's 'pilot game' pyramid scheme, shots of the city from his window, the girl's murder, the trip to Egypt and his parents' conspiracy. Benny's essential element of control is clearly displayed on his video devices: REWIND. The pig's death, for example, can be re-viewed an indefinite number of times, undone, prolonged and abstracted in slow-motion. Rewind entails the ability to control reality, to reverse its progression. As Herbert Hrachovec observes, 'VCRs are symptomatic for a system in which the picture input becomes inconsequential. More interesting are the possibilities of manipulating the input' (1996: 287).

In *Funny Games* (1997), the killer Paul (also played by Arno Frisch) turns the remote on the film itself and rewinds its narrative to erase his victim's rebellion. This notorious act of self-reflexivity casts doubts on who 'wins' in *Benny's Video*. Who manipulates and controls what is 'real'? Who is being manipulated? The title of Michael Haneke's feature names the two main characters: Benny, the pubescent Austrian, and video, in its manifold meanings and implications.

But, in an important sense, it is ultimately Haneke who enjoys the position of Benny; *Benny's Video* maintains perfect surveillance over its characters. This is precisely where Haneke and the theorists overlap in the boldness – or excess – of their approach. Just as one can take Baudrillard, Augé and Deleuze to task for their Parisian solipsism, one must be critical of Haneke's all-or-nothing gambit. The fantasy of *The Matrix* (1999) guides both Haneke and these theorists: that *they* can see a reality even though all others are fooled. This is a similar idea of absolute control to which Benny subscribes.

Re-viewing *Benny's Video* and re-reading Augé, Baudrillard and Deleuze, one finds concerns which trouble us less today. The clear fronts from which they debated – for example, do new media mean freedom or slavery? – have been redrawn or made obsolete. Concerns like Islamist terrorism, global warming and banking collapses have eclipsed or superseded some of these issues; time has clarified others. Critics have interrogated the excesses of Baudrillard, pointing out the way in which his blasé description of contemporary society blithely segues into a wholesale negation of truth and representation, which in turn forecloses the possibility of political agency. In a similar way, from this historical distance we must understand *Benny's Video* and Haneke's cinema of disturbance less as cynical political allegory than as an invitation to reconsider channels of perspective and structures of control. After Augé's supermodernity, Deleuze's sick Eros and Baudrillard's video Narcissus, the crucial question has ceased to be 'what's on?', but rather 'who has the remote?'

Notes
Unless otherwise stated, all translations are by the author.

1   The film comes after *Der siebente Kontinent* (*The Seventh Continent*, 1989) and before *71 Fragmente einer Chronologie des Zufalls* (*71 Fragments of a Chronology of Chance*, 1994).
2   The effect is clearly intentional on Haneke's part, as he reveals in interview: 'Today's children and youth grow up with a medium which treats documentary violence in the same way it treats simulated, fictional violence, in other words Yugoslavia

the same way as the "Terminator". The child, exposed to these different realities, requires help to differentiate in order to develop a normal relationship to reality' (in Donner 1993: 38).

3 In a verdict perhaps more radical than Baudrillard, Roy Grundmann suggests that Benny can in fact distinguish between the real and the virtual: he simply prefers the latter. See Grundmann (2007: 10).

4 As Peter Canning summarises Deleuze: 'Capital, with its differential signifier, is the dynamic temporal form of the "conspiracy of unequal exchange" that coerces and controls the affect and movement of bodies, signs, and images. It is an influencing machine that produces in its own subject the vaguely conscious sensation of a diffuse world conspiracy that is organising the misery' (2000: 346; see also Deleuze 1986: 210–11; Deleuze 1989: 77).

5 There is a real temptation to read this scene as a very Lacanian moment. There is not, however, even a misrecognition in Benny's gaze, nor any sort of recognition. Benny is so semiotically incapacitated, he lacks even the potential of subjectivity. His bodily inscriptions are another futile attempt at communication.

6 Those looking for an Oedipal trajectory here can find one: only in reverse. After the murder, Benny and his mother become the film's couple. This is especially evident in Egypt, when Benny videotapes his mother urinating and sleeps with her in a common bed. The girl is eliminated so that Benny's desire can be displaced to the mother, to whom he previously granted little attention.

7 A useful exercise might be to compare Benny to the teenager Ricky Fitts (Wes Bentley) in *American Beauty* (1999). That character's verisimilitude vis-à-vis Benny suggests either a rather generous case of borrowing by director Sam Mendes and screenwriter Alan Ball, or proves Baudrillard true in his thoughts on the ubiquity of this situation. In that film, the teenager is a drug dealer, an obsessive voyeur who records everything on video, and lives in an oppressive/dysfunctional family situation. The crucial difference is that he strives for the heterosexual coupling he finds with the neighbour's daughter. Benny, in contrast, kills the analogous character.

References

Augé, M. (1995) *Non-places. Introduction to an Anthropology of Supermodernity*. Trans. J. Howe. London: Verso.

Baudrillard, J. (1979) *De la séduction*. Paris: Denoël-Gonthier.

_____ (1983) *Simulations*. Trans. P. Foss, P. Patton and P. Beitchman. New York: Semiotext(e).

_____ (1990) 'Von der absoluten Ware', trans. M. Buchgeister, in H. Bastian (ed.) *Andy Warhol: Silkscreens from the Sixties*. Munich: Schirmer/Mosel, 118–23.

Canning, P. (2000) 'The Imagination of Immanence: An Ethics of Cinema', in G. Flaxman (ed.) *The Brain Is the Screen. Deleuze and the Philosophy of Cinema*. Minneapolis: University of Minneapolis Press, 327–62.

Deleuze, G. (1986) *Cinema 1: The Movement Image*. Trans. H. Tomlinson and B. Hebberjam. London: Athlone Press.

_____ (1989) *Cinema 2: The Time-Image*. Trans. H. Tomlinson and B. Hebberjam. London: Athlone Press.

Deleuze, G. and F. Guattari (2004) *Anti-Oedipus: Capitalism and Schizophrenia*. Trans. R. Hurley, M. Seem and H. R. Lane. London: Continuum.

Denzin, N. (1995) *The Cinematic Society: The Voyeur's Gaze*. London: Sage.

Donner, W. (1993) 'Das Gegenteil von Hollywood', *Tip*, 3 June, 34–9.

Falcon, R. (1998) 'The discreet harm of the bourgeoisie', *Sight & Sound*, 8, 5, 10–12.

Grundmann, R. (2007) '*Auteur de Force*: Michael Haneke's "Cinema of Glaciation"', *Cineaste*, 32, 2, 6–14.

Hrachovec, H. (1996) 'Heimelektronik und Heimnachteil: Michael Haneke's *Benny's Video*', in G. Schlemmer (ed.) *Der neue österreichische Film*. Vienna: Wespennest, 286–99.

Vogel, A. (1996) 'Of Nonexisting Continents: The Cinema of Michael Haneke', *Film Comment*, 32, 4, 73–5.

Funny Games

CHAPTER THIRTEEN

The Ethical Screen:
Funny Games and the Spectacle of Pain

Alex Gerbaz

The use of direct address in *Funny Games*, Michael Haneke's 1997 film about a bourgeois family murdered by two young sociopaths while on holiday, is employed as a device to interrogate the sometimes pleasurable viewing of images of other people's suffering. Haneke uses direct address not only to deconstruct the formulaic family-taken-hostage scenario common to the horror and thriller genres, but also in emphasising the spectator's responsibility to examine the appeal of watching others in pain. I demonstrate this idea by focusing on the 'face-to-face' encounters between viewers and Paul (Arno Frisch), one of the film's psychopathic killers. Drawing on Emmanuel Levinas's philosophy of ethics and the face, I propose that direct address (that is, when characters face the camera) can engage the viewer's sense of responsibility in ways that other cinematic images of faces may not. In this way, the film encourages us to look critically at the mechanisms used to turn violence and pain into popular entertainment. The face-to-face relation between spectators and Paul explicitly prompts reflection on the ethical dimensions of the narrative and, more broadly, of film violence and spectatorship. Often the face in cinema represents a threshold between life and death, and is the singular image that appeals to our sympathy just before a murder or violent act is committed. Perhaps the most disturbing moment in *Funny Games*, however, is not an act of violence but rather the conspiratorial wink that Paul directs at the audience just as the carnage is getting started. By facing the camera, he not only breaks one of the 'rules' of dramatic fictional cinema; he also insinuates that we are on his side rather than that of his victims. Paul's face, its orientation and expression, signifies that viewers *want* to see him commit acts of brutality. And yet Haneke denies us this perverse pleasure by depicting most of the violence offscreen, concentrating instead on the faces of characters as they watch others suffer. This reflects ironically upon the spectator's position as a consumer of violence for the purposes of entertainment. Typically we are the ones looking at images of people in pain (Haneke gives us these images too), but Paul's face becomes a constant reminder that we, the audience, are also being watched. This essay explores ethical and social aspects of film spectatorship, and asks whether or not the cinematic encounter between viewing subject, screen and the human visage can transform or increase awareness of our responsibility towards others in the 'real' world.

Viewers have become fascinated with the screen as a medium that can communicate suffering. Images of fictitious and actual pain are turned into a spectacle: dramatised torture scenes in the cinema; slow-motion replays of sporting injuries on television; beheadings and executions of prisoners on the internet. Whether or not we choose to look at such images, they form a ubiquitous aspect of our visual culture. Screens allow us to watch others suffer while we sit back and do nothing. By 'screening' pain, they at once show it and separate us from it. Using pain as a spectacle has a long history in art. In *Regarding the Pain of Others*, Susan Sontag examines this theme with a focus on war photography, comparing the depiction of modern wartime atrocities to the representation of cruelties and horror in classical art. She suggests that 'the appetite for pictures showing bodies in pain is as keen, almost, as the desire for ones that show bodies naked' (2003: 36); the viewer of pain becomes as much a voyeur as the viewer of pornography. There are two ways in which we usually respond to the spectacle of pain. One is to look away (or cover the eyes); the other is to keep looking. Sontag notes that torment is 'often represented in painting as a spectacle, something being watched (or ignored) by other people' (2003: 38). Why would we look at an image of horror or pain? For Sontag, we have 'the satisfaction of being able to look at the image without flinching', as well as 'the pleasure of flinching' (2003: 37). On the other hand, we may feel shock, and shame at watching (ibid.). That is, when someone sees us looking at pain and doing nothing about it, we feel ashamed.

Being seen as a spectator of pain is ethically problematic. Although not inflicting the pain ourselves, gazing impassively at it suggests indifference to – and perhaps even enjoyment of – the suffering of others. When somebody turns to face us (either the person in pain, or a third party), catches us in the act of looking, our morality comes into question. This 'face-to-face' moment exposes our voyeurism, and provokes us in a way that is similar to an image of cruelty, asking: 'how can you look at this?' Cinema has exploited, in some regards, the fact that such questions can make us uncomfortable. For example, part of the allure of watching a violent or horrific film in a darkened auditorium is that we are unlikely to be caught or confronted by others. Instead, we disappear into the shadows, our faces well-hidden. And by concealing our identities in this way, our sense of responsibility arguably diminishes. In other words, the voyeur does not feel culpable, or accountable, to the same extent as someone who is visible and identifiable. Responsibility has this double meaning, of accepting blame as well as having the ability to respond or act when we become aware of another's suffering.

To be responsible, as Levinas's philosophy implies, starts with not only seeing another person's face, but also showing one's own face. Levinas argues that when faced by another human being we confront something beyond immediate perception: a sense of the Infinite; an intentional life; not another object of perception merely to be observed or played with, but a perceiving subject. However, it is *face-to-face* with others that we discover responsibility: the ability to respond to the absolutely Other, or that which is not fully present in our experience (for example, another person's pain). Our whole ethical life, then, is structured, according to Levinas, around meetings between human faces. Much more than an assemblage of features and expressions, the face signifies that which is essential to society and humanity. It communicates joy as well as suffering, and it warns against violence: 'the face of the other man is for me at one and the same time a temptation to kill and the "thou shalt not kill" by which I am already accused or suspected, but which also already *summons me*' (2002: 535; emphasis in original). The human face expresses emotion and pain, but it also appeals fundamentally to our sense of ethics and responsibility. As responsible subjects, we face others and let them face us too.

Levinas claims that 'the Other faces me and puts me in question' – this face-to-face encounter 'tears consciousness up from its centre, submitting it to the Other' (1969: 207). A disruption of consciousness here means opening up to personal and social responsibility, the Other being that which lies outside of our conscious experience yet to which we are ethically related. In cinema, the face retains a limited ethical dimension as it is mediated by the screen. But just as Levinas argues that the face is ethically privileged amongst other objects, so too it is privileged onscreen when it reaches out to the audience via a direct gaze. Adapting Levinas, I suggest that the frontal facing position onscreen 'puts me in question' in a way that other faces onscreen do not. Direct address questions the spectator's personal enjoyment of the images being presented, and asks him or her to be a more active, critical viewing participant.

Following this, the use of direct address in film and television can, theoretically, instil in viewers a sense of responsibility. For example, television news broadcasters address us, the 'viewers at home', encouraging us to be responsible members of society, even to report criminal activity or suspicious behaviour in the community. Occasionally, they will warn us of upcoming footage that may – and, by implication, should – offend us. Ironically, such alerts often make us pay more attention because they pique our curiosity. In Gaspar Noé's film *Seul Contre Tous* (*I Stand Alone*, 1998), viewers are warned in the final few minutes by a cheeky intertitle onscreen that reads: 'You have 30 seconds to leave the cinema.' This prompts spectators to make a decision whether or not they wish to see the film's disturbing climax of sexual abuse. It also implies that we can escape moral judgement and shame by looking away or going home.

Haneke's *Funny Games*, made in the year before *I Stand Alone*, is equally facetious in reminding viewers that they are watching a 'shocking' film. Its mixture of sadistic violence and self-referential jokes caters ostensibly for the moviegoing public's wish to be horrified as well as amused. However, by focusing on the relationship between entertainment and violence, the film encourages viewers to consider the extent to which the suffering of others is turned routinely into a media spectacle. It also asks us to look critically at our own expectations and desire for cinematic bloodshed. Ironically, though the film does contain harrowingly realistic scenes of human suffering, its acts of violence mostly happen offscreen. Characters' deaths are counterbalanced by off-colour humour and allusions to spectatorship. *Funny Games* was released the year after Wes Craven's *Scream* (1996) which had set a benchmark for postmodern horror. Somewhat like *Scream*, which celebrates the 'rules' of horror movies while humorously pointing them out to the audience, *Funny Games* uses genre conventions in a mocking, self-reflexive fashion. The main difference is that Haneke is not trying to please or reward his audience by appealing to their knowledge of genre codes. Rather, he wants to punish and frustrate us, to have us suffer, like the family in his film.

Funny Games begins by showing a married couple and their young son driving through the countryside in Austria. Husband and wife Georg (Ulrich Mühe) and Anna (Susanne Lothar) select various CDs of classical music, challenging each other to guess the names of pieces, composers, singers and so on. 'Björling and Tebaldi?' 'Of course.' 'An oratorio by Händel?' 'Yes, but which one?' For the first few minutes, Haneke keeps the couple's identity anonymous (we see their hands but not their faces), as if indulging in his own game with the audience. Then, unexpectedly, he cuts to show them smiling. The boy in the back seat, Georgie (Stefan Clapczynski), smiles too. Indeed, it would be difficult to imagine a family that is more comfortable and content than the one presented here. The music sounds beautifully pleasant too. But after a few seconds, the title – *FUNNY GAMES* – appears suddenly onscreen in large, blood-red letters, covering the faces of the characters. The classical music coming from the car's CD player is replaced on the film's soundtrack by the wildly abrasive death-metal of John Zorn. Unaware of the film's abrupt shift in tone, the family keeps smiling away. This initial audiovisual assault introduces the mixture of playfulness and brutality that runs throughout the film. By delaying the appearance of the family's smiling faces, and then overlaying them with bold titles and loud, acerbic music, Haneke not only thumbs his nose at the traditional image of a happy bourgeois family; he also establishes a space for ironic commentary upon the film's characters and events. Haneke is already humiliating the family, even if they do not realise anything is wrong. And he is establishing an unusual amount of suspense (for example, hiding their faces), only to then blatantly spell out the family's approaching demise in large red letters. For the audience, the nature of Haneke's game is starting to emerge: a suspenseful story in which the fate of the characters is predetermined and genre conventions are thrust in our faces.

Upon reaching their holiday house by the river, we are introduced to the character that will be the first to die: the family's dog, Rolfi, begins sniffing around and making a nuisance of itself. The camera pays an excessive amount of attention to this, as if Rolfi were equally important as the human characters. A shot of a bag of golf clubs in a corner of the house ominously links the dog with the first 'funny game' of the film. Rolfi is already interfering (trying to eat food straight from the fridge, and so forth), which is turned into an off-colour joke when Paul later refers to the dog 'getting in the way' of his golf swing. Meanwhile, Georg and his son Georgie take a boat out on the river, while Anna is visited by a young man calling himself Peter (Frank Giering). Peter asks to borrow some eggs, but he 'accidentally' drops them on the floor. He then knocks Anna's cordless phone into a sink of water, causing it to stop working. These little annoyances are mirrored in the audience's building frustration at not getting what they might expect from a violent film or thriller. When Paul arrives, he tells Peter off for being clumsy, but the pair remain in the house and begin to overstay their welcome. There is something unsettling in the way they affect politeness and respect, nonetheless refusing to leave. When Anna's husband returns, they start calling themselves Tom and Jerry, insisting that they will go away only if they are given more eggs. Georg slaps Paul in the face, and they retaliate forcefully. At this stage it becomes clear that Peter/Tom and Paul/Jerry are in complete control of the situation.

Haneke is about to start using Paul as his mouthpiece to converse with the audience. The first instance of direct address is perhaps the most disturbing, and certainly the most unexpected. Paul reveals to Anna and Georg that he has killed the dog, a moment which recalls the canine slayings in such domestic psycho-thrillers of the 1990s as Martin Scorsese's *Cape Fear* (1991) and Barbet Schroeder's *Single White Female* (1992). Haneke delights in building slowly towards Rolfi's death, and then towards the sight of his body, as if perversely encouraging our fascination with it. Anna begins looking for Rolfi in the garden, while Paul directs her by saying 'cold, warm, warmer'. The camera focuses initially on Anna, but as she walks further away Paul steps into the frame's foreground (his back to us). From this position, he watches her with us. Then, just before she finds the dog, Paul turns around slowly and looks straight at the camera. He grins, winks at us, and then looks back towards Anna. Until this moment (about 25 minutes into the film), *Funny Games* has seemed like a mostly conventional psychological thriller or horror movie. But now, a number of questions run through the viewer's mind. Why is this character looking at us? What is he implying about our interest in his sadistic games? We also start looking at faces onscreen differently. Following this initial 'aside' to the audience, it seems as if Paul is always threatening to look at us again. Now that we have been spotted, and identified as possible co-conspirators, we are constantly on the lookout for further signs of recognition – something in the eyes of Paul (or another character) to show that he knows we are here, watching.

Paul has invited us to become his accomplice, to be part of his game. Even though he already has a partner in crime in Peter (who never addresses us directly), he wants to involve the audience for a different reason. Peter is a cipher: an inveterate liar and sociopath with a vacant personality; he is beyond redemption and change. By contrast, Paul seems to recognise that the audience, by and large, consists of complex individuals who feel ambivalent about watching others suffer emotionally and physically. Thus, in the second moment of direct address, several minutes later, Paul speaks to the audience and wants to know whose side we are on. After he and Peter make a bet with Anna and Georg that they will be dead by nine o'clock, Paul says 'What do you think?', turning to face the camera. 'Do you think they've a chance of winning? You are on their side, aren't you? So, who will you bet with?' Paul's invitation to the audience to join in the game is much more explicit now. His question about whether or not we are 'on their side' is a curious one, because it seems as if we have no choice, in fact, but to be on *his* side. He is the only one in the film who looks at us, acknowledges us, and has the

Funny Games (1997): Keeping an eye on us – Paul's first direct address

same capacity as we do to view the film's narrative from the outside, so to speak, or as a text. Paul's asides constitute breaks in the text, pauses at which spectators can take a step back and consider what they are really looking for in the film.

The technique of direct address – when somebody onscreen faces the camera – is seldom used in thrillers, horror films or dramas. In *The Subject of Documentary*, Michael Renov notes that 'in fictional cinematic discourse [it] is rare indeed, except in instances of comedy' (2004: 30). When Charlie Chaplin, say, or Woody Allen turns to face the audience, they are making light of their characters' problems; somehow their pain becomes less serious, less severe. But direct address also reminds the audience that they are spectators, and perhaps we are readier to admit to watching comedies – in which pain and suffering are generally taken less seriously – than to enjoying genres that depict pain with more intensity. There is an element of shame or embarrassment, for example, in confessing to appreciate a film that contains explicit scenes of torture or brutality. More so if someone catches us watching such scenes, or if we are reminded that we are watching by characters within the film.

The role of direct address – and of the face itself – is significant in *Funny Games*. What are the various faces onscreen watching? At a number of points, Paul is looking at us, but more often we are watching him. When other characters die we watch his face for a response – usually there is none. Georgie's face is covered with a bag when Paul and Peter are terrorising his parents, so his facial expressions and responses are not visible either. And we watch Anna's face in close-up, rather than her husband's, when Georg is being tortured. Of course, the first few minutes of the film are all about *not* seeing the family's faces. As viewers, we connect and respond to the human face more strongly than to any other image. Haneke knows this, and by playing with different aspects of the face – hidden, front-on, offscreen – he makes us aware of our different levels of response and engagement.

In many way, *Funny Games* is an anti-horror or anti-thriller, a critique of the genres from which it borrows. Apart from its subversive use of direct address, it takes plot

points and clichés from the kinds of movies in which a family or individual is terrorised by a psychopath, often while on holiday or else in some domestic environment
(for example, Phillip Noyce's *Dead Calm* (1989), *Cape Fear*, *Single White Female*, even
Charles Laughton's *Night of the Hunter* (1955)). It also borrows from the time-worn
'dead-by-dawn' or ticking-clock scenario, in which killers play games with the victims,
postponing their deaths until being foiled at the last minute. In *Funny Games*, this is
turned into an anticlimax when Peter and Paul decide to kill Anna an hour before the
time is up. While murderers are often given a complex (or not-so-complex) backstory
to explain a sociopathic condition (for example, from *Psycho* (1960) onwards), Peter
and Paul toy with their hostages – and, more significantly, with the audience – by
making up stories of childhood abuse before laughing them off as untrue. Haneke uses
these devices to frustrate the audience, giving us pleasingly familiar genre-derived situations and then scrapping them as if they were too absurd to continue with.

Haneke also reverses the convention of having the hostages turn successfully on
their captors. In the film's third moment of direct address, Georgie attempts to escape
from the house in which they are being held captive. Paul chases him, and there is
a long, slow build-up to the eventual confrontation between them. While the boy
hides, Paul puts on some music – the same song by John Zorn that was played over
the opening credits. Georgie finds a rifle, and waits until Paul is only a short distance
away before shooting. Paul stands calmly as Georgie squeezes the trigger. But the gun
misfires. Paul then looks at Georgie – in a close-up point-of-view shot from the boy's
perspective, which means Paul is also looking at us – shrugs, and says 'poof'. There is an
increasing sense that Paul's self-confidence stems from an almost omniscient comprehension of what is possible within the film's narrative framework. He knows the gun
will misfire because he knows the rules of the game. By looking at the camera, he invites
the audience to share his perspective and to accept that these are *his* rules. Nobody is
going to overpower the two villains; there will be no happy ending; and viewers, having
perhaps enjoyed some of the sadistic violence, will not be able ultimately to feel good
about themselves by identifying once more with the victorious heroes.

We gradually become aware of the futility of the family's attempts to escape,
which are depicted in agonising detail: Georg trying to repair a water-damaged phone
with a hairdryer so that he can call for help; he and Anna struggling to move from one
room to another, Georg with a wounded leg; Anna fleeing the house temporarily and
flagging down vehicles on the road. We know all of this is futile because the events
are beyond Anna and Georg's control; Peter and Paul are in charge. This is confirmed
in the fourth direct address, over an hour into the film, when Paul turns to the audience and asks whether or not we are satisfied at the amount the family has suffered:
'Is that enough? We're not even at feature film length yet. You want a proper ending
with plausible plot development, don't you?' Here viewers are being reminded, by
Paul and by Haneke himself, that this whole ordeal, this spectacle of suffering, has
been constructed for our benefit. We expect characters to undergo a certain amount of
torment, but there is also a point at which we want it to stop.

Haneke's film points ironically to the ways that suffering, entertainment and spectatorship seem to go hand-in-hand. In one lingering scene, Peter sits down to watch

Image of pain: Anna's suffering starts to bore her captors

television, and we see slow-motion replays of cars crashing into each other during a professional race. When he shoots little Georgie, blood is splattered across the television screen, symbolising, perhaps, a connection between spectatorship and violence. This has echoes in Haneke's *Code inconnu: Récit incomplet de divers voyages* (*Code Unknown: Incomplete Tales of Several Journeys*, 2000), particularly the scene in which Anne (Juliette Binoche) is ironing a shirt in front of the television at home. Suddenly she hears a child screaming, apparently in another apartment, and a man's voice shouting. She mutes the television and listens intently as the screaming continues for a while and then subsides; she keeps ironing, and then realises the television volume is down, so she turns it back up, interested again in what is onscreen. Throughout this scene we are looking at Binoche, but there is a reflection of the television on the right-hand side of the frame. It is as if she substitutes one attraction for another – the child screaming for the television. In *Funny Games*, we do not witness Georgie's death, but we see the evidence. Rather than showing the murder, Haneke focuses on Paul's preparation of a sandwich in the next room. Because of this concentration on something completely mundane, we become keenly aware of being spectators. Like Binoche's character, we hear an act of violence committed, and we wait and see what happens next. Paul does nothing when the shot is fired – he does not react at all. Haneke frustrates us with this lack of response. He punishes us for wanting to see what has happened, for taking pleasure in the depiction of violence.

Anna seems to have turned the tables when she shoots and kills Peter. At this, Paul looks genuinely surprised. He starts yelling: 'Where's the remote control?' When he finds it, he literally rewinds the scene to the point just before Anna took the gun. This time, Paul grabs the gun and prevents Peter's death. This confirms for us that Paul, and Haneke, plays by his own rules, to the point that he will thwart certain expectations of the genre in order to prolong the suffering of his victims. But he is doing this for the sake of our entertainment – more so, you suspect, than out of any real friendship or affinity with Peter. The remote control scene is also Haneke at his most sadistic. Having presented the audience with a moment of catharsis, with the killing of Peter, Haneke wrenches it back from us, denying viewers any sense of satisfaction at watching an act of violence.

Haneke makes us aware that we are being deprived of a good time. Ironically, when Anna asks her captors why they do not simply kill her right away, Peter replies: 'Don't forget the entertainment value; we'd all be deprived of our pleasure.' But this is precisely what Haneke is doing – or at least, he is encouraging us to feel bad about the pleasure we are deriving from such 'entertainment'. Anna is eventually killed in unspectacular fashion, dumped in the lake almost as an afterthought well before the nine-o'clock deadline. As Peter and Paul sail towards their next destination, they start discussing the difference between film and reality. Are they opposites, like matter and antimatter – or is it less simple to distinguish them? While the audience ponders this question, Peter and Paul arrive at another house. They charm their way inside, before Paul turns to face the camera one last time. He smiles impishly, as if to say 'here we go again'. The shot freezes, and the John Zorn music returns, signalling that the cycle of violence – and the spectacle of pain – will continue.

The five moments of direct address in *Funny Games* are part of a broader strategy on Haneke's part to critique the generic handling of violence and suffering as entertainment, and to encourage viewers to claim responsibility for treating pain as a spectacle. He wants us to suffer because of the suffering that we expect to witness onscreen. He gives us a taste of violence, the anticipation or the idea, but then he prevents us from seeing it. Like the family in the film, he takes us hostage – for one hundred minutes, in a dark room. For ten full minutes of these, we watch Anna and Georg crawl along the floor in pain, in a single, uninterrupted take. We feel this; we empathise; we suffer along with them. Haneke wants the *watchers* to suffer, not to profit from the suffering that they watch. And he turns the tables on us, making Paul the watcher and the audience the watched. Paul talks to us, faces us, just as he talks to his hostages. His direct address makes us uncomfortable, and it encourages us to think ethically. This means thinking about the ethics of spectatorship, of turning violence and pain into entertainment. The violence may not be real in Haneke's film, but Haneke wants us to feel responsible for it. In any case, other people's suffering is a spectacle, and it makes little difference if the pain is real or not: it is all entertainment.

References

Levinas, E. (1969) *Totality and Infinity: An Essay on Exteriority*. Trans. A. Lingis. Pittsburgh: Duquesne University.

_____ (2002) 'Beyond Intentionality', in D. Moran and T. Mooney (eds) *The Phenomenology Reader*. New York: Routledge, 529–39.

Renov, M. (2004) *The Subject of Documentary*. Minneapolis: University of Minnesota Press.

Sontag, S. (2003) *Regarding the Pain of Others*. New York: Farrar, Straus and Giroux.

CHAPTER FOURTEEN

Superegos and Eggs: Repetition in Funny Games (1997, 2007)

David Sorfa

This chapter is a set of ruminations on the repetition of and within the *Funny Games* films. I would like to begin at the obvious place, with Jacques Derrida who argues that it is repetition (or iterability or *différance*) that is the true logic of meaning. He sums up his position in 'Signature Event Context':

> Every sign, linguistic or non-linguistic, spoken or written … in a small or large unit, can be *cited*, put between quotation marks; in so doing it can break with every given context, engendering an infinity of new contexts in a manner which is absolutely illimitable. This does not imply that the mark is valid outside of context, but on the contrary that there are only contexts without any centre or absolute anchorage. This citationality, this duplication or duplicity, this iterability of the mark which is neither an accident nor an anomaly, it is that (normal/abnormal) without which a mark could not even have a function called 'normal'. What would a mark be that could not be cited? Or one whose origins would not get lost along the way? (1990: 2; emphasis added)

There are many ways in which it would be possible to approach the *Funny Games* films using this as a starting point, but the fundamental implication here is that meaning is a slippery beast that changes its form continuously and necessarily – if context is illimitable then meaning cannot be fixed. If the framework for delimiting meaning, pinning it down, is always shifting then meaning itself cannot ever be said to begin meaning.

While it is clear that *Funny Games U.S.* is a repetition of *Funny Games Austria*, as no one calls it, it should be noted that repetition is a recurring trope throughout the film (for convenience I will generally refer to the films in the singular and indicate where I am referring to the two separate films): most obviously the two adolescents are serial killers – they have killed at least two families and are about to kill a third at the end of the film (Haneke says: 'When the film came out I collected seven different newspaper articles from seven different countries describing very similar cases. They were always boys from bourgeois homes, not deprived or drug-addicted, but who just wanted to see what it would be like' (in Falcon 1998:12)); they can repeat a scene (with a *différance*, one might say) if it has not gone the way it should have; they wear the same sorts of clothes – which may remind us of the importance of twins to a certain sub-genre of horror film; the family have gone on holiday before; they have played tennis with their neighbours before, probably more than once; they have played a guessing game about music before. This second repetition of bourgeois rituals is in some way related to the first set of repetitions related to murder.

Let us, however, begin with eggs. In both films a family arrives at a holiday home by a lake and a short while after unpacking, a young man (played by Arno Frisch), dressed in white, comes from their neighbour's house and politely asks for eggs for the next door family's meal. The mother, Anna/Ann (Susanne Lothar/Naomi Watts) gives him the eggs but he breaks them on the way out. He does this again to the second set of eggs. He becomes increasingly insistent for even more eggs, but Anna/Ann asks him to leave only for him to return with his similarly dressed friend and their demands are doubled. Father and son return and the argument over the eggs becomes heated until the father Georg/George (Ulrich Mühe/Tim Roth) slaps one of the men who then retaliates by breaking his leg with a golf club. It is from this point on that the family's fate is sealed.

During this scene there is a close-up of Anna/Ann cleaning up broken eggs from the floor and Haneke's camera lingers on the slimy stuff of the albumen. It is clear that these eggs foreshadow what will happen to each family member in turn: their shells, both metaphorical and literal, will be destroyed and the stuff that indicates their lives will leak out and they will die. Images of bodily fluids appear throughout the film, perhaps most strikingly in the unbroken seven-minute living room shot when the only movement is the trail of snot slowing dripping from Anna's nose. This 'stuff of life' appears regularly in his other films: the spitting in *Code inconnu: Récit incomplet de divers voyages* (*Code Unknown: Incomplete Tales of Several Journeys*, 2000), the ejaculation and vomit in *La Pianiste* (*The Piano Teacher*, 2001), the nosebleeds in *Le temps du loup* (*The Time of the Wolf*, 2003) and the blood spatter in *Caché* (*Hidden*, 2005). These fluids represent a bemusement on the fragility of life. The eggs in *Funny Games* are obviously linked to egos. And where there is an Ego there must be a Superego.

Slavoj Žižek, drawing on Jacques Lacan. describes the Superego as 'the cruel and insatiable agency that bombards me with impossible demands and then mocks my botched attempts to meet them' (2006: 80) and I would like to explore a certain logical route using this quotation as a starting point. And this, of course, takes us straight to hell.

Funny Games (1997): A foreboding of things to come

Funny Games (2007): It is now impossible to put things back the way they were

Funny Games and Possession

If we imagine *Funny Games* to be a devil film rather than a thriller, then the two boys are demons who have possessed the family. The killers appear to be supernatural. They cannot be killed. They can move easily between the diegetic and extra-diegetic worlds (if the diegetic world is earth, does that mean that our spectator world is hell?). They seem to know more about the family than the family does itself (or is it that every family is the same?). Let us then take the familiar reading of possession narratives as some sort of 'return of the repressed' (and, of course, this immediately reminds us of the uncanny, but this is not a reading that I will pursue here): that is, the victim of possession is able

Funny Games (1997): The family cannot understand what is happening to them

Funny Games (2007): The two films are never quite the same but these slight differences merely underline the inevitability of destruction

to express thoughts through the foreign agency of the possessor that would otherwise be inadmissible either to the self or to society at large. In this way the demon is a 'delusion' in Sigmund Freud's sense of this word in *The Future of an Illusion* (1926), since the possession is the expression of a wish fulfilment – in Ken Russell's *The Devils* (1971) and its cognate texts, Sister Jeanne of the Angels (Vanessa Redgrave) wants to be possessed, sexually and literally, by the priest Grandier (Oliver Reed) but can only fulfil her desire through the perverted (in the strict sense) means of the devil (the extent to which Jeanne's possession is conscious or unconscious is another matter entirely).

If we accept that this is so, then which of the family's desires do the two boys fulfil? The family wishes to be punished for their privileged position. They know that their wealth and comfort depends on the poverty and unhappiness of others (an argument that comes up again and again in Haneke's films, particularly in *Code Unknown*, *The Time of the Wolf* and *Hidden*) and thus they wish for due exculpation from this guilt.

If we then go on to reread this within the Freudian structure of Ego, Superego and Id, the subject Ego, aware of the foundational but dangerous and implacable Id, calls forth the punishing Superego to destroy, not the Id, but the state of its own consciousness (since it realises that the Id cannot be destroyed). In this sense, the Supergo, following Žižek perhaps too literally, is the annihilating agency/angel *par excellence*, sent, in fact, by the Id which itself is brought forth by the original guilt of the Ego. I realise that this argument is completely self-fulfilling – the Ego creates the Id; the Id creates the Ego; the Ego creates the Superego; the Id creates the Superego; the Superego destroys both. I believe that there is a way of understanding this if we look at the development of Freud's thinking about the structure of the mind in his very early writings about external and internal stimuli in which consciousness is a by-product – in fact, what Žižek calls the 'symptom' (and later I think the entire system, the 'sinthome' – hence, the Ego – for Žižek, is a symptom and that's why we may as well enjoy it). In order to illustrate this point more clearly I present three diagrams which show the movement from a simple Freudian model through a Žižekian symptom version to the self-annihilating Haneke topography.

If we follow this logic, if we can be said to be operating logically at all by now, then we have a complete collapse of the Freudian topography into a self-annihilating system. If this is so, then we can see a further repetition in Haneke's films. *Funny Games* is now no longer a repetition of itself but rather a repetition of Haneke's first theatrically-released film *Die siebente Kontinent* (*The Seventh Continent*, 1989).

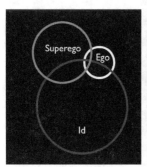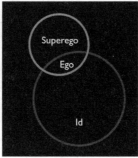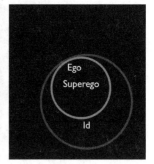

Left to right: Freud; Žižek; Haneke

In this film another bourgeois family – once again mother, father, child – for no apparent reason, lock themselves away in their house, destroy every one of their possessions, except the television set, and finally take overdoses and die while watching Jennifer Rush perform 'The Power of Love' on MTV. Here then the television plays the role of the grotesque Superego – preaching love but demanding death.

In Haneke's films the logic of repetition would seem to form the self-enclosed structure of the subject. The Ego only exists as the symptom of the Id and the Superego

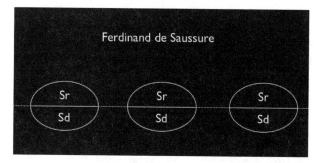

(there may be a problem in my logic here) and is therefore a secondary effect, something derivative rather than original (is this not the definition of repetition?) and it is this derivative-ness that inherently demands the satisfaction of destruction.

In this structural sense, we cannot now talk of intention ('the Ego wants…' or 'the Id wants…') but rather that the very structure that allows these terms to exist is continually imploding into itself. If this were the whole story, of course, nothing would exist and, once again, there would be no problem. I would argue, however, that the way out of this dilemma is through one of the simplest linguistic structures, also vaguely egg shaped, Ferdinand Saussure's sign system (where sr = signifier and sd = signified):

It is in this system, of course, that the repetitive route of our friendly neighbourhood killers is sketched out very clearly and is also the glue that holds the system together (or, which is saying the same thing, destroys it).

The Gift, Hospitality and Sacrifice

Of course the first mistake that the family makes is to invite the killers into their home (like vampires they seem to require explicit permission to enter) and the second is to be generous and give them the eggs. There is a way of understanding this through Jacques Derrida's conception of friendship and hospitality in which hospitality is freely given even to the guest who will destroy and murder you. In fact, the very fundamental proof of hospitality is to invite in one's own murderer (perhaps even in the full knowledge that you will be destroyed). True neighbourliness requires the ultimate sacrifice – such a complete opening up to the Other that it results in self-destruction. I do not think that we need to understand this literally for if we accept the other unconditionally this will necessarily reorient our sense of self in such a way that it is absolutely changed and only metaphorically destroyed.

In the essay 'Why is Every Act a *Repetition?*', Žižek discusses the functioning of the scapegoat:

A 'true' Stalinist would probably say: even if, on the level of immediate facts, the accused are innocent, they are all the more guilty on a deeper level of historical responsibility – by the very insistence on their abstract-legal innocence, they have given preference to their individuality over the larger historical interests of the working class expressed in the will of the Party … This argument clearly resumes the paradox of the sacred space at work in traditional sacrificial logic: as soon as a man finds himself occupying the place of the sacred victim, his very being is stigmatised and *the more he proclaims his innocence, the more he is guilty – since guilt resides in his very resistance to the assumption of 'guilt'*, i.e., the symbolic mandate of the victim conferred on him by the community. What the victim has to do in order to be 'equal to his task' is therefore to assume the burden of guilt in full consciousness of his innocence: the more he is innocent, the greater is the weight of his sacrifice. (2007: 84–5; emphasis added)

References

Derrida, J. (1990 [1972]) 'Signature Event Context', in *Limited Inc.* Ed. G. Graff, trans. A. Bass. Evanston, IL: Northwestern University Press, 1–24.
Falcon, R. (1998) 'The discreet harm of the bourgeoisie', *Sight & Sound*, 8, 5, 10–12.
Žižek, S. (2006) *How to Read Lacan*. London: Granta.
____ (2007) 'Why is Every Act a *Repetition?*' in *Enjoy Your Symptom!: Jacques Lacan in Hollywood and Out*. London: Routledge, 69–112.

CHAPTER FIFTEEN

From Culture to Torture: Music and Violence in Funny Games and The Piano Teacher

Landon Palmer

While music has played an unquestionably vital role in cinema's development as an art form (even silent films, after all, were rarely exhibited without live music), the critical perspective within Michael Haneke's films presumes a conditioned, antici-pated and formulaic use of music within mainstream cinematic practice (to the point of invisibility to the spectator), a systematic employment of music that often directs – even manipulates – the audience's emotions and empathy. The striking, deliberate absence of music in most of Haneke's work reads, at first, as an exemption for the spectator from the traditional aural direction of the filmmaker. However, this 'exemp-tion' is hardly liberating, as the limitations and deconstructive utilities of Haneke's cinematic soundscape can be a discomfiting or jarringly disruptive experience for the spectator.

Haneke asserts repeatedly in interviews that he does not pass judgement on his characters, that he urges those who watch his films to make up their own minds regarding how they interpret what they see (see, for example, Toubiana 2006). His frequent use of the static camera and the long take may suggest, in tandem with this idea, a neo-Bazinian effort to allow the spectator to give their attention to whatever aspect of the frame they please, or a careful desire not to manipulate the spectator's emotions or force their focus of attention through frequent use of the cut.[1] However, Haneke's formal control, while often giving the impression of restraint, frequently stretches these practices to their limits to the point of giving attention to the style itself (for example, the seven-minute static shot in both versions of *Funny Games*, or the narrative segmentation and stylistic 'minimalism' of *Code inconnu: Récit incomplet de divers voyages* (*Code Unknown: Incomplete Tales of Several Journeys*, 2000)). The rare occasions that Haneke does use music in his films are concomitant to these other formal practices: often employed with selective restraint, but deliberately challenging and self-reflexive in intent. Haneke uses this style to comment on cinema itself, engaging in cinematographic 'exercises' that potentially result in the spectator's forced removal from their suspended disbelief. Haneke's methodical formal strategies and self-reflexive narrative deconstruction aim to transcend, or at least make the viewer aware of, the conditioned 'categories' in which such strategies typically manifest themselves within the diegesis of conventional narrative filmmaking.

In other words, Haneke's films aim to 'decondition' the spectator, utilising narrative and form in a way that potentially disrupts what the filmmaker perceives to be common and repeated formulaic tropes within mainstream cinema and their resulting comfort zone of expectation/delivery. The subversion of these expectations ideally creates a more active and self-aware spectator, one who becomes conscious of these conventions and, as a result, questions why such conventions are so passively consumed and enjoyed. Throughout his work, Haneke employs this practice with the intention of inspiring the viewer's awareness of their own passivity and pleasure in their consumption of filmic violence. Haneke's use of disturbing, shocking and often random incidents of onscreen violence is frequently a means to achieve his similarly violent rupturing of our common methodologies of film spectatorship.

One of the signature means with which Haneke executes this layered deconstructive exercise is in his selective use of music. His particular appropriation of music comments on the conventional codes of film music as well as criticises the role of music in culture at large. So when I discuss in this chapter the processes of 'categorisation', I am referring not only to the spectatorial conditioning by mainstream cinema's repeated implementation of a limited number of narrative and formal options (and the ways in which these options are executed that Haneke's work attempts to transcend), but also to the dominant modes of bourgeois cultural consumption Haneke criticises through his use of music (or, a criticism of the categorisation of filmic conventions in tandem with the categorisation of cultural artefacts). This chapter examines the role of music in two of Haneke's films, *Funny Games* and *La Pianiste* (*The Piano Teacher*, 2001), as well as the differing uses of music between the original *Funny Games* and his American remake, *Funny Games U.S.* (2007). I approach Haneke's use of classical music in these two films through the context of his continuing and expanding criticism of the bourgeoisie throughout his filmography, building off of Christopher Sharrett's argument that Haneke's films regularly illustrate the bourgeois appropriation of culture as superficial décor (2006: 8). His application of music and depictions of violence are particularly significant means with which Haneke further exercises a deconstruction of the conditioned norms and expectations of mainstream cinema.

Funny Games

The opening scene of *Funny Games* depicts a cultured, privileged family playing a game on a drive through the countryside to their holiday home. The husband and wife quiz each other on their knowledge of classical music, playing a chosen disc and requesting the name of the composer, composition and date. While this scene's initial use of music is clearly diegetic, the music's volume on the soundtrack remains the same as the camera cuts in and out of the family's car. What we hear, for example, in an overhead shot are not the sounds of the outdoors (cars, birds, wind), but the unbroken sound of classical music by composers Handel ('Cara Salva' from his opera *Atlanta* (1736)), Mascagni ('Tu Qui Santuzza' from his opera *Cavalleria Rusticana* (1890)) and Mozart ('Quintet for Clarinet, 2 Violins, Viola, Violoncello' (1789)), accompanied by the family's continued dialogue. While the classical music continually received in the exterior shots is technically non-diegetic, it still reads as emanating from an unbroken diegetic source. Conversely, the shadows of these exterior shots change during this sequence, signalling that such shots were filmed at different times of day. The changing of shadows at first reads as a simple passage of time, but this initial interpretation of the scene is contradicted by the fact that these shots are accompanied with dialogue and music that suggests continuity rather than ellipsis, attended by the shadows' impossible elongation and reduction. These simple breaks in audiovisual continuity, while not immediately obvious, work as a precursor for the more direct and deliberate breakdown of the relationship between spectator and screen to take place later on in the film.

As the music abruptly transitions non-diegetically to avant-jazz musician John Zorn's chaotic, hardcore sound from his group Naked City over the film's opening credit sequence ('Bonehead', from their appropriately named 1989 album *Torture Garden*), Haneke introduces the practice of disruption that will occupy the narrative of *Funny Games*; that is, as *Funny Games* directly acknowledges the spectator via the insti-gating 'antagonists' of the characters of Paul (Arno Frisch) and Peter (Frank Giering), Haneke aims to disrupt the traditional nature of the spectatorial experience, forcing the viewer out of a state of suspended disbelief. Haneke achieves this by breaking the 'fourth wall' through Paul's direct address to the camera. This character, at different points in the narrative, asks the spectator if they have had enough violence, informs them that the story has yet to end because the film has not reached a satisfactory running time, and even disrupts the linear trajectory of the film itself as he rewinds the events with a remote control to prevent the death of Peter. Haneke's intent with this exercise, which he continued to make clear with the release of the American remake, is to force the spectator to acknowledge the pleasure, or at least the passivity, with which they receive violence depicted onscreen (see Toubiana 2006). Haneke extends this criticism of the passivity of the conditioned spectator to a comparable passivity with which the bourgeois class consumes other forms of culture, specifically classical music.

As Haneke introduces his disruptive exercise in the soundscape of the opening credit sequence, his use of music, and the social criticism within its use, is insepa-rable from his overall formal deconstruction. When Anna (Susanne Lothar) and Georg (Ulrich Mühe) engage in trivia over the content of classical music, they remove such music from its social and historical context. Transitioning between the music of Handel, Mascagni and Mozart, the couple liberally dances across a historically non-linear soundscape of compositions from differing centuries (eighteenth and nineteenth), countries (England, Italy, Germany) and musical movements (Handel's baroque operas, Mascagni's *verismo*, Mozart's classicalism). They also interrupt the music, switching between discs once a composer has been recognised before the song's end, thus further fragmenting these compositions. By trivialising and fragmenting classical music, the couple renders music an object of highbrow mass consumption rather than a revered work of art within an inseparable aesthetic and socio-cultural context. This opening sequence operates as an example of what Christopher Sharrett argues is a criticism of bourgeois values that continues throughout Haneke's work: a criticism of high culture's role in bourgeois society as a 'healthy antidote to a degraded culture industry' (2006: 8). Sharrett contends that Haneke's films display the 'limits of culture', or 'its role in simultaneously offering awareness [of the high arts] while enforcing bourgeois notions of human interaction' (ibid.). The categorisation of such vapid details by Anna and Georg, without truly attempting to understand the meaning or intent of the music, readies the work of art for this type of consumption. Haneke poises classical music and other manifestations of culture as a backdrop for privileged social interaction, utilised to prevent awkward silences during dinner parties or as a distraction that makes a lengthy road trip more enjoyable, rather than an aesthetic experience on its own. Sharett argues further that classical music's tendency to 'seldom be seen as adversarial in nature, or in any sense threatening to state and private power' (ibid.) enables such consumption through the removal of context, social or otherwise. Music used in this way is certainly heard, but hardly listened to.

Furthermore, that the music plays on portable compact discs rather than in a symphony concert hall removes the music from its intended mode of reception and location of power and instead assigns control to the consumer. That two of these excerpts are from operas suggests a further removal from the music's intended medium, rupturing the music's relationship to a meticulously performed narrative. The music no longer belongs to the baton of the conductor, but the dials and devices available to the consumer, which enable Anna and Georg to move between compositions and musical eras at their will. The mechanically (or, in this case, electronically) reproduced work of art in the form of the compact disc enables such a uniquely personal mode of consumption and the resulting schism from its original context.

But the confrontational, experimental qualities of Naked City's hardcore, kinetic collage of contemporary musical genres defies the categorisation that Anna and Georg so readily implement on classical composers. Because Zorn's music is highly improvisational, it cannot be learned, performed, recreated or conveniently historicised in the same way a composition by Mozart can. Zorn's music is also deliberately 'anti-musical': it features an array of guitar, saxophone and indiscernible screams that hardly correspond into a collective sound, much less come together in a harmony or rhythm. It is music that must unavoidably be listened to if played, music that cannot simply fade into the background, and music that would likely never be an appropriate backdrop for conventional social interaction. That the music is used non-diegetically, which

Funny Games (1997): Paul displays narrative agency through the electronic reproduction of John Zorn

creates an absurd audiovisual juxtaposition as it allows the family to interact on their drive as if they were continuously listening to classical compositions, illuminates how Zorn's music cannot believably be juxtaposed with such passive social interaction. And as such music would be disruptive of this type of social interaction, Haneke utilises Zorn's music in this case to similarly disrupt the experience of the spectator.

But Zorn's music also identifies the controlling agent of the film's narrative, Paul. Later in the film, as Paul chases Anna and Georg's son Georgie (Stefan Clapczynski) through the neighbours' house, he puts a CD in a nearby stereo and plays another song from the same Naked City album ('Hellraiser'). This action allows the scene to play out as if the use of music were once again non-diegetic (when it is clearly diegetic), acting as a hard-rock soundtrack to accompany the cat-and-mouse chase between Paul and Georgie. Though the selected piece is unconventional, Haneke juxtaposes the music with a sequence of action in a way similar to the type of sound-track that would accompany a mainstream action film – the type of film that typically uses violence within the established functions Haneke is attempting to deconstruct. Furthermore, Paul's control of the deceivingly diegetic music of this scene signifies his control of the film's narrative in general: his instigation of the family's torture, his solitary agency in being able to address the spectator, and his literal movement of narrative events backward and forward in time. That the film ends with Paul looking at the camera in preparation of torturing yet another family accompanied by the same Naked City track that occupied the opening credits not only renders the music a device to bookend the circular narrative, but signifies the earlier use of the track as an allusion to the unique controlling agency of Paul existing from the very beginning, thereby connecting the violent, confrontational noise of Zorn's music to the violent, confrontational acts of Paul. Zorn's music is also self-reflexive, consciously subverting the expectations and perceived parameters of the medium, just as Paul's instigations of torture are enacted in a way that disrupt the spectatorial experience. Haneke appropriates a disruptive, deviant work of music and implements it here to serve a specific thematic function, and, through the filmmaker's patterning of sonic chaos, Zorn's otherwise subversive music is thus categorised through its deployment as a repeated narrative motif for Paul.

Brian Price argues that violence as depicted in art is decidedly categorised (see 2006: 22). While violence can be portrayed within a narrative as random and without motivation, because of the process and preparation necessary to practise narrative fiction filmmaking, filmic violence is by nature constructed, premeditated and organised. As such, there have arisen conditioned and repeated shortcuts for representing pain on film, from the juxtaposition of shots to the expression of the performer. Price uses the scene early on in *Funny Games* where Paul hits Georg in the leg with a golf club as an instance that utilises several methodologies to signify pain and even motivate empathy, but this scene also illustrates Price's argument that sensorial reactions to mere representations of pain are far from equivalent to the full physical experience (see 2006: 24).[2] But, as Price argues, unlike in conventional depictions of violence, the spectator of *Funny Games* is never granted 'consolation' or relief from such violence through triumph over the antagonists (see 2006: 23). And when removed from such convention, the violence of *Funny Games* becomes disturbing, even infuriating, as Haneke denies the spectator the expected categories of 'justice' typically demonstrated in violent American cinema. Of course, in the 'rewind scene', Haneke intends to tease the audience with relief until Paul once again intervenes.

Haneke exhibits Paul's narrative agency to its fullest extent in the rewind scene, where he saves the life of Peter, whom Anna has shot dead, by rewinding the very film we have been watching. Haneke intended this to be a critical moment where the spectator confronts their enjoyment of witnessing a violent act onscreen, essentially 'applauding an act of murder' (in Toubiana 2006). Haneke's moralistic stance against spectatorial passivity is exercised through Paul, yet the extensive narrative agency of Paul potentially removes the responsibility of authorship from the author. By placing the source of this violence within the persona of Paul, Haneke is able to criticise the spectator for enjoying such violence without having to confront his own complicity in this process as its creative source. Haneke, then, sees his role as filmmaker in the rewind scene as responsible for the condemnation of Peter's murder, but not its initial applause, as if he were, being the entire film's director, somehow the designer of only the latter half of this sequence. Thus, Zorn's music operates less as a signifier of Haneke's creative decision-making and active employment of foreshadowing and motif, and more as a representation of Paul's extensive control of the narrative. As *Funny Games* is most effective as a self-reflexive, extra-diegetic exercise, the force and influence of 'Paul' likewise permeates outside the diegesis.

Haneke's practice of often giving his music a diegetic source in *Funny Games* (usually an electronic source, rather than the physical source of the instrument in *The Piano Teacher*) calls attention to the prevalent uses of music in film to direct, if not manipulate, the viewer's emotional empathy. Traditional orchestral film scores often signal to the spectator the proper times to show certain types of emotion, or sympathise with certain characters while differentiating protagonists from antagonists. But established classical compositions have routinely been appropriated to serve similar thematic aims, and such appropriation can connote a powerful new iconography for these compositions. For example, Richard Strauss's *Also sprach Zarathustra* (1896) is, for some, inseparable from the iconography of Stanley Kubrick's *2001: A Space Odyssey* (1968). But Haneke allows his protagonists to discuss the music and gives them the power to stop and start it at will. In positing music as an ornament for the bourgeoisie rather than its traditional filmic implementation as a thematic cue, leitmotif or an

invisible incitement of an emotional reaction, Haneke does not give these compositions a new context, but removes context as original meaning is lost in the music
through its initial fragmentation and trivialisation. Haneke's thesis in *Funny Games* is
that bourgeois culture has rendered music meaningless. If classical music is used as a
backdrop, or filler, for social occasions, then it is not given enough attention to foreground an inspired discussion of its meaning, as the only context necessary for Georg
and Anna is trivia. In *Funny Games U.S.*, Haneke also criticises another type of music
commonly used for social interaction: pop music.

If there is an even more contrived and coded use of music in mainstream cinematic practice than the orchestral score, it is the use of pop music, for pop music often
articulates emotion bluntly where orchestral scores merely direct it. Within culture at
large, pop is, of course, music manufactured to be received through the controlling
possibilities of electronic reproduction; it is music intended to be consumed via the
car radio, compact disc or iPod, while the receiver of the music can be doing anything
other than simply sitting attentively and listening. With the established verse-cho-
rus-verse pattern of a given song's progression, most pop songs are not only readily
consumable and unchallenging to the listener, but their respective meanings can often
be easily deciphered through song lyrics, allowing them to be plainly interpreted even
as the listener is simultaneously engaging in other activities.[3]

Early on in *Funny Games U.S.*, Ann (Naomi Watts) listens to a generic soft rock
song, 'All to Myself' by Sophie Delila, on a kitchen radio for several minutes until
shutting it off before the song ends. This scene affirms the tune-in, tune-out agency
that pop music as an electronic commodity provides for the listener, but because Ann
sneaks in a cigarette break without George (Tim Roth) noticing in the kitchen before
she prepares a meal, the song also serves a thematic (albeit critical) purpose through
presenting Ann as the familiar cinematic figure of a woman trapped in a domestic
prison. The cigarette in the Austrian version reads as casual and meaningless, especially without the music, but with a decade of successful anti-smoking lobbying in the
United States and Europe between each version of *Funny Games*, the brief cigarette
break by a cultured, middle-class American woman appears dishonest and closeted,
only to be taken advantage of when her husband and child are not around, or as a brief
release from her banal and stifling domestic duties. The intrusion of Paul (Michael
Pitt) and Peter (Brady Corbet), however, prevents any further character development.
Nonetheless, this use of pop music, though brief, does successfully add meaning to
Ann's character as the scene abides by the repeated codes and conventions with which
pop music is so often used in film, while the classical music that opens the film serves
no such purpose.

In Haneke's vision of bourgeois family life, both pop and classical music are used
to accompany social interaction. Musicologist Erkki Pekkilä illustrates this process:

> musical works and styles can now 'travel' from one country to another –
> or even appear everywhere at once. The status of music as a commodity
> has been enhanced and diversified by modes of distribution made possible
> by computers and the Internet. In the universe of new media, differences

between 'highbrow' and 'light' music have almost entirely disappeared, levelled by marketing processes that make no distinction between popular art and music. (2006: vii)

The age of electronic reproduction has allowed for these seemingly contradictory tastes to coexist in modern culture, signified in both versions of *Funny Games* through Ann(a) and Georg(e)'s employment of electronic technology to consume each type of music. Although classical and pop music are posited to serve the same social function (as background décor) in Haneke's interpretation of bourgeois society, pop music, by design, contains meaning, however trite, that is readily interpretable for the contemporary privileged citizen, while classical music is rendered meaningless through its trivialisation and consumer agency via the utilities of electronic reproduction. Thus, Haneke posits that meaning in the era of pop music can only be derived through words rather than the language of music itself.[4]

Just as Haneke's exercise attempts to deconstruct and make the spectator aware of categorised representations of violence and narrative expectations, his social criticism puts those processes of categorising art on display, not only by articulating how classical music is appropriated as a bourgeois decoration, but also by illuminating how different types of music are categorised through their conditioned and repeated utilities in conventional narrative filmmaking.

The Piano Teacher

Haneke continues his critical exercise in *The Piano Teacher*, where classical music and acts of violence also act as co-determinants. While the film, with its self-contained narrative, is not as deliberately self-reflexive as *Funny Games*, similar criticisms on the categorisation of art in culture, conditioned narrative expectations and coded representations of violence are taking place. In fact, one particular sequence of *The Piano Teacher* sees Sharrett's theories of bourgeois adornment of classical music manifested literally. Erika (Isabelle Huppert), the eponymous character, performs music for a private gathering at a luxurious Vienna apartment early on in the film, and the host of the gathering exhibits to Erika's mother his collection of antique musical instruments that decorate his walls, a moment that clearly signifies artefacts of culture as bourgeois décor. What later becomes evident in this film, however, is that Erika's cultured and socially determined musical career stands in stark contrast to several instances of violence and themes of sexuality that become contradictory and counterproductive to the expectations of a classical musician in a rigidly structured bourgeois society.

Haneke opens *The Piano Teacher* by illustrating that, while this may be a movie about music, the spectator should not expect any traditional cinematic implementations of music. The opening credits display Haneke's tendency to restrict music to a purely diegetic use as Erika is shown tutoring several students on the piano. The students' music is interrupted as the film cuts to each title card, eliminating what would otherwise be the utility of the music to accompany an opening credit sequence. However, Haneke abandons his strictly diegetic use of music for one significant sequence where

The violin as an ornament of high culture rather than an instrument of music in *The Piano Teacher* (2001)

Erika is shown rehearsing Franz Schubert's 'Piano Trio in E Flat' (1827) accompanied by several string musicians. The soundtrack of Erika and her accompaniment performing continues as the film cuts to Erika roaming through a pornographic video store, transposing the music to the arena of non-diegesis. The music abruptly stops when she walks into a private viewing booth just as a customer has left. She selects a scene to watch, picks up a tissue from the floor and smells the semen on it. The simulated sexual sounds from the pornographic film are strikingly rhythmic, and these sounds dissolve into the comparatively rhythmic opening chords of 'Im Dorfe', part of Schubert's *Winterreise* (1827), as the film cuts to one of Erika's lessons in the next scene. It is worth noting that Erika's understanding of music, and the way she teaches music, has thus far been presented as strictly objective. She believes in an indisputable right and wrong way to interpret music, not just in hitting the correct notes at the exact rhythm, but employing the proper movement of the body along the way. Classical music then, in order to be acceptably interpreted and performed, must be categorically understood and articulated in performance. Erika's sexual needs, by contrast, cannot be so easily comprehended. Instead, they read as instinctual, irrational and of ambiguous motivation. Huppert's performance gives Erika the same stern, expressionless look when she teaches a student as when she smells semen, which suggests that she treats her career and her sexual repression with the same cold calculation. But her hostility and defensiveness when faced with the real possibility of sex from her student, Walter (Benoît Magimel), suggest a lack of control and understanding regarding sex that finds no analogy in her interpretation of music.[5] This tension provides the film's instigating dichotomy, illustrated through the porn shop sequence's non-diegetic juxtaposition of her music to her unattained pursuit of sexual fulfilment: the social expectations and norms of cultured life Erika must adhere to in her role as a classical musician stand in distinct contradiction to her desire to pursue unorthodox sexual behaviour.

By contrasting the luxurious Vienna apartment Erika performs in to her own apartment, which she shares with her mother, it becomes apparent that Erika performs a social role for the bourgeois class, but is not herself part of that class. The extent of Erika's role within this culture is severely limited and without social mobility, emboldening her existing frustration of working primarily as a teacher rather than a successful performer in her own right. *The Piano Teacher* can then be read as an examination of the repercussions of the strict social norms and expectations implemented by the bourgeoisie upon the producers of culture.

Unlike her vapid bourgeois cohort in this film and the analogous group in *Funny Games*, Erika has a deep and personally meaningful understanding of classical music. When she tells Walter her favourite composers are Schubert and Robert Schumann, Erika compares Schumann's desperate awareness of going mad in his late career to her witnessing her father going through mental illness until his death, citing this as a bond she feels with the composer. While Erika does not articulate such a personal relationship to Schubert, that Schubert's career was underappreciated during his lifetime perhaps provides a more accurate analogy to Erika's own life and career than that of Schumann (and it is Schubert's compositions that Erika performs most often in the film). However, neither Erika nor any other character in the film bothers to articulate Schubert's history. Walter, at one point, addresses the late 'madness' of both Schumann and Schubert, and while both composers did supposedly die of syphilis, by several accounts it is arguable that Schubert was never rendered 'mad' by his sickness (see McKay 1996: 291–3, 319; Gibbs 2000: 93–4, 159–60). This notional analogy, which could have given further explication to the psychology of Erika, is made elusive by the lack of explicit reference. As a result, any meaningful thematic connection between Schubert and Erika can only be inferred by the active and informed spectator. If there does indeed exist such an intentional, direct thematic link between Schubert and Erika, it is one not deliberately articulated by the discourse of the narrative.[6]

It is Erika's apparent lack of a realised connection between Schubert's personal and social crises with her own that articulates the film's attitude towards classical music in contemporary society. That Erika approaches music with cold calculation in mastering a methodical, mathematic interpretation of Schubert signals not only her avoidance, deliberate or not, of defining herself in the potentially destructive personal context of a tortured musician, but also, in terms of a basic historical and cultural understanding, signals the similarly disconnected role of such music within the social interaction of the bourgeoisie at large. While Erika is certainly aware of the history of her favourite composers, her wilful avoidance to define herself in connection with Schubert is inevitable not only because it would be admitting the devastating reality of her own underappreciated career and unfulfilled personal life, but because she is forced, as a piano teacher, to assume the role that high society has placed upon classical music: that of a backdrop for social interaction and staged human connection while having no practical or meaningful significance in contemporary culture (see Sharrett 2006: 8). Thus, even for the informed musician in a culture of uninformed consumers, classical music has a limited role in terms of meaning.

Inherent to Erika's sexual frustration is the violent nature of her sexual desires. Walter reacts in disbelief when Erika confides to him her long-standing secret desire to be struck and beaten consensually as well as engage in other types of aberrant sexual behaviour. Walter's statement, 'Maybe you'd open your cultured mouth and comment on this shit', illustrates the contradiction between Erika's social behaviour (that is, career) and her sexual needs. Haneke tends to favour ambiguity over distinct psychological motivation, so while the filmmaker provides the spectator with several possible explanations for Erika's behaviour – the dead father with a history of mental illness, the overprotective mother, the restrictively mannered society she occupies – these are never posited as direct motivations for any of her actions (see Toubiana 2006). This ambiguity is extended to the film's depiction of violence.

Two instances of self-inflicted violence occur in *The Piano Teacher* that, like the portrayal of violence in *Funny Games*, defy the formally coded norms of representing violence and deconstruct the categories of comprehensibly motivated character action. With regards to the genital self-mutilation that occurs early in the film, the casual nature of the incident, the breadth of its framing, and its seemingly random place within the succession of narrative events (that is, nothing occurs before or after this scene that attempts to directly explicate it) render no simple shortcut for spectatorial understanding of any potential motivation for such a random act of violence. Likewise, the film's final moment, in which Erika stabs herself in the shoulder with a kitchen knife before abandoning her performance, certainly contains a multitude of plausible motivations considering what has occurred previously, but the action itself reads more like an extension of her genital mutilation rather than an ultimate manifestation of her inner pain or an act of closure (it is clearly not an attempt at suicide). The formal restraint and lack of overt psychological justification with which Haneke handles these moments of violence allow his films to disrupt conventional representations of violence exercised through expected patterns of cutting and performance that Price cites as common practice within mainstream cinema. Just as Paul and Peter never explicate the motivation for their instigation of torture,[7] the confounding nature of Erika's behaviour potentially makes the spectator aware of the conventions with which such subjects are often approached in cinema by placing ambiguity where a clichéd and reductive explanatory shortcut would otherwise be. Erika's sexual repression develops from the strictly categorised and socially conditioned regulations by which she is expected to act as a social ornament. As Haneke develops and revisits these criticisms that arguably connect all his films, we can read *Funny Games*, through the bourgeois family's acts of cultural consumption, as displaying the processes through which such categorisation of culture takes place. A reading of these films together reveals the practices of fragmenting and decontextualising cultural artefacts, which can result in the subjugation of the informed and educated interpreters of these artefacts. Haneke's employment of violence in these two films acts as a destabilising agent used to threaten the structure and interrogate the grounds of such social systems – an impenetrable, unintelligible, inevitable phantom force invading the intricately configured categories of bourgeois social ritual. And as Erika, Paul and Peter exist as destabilising forces within the categorised structures of the respective cultural landscapes and narratives they occupy (as represented through their particular relationships with music), their acts of violence similarly destabilise the conventional spectatorial experience.

Notes

1   This is not to suggest that any of Haneke's aims with his use of these formal properties run parallel to André Bazin's theories of realism. Where Bazin advocates the long take, deep focus and sparse editing as the means for a pure cinematic experience, Haneke uses these same tools to create an external, objective schism between

the viewer and the film, thus rejecting Bazin's desired harmony between spectator and screen. I cite Bazin simply to illustrate Haneke's clear favour of the long take and sparse editing.

2   This categorisation of and conditioning to representations of pain could be a cause for the American spectator's alleged desensitisation to depictions of violence onscreen, for these visual shorthands for referencing violence become so repetitive that the capacity of their representation to mimic a full physical sensation continues to atrophy.

3   Admittedly, meaning in such music can also be deciphered simply through the language of music itself, and pop lyrics can sometimes render meaning more elusive than apparent (for example, those of Bob Dylan). But this postulation of pop music as a homogenous medium with uniform practices of meaning dissemination seems particularly appropriate to Haneke's criticism of it, as he outspokenly despises popular music, and is thus inferentially not familiar enough with its varied forms to have a thorough and unproblematic criticism of it.

4   The prevalence of pop music in social/family life was also explored in one of Haneke's earlier films, *Der siebente Kontinent* (*The Seventh Continent*, 1989), which features a scene of a family having dinner while pop plays loudly on the radio, but the music noticeably shifts from the background to the foreground when the conversation suddenly goes uncomfortably silent. In this instance, pop music not only accompanies social interaction, but replaces it.

5   While the rhythmic sexual noises of the pornographic video suggest a connection between her sexual needs to the rhythm of Schubert's music (as this noise smoothly dissolves into 'Im Dorfe'), the simulated sex of pornography is understandably staged, controlled, executed and thus categorised in a way that Erika's sexual fantasies are not.

6   It is worth noting that Sharrett draws a more direct thematic link between Schubert's lonely history and Erika's alienation, even arguing, 'Schubert provides her with a buffer against the world' (2006: 9), whereas my argument maintains that, while Erika is certainly better informed than most of the musicians and music aficionados that occupy her landscape (and an undisputable expert on the composer), she is still too indifferent (wilfully or not) to think of herself as 'like Schubert', which prevents the casual spectator from making such a thematic connection as well. While the connection between Erika and Schubert can be interpreted through what is not directly articulated in Huppert's complex performance (and there is plenty brooding below the surface in each of her rigid facial expressions), any connection between Erika's struggles and the history of Schubert's life can only be made through inference by the spectator familiar with the composer outside the diegesis of the film.

7   In fact, Paul and Peter do just the opposite, spouting off a list of possible character motivations (drugs, closeted homosexuality, childhood abuse) that they ultimately deride, revealing motivation itself as another devious 'game'. This can be read as a criticism for the contrived shortcuts with which conventional cinema attempts to psychologically motivate (even justify) the violent behaviour of certain characters.

However, acts of violence in Haneke's films are always random and ambiguous, leaving the impression that much of the violence in reality exists beyond 'rational' explanation or simple understanding.

References

Gibbs, C. H. (2000) *The Life of Schubert*. Cambridge: Cambridge University Press.
McKay, E. N. (1996) *Franz Schubert: A Biography*. New York: Oxford University Press.
Pekkilä, E. (2006) 'Introduction', in E. Pekkilä, D. Neumeyer and R. Littlefield (eds) *Music, Meaning and Media*. Hakapaino, Helsinki: The International Semiotics Institute, vii–x.
Price, B. (2006) 'Pain and the Limits of Representation', *Framework*, 47, 2, 22–4.
Sharrett, C. (2006) 'Michael Haneke and the Discontents of European Culture', *Framework*, 47, 2, 8–15.
Toubiana, S. (2006) 'Interview with Michael Haneke', *Funny Games*, Kino Video.

The Piano Teacher

CHAPTER SIXTEEN

Images of Confinement and Transcendence: Michael Haneke's Reception of Romanticism in The Piano Teacher

Felix W. Tweraser

Michael Haneke's *La Pianiste* (*The Piano Teacher*), widely acclaimed following its screening at the Cannes Film Festival in 2001 and the most financially successful Haneke film to date on the international market, is a disciplined examination of structures of domination and control in the family and in the institutions of high musical culture in Vienna. In almost every frame the film conveys a sense of confinement, both within the unit of the family and in the rigorous training necessary to become an accomplished concert musician. The visual vocabulary that Haneke employs in *The Piano Teacher* powerfully suggests such confinement within the rigidly hierarchical institutions of contemporary Austrian society, through the *mise-en-scène*, with its emphasis on doors, gates, bars and enclosed spaces such as elevators and closets, to the camerawork, which, with a couple of important exceptions noted below, eschews long establishing shots in favour of medium shots and close-ups to reinforce the idea that the world of the film is like a prison. Scenes located in private spaces – domestic and institutional bathrooms, a bedroom, a booth to view pornographic images, a closet in a locker room – show any sense of actual privacy to be illusory, something Haneke emphasises in the sonic bridges and quick cuts between scenes in public and private places.

In the following, after a capsule summary of the plot and a brief survey of the growing secondary literature on *The Piano Teacher*, I argue that Haneke's disciplined, unforgiving and discomfiting aesthetic works not just as an indictment of advanced

Western capitalism, a subtle commentary on the legacy of authoritarianism and Nazism in Austria or an analysis of the commodification of culture, but also as a notable reinterpretation of the horror and melodrama genres.

Based on the novel *Die Klavierspielerin* (1983), by Nobel laureate Elfriede Jelinek, *The Piano Teacher* recounts an episode in the life of Erika Kohut (Isabelle Huppert), professor of music and pianist on staff at the prestigious Vienna Conservatory. Erika's area of scholarly expertise is Romanticism – her favourite composers are Franz Schubert and Robert Schumann – and she is well-versed in the theoretical reception of the Romantic canon, particularly Theodor Adorno's. A demanding, often cruel, teacher, Erika lives at home with her mother (Annie Girardot), with whom she has a relationship that swings abruptly between abjection and violence. Into this mix comes an engineering student, Walter Klemmer (Benoît Magimel), whose musical talents pique Erika's interest after she listens to him play Schubert at a private salon concert. Walter enrols at the conservatory, over Erika's official objections – his age and other studies preclude a musical career – and becomes her pupil. Initially cool to his romantic overtures, Erika succumbs to his advances right after she has carried out an assault on Anna Schober (Anna Sigalevitch), her most outstanding pupil, and with whom Erika is often seen in the film studying the accompanying part to Schubert's *Lieder*-cycle, *Winterreise* (1827). Hinted at in earlier scenes of voyeurism and self-mutilation, Erika demands that Walter obey sadomasochistic conditions set forth in a letter to him outlining the terms of their relationship. Walter is not open to such demands and, in turn, rejects Erika emotionally, beating and raping her in the film's most harrowing scene. In the final sequence of the film, Erika, about to perform as Anna's stand-in, instead stabs herself in the shoulder and exits the frame, offering a rather enigmatic conclusion. While Jelinek's novel satirises its characters and setting to such a degree that the reader is afforded the comfort of standing outside of its world, Haneke's compositional techniques do not allow the viewer such comfort, and constitute, taken together, a distinctly uncomfortable viewing experience that demands the viewer's reflection on his/her own complicity in its state of affairs.

The Piano Teacher has attracted serious scholarly interest since its release, with interpreters reading the material from a variety of theoretical approaches. Robin Wood's influential analysis connects the themes of violence and domination and the liberating function of the music to a broader indictment of Western culture, 'the very structures of capitalist culture, pervading and corrupting all relationships within it, from the family to the workplace, from parents/children to employers/employees, and then outwards to global politics' (2002: 55). Picking up on Wood's argument and examining the film's relation to genre, Catherine Wheatley places the film in the tradition of the melodrama, finding that Haneke clearly implicates the spectator in his indictment of Western culture: '*The Piano Teacher* functions in many ways as both an updating of the melodramatic genre for the disaffected society of the twenty-first century, and as a deconstruction of the implicit premises and positioning of the spectator' (2006c: 125). Christopher Sharrett explores Haneke's engagement with the generic codes of the horror film, but, like Wood, sees more global elements at work, arguing that the film exists within 'a line of U.S. and European cinema locating mental breakdown and social disorder precisely at the heart of Western bourgeois patriarchal civilisation' (2004a). Jean Wyatt's reading of the film is informed by Lacanian theory; she focuses on the primary mother/daughter relationship, finding Erika's efforts to follow feminine desire overwhelmed by maternal *jouissance*, a battle played out in the Walter/Erika relationship: 'the viewer gets caught up in the oscillation between desire and anxiety provoked by *jouissance* – an oscillation that mimes the tug-of-war in the diegesis between Walter (representative of desire) and Erika (site of *jouissance*)' (2006: 467). Jean Ma places *The Piano Teacher* in the context of the classical romance narrative, particularly its attempt to redeem a damaged social order: 'If the global history of the romance narrative encodes a utopic desire to heal a ruptured social order in the flights and fortunes of individual desire – as evidenced in the genre's marked investment in stories of crossing and passing, across racial, ethnic, national, religious, and class divisions – then *The Piano Teacher* confronts desire with exactly that which it seeks to escape' (2007: 7). Haneke's own remarks about the film, while acknowledging the legitimacy of such critical approaches, include acute observations about the role mass media, notably television in the case of *The Piano Teacher*, play in promoting a culture of consumption and anaesthetising the effects of violence in mass society. Haneke argues:

> I am most concerned with television as the key symbol primarily of the media representation of violence, and more generally of a greater crisis, which I see as our collective loss of reality and social disorientation. Alienation is a very complex problem, but television is certainly implicated in it. We don't, of course, anymore perceive reality, but instead the representation of reality in television. Our experiential horizon is very limited. What we know of the world is little more than the mediated world, the image. We have no reality, but a derivative of reality, which is extremely dangerous, most certainly from a political standpoint but in a larger sense to our ability to have a palpable sense of the truth of everyday experience. (In Sharrett 2004b)

By concentrating on the form of visual transmission and its distance from actual experience, Haneke approximates the disjunctive aesthetic of high modernism, a distinction aptly drawn by Ma: 'what distinguishes Haneke's films and positions them decisively within a strategy of modernist reflexivity, as opposed to postmodern hybridity, is their investigation of the ways in which the effects of violence are inseparable from its forms of circulation and representation' (2007: 10). My reading, while informed by this earlier work, emphasises the formal construction of the visual material in selected scenes, with an emphasis on how Haneke composes the shot and allows it to work in dialogue with the soundtrack. What emerges is a visual and musical vocabulary able to suggest what lies beyond what is seen and heard, and this becomes an important point of identification for the viewer with the film's protagonist.

The composition of several early shots establishes viewer identification with Erika's point of view, while underscoring her often lonely and confined position in mass society. One particularly compelling image from the opening credit montage shows Erika in her office, back turned to the camera and almost entirely in shadow,

Woman at the window: Erika in her office in *The Piano Teacher* (2001)

looking out onto a midday street scene in Vienna. The shot's interior is configured in a horizontal plane that spans a drawing of Robert Schumann, her piano and an unidentified, framed musical score, and which is crossed by a vertical plane of the open window framing Erika's silhouette. The composition itself echoes the familiar contemplative setting of the artist in the paintings of Caspar David Friedrich, in which the lone human figure, back to the viewer, meditates upon a grandly scaled natural scene, but which often simultaneously suggests the limitations of vision and the qualitative differences between perception and experience. Haneke's quotation of Caspar David Friedrich's *Woman at the Window* (*Frau am Fenster*, 1822) seems clear, and links philosophically to the area of Erika's professional expertise: Romanticism. Haneke emphasises the painterly nature of this shot by allowing it to sit in the viewer's visual field a few beats longer than might usually be the case in a more conventional approach, so the viewer has time to contemplate and reflect upon the composition. In Friedrich's interior we are likely in a domestic space, but as is the case with many of his compositions, he draws the viewer to the space beyond the interior/foreground, inviting identification with the contemplative position of the viewing figure within the frame and drawing the viewer's eye to an infinite beyond. A strong vertical orientation in the window frame emphasises the duality of confinement and transcendence, and the viewer shares the painted figure's orientation beyond the boundaries of convention. Haneke's shot also captures the vertical orientation in the window frame, and the viewer is similarly drawn to identify with Erika's view beyond the confines of her office. (This vertical orientation dovetails nicely with many of the other shots in the opening credit sequence, in which hands playing a piano are filmed from above, emphasising through their verticality the confining aspects of the keys.) Yet the scene's suggestion of Romantic transcendence works in ironic juxtaposition with the soundtrack, which consists of ambient traffic noise coming in through the open window, and which contrasts sonically with the montage's clips of Erika tutoring pupils of varying abilities.

Caspar David Friedrich, *Woman at the Window* (1822)
©Nationalgalerie, Staatliche Museen Preußischer
Kulturbesitz

The whole opening credit sequence – introduced by a tight shot of the door to Erika's apartment and concluding with the director's credit following Erika closing her office door, again with the camera focusing tightly on the door itself – acquaints the viewer *in nuce* with the issues at work in the film: the fraught and often violent relationship between mother and daughter, the monotony, terror and control attendant to the musical training at the conservatory and the brief moments of potential transcendence that accompany an otherwise normalised routine. We are introduced as well to the film's key musical passage, the seventeenth song in Schubert's *Winterreise*, 'Im Dorfe', a prototypical Romantic gloss on alienation from middle-class society, heard here in rehearsal performed by Erika's star pupil, Anna Schober. (Anna and her unsympathetic mother form in some ways a mirror image of Erika and hers; Anna's precocious musical talent is destroyed by her mother's mental abuse as well as by Erika's physical assault – Erika had placed shards of glass in Anna's coat during a rehearsal in which Anna has overcome her jitters, thanks in part to attention Walter pays to her, and she performs the piano accompaniment to *Winterreise* with uncommon feeling.) Haneke emphasises the central role played by this song from the cycle:

Of course, the 17th song holds a central place in the film, and could be viewed as the motto of Erika and the film itself. The whole cycle establishes the idea of following a path not taken by others, which gives an ironic effect to the film, I think. It is difficult to say if there is a correlation between the neurosis of Erika Kohut and what could be called the psychogram of a great composer like Schubert. But of course there is a great sense of mourning in Schubert that is very much part of the milieu of the film. Someone with the tremendous problems borne by Erika may well project them onto an artist of Schubert's very complex sensibility. (In Sharrett 2004b)

The music itself provides moments pointing to transcendence from a stultifying world, but at the same time is implicated in the systems of confinement, domination and control that characterise musical education. To Haneke, the proximity of violence and beautiful music and the multivalent nature of musical meaning are characteristically Viennese:

> We are seeing a very Austrian situation. Vienna is the capital of classical music and is, therefore, the centre of something very extraordinary. The music is very beautiful, but like the surroundings can become an instrument of repression, because this culture takes on a social function that ensures repression, especially as classical music becomes an object for consumption. Of course, you must recognise that these issues are not just subjects of the film's screenplay, but are concerns of the Elfriede Jelinek novel, wherein the female has a chance, a small one, to emancipate herself only as an artist. This doesn't work out, of course, since her artistry turns against her in a sense. (In Sharrett 2004b)

The juxtaposition of beauty in the music and abject misery in Erika's personal and professional lives colours the scenic architecture of the film. It also amounts to an oblique reference to Austria's Nazi past, in which visual art and music were put in the service of a genocidal regime. The Nazi aesthetic and authoritarianism permeated all aspects of life and influenced interpersonal attitudes; in a time when public lip-service is paid to coming to terms with this past, the underlying attitudes still express themselves within the family and in interpersonal relations in general.

The film's central character, Erika Kohut, is born into such a family, the age of her mother making it likely that the elder Kohut was socialised during the Nazi era. Erika, in turn, is both dominated (by her mother and, per her own request, by her lover Walter) and dominating (to her students), the particular pathology evident in the scenes with her mother and her students, and it shadows the moments when Erika might transcend familial and professional constraints – interestingly, moments underscored by Haneke's spare employment of long shots from Erika's point of view. Such moments are subtly emphasised by Haneke's composition, for instance, the scene in which Erika, showing interest in Walter, clandestinely follows him to his hockey practice at an ice rink next to the conservatory. Her spying is not immediately apparent, as the viewer sees only a static long shot of two figure skaters practising their routines, who are abruptly interrupted by Walter and his hockey mates. The shot is framed by the vertical bars of the ice rink's gate, but it is only after cutting to an extended reaction shot of Erika in close-up that the viewer realises that the preceding shot was exclusively from her point of view. The image of the hockey players rudely interrupting the beautiful figure-skating routine mirrors the juxtaposition of art and violence suggested throughout the film. Another instance of a long shot from Erika's point of view is the enigmatic final shot, the only time in the film that its professional location, the Vienna conservatory and the adjoining *Konzerthaus*, is seen in such a long shot, and in which Erika finally breaks out of the frame's prison.

Jelinek's novel portrays such confinement, control and domination through the artful employment of linguistic cliché, in part through the literary device of dramatic irony, even in its title, which in the original German conveys an ironic distance from the central character (the more respectful term for Erika's vocation would be *Pianistin*); the language that Erika uses to describe her interior life is itself confining – metaphors of torture and punishment abound – and the reader may plot out an alternative version of events than that seen through Erika's eyes. Haneke resists such 'literary' narrative devices – one might imagine here the use of voice-over clashing with the visual to establish dramatic irony – instead employing the filmic vocabulary of staging, the camera's eye, sound and editing to convey Erika's place within a confining high-brow musical culture; she is a cog in the culture industry (as outlined by Adorno and Horkheimer in *Dialectic of Enlightenment* (1947)), upholding and enforcing its laws and mores. The tension between the liberation offered by creative, in this instance Romantic, art and the institutions that mediate the experience and performance of this art are played out within and upon Erika. Extended tracking shots in scenes following her through Vienna emphasise more its underworld than the sites of its cultural glory and contrast with quieter, more contemplative scenes shot in her office and apartment. Haneke is able to suggest without obtrusive authorial intervention Erika's confinement and the inability to transcend her environment, letting the visual and sonic composition of the scenes articulate the thematic material.

Such narrative restraint is evident in the film's soundtrack, which adheres strictly to its diegesis, consisting only of ambient noise and the music performed either in rehearsal or recital; still, Haneke builds interesting sonic bridges between scenes, most notably in a three-part sequence introduced by Erika's rehearsal of Schubert's Piano Trio in a colleague's apartment. The music continues into the next scene, an extended tracking shot accompanying Erika through a Viennese shopping mall and culminating in her viewing of a pornographic film in a private booth, the music abruptly interrupted by the sound of Erika inserting tokens into the video machine. The change from the Piano Trio to the sounds (and fleeting images) of the pornographic film – no music here – is jarring indeed, but as the camera lingers on Erika viewing the film in an extended reaction shot, Haneke builds another sonic bridge to the next scene, as the music from Schubert's *Winterreise* slowly fills the soundtrack, culminating finally in an abrupt cut to a shot of the rehearsal in which it is being played. This memorable juxtaposition of image and sound from seemingly different worlds effectively undercuts the differences, suggesting subtly the deconstruction of high-cultural discourse, but still leaving open as a possibility the act of original creation (and interpretation) itself. Haneke argues as much when he states: 'Great music transcends suffering beyond specific causes. *Winterreise* transcends misery even in the detailed description of misery. All important artworks, especially those concerned with the darker side of experience, despite whatever despair conveyed, transcend the discomfort of the content in the realisation of their form' (in Sharrett 2004b). The redemptive moments sprinkled throughout the film are conveyed when Erika experiences music in an unmediated form, for instance when she listens to Walter play – here Haneke lingers in extended reaction shots on Isabelle Huppert, who is able to convey with subtle intensity such musical experience – or contemplates life 'beyond the frame', that is, beyond the physical boundaries of her professional and domestic existences.

The thematic core of the novel and film is thus similar: each locates the underlying authoritarian cradle of Austrian society within the nuclear family, and shows how such structures are duplicated in larger social institutions. While Jelinek's novel is more explicit in the suggestion of parallel structures, Haneke's film develops the connection in an understated, visually suggestive way, particularly in the editing strategy, which often cuts quickly between scenes of domestic terror and its reduplication in the professional setting of the conservatory. In response to a question about the role of family in *The Piano Teacher*, Haneke argues:

> I wanted first of all to describe the bourgeois setting, and to establish the family as the germinating cell for all conflicts. I always want to describe the world that I know, and for me the family is the locus of the miniature war, the first site of all warfare. The larger political-economic site is what one usually associates with warfare, but the everyday site of war in the family is as murderous in its own way, whether between parents and children or wife and husband. If you start exploring the concept of family in Western society you can't avoid realising that the family is the origin of all conflicts. I wanted to describe this in as detailed a way as I can, leaving the viewer to draw conclusions. The cinema has tended to offer closure on such topics and to send people home rather comforted and pacified. My objective is to unsettle the viewer and to take away any consolation or self-satisfaction. (In Sharrett 2004b)

The film ends on a note that forecloses reconciliation of conflicts arising in the family but also the conflicts mapped onto professional life. However, it is not necessarily an overly pessimistic conclusion, either; in a nod to the Romantic possibility of transcendence hinted at throughout the film, particularly in the moments of musical sublimity, one may see such a move in Erika's final liberation from the confining frame.

The nuclear family is the primary site of pathology in both novel and film; where the novel has a more expansive account of the father's mental illness and institutionalisation in the state hospital at Steinhof, Haneke strategically employs this information only twice, but at key moments in the film: firstly, when Erika invokes the memory of her father in her first conversation with Walter, perhaps as an attempt to distance herself from his flirtatious overtures and the prosaic setting of the bourgeois salon, also specifically to emphasise her psychic connection to Robert Schumann; and secondly, when Erika's mother invokes his memory to burden her with guilt and control her actions outside of the house. The mother/daughter relationship often presents the transgression of boundaries of propriety, notably in the lack of privacy and the incestuous sharing of the marital bed (particularly the disturbing scene in which Erika tries to return to her mother's womb, expressed, however, as sexual desire). Erika has internalised the disapproving gaze of her mother to the degree that it has become a physical presence within her, hence the emphasis on voiding bodily fluids and the association of expulsion with sexual gratification. Such infantilised moments form three of the film's

A collision of the comic and the disturbing: domestic life in *The Piano Teacher*

most memorably troubling scenes: genital self-mutilation in the apartment bathroom (comically interrupted when her mother impatiently calls Erika to supper); urination while she spies on a copulating couple at a drive-in movie; and regurgitation after performing fellatio on Walter. In this final scene, Erika emphasises that the expulsion renders her 'clean as a baby', something Haneke reinforces in the subsequent shot of Erika stumbling onto the adjoining ice rink into a blinding, all-encompassing light.

In terms of genre, *The Piano Teacher* exhibits elements of the classical melodrama and 'woman's film', as the heroine struggles within a love triangle and juggles personal and professional concerns. Here, however, part of the triangle is formed by Erika's painfully close relationship with her mother, emphasised in the *mise-en-scène* by their sharing of the typically Austrian marital bed – separate mattresses on a single frame – and the abrupt swings between violence and abject apology that characterise their usual domestic encounters. The triangle is introduced in a beautifully conceived staging of Erika (and her mother's) initial encounter with Walter. As Erika and her mother enter an elevator in the building where she is to give her recital, Walter runs up from behind trying to enter the elevator as well, but Erika prevents him from doing so. Mother and daughter's trip in the elevator is then shot from within the carriage and from behind, serving to emphasise the similarities between the two women. At the same time, at each succeeding floor, Walter, who has chosen to run up the stairs, appears and disappears through the elevator window. The confined space of the elevator is emphasised by the static camera position and is an apt metaphorical representation of the fraught mother/daughter relationship, while Walter's attractions – vigour, courtliness, good looks – though apparent to the viewer, cannot violate the closed circle of the mother/daughter bond.

Haneke's film hews closely to the novel's plot points regarding the triangular relationship between Erika, her mother and Walter. (Haneke does not use much from the novel's first half, which supplies more context about Erika's family, her youth and her professional disappointments.) It crystallises key encounters within the melodramatic

Confined space, static camera: Erika and Walter's first sexual encounter in *The Piano Teacher*

triangle: Walter, Erika and her mother meet at a salon-style piano recital hosted by one of Walter's relatives; Erika visits Vienna's pornography shops under the watchful interior eye of her mother; Walter insinuates himself into Erika's personal and professional lives (during a rehearsal of Schubert's *Winterreise* by Erika's star pupil, Anna Schober, and an affected tenor); Erika spies on a copulating couple at a drive-in movie, while Haneke cuts back and forth to a shot of her mother phoning to try to find out her whereabouts; Erika and Walter's first sexual encounter – in a lavatory within the conservatory – comes hard on the heels of her assault on Anna Schober; a second encounter is consummated in a closet adjoining a locker room; Walter's physical assault on Erika occurs in her apartment, as the mother listens from an adjacent room; and, finally, all three are present in the film's last scene, in which Erika, standing in the foyer of the performance hall, where she is scheduled to replace Anna as the accompanist for *Winterreise*, instead stabs herself in the shoulder.

This final scene amounts to a horrific capsule of Erika's damaged primary relationships with her mother and Walter, played out against the somewhat chaotic movements of concertgoers who rush through the foyer before claiming their seats. Coming immediately after the harrowing sequence of rape and violence in the apartment, this scene reunites the three principles at a public institution of musical culture, the *Konzerthaus*, but any change in the dynamics of the triangular relationship is undercut in the snippets of dialogue preceding the performance: Erika's mother undermines others' praise of her daughter with the withering indictment, 'It's only a school concert', and Walter walks calmly past, smiling breezily, offering chit chat, as if nothing has happened. Such preservation of appearances triggers Erika's final break from this untenable situation: she removes the kitchen knife from her purse, calmly stabs herself in the shoulder area – not a life-threatening wound, but one that will make piano-playing most difficult – and walks out of the building. Haneke cuts to the film's final scene, a static long shot of the *Konzerthaus* – 'The final image of *The Piano Teacher* is simply a reassertion of the conservatory, the classical symmetry of that beautiful building in the darkness. The viewer is asked to reconsider it' (Haneke in Sharrett 2004b) – and Erika, here a lone, small figure against the background of an imposing edifice, exits the frame to the viewer's right. One sees here a visual echo of the composition in her office that referenced Friedrich's *Woman at the Window*, and the intimations of anti-domesticity, the life beyond the confines of the home and the workplace that were suggested initially come to their fruition in a subtle, understated gesture. As with the earlier composition in the office, music is absent from the soundtrack, and the viewer is left with the distinct paradox that the music, somehow implicated in the violence and terror just witnessed, has also provided the means for transcending them.

References

Ma, J. (2007) 'Discordant Desires, Violent Refrains: *La Pianiste*', *Grey Room*, 28, 6–29.

Sharrett, C. (2004a) 'The Horror of the Middle Class', *Kinoeye*, 4, 1. On-line. Available at: http://www.kinoeye.com/ (accessed 20 December 2007).

_____ (2004b) 'Michael Haneke: The World that is Known', *Kinoeye*, 4, 1. On-line. Available at: http://www.kinoeye.com/ (accessed 20 December 2007).

Wheatley, C. (2006c) 'The masochistic fantasy made flesh: Michael Haneke's *La Pianiste* as Melodrama', *Studies in French Cinema*, 6, 2, 117–27.

Wood, R. (2002) '"Do I Disgust You?" Or, Tirez pas sur *La Pianiste*', *CineAction*, 59, 54–61.

Wyatt, J. (2006) 'Jouissance and Desire in Michael Haneke's *The Piano Teacher*', *American Imago*, 62, 4, 453–82.

CHAPTER SEVENTEEN

Two Meanings of Masochism in the Language of the Art Critic

Iuliana Corina Vaida

It has become commonplace to use psychoanalysis in the interpretation of artworks, whether to explain the author's intentions, the characters' actions or the general meaning of the story. Hence, there is nothing new about an attempt to employ the psychoanalytic concept of sadomasochism to shed light upon the meaning of two related works: Elfriede Jelinek's novel *Die Klavierspielerin* (1983) and Michael Haneke's film adaptation *La Pianiste* (*The Piano Teacher*, 2001). At the same time, literary critics have already noticed that the theme of sadomasochism plays a key role in Jelinek's work,[1] and film critics have pointed out the presence of sadomasochism in Haneke's films – which is to be expected from a director whose avowed purpose is to document violence in modern Western society. However, in spite of multiple accolades from prestigious international forums – Jelinek received the Nobel Prize for Literature in 2004 and Haneke's film received three top awards at the Cannes Film Festival in 2001[2] – and the subsequent critical interest in the two artists, critics seem to have failed to notice that their works espouse significantly different views of the nature of sadomasochism.

In this chapter I intend to show that Jelinek's novel and Haneke's film *The Piano Teacher* cannot be properly understood by appeal to one and the same psychoanalytical concept of sadomasochism. Working backwards, from the film to the novel as its source of inspiration, I will argue that although an interpretation based on the Freudian concept of sadomasochism, according to which sadism and masochism are two sides of the same coin, works for Haneke's film, it would distort our understanding of Jelinek's novel and minimise the significant differences between the novel and the film – differences that are due, among other things, to the two artists' contrasting *ideological* and *aesthetic* commitments. I will argue that Jelinek's novel is better understood by appeal to Gilles Deleuze's conception of masochism, according to which sadism and masochism are two distinct and irreducible entities, and that Jelinek's affinity, conscious or unconscious, for the Deleuzian theory is due to her radical feminist ideology: in her novel, sadomasochism becomes a metaphor for the incompatibility of man and woman.[3] By contrast, the film's departure from the novel, in particular its affinity with Freudian theory, can be explained as a by-product of Haneke's signature style: his preference for simple plots, the sparse classicist manner of his filming and his anti-psychologism.

Let me begin by briefly outlining the main elements of the story, the way the film presents them. Erika Kohut (Isabelle Huppert) is a professor at the Vienna Conservatory, where she gives piano lessons to generally talented students. A former concert pianist in the making, an expert interpreter of Franz Schubert and Robert Schumann, an exacting teacher, she seems to have sacrificed her personal life on the altar of high culture. She is single, in her late thirties, living with her domineering mother (Annie Girardot) in a small apartment, where they abuse each other physically and verbally, make up and sleep in the same bed. The novel, but not the film, gives us a glimpse into Erika's upbringing, explaining that the sacrifice was not her own choice, but rather a decision made for her, early in life, by her mother. Subjected to an intensive and cruel musical training, denied the simplest joys of childhood and adolescence, Erika gradually turned into a deeply disturbed individual. Her behaviour apparently includes elements of kleptomania (not shown in the film), self-cutting, voyeurism, porn addiction, incestuous impulses towards her mother and sadomasochism. However, in spite of her baggage, she seems to be in control of her life until Walter Klemmer (Benoît Magimel), a handsome and talented student, makes his appearance at the Conservatory and in her life. Walter, thinking himself in love, pursues Erika in spite of the obstacles she places in his way. Eventually, Erika gives in and falls in love. Deciding to trust Walter's proclaimed devotion, she writes him a letter in which she reveals her masochistic fantasies and instructs him how to subject her to pain and humiliation. Disappointed in his romantic expectations, Walter is confused, disgusted and enraged by Erika's assertiveness. A series of odd sexual encounters, unfulfilling for both parties, culminates with Walter raping Erika, who suddenly realises the gap between her fantasies and reality. Both the novel and the film end with Erika attempting to go after Walter to either kill him or throw herself at his feet, and settling instead for the old comforting ritual of cutting herself. The significant differences between the novel and the film will be mentioned in due course.

Freud's Theory of Sadomasochism

In 'The Economic Problem in Masochism', Sigmund Freud remarked that, insofar as it represents the pursuit of physical pain and feelings of distress, which generally signal danger and avoidance, the masochistic instinct is, from an economic point of view, mysterious. Subsequently, Theodor Reik argued that, in some sense, Freud had mis-stated the problem: the masochist does not strive for pain or submission for its own sake, but pain and humiliation are only the means to attaining the original goal of pleasure, the price one has to pay in order to enjoy pleasure. So the mystery to be solved is not why the masochist desires pain and humiliation, but why pleasure can be achieved only through pain and humiliation (see Reik 1941: 187–93).

On the way to solving the mystery, Freud distinguished three forms of masochism: erotogenic, feminine and moral masochism. Erotogenic masochism refers to a physiological mechanism by which a 'peculiar form of sexual excitement' is initially caused in children by certain types of mental or physical pain or discomfort. Insofar as this mechanism survives into adulthood, it provides the physiological basis for psychological masochism (see Freud 1924: 258–9). Feminine masochism refers to the behaviour of men who prefer to play the role of the woman during the sexual act, men who enjoy being the passive participant and desire to be caressed or sexually abused by a dominant woman (playing the role of the father). However, since Freud's term is misleading,[4] I will use the term 'sexual masochism' instead of 'feminine masochism', and consider it applicable to both men and women. Moral masochism refers to a certain attitude towards life, aptly described by Reik as an 'unconscious need for punishment' – a force that drives people 'to deny themselves enjoyment and success, to spoil their chances in life or not to make use of them' (1941: 10). In this case, Freud's term correctly suggests that the masochistic individual suffers from an 'excess of unconscious morality' that makes him behave as if he were held to stringent moral laws and prohibitions and forced to punish himself for disobeying them (ibid.). In moral masochism, the desire for pain has, at least on the surface, lost its connection with sexuality, and therefore moral masochism should be distinguished from sexual masochism.

My focus is on sexual rather than moral masochism, since Erika does not show any clear sign of the latter. If anything, her outward behaviour is that of a sadist.[5] Freud's solution to the mystery of masochism comes in the form of interpreting masochism as a 'turning around' or 'turning inward' of the aggressive impulses of sadism. In a revealing passage, Freud writes:

> If one is willing to disregard a certain amount of inexactitude, it might be said that the death instinct active in the organism – the primal sadism – is identical with masochism. After the chief part of it has been directed outwards towards objects, there remains as a residuum within the organism the true erotogenic masochism, which on the one hand becomes a component of the libido and on the other still has the subject itself for an object. (1924: 261)

The complete explanation of this 'turning inward' involves further theoretical concepts, such as the pleasure principle (Eros) and the death-instinct (Thanatos), ego and superego, which I will not attempt to discuss here. What is important for us is the main thesis of Freud's theory of sadomasochism, which can be formulated as follows: there is such a thing as a sadomasochistic entity – sexual masochism is complementary to, and forms a dialectical unity with, sadism – sadism and masochism are the two

sides of the same coin. They are opposites in a sense that suggests 'possibilities of transformation, reversal and combination' (Deleuze 1991: 68).

The Freudian hypothesis of a sadomasochistic unity has been taken to imply that
the sadist and the masochist are destined to meet (see Deleuze 1991: 40), and that, at
least in theory, they would make a perfect couple. The perfect couple is one in which
the sadistic and masochistic impulses are distributed between the two individuals in
such a way that the sum total of masochistic impulses equals the sum total of sadistic
impulses, even though its distribution between the two individuals may vary. Applying
the Freudian theory to *The Piano Teacher*, we can explain the attraction between Erika
Kohut and her student, Walter Klemmer, as follows. The sadistic side of Erika appeals
to the masochistic side of Walter, while her sexual masochism finds its counterpart in
his sexual sadism. Initially, Walter is attracted to Erika's overtly sadistic behaviour, and
this attraction is a proof of his covert masochism. Once they step into the sexual territory, however, her masochistic demands trigger his deep-seated sadism, which culminates in rape, destroying any possibility of a relationship.

There are two key episodes in the film that anchor the Freudian interpretation.
In the first episode, early in the movie, we see Walter running up the stairs, breathless, trying to catch up with the two Kohut women, mother and daughter, who have
closed the elevator door in his face. They are all going up to an apartment where a
private chamber concert is about to begin and where Erika is going to perform as a
pianist. This short episode epitomises Erika's sadistic behaviour towards her students
in general and Walter in particular. This behaviour is copiously illustrated throughout
the film, especially in the piano lesson scenes, during which Erika enjoys humiliating
her students and crushing their wills. Walter is not spared the brutal treatment which,
it is suggested, is contributing to his attraction to her.

The second key episode is the one in which Erika slips glass splinters into a student's
pocket, punishing her for the attention bestowed upon her by Walter, who joked with
her and sat by her side at the piano to help alleviate her stage fright. The succession
of scenes is breathtaking. As students are leaving the rehearsal hall and going to the
locker room to retrieve their belongings, we hear a piercing scream. Both Erika and
Walter are watching the victim, who is staring in disbelief at her lacerated hand. Erika,
claiming the sight of blood makes her sick, runs to the bathroom, but not before
telling Walter: 'Go to her. Be her brave protector.' For several seconds, we are offered a
close-up of Walter's face. From the blank expression we cannot tell if he is staring at the
scene in front of him or inside his own self. When someone shouts at him, 'Don't stare,
there's nothing to see', Walter finally tears himself from the spectacle and follows Erika
up the stairs to the bathroom, where they have their first sexual encounter. The episode
naturally lends itself to a Freudian interpretation: Walter's masochistic side responds to
the sadistic act which, consciously or unconsciously, he attributes to Erika,[6] and which
arouses him sexually.

It is significant that in the film the victim of Erika's jealousy is a young pianist
who, we have every reason to believe, is very much a copy of Erika herself when she
was young: hardworking, talented, with a 'surprising affinity for Schubert', but shy,
unattractive, dressed in outfits that kill any trace of sex appeal, pushed ahead and

controlled by an overbearing mother. It turns out that Erika's jealousy has a lot to do with this likeness, as well as with the girl's chance to perform in the school's jubilee concert. Thus, Erika's behaviour, as depicted in the film, closely follows the Freudian narrative of the birth of masochism from the primal sadism: the subject's aggressive impulses are first directed at an external object which, by being a mirror image of the subject, foreshadows the inevitable turning around of the aggression against the subject herself.

When we turn to Jelinek's novel, however, we discover a significantly different and more complex story that cannot be properly understood in terms of the Freudian theory.

The Contrast Between the Novel and the Film:
Three Claims Supporting A Deleuzian Interpretation Of The Novel

In what follows, I put forth and defend three distinct claims regarding Jelinek's novel: the first two are mostly clarificatory and prepare the grounds for the third one, which concludes that Freud's theory of sadomasochism fails to provide a satisfactory interpretation of the novel. Then I explain why Gilles Deleuze's theory of masochism is much better suited to make sense of various key episodes in the novel.

(i) Erika's outward behaviour is not that of a sadist. However, she is a sexual masochist; her masochism is related to her self-harming behaviour, as they both originated in her childhood abuse.

Though Erika was abused by her mother as a child, as a mature woman she is no longer a victim, and Jelinek is very good at not eliciting in her readers any sympathy or pity for Erika. However, the facts are chilling. As a child, she was forced to practise for hours on end, denied play, physical activity and interaction with other children. As an adolescent girl with apparently normal desires, she was denied high-heeled shoes and fashionable clothing. What she received in return was the mother's assurance, which became her own, that she was different, special, better than everyone else. But this is very poor nutrition for a child. Jelinek writes, 'HER innocent wishes change over the years into a destructive greed, a desire to annihilate. If others have something, then she wants it too. If she can't have it, she'll destroy it' (1999: 82). As a child, Erika is described as inflicting physical pain on unsuspecting streetcar and trolley riders. She bangs into people, thrusts her fist into them, kicks them in the shin, steps on their toes and pinches them (see Jelinek 1999: 15–17). She despises them and feels the need to punish them (see Jelinek 1999: 21). At 16, Erika punishes the wearer of a fashionable flannel ensemble by discovering and then telling her mother that the girl had earned her clothes by prostituting herself. The girl is expelled from school. Years later, a middle-aged Erika, in love with her student, focuses her jealousy on a girl with whom Walter is flirting, and causes her to injure her hand by sliding glass shards in the pocket of her coat.

Nonetheless, the satisfaction Erika gets from causing pain is different from that of a genuine sadist. Erika is acting like a child envious of those who have things she cannot have, who enjoy freedoms she cannot even dream of. Her behaviour is caused by spite, or envy – not an original outward-directed aggression, like in sadism, but a derivative aggression borne out of frustration and powerlessness.

Though Erika's desire to inflict pain on others is not a form of sadism, her self-cutting and needle-sticking are a form of sexual masochism, understandable in light of her childhood abuse. It has been long recognised that cutting oneself, as well as other forms of self-harm, is the result of childhood trauma, and Erika's childhood is a textbook case of psychological abuse:

> Men and women who experienced childhood trauma feel similar types of pain, but they often express it in different ways. There are many ways to explain why women hurt themselves more often than men do. Men who have been traumatised in childhood are likely to inflict on others what was done to them; they are socialised to act aggressively and to fight back rather than to allow someone to harm or humiliate them. Women are socialised not to fight back; allowing themselves to be hurt or humiliated is far more socially acceptable than being aggressive or violent toward others. Although some women become abusers themselves, it is much more likely that female victims of childhood trauma will inflict pain on themselves. Men act out. Women act out by acting in. (Miller 2005: 5–6)

> The self injurious behaviour serves many functions … [The woman] experiences the behaviour itself as a relationship. It may help her feel alive when she is overwhelmed by feelings of numbness. Paradoxically, it can serve as well to keep her from feeling unbearable tension, rage, or grief. (Miller 2005: 9)

When we encounter Erika, she is a survivor and a highly functional individual. Even though she has to hide her sexual desires, she isn't hiding them from herself, and is taking great risks to satisfy them. The self-cutting has become a successful strategy to cope with pain and to fight numbness. It is also a means of taking back the control over her body – from her mother, from Walter. Even in the end, after Walter rapes and discards her, the wound she inflicts on herself should not be viewed as a suicide attempt: 'Rather than a suicidal gesture, cutting is a symbol of the fight to stay alive' (Strong 1998: xvii).

Because the film offers no explanation for Erika's cruel behaviour towards herself and others, we perceive her behaviour as more gratuitous and repugnant than it actually is. Our perception of Erika as a victim is even more diminished in the film than in the novel, so it is easy to perceive her rape as something that she has brought on herself – something she is partly responsible for.

(ii) Walter is not a sexual masochist and thus, masochism does not play any role in the attraction he feels for Erika. However, there are clear sadistic elements in his personality.

Both in the novel and in the film, Walter's sadism is apparent – although I will argue that the novel suggests that his behaviour is prototypically male rather than sadistic. After a sexual encounter in which he fails to have an erection, Walter blames

Erika's disgusting fantasies and her desire to control him, and decides to reclaim his manhood by violently beating and raping her.

However, Walter's sexual masochism, though recognisable in Haneke's film, is absent from the novel. Jelinek makes it quite clear that Walter's pursuit of Erika is fuelled by his competitiveness and his desire to gain sexual experience by having a relationship with an older woman. As readers, we are allowed to eavesdrop on the characters' inner monologues, which are far from noble. We thus know that Walter's reasons for pursuing Erika have nothing to do with the pleasure of being humiliated; Walter pursues Erika for the sake of the challenge she represents to his masculinity, as his teacher and as an apparently frigid woman, and because he thinks that a relationship with her will give him valuable sexual experience for the future. In the film, because the voice of the all-knowing narrator is replaced with the pure, longing sounds of Schubert's and Schumann's music, we are inclined to attribute to Walter feelings of romantic love mixed with a desire to suffer, instead of dubious motivations and self-serving plans.

The most important evidence to be found in the novel against Walter's masochism is the central episode leading to Erika and Walter's first sexual encounter – an episode significantly different in the novel than in the film. In the novel, Walter is overtly flirting with several young girls, in a final attempt to get Erika's attention. When Erika's jealousy explodes, she does not aim her revenge at the homely piano student in whom she recognises her younger self, but at a well dressed girl, a flutist and a student of fashion design (see Jelinek 1999: 167), who seems to represent everything Erika could not be or have when she was young.[7] In the novel, we also learn that when Erika exits the gymnasium where the orchestra is playing, Walter has already decided to follow her. It is the conductor's glare that keeps him in his seat, while Erika runs to the dressing room, breaks a glass tumbler and slips the splinters into the girl's coat pocket. When she returns, rubbing her hands as if she has just washed them, Walter is again wondering how he can be alone with Erika. The reader has no reason to believe that the girl's pain appeals to his masochism, or that he makes any connection between Erika and the sadistic act. In the novel, Erika does not utter the words 'Go to her. Be her brave protector' that link her to the crime, and there is no indication that Walter is fascinated by the bloody spectacle. The explanation for Walter's pursuit of Erika and the ensuing sexual encounter appears to be devoid of any psychoanalytical depth: Walter has already decided to make one last attempt to get Erika and, when no one is watching, he seizes the opportunity.

As mentioned above, in the film the pretty girl with whom Walter is flirting is replaced with Erika's homely piano student. Possibly in order to simplify the plot and give it more clarity, Haneke makes significant changes in his depiction of the episode. Uncharacteristically, he also yields to the temptation of helping the viewer along the psychologically opaque succession of events, by making Erika utter the words, 'Go to her. Be her brave protector' and offering a close-up of Walter's face. Oddly enough, this one time Haneke departs from his own anti-psychologism, he turns out to be too heavy-handed, leading the viewer to believe that Walter attributes the evil deed to Erika and, consequently, that his attraction to Erika is due to his latent masochism.

*(iii) Freud's hypothesis of a sadomasochistic unity fails to provide a satisfactory expla-
nation of the early failure of the relationship between Erika and Walter.*

Even though the Freudian theory provides an overall satisfactory interpretation
of Haneke's film, by making sense of the main characters' behaviour and their mutual
attraction, a question remains: since the Freudian hypothesis of a sadomasochistic
unity implies that the sadist and the masochist make a perfect couple, how would a
Freudian explain the disastrous early breakdown of the relationship between Erika and
Walter? More generally, the question is: is the Freudian theory capable of explaining
why, in fiction as much as in real life, sexual relations between sadistic and masochistic
individuals fail to work? There is plenty of evidence that appears to falsify the Freudian
hypothesis of a sadomasochistic unity. Take, for example, this passage from Anita Phillips's book *A Defense of Masochism*:

> The sadist and the masochist are an impossible couple. If they were to get
> together, it would probably be due to some mutual misunderstanding and
> misinterpretation … Both want to direct the show, the [sadist] by force, the
> [masochist] by manipulation … The kind of sex we usually call sadomaso-
> chistic is voluntary, consensual and, therefore, directed by masochistic rather
> than sadistic interests. Sadistic interests are not collaborative ones, but rather
> test their effectiveness against the will of another person. Masochism needs
> collusion, because of the risk involved in submission … It is about being hurt
> in exactly the right way and at the right time, within a sophisticated, highly
> artificial scenario. (1998: 11–13)

In fact, the Freudian has an explanation of why sexual relations between a sadist and
a masochist do not work and, in particular, why the relationship between Erika and
Walter has to end so abruptly and painfully. The Freudian argues that, though *in theory*
or *ideally*, the sadist and the masochist make a perfect couple, *in reality* it is likely that
the sadist will get carried away, inflicting more pain than the masochist is willing to
take. The success of the sadomasochistic couple is thus hard to achieve, as it depends
on a succession of fine adjustments between the two protagonists.

However, if we feel more than a little dissatisfied with the Freudian response,
it is because the miscommunication between Erika and Walter is so complete, their
breakup so abrupt and irreversible that, in retrospect, their union seems not just
unlikely, but plainly impossible. Because the Freudian hypothesis of a sadomasochistic
unity is contradicted by so many elements in the novel, we may wonder if an alternative conception of masochism would prove to be more helpful.

In arguing for claims *(i)–(iii)*, I have called into question the adequacy of the
Freudian conception of sadomasochism as the key to understanding Jelinek's novel. In
the remainder of this section, I will argue that Gilles Deleuze's conception of masochism, as presented in his essay 'Coldness and Cruelty', represents a more adequate
basis for a psychoanalytical interpretation of the novel than Freud's theory. According
to Deleuze's view, the sadomasochistic couple is a theoretical, not just practical, impossibility, its failure absolute, not just a matter of degree. Deleuze denies that there is a

sadomasochistic entity, in the form of a perversion or illness, corresponding to the notion of sadomasochism, and claims that the universe of masochism has nothing to do with that of sadism:

> Their techniques differ, and their problems, their concerns and their intentions are entirely dissimilar. It is not valid to object that psychoanalysis has long shown the possibility and the reality of transformations between sadism and masochism; we are questioning the very concept of an entity known as sadomasochism. (1991: 13)

From the several propositions that sum up Deleuze's approach to masochism, I will focus on three, which are the most clearly recognisable in Jelinek's narrative. First, Deleuze explains that the sadist and the masochist are incompatible, their encounter is necessarily explosive and destructive, because they both vie for power in the relationship. Deleuze points out that the sadist enjoys his victim only insofar as she is not consenting, whereas the masochist is looking for a torturer who can be educated, persuaded to follow the masochist's instructions. He concludes that the torturer in masochism is not a sadist, but an element of the masochistic fantasy, a creation of the masochist's imagination. He writes:

> [In masochism we] are no longer in the presence of a torturer seizing upon a victim all the more because she is unconsenting and unpersuaded ... a genuine sadist could never tolerate a masochistic victim ... Neither would the masochist tolerate a truly sadistic torturer. (1991: 40–1)

Second, Deleuze emphasises the centrality of contracts or agreements in enacting the masochistic fantasy. A contract is necessary because the masochist is not searching for just any torturer, but for a torturer who can be educated and drawn into a contractual agreement. The masochist is 'essentially an educator and thus runs the risk inherent in educational undertakings' (1991: 21). Indeed Erika, the educator, is trying to get Walter to agree to a contract before starting a sexual relationship with him – hence, her letter to him. Walter is correct when he senses that Erika, in spite of her desire for submission, is trying to control and dominate him, to educate and mould him into the kind of lover that she needs. But Erika is unexperienced in the field of sexuality and mistaken in her assessment of Walter, who is 'anything but a born follower' (Jelinek 1999: 181), and so her educational undertaking is doomed from the start.

Third, Deleuze claims that the masochistic fantasy is characterised by the centrality of the mother figure and the conspicuous absence of the father. Erika Kohut lives with her mother and even shares a bed with her. The mother has taken on the attributes of the father ever since Erika can remember – she 'alone dictates the shalts and shalt-nots' (Jelinek 1999: 6) and behaves like an 'absolute ruler' (Jelinek 1999: 9). Early in the novel we find out that Erika's father lost his mind and died in an asylum. Later on we learn how the two Kohut women, mother and adult daughter, together disposed of the 'feebleminded and completely disoriented father', by abandoning him in a sanitarium, and then letting him die in a public madhouse (see Jelinek 1999: 91–2).

On the Freudian view, the father figure is central in both sadistic and masochistic fantasies. Freud famously interpreted the masochistic fantasy of 'the child being beaten' as meaning that the masochist, who identifies himself with the child, desires to be beaten/loved by the father.[8] By contrast, Deleuze claims that the mother is the central figure in masochism, and that in the fantasy of the child being beaten 'the father is not so much the beater as the beaten' (1991: 60). What the masochist feels guilty for is 'his resemblance to the father and the father's likeness in him' (1991: 61). As the father 'is excluded and completely nullified' (ibid.), his paternal functions are transferred on to the mother. Accordingly, in Jelinek's novel the paternal functions are shared between mother and daughter. As Allyson Fiddler points out, the relationship between mother and daughter reproduces the 'stereotyped image of overpowering wife and hen-pecked husband' (1994: 131). The mother has moulded her daughter into an 'ersatz husband': the two women share the same bed, and Erika is the breadwinner of the household while her mother takes care of her and does the housework (see Fiddler 1994: 130–1).

These are three major reasons suggesting that the Deleuzian conception of masochism provides a better interpretation of Jelinek's novel than the Freudian conception. On the Deleuzian interpretation, the failure of Erika and Walter to understand each other is not just an unfortunate occurrence, but a necessary outcome. In Deleuze's words, the sadist and the masochist 'represent parallel worlds, each complete in itself, [so that] it is both unnecessary and impossible for each to enter the other's world' (1991: 68).

Beyond the Psychoanalytical Explanations:
Jelinek's Feminist Ideology Versus Haneke's Old-School Aesthetics

Echoing Deleuze's words quoted above, Jelinek describes man and woman as 'each welded to his or her own little love planet, two ice flows, which are inhospitable continents, repelling one another and drifting apart' (1999: 240). Her view of the possibility of a happy union between man and woman is bleak: 'The opposite sex always wants the exact opposite' (1999: 143). One could argue that Jelinek's real topic is not the sadomasochistic couple, but the relationship between man and woman in general, and that the theme of the impossibility of the sadomasochistic couple is a metaphor for the impossibility of a satisfying relationship between man and woman in a patriarchal society.

Accordingly, while the Freudian interpretation is stuck in the dynamic of the sadomasochistic couple, the Deleuzian interpretation allows us to see Erika not just as a pathological case, but as a woman whose sexual desires fail to conform to the strict and unimaginative norm allotted to women in a male-dominated society. Moreover, it allows us to see Walter not as a sadist, but as a typical man. After all, it is difficult to regard him as a sadist, when his entire behaviour, with the exception of the rape act, falls within the limits of what passes for normal male behaviour in our society:

full of energy, aggressive, competitive, with an all-encompassing sense of entitlement and completely lacking in self-doubt. We can imagine that Walter is the product of an upbringing similar to that of Erika's cousin, an upbringing during which he was encouraged to explore, to take physical challenges, to rebel against authority and to stop at nothing in order to get what he wants.[9] This kind of upbringing, which has produced, over generations, a multitude of well-adjusted, highly-successful men at the top of the social and professional hierarchy, could not be more different from what Erika experienced at the hands of her mother.

This suggests that the Deleuzian conception of masochism may allow us to integrate Jelinek's *ideological* commitments, her radical feminism, into the psychoanalytical interpretation of her novel – in a manner that the Freudian conception is incapable of. To see how this is possible, we need to start by acknowledging that, in *The Piano Teacher*, the feminist ideology is present as more than the sum total of sordid incidents and inflaming sarcasms about men and women, which are characteristic of Jelinek's style. Its presence is manifest in the subtle distortion that the narrative induces in our perception of normalcy and disease, even of right and wrong: because we are shocked and outraged by Erika's behaviour, because we perceive her as sick and perverse, we accept Walter's aggression, even in the form of rape, as almost natural and understandable. On reflection, this reveals the influence that the structure of power in society has on our perception: the main reason why we perceive Walter as normal is that the spectrum of sexual behaviours that are regarded as normal and acceptable for men is much wider than for women. Jelinek's point is not just the old feminist adage that, in a male-dominated society, sadistic behaviour has more positive connotations than masochistic behaviour. Her point is that, whether sadistic or not, men always have more opportunities than women to get their sexual preferences satisfied while still remaining within the limits of what is normal and acceptable.

Jelinek goes to great lengths in her novel to describe how men are catered to, offered various sexual outlets, inside and outside of marriage. Not only do they expect their women to conform to their desires and fantasies, they also have a whole industry of prostitutes, peep-shows and pornographic movies devised entirely for their consumption. By contrast, there is a very narrow spectrum of sexual behaviours regarded as normal and acceptable for women. As is appropriate with the powerless and the oppressed, they are forced into conformity and uniformity, their various sexual needs ignored.

The contrast between the different ways we perceive the behaviour of men and women is brought out by the parallel stories of Erika's voyeuristic adventure in Prater Park and Walter's revenge trip into the city park. Erika goes to Prater Park at night in order to spy on couples having sex. When she inadvertently betrays her presence, the man of the couple pursues her aggressively, if unsuccessfully, and Erika is lucky to come out of her adventure alive. There is no doubt that her behaviour is wrong. But when Walter, angry after his failure to achieve an erection with Erika, goes into the city park, also at night, with the intention to kill an animal, we hesitate in our judgement that what he is doing is wrong. We try to understand him and excuse his rage: after all, he is recovering from his 'first terrors of impotence' (Jelinek 1999: 244), caused by

Erika's aberrant behaviour! When, instead of birds, he stumbles upon a young couple making love, he sees himself in the position of order restorer, defender of municipal property, enforcer of the law. He is a punisher, shrieking with righteous indignation. He thinks he is in the right, and his sense of entitlement, his lack of self-doubt, almost convinces us that he is.

Though Erika's masochistic sexuality is the result of her childhood abuse, this does not mean that it is necessarily self-destructive: Erika wants to enact her sexual fantasies, and she hopes that love and understanding will make that possible. When Walter comes along and proclaims his love to Erika, assuring her that 'he has never shied away from any risk – the bigger, the better' (Jelinek 1999: 196), Erika thinks this is her chance to enact her sexual fantasies. However, Walter turns out to be 'anything but a born follower' (Jelinek 1999: 181), and is very sensitive to Erika's attempts to lead him: 'This woman has not a spark of submission … He must go no further with her' (Jelinek 1999: 179). While Erika dreams of moulding him into the lover she needs, Walter also dreams of changing Erika, in ways that go beyond her role as his lover. He dislikes her clothes, and intends to change her style. He has no doubts he holds the standard of what she ought to become: 'This finery, this frippery, which Walter feels disfigures her, must be discarded at once! For his sake!' (Jelinek 1999: 203).

In the end, by raping Erika, Walter demonstrates that he has no desire and no need to change for her sake: 'I am I … He threatens the woman: She has to take him just as he is. I am as I am' (Jelinek 1999: 270). Erika's rape corresponds to what Deleuze calls, in his theory of masochism, 'the aggressive return of the father' (1991: 65); Walter's 'I am I' symbolically recalls the God of the Old Testament. Deleuze argues that the return of the father is a 'constant threat from the side of reality to the masochist's world' (ibid.) – the reality being the patriarchal order that the masochist has tried to protect himself against by means of the contract.

Deleuze's theory of masochism allows us to understand why it is impossible for a masochistic woman to fulfil her fantasies in a male-dominated society. According to Deleuze, the main character in the masochistic fantasy can only be played by a very special kind of woman:

> Masoch and his heroes are constantly in search of a peculiar and extremely rare feminine 'nature'. The subject in masochism needs a certain 'essence' of masochism embodied in the nature of a woman who renounces her own subjective masochism. (1991: 42–3)

It follows that, in order to fulfil her fantasies, a masochistic woman would have to find a man who embodies the 'essence' of masochism and at the same time is willing to renounce it, or at least postpone his own satisfaction for the sake of the woman's pleasure – an impossible task in a patriarchal society, in which men neither want to nor have to put their desires on hold for the sake of women.

I have argued that Jelinek relies on the Deleuzian conception of masochism because of her *ideological* commitments – because it reinforces her feminist intuitions. Turning back now to Michael Haneke's film adaptation, we notice that its departure from the novel, its rendition of the story in accordance with the Freudian theory of sadomasochism, is closely related to the characteristics of Haneke's style, especially his preference for simple plots and his clear, concise approach. Thus, in the remainder of this essay I will argue that Haneke's appropriation of the Freudian conception of sado-masochism is, rather than a matter of what the director holds true, a by-product of his *aesthetic* commitments. Haneke has, consciously or subconsciously, embraced Freud's theory because it allows him to make a film which, with classical elegance, delivers a disturbing and subversive message.

Whether or not we count simplicity among the criteria of truth, we generally see it as an attractive, good-making feature of any theoretical construction. Thus, we cannot deny that one of the great attractions of Freud's theory of sadomasochism is its elegant simplicity. For Michael Haneke, who works within the bounds of modernist/classical art forms, Freud's beautifully simple theory serves the need to condense the material of the novel, bring clarity to and unify the plot. The music of Schubert and Schumann also help anchor the film in the great classical tradition. Haneke's unique talent is to infuse great emotional tension and shocking power into a style of filming characterised by classical simplicity, rationalist clarity, precision and restraint. However, in this case the classical values are achieved by sacrificing Jelinek's insight that 'reality is dishev-elled' (2004), too complex to be conveyed in any elegant and simple form.[10] If the values of elegance and simplicity can only be achieved by sacrificing parts of reality, Jelinek has good reasons to reject them: what is most likely to be sacrificed is women's reality, the ways in which they are different from men.

One of the main elements of Haneke's style is his anti-psychologism. Regarding this aspect of his films, Haneke once said in an interview: 'I try to make anti-psycho-logical films with characters who are less characters than projection surfaces for the sensibilities of the viewer; blank spaces force the spectator to bring his own thoughts and feelings to the film. Because that is what makes the viewer open for the sensitivity of the character' (in Frey 2003). As Mattias Frey notes, Haneke 'goes to extremes in withholding information in order to compel the spectator to "think with" and "feel with" the film, instead of simply consuming it' (2003). But no matter how well this technique has served him in the past, in his polemic with American cinema and his criticism of modern society, its effect in *The Piano Teacher* is, at least compared to Jelinek's novel, a rather conservative affirmation of traditional ways of thinking, a bow in the direction of patriarchal values and old-school psychoanalysis. Confronted with 'blank spaces' and outrageous and inexplicable behaviour, forced to bring his own thoughts and feelings to the film, the spectator is likely to fall back onto old theories and traditional ways of thinking about men and women.

In conclusion, intentionally or not, Haneke's film is an exercise in how form can affect content, in how classical conventions and stylistic clarity can go along with our sexist perception of reality, and support traditional patriarchal values. However, Haneke's film remains a highly coherent and unitary work of art, drawing strength from the brilliant performance of its actors, as well as from the music of Schubert and Schumann. Though distinct, in style and ideology, from Jelinek's novel, it is equally fascinating, and is best viewed as a work of art in its own right.

I have argued for the importance for the art critic to distinguish between two concepts of masochism, one corresponding to Freud's theory of sadomasochism and the other to Deleuze's theory of masochism. I have followed the implications of this distinction in the case of two artworks, Elfriede Jelinek's novel and Michael Haneke's film adaptation, arguing that, though closely related, the two cannot be properly understood by appeal to the same conception of masochism. Though the Freudian conception allows us to understand Haneke's film, it encounters serious difficulties when applied to Jelinek's novel. In Haneke's film, Erika's sadomasochistic behaviour is extreme and easily recognisable, but Walter, in spite of his happy-go-lucky façade, is also suffering, latently, from the same affliction. The relationship, which begins with the sadistic side of Erika's behaviour exercising its attraction on the masochistic side of Walter's personality, is going to end when her sexual masochism triggers his latent but powerful sadism. In contrast with the film, the novel suggests that Erika is not genuinely sadistic, that Walter has no masochistic traits and that not even the label 'sadistic' may be applicable to him. Thus, the Freudian interpretation becomes inadequate and we are compelled to search for an alternative – in this case, provided by the Deleuzian conception of masochism.

Author's note

I am indebted to Allan Casebier with whom I had numerous helpful discussions. His suggestions were invaluable, and so was his encouragement while I was writing this article.

Notes

1   Allyson Fiddler quotes Elfriede Jelinek saying 'Sado-Masochismus ist mein Thema Nummer eins' (1994: 146).

2   Grand Jury Prize, Best Actress and Best Actor Awards.

3   To my knowledge, Fiddler is the only one who notes that *The Piano Teacher* disproves 'the traditional Freudian view that sadism and masochism are simply two sides of the same phenomenon', and subscribes to Gilles Deleuze's opposing view that 'although on the surface there would seem to be much in common between [sadism and masochism], they are, in fact, derived from quite different deep structural roots' (1994: 151). However, Fiddler does not take her observation beyond a brief discussion of the novel's 'letter episode', in which she points out that, in search of her sexual identity, Erika needs to 'reproduce the structures of masculine dominance' (1994: 152).

4   The term is more misleading today than in Freud's time, not only because the sexual perversion is present in both men and women, but also because it originally referred to a sexual perversion in men (not in women), characterised by behaviour believed by Freud to be similar to the sexual behaviour of the 'normal' woman, thus implying that masochism is natural and 'normal' to women.

5   The only episode in Erika's life suggesting she might be a moral masochist is her mysterious failure as a concert pianist and her subsequent resignation to the life of a piano teacher. However, the failure may also have a different explanation: she may just not be talented enough (her mother is obviously delusional when she claims Erika is a genius), or she may have decided she did not want the life of a concert pianist.

6   In the film, Erika's words make a clear connection, based on jealousy, between herself and the victim, whereas in the novel Erika is not saying anything. This turns out to be one of the key differences between the film and the novel.

7   The girl is wearing a miniskirt, showing her legs 'almost up to where they end and run into the body' (Jelinek 1999: 160). Later, in the locker room, Erika recognises the girl's coat 'because of the fashionably loud colour and because of the new stylish mini-shortness' (1999: 166).

8   According to Freud's theory, the etiology of the perversion links it to the original sadism: the masochist started by wishing to take the place of the father, by killing or castrating him, but then feelings of guilt and the fear of castration make him abandon the sadistic impulse and ask for the father's love, by taking over the passive role of the mother.

9   The cousin, who once visited Erika at a holiday location in the Alps, is described as gaining the admiration of Erika's mother and grandmother with his display of vitality, humour and rebelliousness. In the meantime, the women force Erika to spend all her time in the house, isolated from her peers, practising the piano. The older women's view seems to be that a man who has a successful career ahead of him can and should enjoy the pleasures of life while he is young, whereas a woman can only attain success in her career if she sacrifices her sexuality. They fear, maybe correctly, that love and the attention of men will endanger a young woman's sense of self and her determination to succeed.

10 In her Nobel Prize Lecture, Jelinek speaks of the untidy nature of reality:

'It's so very dishevelled. No comb, that could smooth it down. The writers run through it and despairingly gather together their hair into a style, which promptly haunts them at night. Something's wrong with the way one looks. The beautifully piled up hair can be chased out of its home of dreams again, but can anyway no longer be tamed ... It simply won't be tidied up. It doesn't want to. No matter how often one runs the comb with the couple of broken off teeth through it – it just doesn't.' (2004)

References

Deleuze, G. (1991 [1967]) 'Coldness and Cruelty', in *Masochism*. Trans. J. McNeil. New York: Zone Books, 9–138.

Fiddler, A. (1994) *Rewriting Reality. An Introduction to Elfriede Jelinek*. Oxford and Providence: Berg.

Freud, S. (1924) 'The Economic Problem in Masochism', in *Collected Papers*, Volume II, translated under the supervision of J. Riviere. London: Hogarth Press and The Institute of Psycho-Analysis, 255–68.

Frey, M. (2003) 'Michael Haneke', *Senses of Cinema*. On-line. Available at: http://www.sensesofcinema.com/contents/directors/03/haneke.html (accessed 10 October 2008).

Jelinek, E. (1999) *The Piano Teacher*. Trans. J. Neugroschel. London: Serpent's Tail.

———— (2004) *The Nobel Prize Lecture*. On-line. Available at: http://nobelprize.org/nobel_prizes/literature/laureates/2004/jelinek-lecture-e.html (accessed 10 October 2008)

Miller, D. (2005) *Women Who Hurt Themselves*. London: Basic Books.

Phillips, A. (1998) *A Defense of Masochism*. New York: St. Martin's Press.

Reik, T. (1941) *Masochism in Modern Man*. Trans. M. H. Beigel and G. M. Kurth. New York and Toronto: Farrar & Rinehart.

Strong, M. (1998) *A Bright Red Scream. Self-Mutilation and the Language of Pain*. New York: Penguin.

Hidden

CHAPTER EIGHTEEN

Subject to Memory? Thinking after Hidden

Nemonie Craven Roderick

In the Beginning ... Silence

Caché (*Hidden*, 2005) begins with a silence which, like that of the 'il y a', the existential state described by Emmanuel Levinas in some of his earliest works, lacks peace, and could be seen, rather, to constitute 'an undetermined menace' (1978: 60).[1] This murmuring, increasingly unsettling silence begs a question: the disembodied 'Et alors?' I hear voiced, and which, indeed, I had silently voiced, or, perhaps, the 'Who's there?' with which *Hamlet* opens and unfolds its many questions – 'Speak, speak. I charge thee, speak.' For the time of this film is out of joint and its coherence, therefore, elusive to my grasp. The 'something rotten' at the heart of *Hidden*'s vision of a state, France, founded on the death of a king and of so many others, creates a haunted perspective by means of which sovereignty – including the sovereignty of history – is undone, and yet by means of which I become a vigilant spectator.[2]

The film critically engages conceptualisations of history and memory, as the past re-emerges as a question and a power in its movement through various individuals and groups of individuals – Georges (Daniel Auteuil), Anne (Juliette Binoche), Majid (Maurice Bénichou), the spectator (myself and others) – who become subject to interrogation or subject to memory: who are, in various ways, called to respond. I think here of Walter Benjamin's sixth thesis on the philosophy of history:

> To articulate the past historically does not mean to recognise it 'the way it really was' (Ranke). It means to seize hold of a memory as it flashes up at a moment of danger. Historical materialism wishes to retain that image of the

past which unexpectedly appears to a man singled out by history at a moment of danger ... Only that historian will have the gift of fanning the spark of hope in the past who is firmly convinced that *even the dead* will not be safe from the enemy if he wins. And this enemy has not ceased to be victorious. (1999: 247; emphasis in original)

Is the 'image of the past' Benjamin refers to a form of what Martha Nussbaum, after the Stoics, might call a 'cataleptic impression'? Diverging from the Stoic account – that 'all our knowledge of the external world is built upon the foundation of certain special perceptual impressions: those which, by their own internal character, their own experienced quality, certify their own veracity' (1990: 265)[3] – Nussbaum states that the 'cataleptic impressions in this case ... are emotional impressions – specifically, impressions of anguish' (1990: 266). As an example, she cites Marcel's reaction, in Proust's *Albertine disparue* (1925), to the news that 'Mademoiselle Albertine has gone'. It is on hearing this that 'Marcel knows, and knows with certainty, without the least room for doubt, that he loves Albertine' (Nussbaum 1990: 261).

Might Benjamin's 'image of the past' be an image of injustice?[4] The image of an other's anguish, to which the historical 'Messiah' is compelled to bear witness? 'Historical materialism wishes to retain that image of the past which unexpectedly appears to a man singled out by history at a moment of danger'. As Susan Sontag writes: 'no "we" should be taken for granted when the subject is looking at other people's pain' (2003: 7). I think now of Antigone, figuring courage and an experience of injustice uniquely her own; of Phocion's widow as described by Gillian Rose after Plutarch: gathering her husband's ashes 'for if they are left unconsecrated, his unappeased soul will wander forever' (Rose 1996: 23).[5] I remember the image of Majid, as a child, coughing up blood; Majid, as a man, slitting his own throat in a spectacular, petrifying display. I remember Georges left, alone, with this scene, and myself as his spectatorial shadow.[6] Do these images contain what David Simpson might call a 'purposive shock' – a 'power to move and move to action?' (2006: 129). Paul Gilroy has criticised the representation of Majid's suicide as 'an exclusively aesthetic event', which denies Majid a voice (2007: 234). But does this reading overlook Majid's claim to integrity? Does it overlook the significance of his claim to an absolute silence, and his resistance to interrogation? Majid's act speaks, and speaks of countless acts many would dismiss as 'senseless'.[7] On 10 June 2006, three inmates of the US base at Guantánamo Bay were found dead after having committed suicide in an act described by the camp commander Rear Admiral Harry Harris as one of 'asymmetrical warfare' (BBC 2006). In the absence of *habeas corpus*, it is possible to reclaim the body. And it is possible that there is a version of truth in such testimony, to which we or, again, I, in my singularity, might bear witness.

In the case of Georges, however, it appears that the impressions he is subject to move him towards a more active forgetting. When Majid's son (Walid Afkir) confronts Georges at his place of work, Georges once again refuses any responsibility for Majid's 'sad and ruined' life. At the end of the film, Georges attempts to take refuge in the anonymity of sleep from the images that haunt him, by taking 'deux cachets' – sleeping pills. *Even the dead* will not be safe. Libby Saxton has described Haneke's aesthetic construction in general as an attempt to 'implicate the body of the viewer-witness, a body habitually preserved as inviolable by the signifying procedures of dominant forms of cinema. In according a spectrum of spectators physical presence on-screen, Haneke's films insist on spectatorship as an embodied, corporealised experience, as an encounter between vulnerable bodies' (2008: 89). If I figure Georges' spectatorial shadow, to what extent am I also implicated in this active forgetting?

Thence Came a Spirit…

I introduce these questions in order to draw Haneke's perhaps aporetic film into current debates in the field of ethics and politics, which touch on a conceptualisation of 'aesthetic experience' which follows the etymology of 'aesthetic', from the Greek *aisthánesthai* – 'to perceive sensuously'.[8] David Simpson, in his recent work *9/11: The Culture of Commemoration*, has argued that 'the time *is* out of joint, which means that we must work all the harder to find its history and to dispel its mysteries' (2006: 170; emphasis in original). Yet he has cautioned against the privileging of aesthetic experience he reads in the work of Nussbaum and Terry Eagleton. Eagleton, he points out, has recently turned 'against theory', making a 'renewed case for the power of literature as the medium better suited to our human needs, better able to cultivate the desired sympathy or compassionate identification with the demise of physical suffering' (2006: 125).[9] Yet Simpson draws on William Wordsworth for evidence that art might blunt our sensitivity to suffering. In 'The Prelude', Wordsworth 'tried to explain why the sight of the "ghastly face" and "spectre shape" of a drowned man surfacing on the lake of Esthwaite did *not* startle or surprise him':

> And yet no vulgar fear,
> Young as I was, a child not nine years old,
> Possessed me, for my inner eye had seen
> Such sights before among the shining streams
> Of fairyland, the forests of romance –
> Thence came a spirit hallowing what I saw
> With decoration and ideal grace,
> A dignity, a smoothness, like the words
> Of Grecian art and purest poesy. (See Simpson 2006: 126 – 27; emphasis in original)

Simpson asks, therefore: 'Are the drowned man and the falling towers instances of what we call, after Baudrillard, the *simulacrum*, the sign without a signified, the image emptied of any connection to the real? … Are we trapped by the repetition of the spectacle as a commodified form able to digest whatever associates with it in the realm of new experience, making such experience never new and never shocking?' (2006: 129). Are we immune even to what Gilroy dismisses as 'an exclusively aesthetic event'? And to what extent might this immunity have been built through an immersion in the aesthetic element?

Nussbaum, however, expresses similar scepticism about aesthetic experience. Indeed, her essay 'Love's Knowledge' is preoccupied by the problem of scepticism: 'We said that the cataleptic impression can coexist with scepticism about the feelings of the other. In fact, it implies this scepticism. For on the cataleptic view an emotion can be known if and only if it can be vividly experienced. What you can't have you can't know. But the other's will, thoughts and feelings are, for Marcel, paradigmatic of that which cannot be had. They beckon to him out of Albertine's defiant, silent eyes at Balbec, a secret world closed to his will, a vast space his ambitious thoughts can never cover' (1990: 271). As Emmanuel Levinas has written: 'Proust's most profound lesson, if poetry can contain lessons, consists in situating reality in a relation with something which for ever remains other, with the Other as absence and mystery, in rediscovering this relation in the very intimacy of the "I"' (1989: 163). For Levinas, 'I am therefore necessary to justice, as responsible beyond every limit fixed by an objective law' (1969: 245). The 'I' is that without which the other and, in particular, the other of history is lost. Nussbaum concludes her discussion of love's knowledge and literature with the observation that 'it was philosophy, and not the story, that showed us the boundaries and limits of the stories' (1990: 283). It is 'perhaps in the attentive – or I might even (too naively?) say loving – conversation of philosophy and literature with one another we could hope to find, occasionally, mysterious and incomplete, in some moments not governed by the watch, some analogue of the deliberate fall, the aim for grace' (1990: 284).

The Past in the Present

In an attempt to read *Hidden* through the lens of 'trauma theory', Guy Austin describes what he sees as 'the return of the body, of emotion and potentially also of politics, to the domain of theory from whence these concerns had been exiled by deconstruction' (2007: 530). Yet in order to think through the role of aesthetic experience for a subjectivity, at risk, 'at a moment of danger' in history, I have already turned to the work of Emmanuel Levinas, whose philosophy was so central to the thinking of Jacques Derrida. Levinas's 1974 text *Otherwise than Being or Beyond Essence* is dedicated to 'the memory of those who were closest among the six million assassinated by the National Socialists, and of the millions of all confessions and all nations, victims of the same hatred of the other man, the same anti-semitism' (1981: n.p.).[10] There is a visceral emphasis on sensibility in Levinas's work. In his 1972 text 'Truth of Disclosure and Truth of Testimony', Levinas describes the experience of our radical responsibility towards 'the Other' as an alienation in 'the depths of' identity: '*The soul is the other within me*, a sickness of identity; its being out of phase, its diachrony, gasping, shuddering ... A sensibility perhaps, coming back to the for-the-other of maternity ... A subjectivity of human flesh and blood more passive in its extradition to the other than the passivity of the effect in a causal chain' (1996a: 102). Subjectivity in Levinas's work is described in terms of 'vulnerability, exposure to outrage, to wounding' and, importantly, as a 'trauma of accusation suffered by a hostage to the point of persecution' (1996b: 121).

Levinas's work is an attempted renewal of philosophy in the face and in the aftermath of horror, in which philosophy is redefined as 'the wisdom of love at the service of love' (1981: 162). Levinas's work seeks to move beyond phenomenology as a philosophy of present perception, by introducing the haunting figure of the Other – entering into 'a kingdom of an invisible King' (1981: 52). Levinas may describe the ethics he posits in terms of an 'optics' (see Levinas's preface to his own work of 1969), but the face of the Other, which constitutes a breach in any totalising ontology by the epiphany of infinite time it prompts, is that which occupies an ambiguous position in the realm of the senses. In *Otherwise than Being*, Levinas seeks to think an abso-lute alterity, which throws the sovereign 'I' into question, introducing a diachrony – a double time – irreducible to any present or presence, which Sarah Cooper has expressed in terms of 'the ethical rip in the fabric of time' (2006: 28).

I wish to draw attention to the sense in which 'memory' – an image of the past – might be linked to sensibility, and also to ethics and politics understood after Levinas as a passivity coupled with activity (the response of our responsibility). I wish to consider memory as an experience of 'purposive shock', which might change my relationship, as an individual, with history. Hue-Tam Ho Tai has noted the increasingly significant role memory has played in historiography after Pierre Nora's *Lieux de mémoire* project, exploring the 'construction of the French past' through 'questions it poses about nation, nationalism, and national identity, as well as its implications for the conceptualisation of the relationship between history and memory' (Tai 2001). She cites also the impor-tance of scholarship in Holocaust studies, where 'memory – localised, diffuse, polysemic – is thus often seen as undermining nationalising, totalising projects'. Robert Eagle-stone's important work *The Holocaust and the Postmodern*, against historicism (which, he emphasises, 'is not the same as "not believing in the past"'), 'is a way of rejecting the claims of the discipline of history to the mastery of that past as if it were a science' (2004: 171). Eaglestone draws on Levinas's reconceptualisation (or rehabilitation) of 'truth' as 'witnessing' which, he argues, 'comes to be understood, in one context and series of debates, as memory' (ibid.). In thinking about memory as linked to sensibility, and so to the aesthetic, however, I am forced to ask, with Nussbaum, how to delimit the boundaries and limits of stories. As David Simpson states, in questioning the picture of our responsiveness to the past he finds in 'the culture of commemoration' post-9/11:

> Photographs of the dismembered, the dead, and the dying will not in them-selves change the terms of the culture of commemoration, whose nationalised or mediatised attributes have usually proved more powerful than any claims for common human sympathies or responses. But if any inquiry into these consequential matters is to be other than radically foreshortened, there is a need for more images and more words. (2006: 119)

Subject to Memory?

Hidden threads the past through the present, and it is brought to bear upon individuals and groups of individuals, intertwining guilt and commemoration. Into this web are various other threads of history woven and unravelled. On October 17 1961, the FLN

(*Front de Libération Nationale/National Liberation Front*) organised a demonstration in Paris against a curfew applicable to so-called 'French Muslims of Algeria'. It has been estimated that around 200 demonstrators were murdered that day by the Parisian police force, then under the leadership of Maurice Papon.[11] In the 1990s Papon was imprisoned following his conviction for crimes against humanity after an assessment of his role in the Vichy regime during World War Two. That the Parisian police force was, at the time of the Algerian war of independence, institutionally racist is a fact that has been addressed only relatively recently, and the process of commemorating the events of 1961 has been slow. Only in 1999 was Papon also convicted of an active role in what is now perceived to have been a brutal massacre of peaceful demonstrators. Some demonstrators were thrown from bridges after having been beaten unconscious, and bodies were seen floating in the Seine near the Quai d'Orfèvres, centre of the Parisian police force. Only on 17 October 2001 was a commemorative plaque placed on the Pont Saint-Michel in the centre of Paris although, as the number of dead is still under dispute, it is dedicated 'À la mémoire des nombreux Algériens tués lors de la sanglante repression de la manifestation pacifique du 17 octobre 1961'.

In what ways am I subject to memory? I might be subject to laws established in the service of memory. For example, the law of 12 October 2006 passed by the French Senate against any contestation of the Armenian genocide.[12] Law provides the means to inflect the picture of our responsiveness to the past. Bernard Dréano, however, has argued that this law 'feeds nationalisms' (2006) and, indeed, we have recently seen the political import of this particular question re-emerge (see Cornwell 2007). Dréano also refers to the now repealed law of 23 February 2005, by means of which law might have erased the memory of crimes committed during the Algerian war of independence, making the point that law can at times obstruct certain historical claims[13] – such as those made in the struggle for Turkey's recognition of the Armenian genocide. As Eric Heinze has commented, in another context, 'US law protects hate speech; France routinely punishes it. Yet, given the recent episodes of ethnic unrest in France … no one can seriously argue that its bans on hate speech have been more successful in promoting racial tolerance than American freedoms have' (2006).

Dréano has drawn out the connection between questions of historical memory and the politics of art in noting that 12 October 2006 was also the date on which Turkish writer Orhan Pamuk was awarded the Nobel Prize for Literature, dividing opinion in Turkey. Pamuk chose to comment on the murder, in 1915, of '30,000 Kurds' and 'a million Armenians' in an interview with Swiss magazine *Tages-Anzeiger*, at considerable personal risk. As he put it in his Nobel Lecture (in a different context), we are constantly reminded 'that writing and literature are intimately linked to a lack at the centre of our lives, and to our feelings of happiness and of guilt' (2006).

The Play's the Thing…

Haneke may not need to draw on the same resources of courage as Pamuk, but he has nonetheless been recognised, in the words of Mark Cousins, as 'the great disconcerter of European metropolitan elites' (2007: 225). It is clear that his work engages a particular group identity. Yet might it not be the case that an identification with the milieu of Georges and Anne (I am their spectatorial shadow) could be coupled with a masochistic enjoyment of guilt, a safe defusing of responsibility in what Levinas has called 'the aesthetic element'? A safe arena for the kind of hand-wringing that Paul Gilroy compares to 'shooting crabs in a barrel'? (2007).

'Why does the other concern me? What is Hecuba to me?' asks Levinas in *Otherwise than Being* (1981: 117), paraphrasing Hamlet's 'What's Hecuba to him, or he to her,/That he should weep for her?', soliloquised in contemplation of the performance of his beloved player and the possibility that,

'The play's the thing
Wherein I'll catch the conscience of the King.'

In his 1948 essay 'Reality and its Shadow', Levinas questions the role of art with respect to our capacity to do justice to the Other, particularly by describing the captivating effect of the 'aesthetic'. For Levinas, 'the aesthetic element' is one of 'sensation': 'Sensation is not a residue of perception, but has a function of its own – the hold that an image has over us, a function of rhythm' (1989b: 134). 'Rhythm represents a unique situation where we cannot speak of consent, assumption, initiative or freedom, because the subject is caught up and carried away by it. The subject is part of its own representation. It is so not even despite itself, for in rhythm there is no longer a oneself, but rather a sort of passage from oneself to anonymity' (1989b: 133). In a text from 1958, Martin Buber's 'I-Thou' relation is said to be revealed in what Buber called '*Umfassung*' – 'the embrace'. Levinas is keen to distinguish this relation from 'the psychological phenomenon' of '*Einfühlung*' – 'empathy' – where the 'subject puts itself completely in the other's place, thus forgetting itself' (1989c: 68). On the contrary, '*Umfassung*' is described as a relation wherein 'the I sharply maintains its active reality' (ibid.). Similarly, in 'Reality and its Shadow', against the implications of aesthetics as potentially absorbing, Levinas pitches a concept of 'criticism' as that which might introduce the time of 'the Other' into what Levinas calls the 'between time' of art – which he describes as 'inhuman' and 'monstrous'. For Levinas, the 'most lucid writer finds himself in the world bewitched by his images' yet the 'most forewarned, the most lucid writer none the less plays the fool' (1989b: 142 – 43). Haneke could be seen to play the knowing and silent fool to the history *Hidden* engages – implicating the Western spectator (myself and others) in this history. Yet any straightforward spectatorial identification has been complicated throughout Haneke's oeuvre.

In *The Drowned and the Saved*, Primo Levi, who survived the genocide perpetrated by the Nazis and imprisonment at Auschwitz, writes about an encounter with a young schoolboy who 'asked me the obligatory question: "But how come you didn't escape?"' (Levi 1989, cited by Eaglestone 2004: 19). As Robert Eaglestone points out, 'used to romantic prison fictions, the boy identifies himself with the captive Levi and imagines a storybook escape' (2004: 20). Levi writes that he 'would like to erect a dyke against' the trend towards a representation of the experience of the camps that might encourage any form of identification. It is:

part of our difficulty or inability to perceive the experience of others, which is all the more pronounced the further these experiences are from ours in time, space or quality. We are prone to assimilate them to those related ones, as though the hunger in Auschwitz were the same as that of someone who has skipped a meal, or as though escape from Treblinka were similar to an escape from any ordinary gaol. (Cited in Eaglestone 2004: 22)

I remember here my desire for the tortured family in *Funny Games* (1997) to escape, and the feeling of spectatorial humiliation I experienced when they inevitably failed to do so. Haneke complicates identification, and I am caught out in my movement between self and other, across a boundary as fragile as the limits of stories.

Libby Saxton's work on filmic representation offers an invaluable resource for thinking through the sense in which *Hidden* immediately solicits and then throws into question the role of the spectator. Saxton has, for example, argued that, during *Hidden's* opening sequence, 'the absence of a counter-shot disrupts the mechanisms through which cinema habitually sutures its spectators seamlessly into its diegetic fictions, preventing us from making sense of the space outside the frame' (2008: 106). This observation is part of an analysis of the various absences or non-representations within Haneke's oeuvre.[14] Haneke's aesthetic construction offers experiences which are not simply alienating, and certainly not solipsistic – but solitary. In *Hidden*, we, as spectators, or again, I, in my singular responsibility, suddenly and shockingly encounter that which Simon Critchley describes as 'radically resistant to the order of representation' (1997: 26): death, in the form of a suicide. In its representation of absence, the absolute silence of Majid's death, *Hidden* could be seen to announce the duality which Levinas describes as developing from an experience of an other's death to the relation with the irreducible Other (see Levinas 1983: 20) – opening 'the ethical rip in the fabric of time'. It gives us this time, out of joint. In *Hidden*, the Other is eventually hidden – and this absence is a haunting.

Levinas writes, 'the self is through and through a hostage, older than the ego, prior to principles. What is at stake for the self, in its being, is not to be. Beyond egoism and altruism it is the religiosity of the self' (1981: 117). In the *Discourse on Inequality* Jean-Jacques Rousseau famously argues that 'human governments need a basis more solid than reason alone' (1994: 77) and that 'if I am obligated to do no evil to my fellow man, it is less because he is a rational being than because he is a sentient being' (1994: 2). Yet I seek to clarify, as Howard Caygill has done, that *Otherwise than Being*, despite describing a subjectivity bound to the Other in sensibility, does not posit subjectivity as 'subject to heteronomy' (2002: 148). Levinas looks towards the 'possibility of finding, anachronously, the order in the obedience itself, and of receiving the order out of oneself, this reverting of heteronomy into autonomy, is the very way the Infinite [takes place]' (1981: 148 – translation modified by the author).[15] The 'I' is that without which the other is lost. Thus, I would suggest, there is an echo of Benjamin's 'man singled out by history at a moment of danger' in Levinas's particular messianism: 'Messianism is therefore not the certainty of the coming of a man who stops History. It is my power to bear the suffering of all. It is the moment when I recognise this power and my universal responsibility' (1990a: 90). Levinas's philosophy, as with our thinking after watching *Hidden*, does not end with, but begins by placing 'emotion or anguish at the heart of consciousness' (2000: 211).

Notes
Unless otherwise stated, all translations are by the author.

1   As Colin Davis points out, the '*il y a* names what Levinas calls "existing without existents [*un exister sans existant*]": an anonymous, impersonal *existing* (the verbal form is important here) before the constitution of the individuated human subject' (1996: 23; emphasis in original).

2   Insomnia is a central part of Levinas's account of 'hypostasis' or what Davis calls 'the constitution of the individuated human subject' as described in *De l'existence à l'existant* (Levinas 1963). In the series of lectures *God and Onto-theo-logy* (delivered between 1975–76, Sorbonne, Paris) Levinas, in a lecture entitled 'In Praise of Insomnia', compared his 'meta-category' of insomnia to 'the Cartesian idea of the infinite, in which the cogito bursts under the impact of something it cannot contain' (2000: 212).

3   In a footnote (see 1995: 265), Nussbaum explains that, '"Cataleptic" is the Greek *katalēptikē*, an adjective from the verb *katalambanein*, "apprehend", "grasp", "firmly grasp". It is probably active rather than passive: "apprehensive", "firmly grasping (reality)".'

4   Citing E. Ann Kaplan (2005), Guy Austin writes, 'Kaplan establishes the concept of the "vicarious trauma" experienced by the reader or the viewer when confronted with trauma narratives, and seeks to distinguish between the effect of witnessing, which "involves not just empathy and motivation to help, but understanding of the structure of injustice", and what she terms the "empty empathy", which tends to be elicited by images of suffering provided without a context or background knowledge' (2007: 530). This distinction will be pertinent to my discussion of Emmanuel Levinas's thoughts on 'the aesthetic element'.

5   To see the painting by Poussin that Rose is discussing, visit: http://www.liverpool-museums.org.uk/walker/collections/17c/poussin.asp. In *Antigone's Claim*, Judith Butler asks whether 'Antigone herself might be made into a representative for a certain kind of feminist politics' (2000: 2).

6   I shadow the positions of Georges and Anne at the outset of the film. I share in their point of view. Eventually, Georges' meeting with Majid is re-played on their television screen – his lying revealed to Anne in their family home. The angle of filming in the first encounter between Georges and Majid is paralleled in the framing of Majid's suicide. This leaves me asking: will this footage ever find its way into the wider world?

7   I assume that readers will feel familiar with this language, as Haneke seems to do when Georges suggests that Anne's distress (caused by his unwillingness to share his suspicions about Majid) is the reaction sought by Majid, whom he assumes

to be responsible for sending the videos and drawings which, in Anne's words, 'terrorise' them. In the face of terror, we are supposed to 'keep calm and carry on' – whereas Anne is perhaps representative of many in wanting to interrogate the situation more thoroughly.

8   As Peter de Bolla points out in an abstract of his highly pertinent scholarship: 'Over the last twenty years or so it has become a commonplace in discussions of "aesthetics" or of "art" in the most general sense to note that the term "aesthetics" was only very recently invented by Alexander Baumgarten in 1735, where it appears in his *Meditationes philosophicae de nonnullis ad poema pertinentibus*. But the force of this observation in regard to the relative youth of the concept is rarely, if ever, commented upon. As many philosophers and critics have pointed out, Baumgarten's use of the term was not primarily angled at what today might be unproblematically called "artworks" – say, paintings in the European grand master tradition – since his new kind of investigation was to be a "science of sensual recognition", that is, a general inquiry into how we come to know the world from the evidence of our senses' (2002: 19).

9   Simpson refers particularly to Eagleton (2002); see also Eagleton (2003).

10 In the autobiographical text 'Signature' Levinas writes that his intellectual 'biography' 'is dominated by the presentiment [note here the emphasis on sentience] and the memory of the Nazi horror' (1990b: 291).

11 I draw here on the work of historian Jean-Luc Einaudi. See, for example, Einaudi and Kagan (2001).

12 See http://www.senat.fr/leg/ppl06-020.html

13 For an initial reaction to the repealed law of 23 February 2005, see Liauzu (2005).

14 Catherine Wheatley (2006a), for example, has called attention to the 'unseen obscene' in *La Pianiste* (*The Piano Teacher*, 2001), and Saxton has suggested that, also in *The Piano Teacher*, 'Erika's face is less a window on her soul than a mask which conceals it from sight, or a blank screen which, like so many of Haneke's images, solicits the spectator's projections' (2008: 84). See also Saxton (2007).

15 The Infinite is here to be understood as the epiphany of the irreducible alterity of the Other – and in terms of ethics.

References

Austin, G. (2007) 'Drawing Trauma: Visual Testimony in *Caché* and *J'ai 8 Ans*', *Screen*, 48, 4, 529–36.

BBC News (2006) 'Triple Suicide at Guantanamo Camp'. On-line. Available at: http://news.bbc.co.uk/1/hi/world/americas/5068228.stm (accessed 11 June 2006).

Benjamin, W. (1999 [1940]) 'Theses on the Philosophy of History', in *Illuminations*. Trans. H. Zorn. London: Pimlico, 245–55.

Bolla, P. de. (2002) 'Towards the Materiality of Aesthetic Experience', *Diacritics*, 32, 1, 19–37.

Butler, J. (2000) *Antigone's Claim: Kinship between Life and Death*. New York: Columbia University Press.

Caygill, H. (2002) *Levinas and the Political*. London and New York: Routledge.

Cooper, S. (2006) *Selfless Cinema? Ethics and French Documentary*. London: Legenda.

Cornwell, R. (2007) 'Bush and Congress Dispute Armenian "Genocide" Status', *Independent*, 11 October. On-line. Available at: http://www.independent.co.uk/news/world/americas/bush-and-congress-dispute-armenian-genocide-status-394621.html (accessed 11 October 2007).

Cousins, M. (2007) 'After the end: word of mouth and *Caché*', *Screen*, 48, 2, 223–6.

Critchley, S. (1997) *Very Little … Almost Nothing: Death, Philosophy, Literature*. London: Routledge.

Davis, C. (1996) *Levinas: An Introduction*. Cambridge: Polity.

Dréano, B. (2006) 'Négation Du Génocide Arménien: Cette Loi Alimente Les Nationalismes', *Politis*, 922, 19 October. On-line. Available at: http://turquieeuropeenne.eu/article1561.html (accessed 19 October 2006).

Eaglestone, R. (2004) *The Holocaust and the Postmodern*. Oxford and New York: Oxford University Press.

Eagleton, T. (2002) *Sweet Violence: The Idea of the Tragic*. Oxford: Blackwell.

_____ (2003) *After Theory*. New York: Basic Books.

Einaudi, J.-L. and É. Kagan (2001) *17 Octobre 1961*. Arles: Actes Sud/Solin.

Gilroy, P. (2007) 'Shooting crabs in a barrel', *Screen*, 48, 2, 233–5.

Heinze, E. (2006) 'Self-Righteous Editors', *London Review of Books*, 28, 16, 17 August. On-line. Available at: http://www.lrb.co.uk/v28/n16/letters.html (accessed 26 March 2009).

Kaplan, E. Ann (2005) *Trauma Culture. The Politics of Terror and Loss in Media and Literature*. New Brunswick, NJ: Rutgers University Press.

Levi, P. (1989) *The Drowned and the Saved*. Trans. R. Rosenthal. London: Abacus.

Levinas, E. (1963) *De l'existence à l'existant*. Paris: Vrin.

_____ (1969) *Totality and Infinity: An Essay on Exteriority*. Trans. A. Lingis. Pittsburgh: Duquesne University Press.

_____ (1978) *Existence and Existents*. Trans. A. Lingis. The Hague: Martinus Nijhoff.

_____ (1981) *Otherwise than Being or Beyond Essence*. Trans. A. Lingis. Pittsburgh: Duquesne University Press.

_____ (1983) *Le Temps et l'autre*. Paris: Quadrige Grands Textes.

_____ (1989a [1947]) 'The other in Proust', trans. S. Hand, in S. Hand (ed.) *The Levinas Reader*, Oxford: Blackwell, 160–5.

_____ (1989b [1948]) 'Reality and Its Shadow', trans. A. Lingis, in S. Hand (ed.) *The Levinas Reader*, Oxford: Blackwell, 129–43.

_____ (1989c [1963]) 'Martin Buber and the Theory of Knowledge', trans. S. Hand, in S. Hand (ed.) *The Levinas Reader*, Oxford: Blackwell, 59–74.

_____ (1990a [1963]) 'Messianic Texts', trans. S. Hand, in *Difficult Freedom*. Baltimore: The Johns Hopkins University Press, 59–95.

_____ (1990b [1963]) 'Signature', trans. S. Hand, in *Difficult Freedom*. Baltimore: The Johns Hopkins University Press, 289–95.

_____ (1996a [1972]) 'Truth of Disclosure and Truth of Testimony', trans. I. MacDonald and S. Critchley, in S. Critchley, R. Bernasconi and A. T. Peperzak (eds) *Basic Philosophical Writings*. Bloomington and Indianapolis: Indiana University Press, 98–107.

_____ (1996b [1970]) 'Essence and Disinterestedness', trans. A. Lingis, with revisions by S. Critchley and A. T. Peperzak, in S. Critchley, R. Bernasconi and A. T. Peperzak (eds) *Basic Philosophical Writings*. Bloomington and Indianapolis: Indiana University Press, 109–27.

_____ (2000) *God, Death and Time*. Trans. B. Bergo. Stanford: Stanford University Press.

Liauzu, C. (2005) 'Une loi contre l'histoire', *Le Monde diplomatique*, April. On-line. Available at: http://www.monde-diplomatique.fr/2005/04/LIAUZU/12080 (accessed 10 October 2008).

Nussbaum, M. (1990) 'Love's Knowledge', in *Love's Knowledge: Essays on Philosophy and Literature*. Oxford; New York: Oxford University Press, 261–85.

Pamuk, O. (2006) 'My Father's Suitcase', Nobel Prize Lecture. On-line. Available at: http://nobelprize.org/nobel_prizes/literature/laureates/2006/pamuk-lecture_en.html (accessed 22 November 2008).

Rose, G. (1996) *Mourning Becomes the Law: Philosophy and Representation*. Cambridge: Cambridge University Press.

Rousseau, J.-J. (1994) *Discourse on Inequality*. Trans. F. Philip. Oxford and New York: Oxford University Press.

Saxton, L. (2007) 'Secrets and Revelations: Off-Screen Space in Michael Haneke's *Caché*', *Studies in French Cinema*, 7, 1, 5–17.

_____ (2008) 'Close Encounters with Distant Suffering: Michael Haneke's Disarming Visions', in K. Ince (ed.) *Five Directors: Auteurism from Assayas to Ozon*. Manchester: Manchester University Press, 84–111.

Simpson, D. (2006) *9/11: The Culture of Commemoration*. Chicago and London: University of Chicago Press.

Sontag, S. (2003) *Regarding the Pain of Others*. New York: Farrar, Straus and Giroux.

Tai, H.-T. H. (2001) 'Remembered Realms: Pierre Nora and French National Memory', *American Historical Review*, 106, 3. On-line. Available at: http://www.historycooperative.org/journals/ahr/106.3/ah000906.html (accessed 26 March 2009).

Wheatley, C. (2006a) 'Unseen/Obscene: The (Non) Framing of the Sexual Act in Michael Haneke's *La Pianiste*', in M. Seabrook, A. Lewis, L. Bolton and G. Kimber (eds) *Framed!* London: Peter Lang, 127–44.

CHAPTER NINETEEN

Digital Cinema and the 'Schizophrenic' Image: The Case of Michael Haneke's Hidden

Ricardo Domizio

In cultural and critical circles the dramatic voices proclaiming the more far-reaching effects of the digital 'revolution' have died down and the 'digital creep' into all areas of media and cultural production is all but complete. In the case of cinema, however, despite the fact that digital methods dominate certain aspects of film production, and continue to make inroads into distribution and exhibition, predictions about the 'death of cinema' now seem premature. Interestingly, as we approach the end of the first decade of the new millennium, high-end cinema production has been remarkably resilient in clinging to old 'analogue' technologies of celluloid-based principle photography. Whether this is to do with a 'rational' calculation regarding image resolution versus cost, or more to do with a preference based on filmmakers' 'faith' with any putative metaphysical quality of film, time will tell. A few big-name directors, like Michael Mann, Abbas Kiarostami and David Lynch, have 'crossed over' to digital filming, whilst a few more, like Michael Winterbottom and Mike Figgis, actively celebrate new media and thrive on the 'ethics' and potential of the digital camera. Michael Haneke's first digital production, *Caché* (*Hidden*, 2005), took the Best Director Award at the Cannes Film Festival in its year of release. Although I will view *Hidden* as an index of the passage from film to digital cinematography it is by no means a principled move on the part of the filmmaker – for the remake of his 1997 film *Funny Games* (*Funny Games U.S.*, 2007) Haneke returned to 35mm film stock.[1] Even so, the 'digitality' of *Hidden* is appropriate enough for a film which, as we shall see, stages the cultural apprehension surrounding the ubiquity of images and their 'schizophrenia' in the digital era.

Haneke's reputation has grown as a 'cerebral' or philosophical film director, exploring some defining themes of contemporary Western European society and embedding his films with qualities that are unmistakeably 'cinematic' and, at the same time, 'conceptual'. The typical Haneke film exhibits a distinctive self-consciousness in the cinematic image and demands a certain recognition of our – that is, the specta-tor's – implication in the narrative conundrums, which are variously psychological, political and philosophical. At the same time his filmmaking counters, or rather criti-cally engages, certain aspects of contemporary 'entertainment' cinema, especially as it pertains to the pre-packaged representation of physical and psychological violence. In presenting a cinema of questions rather than answers, a Haneke film is never an 'easy ride'. This perception of the director – as setting a challenge to 'cinema', but also to politics and philosophy – is bolstered by the various interviews Haneke has given where he voices his recurrent concerns about the 'dishonesty' of narrative cinema, the ethics of screen violence, and more generally on the key philosophical theme of the void between a ubiquitous mediascape of 'representation' and an intractable 'reality'. But the earnest thematics of his films are just one dimension of his rejection of the 'mainstream'. Visually, Haneke has developed a stylistic economy that articulates his oppositional stance in a pared down, 'glacial' aesthetic, at odds with most 'embodied' filmmaking today, and instead recalling a fascination with the 'metaphysics of the image', similar to modernist auteurs like Michaelangelo Antonioni or Yasujirō Ozu. Like the modernists, Haneke's conceptual investment into the image-structure of his films belie their typically restrained formal qualities, characterised in visual terms by long takes, a 'listless', observational camera and a tendency towards a blue tonal palette that lends the image the faint edge of crystalline sharpness and 'objective' distance. Like the art cinema auteurs, then, Haneke's is a cinema of thought, one that, even as it in many ways relies on 'genre' cinema, defies conventional approaches and responses to the cinematic object. And it is precisely Haneke's cool but meticulous attention to the cinematic image – in terms of both cultural artefact and conceptual tool – that makes *Hidden* a vital text in the emerging canon of 'digital cinema'. My aim, therefore, is to use Haneke's work to explore and to theorise the move from film to digital in terms of the constitution and deployment of the cinematic image.

At stake here is not a new ontology of film as such, but a recognition that under the transformational law of digital media the image has no centre, in terms of 'iden-tity', and no limits, in terms of 'effects'. We are witnessing more than the expansion of a new ubiquitous 'mediascape' of images, but the creation of a world of immanence of visual forms that is both deprivileging and liberatory: deprivileging in the removal of any hierarchy or 'representational function' in the image; liberatory in that, despite the levelling process described, a new kind of politics, prior to 'narrative' or 'genre', is released in the image. I take *Hidden* to be an example of a film that in its visual constitution establishes its own relation to 'digitality' and, further, is able to offer a new way of thinking about 'digital cinema' and the digital moving image generally. The film's standing as a text in which the interplay of images takes on a central and disturbing role is without doubt. But reading *Hidden* against two films that precede it in Haneke's oeuvre, namely *Benny's Video* (1992) and *Funny Games*, proves to be effective in revealing the change in the constitution and deployment of the cinematic image from pre-digital to digital cinema. Precisely because in each of these works Haneke employs a distinct visual methodology that is strictly related to their respective narrative strategems, the differences in the image-matrix of the films becomes apparent. In *Benny's Video* the visual methodology relies on an image that is fetishised through a distinction between the 'smooth' cinematic image of the diegetic world and the 'rough' electronic media of television, home movies and trash-video rentals; in *Funny Games* it lurks in a narrative image that feeds the spectator's appetite for gratuitous thriller sensations, only for it to 'bite back'; in both these films the textuality of the image in some way seeks to separate itself out as something other than purely or naïvely cinematic. In turning his thematic eye back onto the commodified effects of the cinematic image itself, the films become metacinematic. Finally, in *Hidden* we have perhaps the most metacinematic film of all but, in contrast with the previous, one whose images no longer distinguish themselves as something 'other'. On the contrary, the images in this film are not abstracted from some master-plan, but are internal to its dynamic, seeming to emerge logically, if not organically, from the same visual ground. This is not to say we have a singular or unitary articulation of the image; we have in fact a menagerie of visions: a veritable merry-go-round of images, provocative and banal, technologically produced and 'primitive', concrete and unanchored – images that constantly feedback to alter our understanding of the film and our relationship to what we are seeing. Whereas in *Benny's Video* and *Funny Games* the particular deployment of the cinematic image is part of the conceit (forcing us to recognise its separateness from 'reality'), in *Hidden*, by contrast, the issue of the image is not a narrative 'device' but is rather subsumed into the fabric of the film, giving substance to the claim that in *Hidden* there is no longer an 'outside' to the image.

What differentiates *Hidden* from these previous films, then, is not its elevation of the image itself to a concrete problematic of the film – the issue of where images 'come from' is at the heart of *Hidden*'s mystery – rather it is the treatment of the visual domain as immanent to both the world of the film and to its aesthetic construction. This 'seamlessness' of form and content can, of course, be viewed as part of the developmental arc of authorial style, but I want to look at this immanence as a particularly incisive indicator of change more generally in our image culture, that is as an effect of the move from analogue to digital cinema. Although, in making *Hidden*, Haneke has not overtly expressed any wider ambition to explore the possibilities of digital filmmaking or to test out the conditions specific to digital cinema, his intrinsic fascination with the cinematic image as such, together with the trace of 'digitality' residing in the film's structure, make it something of a model, conscious or not, for digital cinema.

Although already his fourth feature film, *Funny Games* was the first to garner a wide international reputation for Haneke and, later, achieve something of a critical standing itself despite, or perhaps because of, the considerable controversy that issued in its wake. The initial furore over the film was due to what was widely reported as an audacious, not to say 'dictatorial', use of violence. Dictatorial not in the sense of the film's gleeful cat-and-mouse manipulation of audience expectations, but rather in appearing to use cinematic violence as a weapon against the naïve or implicated spectator, reversing the thriller-pleasure cathexis and forcing the audience to confront the base 'logic' of their own desires. The plot revolves around two innocent-looking, clean-cut young men who, for no apparent reason (and the pointlessness is partly the point), engage in the unremitting and sadistic brutalisation of an archetypal bourgeois family in their isolated holiday home. The torture inflicted on the unsuspecting family is calculated to build, layer upon layer, into an excruciating offering to the horror-thriller appetite that touches the very limit-point of genre. But its ultimately dissatisfying, unredemptive ending was seen by most as a contemptuous (and unnecessary) assault on the spectator. In refusing to give the audience 'what they want' (or perhaps in giving them too much?) Haneke was deemed to have revoked the contract between director and spectator and to have rewritten generic codes unilaterally.

One of the indicators of this genre-breaking urge is when the putative leader of the assailants, Paul (Arno Frisch), turns towards the camera and, in a Brechtian break with narrative transparancy, teases the audience with the same kind of 'games' that he uses against his in-film victims. Near the end of the film Paul turns to us to ask: 'We haven't reached feature-film length yet … You want a real ending with plausible plot development, don't you?' This playing with spectator knowledge and expectations of the thriller genre breaks the solipsistic flow and throws the film into a critical reflection on genre. But this rhetorical 'performance' of the cinematic image is more than a spurious appendage or an empty ruse. On the contrary, it is the very point of the film. In both a formally experimental and confrontational sense, the manipulation of the thriller-image is intended to draw out the lines of cinematic terror to their unwelcome but logical conclusion, and thus to create a formal point zero for the genre. The purpose in *Funny Games* is not to provide a more 'honest' narrative, but rather to critique the normative assumptions and consumption of the thriller-image by using the cinematic image against itself. Haneke is metaphorically saying: 'this is what you want … go on then, have it.'

If we go back to *Benny's Video* we find that Haneke had already thematised the media-mediated violence and the dangers inherent in the position of passive or absorbed spectatorship. We recall that Benny (Arno Frisch), the withdrawn and catatonic teenage anti-hero is himself utterly seduced by the video image to the point where the distinction between reality and representation is in danger of collapsing completely (only to be re-established at a higher, 'textual' level). Benny is not only a consumer of the image in the form of the rented video-trash that he watches daily, he is also a producer in the sense that he avidly films the prosaic and empty 'reality' that comes within the orbit of his reclusive existence. From his production centre of a bedroom, the cameras are permanently recording his surroundings. Benny even prefers the view from his bedroom window via the video monitor rather than through 'unmediated' phenomenological perception, thus unmasking a voyeuristic fascination that, for many, defines the cinematic image itself. Over and above this 'everyday' footage, however, Benny's favourite video is his own recording of the killing of a pig shot on his video-8 camera at a local farm. The video bears the usual hallmarks of

amateur 'home-video' – jerky hand-held camera, grainy, low-quality image, a vora-
cious 'consumption' of the visual object. Thus, a gulf in representation exists between
the video image supposedly shot by Benny and the pristine smoothness of the diegesis
directed by Haneke. This distinction between the two kinds of image is more than
a device. Benny is captivated by the pig footage and constantly rewinds and replays
the death throes of the animal in slow-motion, thus hinting at a latent pathology in
his character. But Haneke insists that this 'illicit' craving for disturbing and violent
imagery is not just a question of personal psychology, it is linked to a much wider and
socially sanctioned concatenation of violent apparitions that exists in the commodified
'mediascape': images of war and violence in the television news bulletins that pervade
the family home, and the 'video nasties' that Benny freely rents from his local video
shop. Not only immersed in, but also subsumed by imagistic violence, Benny finds
that the only taste of 'reality' is in actually performing the pig-killing act he is so captivated by, only this time on a human subject. In the film's most disturbing scene we
witness (on Benny's video monitor, naturally) his killing of a girl that he opportunisti-
cally meets outside the video shop and invites back to his room. But rather than seeing
the killing directly, we hear the messy and prolonged death of the girl, for the actual
murderous act is slightly to one side of the locked-off video camera. After the killing,
Benny goes back to his listless existence, with only nominal signs of consciousness of
the magnitude of his actions. For Benny, the worlds of reality and representation are
blurred to say the least. But in keeping the two levels discrete, Haneke forces the spectator to perceive and recognise the distinction between the debased and edgy 'heat' of
electronic representation and the coolness of filmed reality. The cinematic image here
is deployed effectively as a critique of the 'lower forms' of moving-image culture and
Haneke trusts that we recognise the dangers of entrapment and stick to the 'right side'
of the divide.

Funny Games removes the distancing layer of narrative – no longer are we buffered
from the engulfing violence of the mediascape as we are in *Benny's Video*, and no longer
are we offered a choice between one type of image and another. The cinematic image is
now more 'unitary' but no less contrived. A combination of direct address-to-camera
and the self-consciousness of an overly plot-driven narrative is enough to reveal the
'funny games' being played not only on our despairing family, but on the spectator as
well. However, the most audacious 'trick' purveyed by Haneke is the moment near the
end of the film where the by now desperate and dishevelled mother Anna (Susanne
Lothar) snatches a shot-gun from the living room coffee table and lets one of the
gruesome assailants, Peter (Frank Giering), have it. Even as the audience is about to
applaud the just deserts meted out to the evil-doers and look forward with relief to the
narrative 'pay-back', Paul grabs the video remote control from the sofa and hits rewind.
In a moment of jaw-dropping conceit the film image stops dead and spools backwards
to the point before Anna reaches for the gun, and then commences normal 'playback',
only this time (in an 'alternative' ending) Paul thwarts her attempt to snatch the gun.
To deny the audience such a staple feature of 'final girl' antics is one thing but the
hurling of the film from any pretence of diegetic verisimilitude by such a 'trick' is
quite another.[2] In this flagrant violation of the codes of genre cinema, or in rupturing

the phenomenological 'integrity' of the film, Haneke first reveals, and then takes to an extreme conclusion, the clichés, the 'funny games', that are usually played on us by cinematic narrative and, by extension, other media.

In setting many of his narratives in the very seat of the bourgeois family (read: white, Western) Haneke is claiming a representative function for these films, a 'politics' if you will. The archetypal middle-class family unit – the embodiment of 'respectable' society for centre-right social democratic parties – is bracketed off and tested *in extremis*, subjected to violent assault from the 'outside'. But more than an attack on the institution of the nuclear family, the films represent a more subtle instruction on the uses and effects of the cinematic image itself. In *Benny's Video* the home video aesthetic is linked to the trash-video culture that Benny consumes every day and contrasted with the 'professional' cinematic image that frames it. And in *Funny Games*, too, we can think of the narrative 'devices' – the wink-to-camera, the 'unkind' rewind – as constituting a type of cinematic image, one that has the all-too obvious signs of directorial control. In both films, then, Haneke is mobilising the film image in a discernibly 'external' way. That is, there is a continual process of establishing a putative 'nomalised' cinematic image in relation to its 'other' (the home video, the video nasty, the overwrought genre-image). This 'externality' of visual form is used to enable a 'spectator-consciousness', a self-awareness of the spectator-as-consumer, of genre, of pleasure, of the seductiveness of cinematic violence. The feeling, though, is of an overtly 'constructed' transparency or, to put it another way, a particular 'programmatic' and enforced deployment of images, a doxa where diverse image-types are brought self-consciously into dissonance.

In *Hidden* Haneke replays the themes of the shattering of bourgeois complacency and self-righteousness and, as in *Benny's Video* and *Funny Games*, this shattering takes the form of a threat to the archetypal nuclear family: Mama, Papa and young teenage son. But where the earlier films conjure up their threat from the 'outside', in *Hidden* the threat is envisioned as something that is already immanent to the family, 'hidden' within the childhood history of the father figure. Correspondingly, the visual aesthetic of the film sees not the external application of cinematic 'device' but rather the 'self-generation' of a quiet succession of image-types that are driven by an autonomous logic which is internal to the movement of its narrative. The expressive capacity of the film is not dictated, as in the earlier films, by the linearity of genre, plot or polemic. Rather, it can be read in aesthetic terms as a circularity in the flow of images, an internal 'productiveness' of film form or, in other words, as a function of the 'digitality' of the cinematic image.

It is clear from the beginning that *Hidden* is founded upon a different regime of cinematic image than the earlier works, and correspondingly calls for an altered spectator response. The famous first shot of the film provides a taste of things to come: an image which is already more seeded in its openness and ambiguity than the typical establishing shot. The 'unremarkableness' of the image is the first thing to remark upon: a long shot of an apartment from the other side of a quiet residential street. Nothing happens, which is to say, nothing *cinematically* happens: a man walks past the field of vision, a woman eventually leaves the apartment, a cyclist glides by, the faint sound of distant traffic and bird calls is heard. The shot is held for far too long, is far too static and is far too 'pedestrian' in framing and feel, eventually assuming a distorting and disorientating effect rather than an establishing one. After a few minutes a man speaks over the image, then a woman, and suddenly the previously detached camera gaze cuts to a much more recognisably 'cinematic' shot following a character that we later learn is the nominal head of our family, Georges (Daniel Auteuil), and mobilising the beginnings of our identification with him. Haneke then cuts back to the same static opening shot of the street and we finally realise that we are watching a second-order representation, a film-within-a-film – confirmed when the image fast-forwards, rewinds and then pauses. This opening shot in fact shows the contents of an anonymous videotape sent to our archetypal bourgeois family – for what purpose remains unclear throughout the film.

For a director as concerned with the issue of 'representation' as Haneke, the motif of the film-within-a-film is something of a defining problematic for cinema, and one that he returns to in many of his films. In *Benny's Video*, for instance, Benny's video-recordings of 'life' outside of his bedroom window denote the banality of representing 'reality' and recall a 'surveillance' aesthetic which is similar to the opening of *Hidden*. Where the two films differ, however, is that in *Hidden* this second-order representation is not 'framed' within the master-representation. In *Benny's Video* Haneke is always careful to indicate the difference between film world and 'representation' (for example, video, television). The effect of this is to always privilege the pristine image of the diegesis (filmed on 35mm film stock) with respect to the compromised video/television image. Instead, in *Hidden*, this visual difference is eliminated: the single frame and the singular image contain both orders of representation. There is no distinction aesthetically, or in terms of 'status', between the diegesis and the videotaped footage contained within it. In terms of the image, the two phenomenological layers collapse into one seamless layer. Later we are foxed by the same technique, suddenly becoming aware that what we are watching is, again, a videotaped image 'within' the diegetic world. The succession of familiar framings, repeated compositions or recurring images succeeds in undermining our confidence that any image in the film contains the truth it appears to show. Time and again we have the same interweaving of the orders of representation where the videotape, reveries, memories, pictures, repetitions, all assume the form of diegetic reality only to flip into another state that leaks back to destabilise the distinction between 'being' and 'representation'. This is quite different to the image-strategies in *Benny's Video* and *Funny Games*, where the disconcerting image is overdetermined, which is to say, forced into its bifurcated condition or its outright fakeness.

How can we think this change in Haneke's work from construction to immanence? Or, put another way, how can we account for the radical ambiguity of the image as something that is internal to its constitution, rather than imposed from the outside? One way to understand such a change is to place it within an empirical analysis of the recent history of image culture more generally, that is, within the context of the digital era. As mentioned above, *Hidden* is Haneke's first digital film and I believe the newfound instability in the cinematic image can be attributed to the workings of 'digitality'. This is not a reductive move in the sense of predicating a new visual alterity on 'technological effect'. Rather it is an attempt to theorise the inestimable change in methods, procedures and uses of images in the post-digital era in terms of the image itself. In order to do this I turn to Gilles Deleuze and Felix Guattari's writings on capitalism and schizophrenia to offer a new way of thinking about digital images. To comprehend digital cinema as a manifestly 'schizophrenic' image, a brief detour into two founding concepts are necessary. Firstly, *capitalism*: the two volumes of Deleuze and Guattari's *Capitalism and Schizophrenia* offer their most authoritative, if eclectic, exposition of capitalism's insidious and omnipresent force. More than just a political or economic order, capitalism is also a massive machine that shapes and channels the chaotic flux of the natural and human world and 'captures' it for its own ends. It paradoxically achieves its all-pervasive effect by freeing up closed systems. Any social order must structure the vicissitudinary flows of the world in order to have a chance of enduring and reproducing (this structuring forms the realm of politics, tradition, authority, institution and culture). Deleuze and Guattari call this process of structuring 'coding'. They conceive coding as restrictive but at the same time necessary in order to enable the functioning of a socius. So-called primitive societies, for instance, code their world and relations within it through kinship systems: networks of blood relations (filiation) and marriage relations (alliance) that channel and order the flow of goods, people, privileges and social standing. In contradistinction 'despotic' regimes institute a rigid overcoding of their societies with reference to the absolute strictures and megalomaniac rule of the despot. The heterogeneous fluxes of exchange and relations inherent in the socius are seized and shackled by a despotic administration that dreads unsupervised diversity, heterogeneity and freedom.

Capitalism, for Deleuze and Guattari, represents a radical break to this basic coding operation of the nature of society. In saying this it is not their intention to naturalise capitalism as an evolutionary end-point in history or economics, much less to claim that capitalism is more 'liberating' or 'civilised' than any order that precedes it. Rather, from an immanent analysis of social orders, capitalism, unlike other systems, depends on a never-ending, always expanding connection to forces of production and expenditure that is fundamentally unreceptive to final regulation, restriction and channelling. Instead, therefore, of coding flows, capitalism necessarily works through a regime of decoding. Which is to say that it unlocks rigid arrangements and stratified relationships in society so that it can commodify and extract surplus value on new arrangements and relationships. In this way capitalism unleashes vast new flows 'of property that is sold, flows of money that circulates, flows of production and means of production making ready in the shadows, flows of workers becoming deterritorialised' (Deleuze & Guattari 2004: 244).

However, in order to extract surplus value from the decoded flows a recoding, however provisional, is necessary, and for capitalism this specific process is termed 'axiomatisation'. Axioms are abstractions that evacuate flows of their unique meanings in any given coded context and replace them with a regime of quantitative equivalence in the form of monetary value. But in reducing the physical and social world to flows of capital, the codes and signifying practices that previously defined the world suddenly become unrecognisable. This process describes the operation of 'market forces' in capitalism, and it is precisely this incessant force of abstracting social codes and qualitative value into quantitative units that produces a 'schizophrenic' effect.

The second term that requires explication is *desire*. Desire is not limited to the sexual dimension that Freudian psychoanalysis, within the orbit of the Oedipal family structure, would have it but instead is conceived as a much wider motivating force that invests the whole of the social domain. Desire is, according to Deleuze and Guattari, the whole of production, or 'desiring-production', a positive and primary force, rather than one based on Lacanian lack. It is, in fact, the category of desire and desiring-production that is captured and subjected to social coding by any political order. Schizophrenia, then, defines the spontaneous or unpredictable forms of desire that is produced when freed from social coding, that is, produced by capitalism.

For Deleuze and Guattari, then, schizophrenia describes a historical formation, not a psychological condition, and although their analysis predates the onset of what was commonly termed the 'information age' or the 'digital revolution' it is clear that capitalism has, in the meantime, not only survived but thrived, extending its frontiers and reinvigorating its ability to harness desire – literally capitalising on the various transformations of every niche of culture and production wrought by digital technologies. One could even conclude that capitalism has found an ally in the digital machine, increasing productivity and aiding the flow of money, goods and labour. The reason for this productive relationship is, at heart, simple: in operating under the same axiomatic logic as capitalism digitisation facilitates the latter's power and virulence. That is, just as capitalism converts qualitative value into quantitative monetary value, digitisation converts information into binary units that can be (or, better, *must* be) manipulated, copied and transformed. If we take the case of the digital image, digitisation evacuates the perceptual visual field of its specific meanings and contexts, scanned and quantified into data-sets that designate each pixel. Once converted into inert binary information, the data can be processed and output to suit whatever bureaucratic or cultural recoding necessary in the new (but always provisional) context. The schizophrenia of the digital image is in this sense the intrinsic by-product of this decoding process – the spark that incites, in an irreducibly unpredictable way, the next image. It is defined by more than a 'postmodern' trend towards discontinuity, simulation or self-conscious 'playfulness' (exactly the characteristics noticeable in *Benny's Video* and *Funny Games*). Rather it is a radical ambiguity or alterity that is released from the image itself. Schizophrenia is the tendency of the digital image but also the limit-point where it loses all control. It is, for Brian Massumi, a scrambling of signifying codes constituting a 'breakaway into the unstable equilibrium of continuing self-invention' (1992: 92).

What *Hidden* shows us is what happens at this limit-point: not a parade of spectacular or fantastical visions, as is the usual expectation when one talks of 'digital cinema', but a slowly rising scale of uncanniness within the image. We are confronted, even in the most outwardly straightforward of scenes, with a sensation of recognition 'undone', resulting finally in an absolute indeterminacy to the image. Our responses to the film as a whole are as befuddled and disorientated as Georges' are to the array of diegetic images sent to his family home and workplace. The digital image is not mobilised by Haneke to shock or to amaze. Even the most startling moment in the film (where Georges' nemesis commits his stunning act of violence) is rendered with the same detachment and studied banality as the opening scene described previously (is it diegetic 'reality' or videotaped representation?). In its own quiet and insidious way the unsettling quality of the image in *Hidden* is the cinematic form of the appearance of schizophrenia.

Ultimately, rather than conforming to a conventional linear causality *Hidden*'s logic is 'digital', which is to say its images bespeak circularity and repetition. Image begets image in a dangerous proliferation that renders the usual grounding concepts like 'origins', 'referentiality' and 'representation' meaningless. What we are faced with instead is the immanence of the image in the digital context, an immanence which, far from flattening out any possibility of resistance or opposition, enables a politics of alienation and otherness to emerge from its very alterity. The paradox of *Hidden* is that the film seems utterly plausible from the aesthetic point of view and yet the 'mystery of the image' remains beyond its denouement (who sent the tapes? Who made the drawings? What is the 'reality' of the image?). I have tried to argue that far from being an 'irrational' outcome of the film, this ambiguity is an inherent effect of the 'schizophrenic' condition of the digital image. In the end this digitality proves itself as the other subject of *Hidden*.

Notes

1   Haneke remade this film for a 'Hollywood' audience and so, with considerable irony, brought home his critique of cinematic violence to the centre of his original target.

2   The 'final girl' is the sole-surviving female protagonist of many a 'slasher film' as theorised by Carol Clover (1992).

References

Clover, C. (1992) *Men, Women and Chain Saws: Gender in the Modern Horror Film*. Princeton, NJ: Princeton University Press.

Deleuze, G. and F. Guattari. (2004) *Anti-Oedipus: Capitalism and Schizophrenia*. Trans. R. Hurley, M. Seem and H. R. Lane. London: Continuum.

Massumi, B. (1992) *A User's Guide to Capitalism and Schizophrenia*. Cambridge: MIT Press.

CHAPTER TWENTY

Hidden Shame Exposed: Hidden and the Spectator

Tarja Laine

This chapter investigates what I consider the most interesting aspect of Michael Haneke's film *Caché* (*Hidden*, 2005) (and the director's films in general); namely the strategies the film uses to confront the spectators with their own engagement with visual displays. The narrative theme of this multilayered masterpiece is what happens when a personal (and national) shame that is safely hidden suddenly surfaces. The plot revolves around mysterious surveillance tapes that are left anonymously on the doorstep of Georges (Daniel Auteuil) and his wife Anne (Juliette Binoche), and the question of their dispatcher's identity. The names Georges and Anne can be seen as a reference to the terrorised couple, Georg and Anna, in Haneke's other domestic thriller *Funny Games* (1997). But whereas *Funny Games* expanded the diegesis to include the audience through direct address, in order to render the viewers complicit in the violence perpetrated on its victims, in *Hidden* it is the victims themselves who are now in the wrong, driven by their post-colonial guilt.

Like *Funny Games*, *Hidden* is not a closed system of the diegesis (the world of the film) and the non-diegesis (the world of the viewer), but a dynamic space where both the diegesis and the non-diegesis overlap and penetrate each other, but without a mediating in-between space. And as in *Funny Games*, Haneke once again criticises and rearticulates the ways in which we, the spectators, engage with cinematic fiction. In many of Haneke's films, a reciprocal looking relationship is established between the film and its spectator. This means that in most of his films, but especially in *Hidden*, spectatorship is not a simple or a straightforward matter, but a process of creative engagement that demands a certain degree of effort from the spectator. Furthermore, Haneke's films often set up a kind of 'reciprocal alteration' between the film and the spectator that requires mutual recognition of both parties with the conscious intention of understanding the dynamic tension between each party. In *Hidden*, this is established through disturbing the act of viewing and bringing about an effect of doubt regarding the status of the image, especially in its flowing together of the diegesis and the non-diegesis.

The film opens with what seems like a classical establishing shot of Georges and Anne's Parisian residence, safely hidden behind a locked gate and a front garden, with minimal movement within the frame. The shot lasts about three minutes, up to the point where we suddenly hear a piece of diegetic offscreen dialogue that somehow appears to originate from behind our backs. This localisation of sound right behind us is then justified as the image freezes, then speeds up and fast-forwards, revealing that the image is not just any image, but an image in the process of being viewed, and not only by us, but by the diegetic characters as well. The image turns out not to have been a regular establishing shot (on which the opening credits unfold one letter at a time, from left to right, slowly filling the frame and contributing to the spectator's erroneous judgement about the diegetic status of the shot), but a television screen showing footage of the first surveillance tape. It is particularly interesting that sound is privileged over image in the trustworthiness applied to the diegetic status of the shot.

Similarly, mostly static establishing shots and surveillance images of the house, as well as of other locations, occur throughout the film, and their diegetic status, too, remains unclear. The film is shot in high-definition digital video, which further disturbs the act of viewing. The quality of the surveillance images is not only perfectly identical to the regular shots, the images filmed through a window or a windscreen also merge seamlessly with the rest of the footage, including the television image of

Caché (2005): A diegetic frame within, or a non-diegetic frame beyond the film?

Georges presenting his weekly literature programme (but which nevertheless can track Georges receiving a phone call outside the studio setting). The doorbell rings, but there is no one at the door. The point-of-view shot by an anonymous camera operator is just about similar to the shot seeming to be from Georges' point of view in the same corridor (even though the latter is not a real point-of-view shot since Georges appears in the frame at the end of it). Very much aware of themselves, the spectators come to doubt the diegetic status of every image, every sound and every incident. Characteristic for the cinema of Haneke, these instances are moments when the diegesis and the non-diegesis cancel each other out. Or rather, these are moments of reciprocal alteration, in which the diegesis and the non-diegesis modify each other by folding over and negotiating with each other.

The surveillance tapes feature what appears to be footage from a hidden (but omniscient) camera; throughout the whole film, the camera has access to both the most public and the most private places, sometimes filming from positions that are physically impossible within the diegesis, but neither the camera nor its operator are visible to the protagonists or to the spectator. Who filmed and sent the tapes? Why does the presence of the camera go unnoticed by Georges and Anne? It would be an easy solution to conclude that the camera is simply hidden from sight as in candid camera or reality television shows (the fact that the film never reveals who is observing the family would seem to support this idea). But the camera could also be considered as situated in the space where the diegesis and the non-diegesis flow into each other, establishing a co-creative, dynamic relation between the diegesis and the non-diegesis. This reciprocal alteration, where the diegetic and the non-diegetic co-creatively shape one another, can be thought of as an internal, dynamic resonance, rather than an external cause and effect relationship.

As noted before, the dynamic interplay between the diegesis and the non-diegesis is present in *Funny Games* as well, in which the spectator can move between the diegesis and the non-diegesis together with the torturers. This renders the spectator an accomplice to the Schobers' torture (see Sorfa 2006: 98). But whereas there is a visible movement in *Funny Games* between the diegesis and the non-diegesis, in *Hidden* the 'here' of the spectator's experience and the 'there' of the cinematic world flow together *internally* in and through the affective operations incarnated in the film's invisible camera operator and 'taken in' by the spectator. David Sorfa makes a similar point by writing that 'It is the desire of cinema itself that sends these tapes to the *Hidden* family' (2006: 102). In these operations, the spectator and the film coexist through reciprocal alteration that enhances both the human and the cinematic viewing subject (to use Vivian Sobchack's terminology). Reciprocity knits together the texture of the whole affective operation which no longer exists in between the 'here' and the 'there', but as a simultaneity and a coexistence.

The reciprocal alteration of the diegesis and the non-diegesis creates a viewpoint with a heightened sensitivity to mutual affirmation of the human and the cinematic subject, and an added intention of understanding and enhancing both of them. For instance, the opening shot of *Hidden* discussed above is both diegetic (the footage of Georges and Anne's house is footage of their actual house within the world of the film and the footage can also be seen by the protagonists) and non-diegetic (the invisible camera operator who records the surveillance footage is not a figure within the world of the film). But neither is the invisible camera operator the actual, historically real filmmaker ('Haneke') himself within the world of filmmaking. Rather, the observer is the cinematic subject, as its own creation, which the spectator nevertheless 'takes in'. This alteration of the diegesis and the non-diegesis shakes us, the spectators, into realising that all looking always contains the possibility of being looked at, and that this possibility is the reciprocity that is constitutive for each of us. And, as many critics have noted, even the name of the street where Georges and Anne live, Rue des Iris, can be understood as a reference to this ontology of looking.

An important issue with regard to the tapes, then, is the fact that they are made available to those under surveillance. Georges is meant to know that he is being watched, and, in this knowledge, to recognise and accept the responsibility for his past actions. In a crucial scene Georges visits Majid (Maurice Bénichou) for the first time to accuse him of terrorising his family with the tapes. Georges' visit appears to have been filmed without either character's knowledge. Later, the mysterious tape is sent to Anne, to whom Georges did not tell the truth about his confrontation with Majid. On this tape, we witness Georges accusing and threatening Majid; after Georges' departure, Majid weeps inconsolably in his solitude. He is viewed in his low-rent apartment in Romainville, in the eastern suburbs of Paris, geographically distant, and symbolically even further removed from the chic *arrondissement* where Georges and Anne reside. In this scene, there is emotional proximity, but only to the extent that the emotionally intimate encounter with Majid's raw subjectivity on tape emphasises Georges' refusal of acknowledgement and its (repressed) emotional impact on both Majid and Georges. By producing another mysterious tape, the film allows Georges and Majid to 'meet', but only through the affective operations that *Hidden* establishes in its reciprocal alteration of the diegesis and the non-diegesis, sensed by the spectator.

Similarly, Georges' refusal to acknowledge his own traumatic memory surfaces only in and through the reciprocal alteration of the diegesis and the non-diegesis. In Georges and Anne's house, we twice witness a young Arab boy who seems to be bleeding from his mouth (the mysterious tapes are wrapped in childish drawings of a figure whose mouth is similarly smeared with blood). Later we find out that this boy is a vision from Georges' repressed memory of Majid when Georges was six years old. The appearance of young Majid (Malik Nait Djoudi) further enhances the shared existence of the diegesis and the non-diegesis, and, as a result, reality and representation, vision and dream, memory and imagination all gain the same ontological status. The childish drawings demand recognition from Georges, but it is this scene that

> almost picks open Georges' memory at that point, cutting into his mind, his memory cache. And in giving us Majid for only a second the film makes us realise how hidden this memory is, how repressed and locked away it is. … It is the film itself, as past rising up to the present, that accuses Georges. (Frampton 2006: 144)

For us, the spectators, it is clear how repressed Georges' memory is, because it is in and through our lived body that the diegesis and the non-diegesis flow together, bringing the past to the surface in the present. Our attention is directed to all the hidden and unhidden memories at once, and, as a result, we are invited to grasp all the different viewpoints through these memories. By the folding together of the diegesis and the non-diegesis, the past breaks through into the present in order to bring the protagonists in *Hidden* together, but it is ultimately in vain. The film itself sends the tapes to Georges as invitations to remember and acknowledge, as if he really had the freedom to accept them within the film's story world. By addressing Georges in a similar manner as the spectator, *Hidden*'s invisible camera operator treats both of them as equals, almost as if the spectator and Georges both had the power to control what they see or even to alter the course of events. Sorfa calls this phenomenon 'the double bind of the engaged' (2006: 94) and it adds to the reciprocal alteration of the film, namely the coexistence of both the spectator and Georges with the film. Therefore, although the tapes cause Georges and Majid's paths to cross, they do not meet in any 'real' sense of the word, because Georges refuses to accept the tapes as an invitation to acknowledge. Instead, he believes them to be a straightforward threat. Miscommunications and misunderstandings remain the narrative forces of the film, as residues of reciprocal alteration. For the spectator, however, these residues enable moments of added intention of understanding the complex interactions between the protagonists that the mysterious tapes have set in motion.

Shared Concern

As I have argued above, the reciprocal alteration of the diegesis and the non-diegesis in *Hidden* requires an exceptionally creative kind of engagement on the part of the spectator with the enigmatic network in which Georges stands out as the central figure. Majid's parents worked for Georges' family before they died in the police massacre during a demonstration against a discriminatory curfew in Paris, which resulted in Georges' parents taking in Majid.[1] In the film, Georges has guilty dreams about deceiving Majid into killing a rooster, which results in Majid being hastily sent off to an orphanage, and thereby being deprived of a good education and a better future. The dream scene starts shockingly with an abrupt close-up of an axe cutting off the head of the rooster; the young Georges watches the event in a state of fright. An exchange of looks is established between Georges and Majid through a series of shot/reverse point-of-view shots; from Georges' point of view, the dream-Majid approaches the camera with his axe raised, so that he literally 'swallows' the image in the end, in an extreme close-up. This scene is a forceful demand of recognition of guilt, showing Georges haunted by his past, his memory and his knowledge. It is also a forewarning of shocking events yet to come. Towards the end of the film, Majid asks Georges to come to his apartment. As soon as Georges arrives, Majid says: 'I asked you to come because I wanted you to be present.' In an abrupt gesture, Majid then slits his throat, his blood spraying all over the walls. Majid's suicide is an extreme demand of recognition, but again and again Georges refuses to acknowledge this demand or admit his feelings of guilt to his mother (Annie Girardot), to Anne, to Majid, to Majid's son (Walid Afkir), or even to himself.

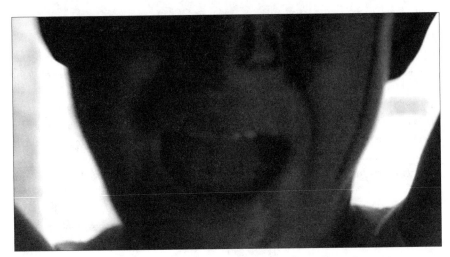

Guilt swallows in *Caché* (2005)

It is interesting to note the fact that the last (dramatic) meeting between Georges and Majid is filmed in exactly the same style as the secretly filmed footage that followed their first confrontation (by contrast, the first actual confrontation used shot/reverse-shots and multiple camera angles). Again, this reinforces the questioning of the diegetic status of the image, allowing the non-diegesis to flow together with the diegesis in order to hold Georges responsible for Majid's suicide. According to Elizabeth Ezra and Jane Sillars, this scene also

> lends a sense that Majid's act is historically and ideologically overdetermined, forced into being by the representational power of Georges' fantasy, always already having happened ... Georges' refusal as an adult to acknowledge the effects of his earlier actions suggests a parallel with the postcolonial metropolitan who is neither wholly responsible for, nor wholly untainted by, past events from which he or she has benefited. (2007: 219)

Majid's act is overdetermined in that it is caused by repressed traumas on many different levels, but it is also overdetermined because the invisible camera operator always already knew that Georges would choose to ignore the significance of the tapes (and thereby to prevent change), even before sending them. The invisible camera operator knew this because he is simultaneously a diegetic and a non-diegetic figure (and simultaneously neither). Georges' attitude can therefore indeed be read as an analogy for the French national imaginary and its undercurrent of guilt and shame for the treatment of Algerians in France. Max Silverman writes:

> *Hidden* is a commentary on a France (at least in the form of Georges) so incapable of dealing with difference unless it is kept strictly at arms-length, and so anaesthetised against its own guilt and responsibility in relation to past events, that only a dismantling of the erected barricades will open up hidden truths. (2007: 249)

Silverman argues that Georges is not an allegory of France *per se*, but only of a certain generation of Frenchmen. Georges is an allegory of the France that refuses to take responsibility for something that happened in the past, since France is not the same nation any longer. The function of the tapes is unambiguous both within and beyond the diegesis: it is a way of demanding recognition for the French national shame that has long been hidden in plain sight. This is *Hidden*'s political reason for being. But by positioning the spectator as a locus for the folding together of the diegesis and the non-diegesis, Haneke attempts to establish an exchange of recognition of this guilt for the spectator as well. This exchange manifests itself in the demand for reciprocal visibility without which human interaction would not be possible. By demanding recognition from Georges, Majid demands to be perceived, and therefore to be. But Georges' refusal denies Majid not only his past, but also his future.

In an interview about the film, Haneke has stated that Georges' guilt is traumatic, because he refuses to see and accept that his selfishness has destroyed a human life. Instead, he prefers to keep the secrets as they are, out of sight, buried deep under the façade of his 'stable' bourgeois family. The exchange of recognition that Haneke sets up in his film is not only positive. It would be easy for the spectator to adopt a position of moral outrage towards Georges' bourgeois hypocrisy (Jean-Paul Sartre would say that Georges lives in 'bad faith'). But the truth is that it is relatively effortless (at least for this filmgoer) to imagine how Georges feels in his attempt to protect himself and his family without viewing things from his moral position. I do not need to approve of Georges' decision to live in denial in order to be able to recognise his behaviour as the actions of another person fundamentally like myself in his basic humanity. Georges' past wrongdoing is, in fact, the normal selfishness of a six-year-old child, regardless of its huge consequences.[2] Things become complicated only when Georges refuses to acknowledge his guilt as an adult. Georges blames his past behaviour on the fact that he was a child, and does not take responsibility for it in the present either. This is what *Hidden* does: it invites us to see through the excuses, and not only in the film, but in our own lives as well.

This complicated engagement allows the emergence of multiple viewpoints that originate through reciprocal alteration and mutual recognition in a self-reflective sense, instead of from a position of easy middle-class morality. The mirror that Haneke's film holds in front of Georges is also held in front of his target audience of liberal European intellectuals, as reflected in the dinner parties that Georges and Anne regularly host. Haneke's mirror presents his audience with their own image, which, like Georges', is not necessarily what they took it to be. This challenges the spectators to acknowledge that image and to change it, or to agree with it and keep on living a lie. Like so often in the cinema of Haneke, the spectators are invited to question and redefine their own relationship with the events depicted and represented in the media, regardless of whether or not they have had a 'first-hand' experience of them. In *Hidden*, this is done by channelling the folding of the diegetic and the non-diegetic into each other through the spectators, so that they feel the reciprocal alteration of human interactions that shape the protagonists' realities to the point of Majid's suicide.

Hence, this means that we, as spectators, are also responsible for the events depicted in *Hidden*, because the invisible camera operator is always there, recording history that defines us and looks back at all of us, even though we would not always be aware of its look. We are all responsible, because we all have the responsibility to think of ourselves in relation to representations of things past. In *Hidden*, the spectator has the responsibility to think, but this thinking is not achieved through visual pleasure or the satisfaction of narrative desire. Rather, it is achieved through the effects and affects of reciprocal alteration that make everyone a part of everyone else's world, and that makes discrimination the concern of us all.[3] Georges, however, negates his responsibility both as an actor and as a witness, and therefore, for him, everything remains the same in the end: his past as hidden, but nevertheless as haunting, as it ever was. Indeed, in the brilliant final shot of the film, the sons of both Majid and Georges are brought together for the first time (at least for us), in a static long shot of the school Pierrot (Lester Makedonsky) attends. Not much happens in this shot, and one has to observe it very closely to see that the shot is actually about the two boys. The stillness of the shot makes it similar both to the secretly filmed footage and to the regular establishing shots that recur in the film, producing again an effect of doubt about the diegetic status of the image. But in this last image, the past is not looking at the present, but into the future. Or better yet: in this last image the past and the future appear together, not as a denied memory, but as a mutual enrichment; always acknowledging, encountering, modifying and reconfiguring each other.

When the past is in reciprocal alteration with the future like this, it can indeed open up new possibilities for unexpected alliances instead of merely exposing shameful national secrets or individuals.[4] Admittedly, this reading might seem too optimistic, utopian even, especially given the fact that Haneke won the Best Director Award for his film at the Cannes Film Festival just a few months before the ethnic riots in France in October and November 2005.[5] However, in Haneke's film lies the possibility of viewing the events from the perspective of shared concern. The shared concern is the reciprocity through which the individuals meet, but for a shared encounter to occur, the individuals need to 'exit themselves'. This is precisely the configuration Haneke sets up in this film, not only on the thematic level, but on the spectatorial level as well, since in *Hidden* the process of viewing becomes a matter of the diegetic and the non-diegetic flowing together in reciprocal alteration that carries the spectator from the position of 'here' to 'there'.

Author's note
Many thanks to Wim Staat, Dan Hassler-Forest and Tom van Klingeren.

Notes

1   Much has been written about *Hidden* in connection to this violent attack against the peaceful demonstrators in which approximately 200 French Algerians were killed. This took place on 17 October 1961, and was ordered by Maurice Papon, a former Nazi collaborator and then the chief of the Parisian police. Not only was the French government reluctant to investigate the event, but it also remained

silent about what happened. Furthermore, despite the extent of the massacre, the press coverage of it was scarce, downplayed in the media due to the censorship by several levels of the French authorities. This extensive cover-up was made possible through emergency laws from 1955 that allowed authorities to withhold information from the public.

2   Even though, as Giuseppina Mecchia notes when writing on *Hidden*, some children do have the power to be particularly malicious towards other children 'because they are supported by an adult system founded on underlying prejudice, violence, and racism' (2007: 140).

3   According to Sorfa, this trend in Haneke's cinema started in *Code inconnu: Récit incomplet de divers voyages* (*Code Unknown: Incomplete Tales of Several Journeys*, 2000): 'everyone is by necessity connected to everyone else and ... there is no position of non-complicity: everyone must share the blame' (2006: 99).

4   For Silverman, one possible interpretation of the ending is that 'the colonial barriers and atavistic reflexes of previous generations may be loosening through dialogue and a new attitude to difference' (2007: 249).

5   The riots in 2005 were triggered by the accidental death of two teenagers of North-African descent who were electrocuted in a power station while trying to run away from the police. Yet the escalation of the riots was not so much the accident as such, but the way in which the incident was dealt with. Outrage followed especially when then-Minister of the Interior (and now President) Nicolas Sarkozy repeatedly called the rioters 'scum' and 'immigrants' (particularly interesting, given that Sarkozy himself, like most of the rioters, was born in France of immigrant parents).

References

Ezra, E. and J. Sillars (2007) '*Hidden* in Plain Sight: Bringing Terror Home', *Screen*, 48, 2, 215–21.

Frampton, D. (2006) *Filmosophy: A Manifesto for a Radically New Way of Understanding Cinema*. London: Wallflower Press.

Mecchia, G. (2007) 'The Children are Still Watching Us, *Hidden/Hidden* in the Folds of Time', *Studies in French Cinema*, 7, 2, 131–41.

Silverman, M. (2007) 'The Empire Looks Back', *Screen*, 48, 2, 245–9.

Sorfa, D. (2006) 'Uneasy Domesticity in the Films of Michael Haneke', *Studies in European Cinema*, 3, 2, 93–104.

The White Ribbon

CHAPTER TWENTY-ONE

The White Ribbon in Michael Haneke's Cinema

John Orr

Filmed over the summer of 2008 in Lübeck, Leipzig and rural locations in Branden-berg, Northern Germany, Haneke's 2009 Palme d'Or winner *Das weiße Band* (*The White Ribbon*) is a radical departure from his previous films. It is shot in a rich, highly textured black-and-white and the action takes place in a village in Northern Germany just prior to World War One. Where we perhaps assumed that Haneke was by inclination a colour director he changes format. Where we always thought his films were dark fables about the present or the future, he goes back to the past. Where we had become accustomed to the aggressive reflexivity of his media-conscious narratives in the electronic age, this is practically a pre-motorised world. Where we might have assumed his career's Franco-Austrian axis was set in stone, he makes his first feature film set and shot in Germany – then Prussian Germany in a region of the country that later become part of the DDR during the long period of the Cold War. In every way the changes confound us, but Haneke had already spoken about plans for adapting Robert Musil's *Young Törless*, or *Die Verwirrungen des Zöglings Törless* (*The Confusion of Young Törless*, 1906), a much earlier evocation of authoritarianism and cruelty in the Prussian mindset at the start of the last century. And in some ways the spirit of the Austrian writer seems to echo throughout this work, as do the fictional chronicles of Thomas Mann.

In the New German Cinema of the 1960s and 1970s the early century period had been accessed too – one thinks of Volker Schlöndorff's 1965 version of the

Musil novella – but above all Haneke's film seems in line with two very different products of the modernist movement: Schlöndorff's adaptation of Marguerite Yourcenar's *Le Coup de grâce*, (*Der Fangschuss* (*Coup de grâce*), 1976) brilliantly scripted by Margaretha Von Trotta and Jutta Brückner, and Edgar's Reitz's nine-part television series *Heimat* (1979–1984) that obtained a cinema release because of its widespread impact. Stylistically, these two artworks are like day and night, but Haneke crucially combines elements of them in his highly original masterpiece. Set in the Baltic in 1919, *Le Coup de grâce* is detached, elliptical, even cold in the study of a covert bisexual triangle beset by conflicting political loyalties of Left and Right. But it oozes a violent tension that is nowhere fully explained and broods on space and place in way that makes it eerie and atmospheric especially in its winter settings. Haneke makes a summer film that folds over into winter, and here, too, ice also eats into the soul, as the sense of atmospheric menace is equally powerful. While the 1976 film's setting is an isolated country house in the middle of disputed territory, Reitz's epic is the opposite – a stolid recognisable German village with a knowable community. This, too, is Haneke's start and genre positioning. But his film differs because the other two begin in 1919, so that *The White Ribbon* is a verge-of-war fable that can be read as a prequel to either or both. (It is worth noting also that Haneke, often called 'a second-generation modernist', is roughly the same age as most New German Cinema directors, including Schlöndorff, who often called on Jean-Claude Carrière for screenplay assistance – as Haneke did in *The White Ribbon*).

So, to sum up first and then elaborate: like the Reitz epic, Haneke has constructed a revisionist Heimat film with an original screenplay and a narrator involved in the story itself, for Reitz the village idiot, for Haneke the teacher (Christian Friedel) at the village school reflecting back on the events of the time as an ageing man (Ernst Jacobi). But in setting, the Austrian forsakes the Alpine original of the Heimat genre and the Bavarian setting of most revisionist remakes of the 1970s (see Elsaesser 1989: 141–9) in favour of the flat plains of rural Northern Germany. Like *Le Coup de grâce* he revisits history atmospherically in luminous monochrome and uses distancing effects to undermine the realism of motive and event. In the detail of setting, costume and speech there is a naturalistic precision that is juxtaposed against the opacity of the events themselves. Everything is elliptical: we seem to be in the position of many a witness at a street accident. The crucial event happens moments before our eyes and ears tune in to it and we seem to be forever arriving that split second too late. This structural withholding thus follows closely in the footsteps of his previous European film *Caché* (*Hidden*, 2005), where the image is often just out of range of the eye and life one step ahead of art, when for reassurance as spectators we usually demand everything in range of the eye and art one step ahead of life. It also differs from the earlier offscreen violence of the Austrian films that compensate for the absence of seeing, as Brigitte Peucker notes, through the onslaught of sound (see 2007: 132). In *Funny Games* (1997) the cries of the suffering are turned up and clearly heard because we are in the same house and usually the same room at the same time. Here, by contrast, where we arrive after the event, Haneke maintains equal balance between sight and sound, and the effect is just right.

Now to the story itself in a film lasting 145 minutes, the longest of Haneke's features to date. In the small agricultural village of Eichwald, where most of the inhabitants seem to work for the local baron and landowner (Ulrich Tukur) and attend the Lutheran village church, a series of puzzling and violent events take place – largely offscreen – in the period between 1913 and 1914. At the start the village doctor (Rainer Bock) is knocked off his horse and badly injured through the impact of a cable stretched across the track between two trees. The culprit is never found. There follows a series of incidents that are never fully explained. Are they linked? Is there some kind of chain reaction? We never know. But soon after, a farm worker's wife is badly injured by falling through the rotten floor of a sawmill; her son then destroys the Baron's cabbage crop ready for harvesting, and her husband – as a response to both or neither? – kills himself. The Baron's young son is kidnapped, hung upside down in the barn and beaten before being found and rescued, but by whom? Soon after, the barn is burnt down. Horrors outside the home are matched by domestic horrors within. The Doctor appears to have sexually abused his daughter though we cannot be sure, while of one thing we can be certain: the Pastor (Burghart Klaußner) uses physical punishment without remorse on his young children – hence the title of the film. The 'white ribbon' is the emblem of innocence that his children have forfeited by minor transgressions; henceforth it is worn as an armband of shame until the hapless child is judged by the vindictive cleric to have 'reformed'.

If the causal linkages were there, either as transparent events witnessed, or even suspected, by the pillars of the community then we have the basis for some kind of revenge movie, or a happy ending where the incorruptible schoolteacher finds out the full truth. But Haneke has systematically uncoupled all the links in the causal chain, a veritable feast for ravenous Deleuzians. Meanwhile evil – a bona fide absolute – is ubiquitous: it is everywhere and nowhere at the same time. And let us consider the eminent locals, who in the Teacher's onscreen narration are given titles but no names (Baron, Baroness, Doctor, Steward, Midwife, Pastor) – a self-conscious nod by Haneke to the 'social types' of expressionist drama of the period – all lack the unity we associate with those who regulate community life according to their own dicta. Haneke successfully blends the anti-psychology of the dramatic 'type', where the surname is nothing and the title everything, into the excessively formal social etiquette of the time. Obsessed by formal correctness, everyone is looking over their shoulder at the same time, fearful of being exposed, while soon after the unexplained kidnap and torture of her son the attractive Baroness (Ursina Lardi), unhappy in marriage, leaves the Baron to go and live in Italy. Echoing *Hidden* there are certainly clear tensions of class, but equally there are tensions of generation, of peasants versus masters, adults versus children. On the edge of a war that comes from the outside, the question is obliquely posed: are the village children hapless innocents or are they veritable monsters who will soon come into their own in the wreckage of postwar Germany?

The White Ribbon differs from *Hidden* in one important respect. Apart from the Teacher, an outsider to the village who lives in a nearby town and plays the role of a semi-naïve narrator, there is no central locus for the understanding of disaster.

In *Hidden* the focus is the besieged family of Georges (Daniel Auteuil) with whose predicament spectators can sympathise even when they distance themselves from the protagonists; but here there is no nucleus of perception or investigation that can direct the spectator. The Teacher narrates but does not investigate. Nor, it seems, does anyone else. If everyone in the village has their own secrets to conceal, how diligent will they be in pursuing the secrets of others? We are completely on the outside but close enough as intimate witnesses to be truly disturbed by events that seem to have paralysed the commonsense quest for knowledge. We do, however, expect onscreen narration to guide us to a revelation at hand. A good comparison can be made here with Joseph Losey's film of L. P. Hartley's 1953 novel *The Go-Between* (1971), where an ageing narrator revisits the scene of his youth and his unwitting role in a tragic love affair, only revealed at the very end. While Losey (with a film set in the same prewar period) gives us the revelation and its tragic consequence, Haneke's ageing Teacher skirts courteously around the edge of the abyss. There is no revelation at hand. The framing narrative makes us none the wiser than the story itself. For the Teacher looking back is more concerned in the end with his own missed opportunity by which he is still traumatised. His engagement to the Nanny (Leonie Benesch) of the Baron's children is fatally postponed for a year owing to the truculence of her father. In the meantime war breaks out and changes everything. He never returns to the village again.

The film brings to full fruition in practice the polemical Haneke who had demanded in his film aesthetics the intelligent participation of the spectator in the outcome of the narrative. No entertainment, no distraction, no relaxation. Catherine Wheatley has recently claimed that Haneke's films offer the genuine prospect of a moral spectatorship that transcends the entertainment mode by which Hollywood lures us into the uncritical acceptance of violence and atrocity, an aesthetic that Haneke usually instigates through ironising generic conventions (see 2009: 78–88). But only late on in his career, I would argue, does he truly achieve his objective. Gone is the earlier rash metaphor of 'raping the spectator into awareness', which twice imploded with *Funny Games*, the first time as art, the second time, in the American remake, *Funny Games U.S.* (2007), as farce. With *Code inconnu: Récit incomplet de divers voyages* (*Code Unknown: Incomplete Tales of Several Journeys*, 2000), *Hidden* and *The White Ribbon*, Haneke has opted for a softer, sinuous but more complex strategy of seducing the spectator into judgement. And it works. The mature Haneke has largely resisted the temptation to reduce shock to sensation: the event that shocks still remains as crucial to his cinema as the mystery of its origin. But he has now discovered that mystery is more disturbing than the un-pleasure of repellent sensation. Conflating both we could say that in the mystery of un-pleasure lies the propinquity of evil. The shock aesthetic propels us towards this discovery but as spectators we are now on our own, autonomous beings having to chart un-navigated waters. Thus Haneke's aesthetic works both through the existence of evil and through the mystery of evil, of which human cruelty is overt manifestation. We are in search not so much of the Hidden God as the Hidden Satan. The existentialism of judgement is matched by the fundamentalism of that to be judged. The modern and the archaic coexist in uneasy proximity and in Haneke at his very best tension thrives shimmering across the surface of the screen.

On the acting front, an abrupt departure from recent practice is also to be noted. Gone is the seductive stardom of Juliette Binoche, Isabelle Huppert and Naomi Watts. The acting ensemble rules and here the children are as integral as the adults to Haneke's project. In directing both simultaneously in this symbiotic mix of tension and suspicion, the children are iconic equals, never clumsy, cute or overly endearing. Haneke avoids sentimentality with professional rigour and the bleak austere childhood in such a strict Lutheran culture has about it more than an echo of Ingmar Bergman; the autobiographical Bergman as the son of a Lutheran pastor, that is, in Michael Winterbottom's documentary *Ingmar Bergman: The Magic Lantern* (1989), and not the period films that Bergman sets in the radiant summers of the early twentieth century. Of course, Bergman's childhood is inter-war, but the way in which the severe discipline of family, father and faith lead on into the release of gratuitous cruelty of which young boys such as he and his brother are capable, seems to have more than an echo here in Haneke's preoccupations. One could also add that Bergman's teenage years provide this film with an offscreen postscript: the Swede's first visit to Germany was to produce an infatuation with Hitler that lasted for some time. So this film is less homage to Bergman, whom Haneke admires, than deconstruction of Bergman, which gives it added bite. For the Swede, Scandinavian midsummer is both consolation and transcendence of long winter light. But further south the look of Haneke's film, superficially close to Bergman, denies both as late summer segues into winter. Nonetheless, *The White Ribbon* places Haneke closer to Bergman than any other of his films, as well as to the varied work in New German Cinema of early Schlöndorff, von Trotta in the very Lutheran *Die Bleierne Zeit* (*The German Sisters*, 1981) that Bergman so admired, Reitz and Jean-Marie Straub, in particular the abstract generational conflict of *Nicht versöhnt oder Es hilft nur Gewalt wo Gewalt herrscht* (*Unreconciled*, 1965).

For Haneke, the Austrian born in Munich, this then may be something of a return to origins, an ironic revisiting of *Heimat*; but it is more of a discovery, a move into history that is both familiar and unfamiliar at the same time. It is a step into the unknown; at the same time it glosses a previous fictional and filmic history and echoes of that resonate throughout the picture. It has wrong-footed completely, however, those who see Haneke's work as solely attuned to murderous acts mediated by electronic culture's latest fix. The trip wire set for the horse's hooves is centuries old as is the unseen act of arson that torches the barn. This generically is Haneke's history of violence and shows that his pessimism about the human condition goes beyond its very specific Adornian incarnation – the aphoristic savaging of commodity capitalism. You might say here that Theodor Adorno spirals backward into Friedrich Nietzsche, yet at the same time Haneke subtly undermines the demonic gesture in his search for the hidden Satan, for if the Devil remains 'hidden', how do we know the Devil exists?

References

Elsaesser, T. (1989) *New German Cinema: A History* London: Macmillan.

Peucker, B. (2007) *The Material Image: Art and the Real in Film* Stanford: Stanford University Press.

Wheatley, C. (2009) *Michael Haneke's Cinema: The Ethic of the Image* Oxford: Berg-bahn Books.

FILMOGRAPHY

[Based on the data from the films' credits and various published German and English sources.]

1974

After Liverpool (aka *...und was kommt danach?*) (TV)
89 minutes
Director: Michael Haneke
Producer: Horst Bohse
Screenplay: James Saunders (trans. Hilde Spiel)
Cinematography: Jochen Hubrich, Günter Lemnitz, Gerd E. Schäfer
Editor: Christa Kleinheisterkamp
Cast: Hildegard Schmahl, Dieter Kirchlechner
Country: Austria
Language: German

1976

Sperrmüll (TV)
80 minutes
Director: Michael Haneke
Screenplay: Alfred Bruggmann
Cinematography: Henric von Bornekow
Cast: Ernst Fritz Fürbringer, Tilli Breidenbach, Karlheinz Fiege, Suzanne Geyer
Country: West Germany
Language: German

1976

Drei Wege zum See (*Three Paths to the Lake*) (TV)

97 minutes

Director: Michael Haneke

Producer: Rolf von Sydow

Screenplay: Michael Haneke, Ingeborg Bachmann (short story)

Cinematography: Igor Luther

Editor: Helga Scharf

Cast: Ursula Schult, Guido Wieland, Walter Schmidinger, Bernhard Wicki

Country: Austria/West Germany

Language: German

1979

Lemminge, Teil 1 Arkadien (TV)

113 minutes

Director: Michael Haneke

Production Company: Schönbrunn-Film, Sender Freies Berlin, Österreichischer Rundfunk (ORF)

Screenplay: Michael Haneke

Cinematography: Walter Kindler, Jerzy Lipman

Editor: Marie Homolkova

Cast: Regina Sattler, Christian Ingomar, Eva Linder, Paulus Manker, Christian Spatzek, Elisabeth Orth

Country: Austria/Germany

Language: German

Lemminge, Teil 2 Verletzungen (TV)

107 minutes

Director: Michael Haneke

Production Company: Schönbrunn-Film, Sender Freies Berlin, ORF

Screenplay: Michael Haneke

Cinematography: Jerzy Lipman

Editor: Marie Homolkova

Cast: Monica Bleibtreu, Elfriede Irrall, Rüdiger Hacker, Wolfgang Hübsch, Norbert Kappen, Guido Wieland, Vera Borek, Wolfgang Gasser, Julia Gschnitzer, David Haneke

Country: Austria/Germany

Language: German

1983

Variation (TV)

98 minutes

Director: Michael Haneke

Production Company: Sender Freies Berlin

Screenplay: Michael Haneke

Cinematography: Walter Kindler

Editor: Barbara Herrmann

Cast: Elfriede Irrall, Suzanne Geyer, Hilmar Thate, Monica Bleibtreu
Country: Germany
Language: German

1984

Wer war Edgar Allan? (*Who was Edgar Allan?*) (TV)
83 minutes
Director: Michael Haneke
Producers: Neue Studio Film, Zweites Deutsches Fernsehen, ORF
Screenplay: Michael Haneke, Hans Broczyner, Peter Rosei (novel)
Cinematography: Frank Brühne
Editor: Lotte Klimitschek
Cast: Paulus Manker, Rolf Hoppe, Guido Wieland
Country: Austria/Germany
Language: German

1986

Fräulein (TV)
108 minutes
Director: Michael Haneke
Producer: Ulrich Nagel
Screenplay: Michael Haneke, Bernd Schröder (concept)
Cinematography: Walter Kindler, Karl Hohenberger
Editor: Monika Solzbacher, Monika Schreiner
Cast: Angelica Domröse, Péter Franke, Lou Castel, Heinz-Werner Kraehkamp, Cordula Gerburg, Margret Homeyer
Country: Germany
Language: German

1989

Der siebente Kontinent (*The Seventh Continent*)
90 minutes
Director: Michael Haneke
Producers: Veit Heiduschka, Wega Film
Screenplay: Michael Haneke
Cinematography: Anton Peschke
Editor: Marie Homolkova
Cast: Dieter Berner, Leni Tanzer, Birgit Doll
Country: Austria
Language: German
Awards: Ernest Artaria Award, 1989 (Locarno International Film Festival)

1991

Nachruf für einen Mörder (*Aftermath of a Murder*) (TV)

110 minutes

Director: Michael Haneke

Production Company: ORF

Screenplay: Michael Haneke

1992

Benny's Video

105 minutes

Director: Michael Haneke

Producers: Veit Heiduschka, Michael Katz, Bernard Lang, Gebhard Zupan, Wega Film

Screenplay: Michael Haneke

Cinematography: Christian Berger

Editor: Marie Homolkova

Cast: Arno Frisch, Angela Winkler, Ulrich Mühe, Ingrid Stassner

Country: Austria

Language: German

Awards: Vienna Film Award, 1992 (Viennale); FIPRESCI Prize, 1993 (European Film Awards)

1993

Die Rebellion (*The Rebellion*) (TV)

90 minutes

Director: Michael Haneke

Production Company: ORF

Screenplay: Michael Haneke, Joseph Roth (novel)

Cinematography: Jirí Stihr

Editor: Marie Homolkova

Cast: Branko Samarovsk, Judit Pogányi, Thierry Van Werveke, Deborah Wisniewski, Katharina Grabher, August Schmölzer

Country: Austria

Language: German

Awards: Best TV Film, 1994 (Austrian People's Education TV Award); Best Teleplay, 1994 (Baden-Baden TV Film Festival).

1994

71 Fragmente einer Chronologie des Zufalls (*71 Fragments of a Chronology of Chance*)

96 minutes

Director: Michael Haneke

Producers: Veit Heiduschka, Willi Seigler, Wega Film

Screenplay: Michael Haneke

Cinematography: Christian Berger

Editor: Marie Homolkova

Cast: Gabriel Cosmin, Urdes Lukas Miko, Otto Grünmandl, Anne Bennent, Udo Samel, Branko Samarovski, Georg Friedrich, Claudia Martini
Country: Austria
Language: German
Awards: Best Film, Best Screenplay, Prize of the Catalan Screenwriter's Critic and Writer's Association, 1994 (Sitges – Catalonian International Film Festival)

1995

Lumière et compagnie (*Lumière and Company*)
1 minute
Director: Michael Haneke
Producers: Ángel Amigo, Anne Andreu, Humbert Balsan, Neal Edelstein, Fabienne Servan-Schreiber, Soren Staermose
Screenplay: Michael Haneke
Cinematography: Michael Haneke
Editor: Michael Haneke
Country: Austria

1997

Funny Games
108 minutes
Director: Michael Haneke
Producers: Veit Heiduschka, Wega Film
Screenplay: Michael Haneke
Cinematography: Jürgen Jürges
Editor: Andreas Prochaska
Cast: Susanne Lothar, Ulrich Mühe, Arno Frisch, Franck Giering
Country: Austria
Language: German
Awards: Best Director, 1997 (Chicago International Film Festival); Critics' Award, 1998 (Fantasporto); International Fantasy Film Special Jury Award, 1998 (Fantasporto); FIPRESCI Prize, 1997 (Flanders International Film Festival)

Das Schloß (*The Castle*)
123 minutes
Director: Michael Haneke
Producers: Christina Undritz, Bayerisher Rundfunk, Wega Film, Arte, ORF
Screenplay: Michael Haneke (adapted from a novel by Franz Kafka)
Cinematography: Jirí Stihr
Editor: Andreas Prochaska
Cast: Susanne Lothar, Ulrich Mühe, Franck Giering, Felix Eitner
Country: Germany/Austria
Language: German

Awards: Best TV Film, 1998 (Austrian People's Education TV Award); Special Award, 1998 (Baden-Baden TV Film Festival)

2000

Code inconnu: Récit incomplet de divers voyages (*Code Unknown: Incomplete Tales of Several Journeys*)
118 minutes
Director: Michael Haneke
Producers: Yvonn Crenn, Christoph Holch, Marin Karmitz, Thilo Kleine, Titi Popescu, Alain Sarde, Michael Weber, Bavaria Film, Canal +, Filmex, France 2 Cinéma, Les Films Alain Sarde, MK2 Productions, Romanian Culture Ministry, Zweites Deutsches Fernsehen, arte France Cinéma
Screenplay: Michael Haneke
Cinematography: Jürgen Jürges
Editors: Karin Martusch, Nadine Muse, Andreas Prochaska
Cast: Juliette Binoche, Thierry Neuvic, Alexandre Hamidi, Ona Lu Yenke, Luminita Gheorghiu, Walid Afkir, Maurice Bénichou
Country: France/Germany/Romania
Language: French
Awards: Prize of the Ecumenical Jury, 2000 (Cannes Film Festival)

2001

La Pianiste (*The Piano Teacher*)
131 minutes
Director: Michael Haneke
Producers: Veit Heiduschka, Michael Katz, Christine Gozlan, Yvon Crenn, Bayerischer Rundfunk, Canal +, Centre National de la Cinématographie, Eurimages, Les Films Alain Sarde, MK2 Productions, P.P. Film Polski, Wega Film, arte France Cinéma, arte, ORF
Screenplay: Michael Haneke (adapted from a novel by Elfriede Jelinek)
Cinematography: Christian Berger
Editors: Nadine Muse, Monika Willi
Cast: Isabelle Huppert, Benoît Magimel, Annie Girardot
Country: France/Austria
Language: French
Awards: Grand Jury Prize, 2001 (Cannes Film Festival); Best Foreign Film, 2002 (German Film Awards)

2003

Le temps du loup (*The Time of the Wolf*)
110 minutes
Director: Michael Haneke
Producers: Veit Heiduschka, Michael Katz, Margaret Ménégoz, Michael Weber, Bavaria Film, Canal +, Centre National de la Cinématographie, Eurimages, France 3 Cinéma, Les Films du Losange, Wega Film, arte France Cinéma
Screenplay: Michael Haneke
Cinematography: Jürgen Jürges

Editors: Nadine Muse, Monika Willi
Cast: Isabelle Huppert, Olivier Gourmet, Daniel Duval, Patrice Chéreau, Anaïs Demoustier, Hakim Taleb, Lucas Biscombe, Maurice Bénichou, Béatrice Dalle
Country: France/Austria/Germany
Language: French
Awards: Best Screenplay, 2003 (Sitges – Catalonian International Film Festival)

2005

Caché (*Hidden*)
117 minutes
Director: Michael Haneke
Producers: Valerio de Paolis, Veit Heiduschka, Michael Katz, Margaret Ménégoz, Michael Weber, Les Films du Losange, Wega Film, Bavaria Film, BIM Distribuzione
Screenplay: Michael Haneke
Cinematography: Christian Berger
Editors: Michael Hedecek, Nadine Muse
Cast: Juliette Binoche, Daniel Auteuil, Maurice Bénichou
Country: France/Austria/Germany/Italy
Language: French
Awards: Best Director, FIPRESCI Prize, Prize of the Ecumenical Jury, 2005 (Cannes Film Festival); Best Director, 2005 (Chlotrudis Award); Best Feature Film, 2005 (Diagonale Austrian Film Festival); Best Director, FIPRESCI Prize, 2005 (European Film Awards); Best Foreign Language Film, 2006 (Film Critics Circle of Australia Awards); Best Screenplay, 2006 (Lumiere Awards); 50th Anniversary Prize, 2006 (Valladolid International Film Festival); Best Screenplay, 2006 (Étoiles d'Or)

2007

Funny Games U.S.
111 minutes
Director: Michael Haneke
Producers: Rene Bastian, Christian Baute, Chris Coen, Hamish McAlpine, Linda Moran, Jonathan Schwarz, Andro Steinborn, Naomi Watts
Screenplay: Michael Haneke
Cinematography: Darius Khondji
Editor: Monika Willi
Cast: Naomi Watts, Tim Roth, Brady Corbett, Michael Pitt
Country: USA
Language: English

2009

Das weiße Band, Eine deutsche Kindergeschichte (*The White Ribbon*)
144 minutes
Director: Michael Haneke
Producers: Stefan Arndt, Veit Heiduschka, Michael Katz, X-Filme Creative Pool, Wega Film, Les Films du Losange, Lucky Red, Canal +

Screenplay: Michael Haneke

Cinematography: Christian Berger

Editor: Monika Willi

Cast: Christian Friedel, Ulrich Tukur, Josef Bierbichler

Country: Austria/Germany/France/Italy

Language: German

Awards: Palme d'Or, FIPRESCI Prize, 2009 (Cannes Film Festival; Best European Film, Best Director, Best Screenwriter, 2009 (European Film Award); Best Foreign Language Film, 2009 (Golden Globe Awards)

BIBLIOGRAPHY

Adorno, T. (1984) *Aesthetic Theory*. Trans. C. Lenhardt. London: Routledge & Kegan Paul.

_____ (1992) 'On Dickens' *The Old Curiosity Shop*', in *Notes to Literature vol. 2*. Ed. R. Tiedemann, trans. S. W. Nicholsen. New York: Columbia University Press, 171–7.

Ang, I. (1992) 'Hegemony-in-Trouble: Nostalgia and the Ideology of the Impossible in European Cinema', in D. Petrie (ed.) *Screening Europe: Imaging and Identity in Contemporary European Cinema*. London: British Film Institute, 21–31.

Anon. (1997) 'Michael Haneke verfilmt Franz Kafka', *Skip*, 4/97, 118.

_____ (2003) '*Le temps du loup*', *Positif*, 512 (October), 51.

Arthur, P. (2005) 'Endgame', *Film Comment*, 51, 6, 24–8.

Augé, M. (1995) *Non-places. Introduction to an Anthropology of Supermodernity*. Trans. J. Howe. London: Verso.

Austin, G. (2007) 'Drawing Trauma: Visual Testimony in *Caché* and *J'ai 8 ans*', *Screen*, 48, 4, 529–36.

Bachmann, I. (1978 [1972]) *Drei Wege zum See*, in *Ingeborg Bachmann. Werke* (vol. 2). Eds C. Koschel, I. von Weidenbaum and C. Münster. Munich: Piper, 394–486.

Badiou, A. (2007) *The Century*. Trans., commentary and notes A. Toscano. Cambridge and Malden: Polity Press.

Balibar, E. (2003) *We, the People of Europe?: Reflections on Transnational Citizenship*. Princeton: Princeton University Press.

Baudrillard, J. (1979) *De la séduction*. Paris: Denoël-Gonthier.

_____ (1983) *Simulations*. Trans. P. Foss, P. Patton and P. Beitchman. New York: Semiotext(e).

_____ (1990) 'Von der absoluten Ware', trans. M. Buchgeister, in H. Bastian (ed.) *Andy Warhol: Silkscreens from the Sixties*. Munich: Schirmer/Mosel, 118–23.

Bazin, A. (1997) '*Un condamné à mort s'est échappé*', in *Robert Bresson: Eloge*. Milan and Paris: Mazzotta and Cinémathèque Française, 30–2.

BBC News (2006) 'Triple Suicide at Guantanamo Camp'. On-line. Available at: http://news.bbc. co.uk/1/hi/world/americas/5068228.stm (accessed 11 June 2006).

Benjamin, W. (1963) *Das Kunstwerk im Zeitalter seiner technischen Reproduzierbarkeit*. Frankfurt: Suhrkamp.

_____ (1999 [1940]) 'Theses on the Philosophy of History', in *Illuminations*. Trans. H. Zorn. London: Pimlico, 245–55.

_____ (2003 [1940]) 'On the Concept of History', in *Selected Writings*, Vol. 4. Ed. H. Eiland and M. W. Jennings, trans. H. Zohn. Cambridge: Harvard University Press, 389–400.

_____ (2004 [1935]) 'The Work of Art in the Age of Mechanical Reproduction', in L. Braudy and M. Cohen (eds) *Film Theory and Criticism*, sixth edition. New York: Oxford University Press, 791–811.

Beugnet, M. (2007) 'Blind spot', *Screen*, 48, 2, 227–31.

Bingham, A. (2004) 'Life, or something like it: Michael Haneke's *Der siebente Kontinent* (*The Seventh Continent*, 1989)', *Kinoeye*, 4, 1. On-line. Available at: http://www.kinoeye.org/04/01/bingham01_no2.php (accessed 17 January 2008).

Birch, N. (2006) 'Pamuk's Nobel Divides Turkey', *Guardian*, 13 October. On-line. Available at: http://www.guardian.co.uk/books/2006/oct/13/nobelprize.turkey (accessed 26 March 2009).

Bolla, P. de (2002) 'Towards the Materiality of Aesthetic Experience', *Diacritics*, 32, 1, 19–37.

Bradshaw, P. (2008a) 'Haneke's House of Horrors', *Guardian*, 30 April. On-line. Available at: http://www.guardian.co.uk/film/filmblog/2008/apr/30/hanekeshouseofhorrors (accessed 28 November 2008).

_____ (2008b) 'Portraits of Binoche', *Guardian*, 5 September. On-line. Available at: http://www.guardian.co.uk/film/filmblog/2008/sep/05/binochepaintingsatbfisouth (accessed 11 November 2008).

Branigan, E. (1984) *Point of View in the Cinema: A Theory of Narration and Subjectivity in Classical Film*. Berlin: Mouton De Gruyter.

Bresson, R. (1977) *Notes on Cinematography*. Trans. J. Griffin. New York: Urizon Books.

Butler, J. (2000) *Antigone's Claim: Kinship Between Life and Death*. New York: Columbia University Press.

Canning, P. (2000) 'The Imagination of Immanence: An Ethics of Cinema', in G. Flaxman (ed.) *The Brain Is the Screen. Deleuze and the Philosophy of Cinema*. Minneapolis: University of Minneapolis Press, 327–62.

Cartmell, D. (1999) 'Introduction', in D. Cartmell and I. Whelehan (eds) *Adaptations. From Text to Screen, Screen to Text*. London and New York: Routledge, 23–8.

Cavell, S. (1971) *The World Viewed*. New York: Viking Press.

Caygill, H. (2002) *Levinas and the Political*. London and New York: Routledge.

Chatman, S. (1999 [1990]) 'The Cinematic Narrator', in L. Braudy and M. Cohen (eds) *Film Theory and Criticism*, fifth edition. New York and Oxford: Oxford University Press, 473–86.

Chion, M. (1999) *The Voice in Cinema*. New York: Columbia University Press.

Cieutat, M. (2000) 'Entretien avec Michael Haneke: La fragmentation du regard', *Positif*, 478, 25–9.

Cieutat, M. and P. Rouyer (2005) 'Entretien avec Michael Haneke: On ne montre pas la réalité, juste son image manipulée', *Positif*, 536, 21–5.

Clover, C. (1992) *Men, Women and Chain Saws: Gender in the Modern Horror Film*. Princeton, NJ: Princeton University Press.

Cockrell, E. (2006) 'Michael Haneke', *Guardian International Film Guide 2006*. London: Guardian Books, 23–8.

Combs, R. (2002) 'Living in Never-Never Land', *Film Comment*, 38, 2, 26–8.

Conley, T. (2008) 'Fabulation and Contradiction: Jacques Rancière on Cinema', in T. Trifonova (ed.) *European Film Theory*. New York: Routledge, 137–50.

Cooper, S. (2006) *Selfless Cinema? Ethics and French Documentary*. London: Legenda.

Cornwell, R. (2007) 'Bush and Congress Dispute Armenian "Genocide" Status', *Independent*. On-line. Available at: http://www.news.independent.co.uk/world/americas/article3047633.ece (accessed 11 October 2007).

Cousins, M. (2007) 'After the end: word of mouth and *Caché*', *Screen*, 48, 2, 223–6.

Critchley, S. (1997) *Very Little … Almost Nothing: Death, Philosophy, Literature*. London: Routledge.

Cunneen, J. (2003) *Robert Bresson: A Spiritual Style in Film*. New York and London: Continuum.

Dassanowsky, R. (2007) *Austrian Cinema: A History*. Jefferson, NC and London: McFarland, 253–63.

Davis, C. (1996) *Levinas: An Introduction*. Cambridge: Polity.

Dayan, D. (1976) 'The Tutor Code of Classical Cinema', in B. Nichols (ed.) *Movies and Methods: I*. Berkeley: University of California Press, 483–51.

De Angelis, M. (2007) *The Beginning of History*. London: Pluto.

Debord, G. (1967) *The Society of the Spectacle*. On-line. Available at: http://situationist.cjb.net (accessed 17 January 2008).

_____ (1990) *Comments on the Society of the Spectacle*. Trans. M. Imrie. London and New York: Verso.

Deleuze, G. (1986) *Cinema 1: The Movement Image*. Trans. H. Tomlinson and B. Hebberjam. London: Athlone Press.

_____ (1988) *Bergsonism*. New York: Zone Books.

_____ (1989) *Cinema 2: The Time-Image*. Trans. H. Tomlinson and B. Hebberjam. London: Athlone Press.

_____ (1991 [1967]) 'Coldness and Cruelty' in *Masochism*. Trans. J. McNeil. Zone Books: New York, 9–138.

_____ (1994) *Difference and Repetition*. New York: Columbia University Press.

_____ (2001) *Logic of Sense*. London: Athlone Press.

Deleuze, G. and F. Guattari (2004) *Anti-Oedipus: Capitalism and Schizophrenia*. Trans. R. Hurley, M. Seem and H. R. Lane. London: Continuum.

Denzin, N. (1995) *The Cinematic Society: The Voyeur's Gaze*. London: Sage.

Derrida, J. (1990) 'Signature Event Context', in *Limited Inc*. Ed. G. Graff, trans. A. Bass. Evanston, IL.: Northwestern University Press, 1–24.

_____ (1997) 'Politics and Friendship: A Discussion with Jacques Derrida'. Centre for Modern French Thought, University of Sussex, 1 December. On-line. Available at: http://hydra.humanities.uci. edu/Derrida/pol+fr.html (accessed 8 June 2010).

_____ (2001) 'On Cosmopolitanism', in *On Cosmopolitanism and Forgiveness*. Trans. M. Dooley and M. Hughes. London and New York: Routledge, 3–24.

Derrida, J. and A. Dufourmantelle (2000) *Of Hospitality: Anne Dufourmantelle Invites Jacques Derrida to Respond*. Trans. R. Bowlby. Stanford: Stanford University Press.

Diethardt, U. (1995) 'Literatur folgt einer anderen Struktur als Film', in U. Diethardt, E. Polt-Heinzl and C. Schmidjell (eds) *Fern-Sicht auf Bücher. Materialienband zu Verfilmungen österreichischer Literatur*. Vienna: Dokumentationsstelle für Neuere Österreichische Literatur, 11–22.

Doane, M. A. (1990) 'Information, Crisis, Catastrophe', in P. Mellencamp (ed.) *Logics of Television: Essays in Cultural Criticism*. Indianapolis: Indiana University Press, 222–39.

Donner, W. (1993) 'Das Gegenteil von Hollywood', *Tip*, 3 June, 34–9.

Dréano, B. (2006) 'Négation du génocide arménien: cette loi alimente les nationalismes', *Politis*, 922. On-line. Available at: http://www.politis.fr/article1846.html (accessed 19 October 2006).

Eaglestone, R. (2004) *The Holocaust and the Postmodern*. Oxford: Blackwell.

Eagleton, T. (2002) *Sweet Violence: The Idea of the Tragic*. Oxford: Blackwell.

_____ (2003) *After Theory*. New York: Basic Books.

Einaudi, J.-L. and É. Kagan (2001) *17 Octobre 1961*. Arles: Actes Sud/Solin.

Eisenman, P. (2008) 'The Eisenman-Haneke Tapes', *Iconeye*, 55, January. On-line. Available at: http://www.iconeye.com/index.php?option=com_content&view=article&id=3062:the-eisenman-haneke-tapes (accessed 19 September 2008).

Engelberg, A. (1999) 'Nine Fragments about the films of Michael Haneke', *Filmwaves*, 6, 4, 32–4.

Ezra, E. and J. Sillars (2007) '*Hidden* in plain sight: bringing terror home', *Screen*, 48, 2, 215–21.

Falcon, R. (1998) 'The discreet harm of the bourgeoisie', *Sight & Sound*, 8, 5, 10–12.

Felix, J. and M. Stiglegger (2003) 'Austrian psycho killers & home invaders: the horror-thrillers *Angst & Funny Games*', in S. J. Schneider (ed.) *Fear Without Frontiers: Horror Cinema Across the Globe*. Surrey: FAB Press, 175–84.

Fiddler, A. (1994) *Rewriting Reality. An Introduction to Elfriede Jelinek*. Oxford and Providence: Berg.

Flos, B. (1991) 'Ortsbeschreibungen', in A. Horwath (ed.) *Der siebente Kontinent. Michael Haneke und seine Filme*. Vienna: Europaverlag, 165–9.

Foster, H. (1983) 'Postmodernism: A Preface', in *The Anti-Aesthetic: Essays on Postmodern Culture*. Port Townsend, WA: Bay Press, ix–xvi.

Foundas, S. (2001) 'Michael Haneke: The Bearded Prophet of *Code Inconnu* and *The Piano Teacher*', *indiewire*. On-line. Available at: http//www.indiewire.com/people/int_Haneke_Michael_011204.html (accessed 14 September 2004).

Frampton, D. (2006) *Filmosophy: A Manifesto for a Radically New Way of Understanding Cinema*. London: Wallflower Press.

French, P. (2006) '*Hidden*', *Observer*, 29 January. On-line. Available at: http://www.guardian.co.uk/film/2006/jan/29/philipfrench1 (accessed 11 November 2008).

Freud, S. (1924) 'The Economic Problem in Masochism', in *Collected Papers*, Volume II, translated under the supervision of Joan Rivière. London: Hogarth Press and The Institute of Psycho-Analysis, 255–68.

_____ (1961) *Civilization and Its Discontents*. Ed. and trans. J. Strachey. New York: W. W. Norton.

Frey, M. (2002) 'Supermodernity, Capital, and Narcissus: The French Connection to Michael Haneke's *Benny's Video*', *Cinetext*. On-line. Available at: http://cinetext.philo.at/magazine/frey/bennys_video.pdf (accessed 10 October 2008).

_____ (2003) 'Michael Haneke', *Senses of Cinema*. On-line. Available at: http://www.sensesofcinema.com/contents/directors/03/haneke.html (accessed 10 October 2008).

_____ (2006) '*Benny's Video, Caché*, and the Desubstantiated Image', *Framework*, 47, 2, 30–6.

Frodon, J.-M. (2005) 'Un pacte de croyance', *Cahiers du cinéma*, 603, 28–30.

Genette, G. (2004) *Métalepse: De la figure à la fiction*. Paris: Edition du Seuil.

Gibbs, C. H. (2000) *The Life of Schubert*. Cambridge: Cambridge University Press.

Gilroy, P. (2007) 'Shooting crabs in a barrel', *Screen*, 48, 2, 233–5.

Gravel, J.-P. (2006) 'Le cinéma du soupçon', *Cinébulles*, 24, 2, 6–13.

Greuling, M. (2003) 'Michael Haneke: Der Ohrenmensch', *Celluloid. Die Österreichische Filmzeitschrift*, January/February, 10–13.

Grønstad, A. (2008) 'Downcast Eyes: Michael Haneke and the Cinema of Intrusion', *Nordicom Review*, 29, 1, 133–44.

Grundmann, R. (2007) '*Auteur de Force*: Michael Haneke's "Cinema of Glaciation"', *Cineaste*, 32, 2, 6–14.

Guilloux, M. (2000) '"Rencontre" with Michael Haneke', *L'Humanité*, 15 November, 2–3.

Haneke, M. (n.d.) 'Notes to *Der siebente Kontinent*', Vienna, Wega Film.

_____ (n.d.) 'Notes to *71 Fragmente einer Chronologie des Zufalls*', Vienna, Wega Film.

_____ (1992) 'Film als Katharsis', in F. Bono (ed.) *Austria (in)felix: Zum österreichischen Film der 80er Jahre*. Graz: Edition Blimp, 89.

_____ (1995) 'Schrecken und Utopie der Form', *Frankfurter Allgemeine Zeitung*, 6.

_____ (1998a) 'La negazione è l'unica forma d'arte che si possa prendere sul serio', in A. Horwath and G. Spagnoletti (eds) *Michael Haneke*. Turin: Lindau, 44–5.

_____ (1998b) 'Terror and Utopia of Form, Addicted to Truth: A Film Story about Robert Bresson's *Au Hasard Balthasar*', in J. Quandt (ed.) *Robert Bresson*. Ontario: Wilfred Laurier Press, 551–9.

_____ (2000) '*71 Fragments of a Chronology of Chance*: Notes to the Film', in W. Riemer (ed.) *After Postmodernism: Austrian Film and Literature in Transition*, Riverside, CA: Ariadne Press, 171–5.

_____ (2005) 'Family is Hell and So is the World', *Bright Lights Film Journal*. On-line. Available at: http://www.brightlightsfilm.com/50/hanekeiv.htm (accessed 11 November 2008).

Harbord, J. (2004) 'The Poetry of Space: The Geography of Uncertainty: Thoughts on Cities and Cinema', *Vertigo*, 2, 6, 3–4.

Hardt, M. (1993) *Gilles Deleuze: An Apprenticeship in Philosophy*. Minneapolis: University of Minnesota Press.

Hardt, M. and A. Negri (2000) *Empire*. Cambridge, MA: Harvard University Press.

Hart, G. K. (2006) 'Michael Haneke's *Funny Games* and Schiller's Coercive Classicism', *Modern Austrian Literature*, 39, 2, 63–75.

Heimerl, T. (2005) 'Vom Kampf der Geschlechter zu Pathologie der Liebe', in Christian Wessely, Gerhard Lardner and Franz Grabner (eds) *Michael Haneke und seine Filme*. Marburg: Schüren, 193–217.

Heinze, E. (2006) 'Self-Righteous Editors', *London Review of Books*, 28, 16, 17 August. On-line. Available at: http://www.lrb.co.uk/v28/n16/letters.html (accessed 26 March 2009).

Henderson, B. (1999 [1970]) 'Towards a Non-Bourgeois Camera Style', in L. Braudy and M. Cohen (eds) *Film Theory and Criticism*, fifth edition. New York and Oxford: Oxford University Press, 57–67.

Hoberman, J. (2002) 'Prisoner's Songs', *Village Voice*, 27 March. On-line. Available at: http://www.villagevoice.com/film/0213,hoberman,33363,20.html (accessed 20 December 2007).

Holmes, D. (2005 [2001]), 'Michael Haneke: Code Unknown', in Kevin Conroy Scott (ed.) *Screenwriters' Master Class: Screenwriters Discuss Their Greatest Works*. London: Faber, 91–107.

____ (2007) 'Literature on the Small Screen. Michael Haneke's Adaptations of Josef Roth's *Die Rebellion* and Kafka's *Das Schloß*, in J. Preece, F. Finlay and R. Owen (eds) *New German Literature. Life-Writing and Dialogue with the Arts*. Oxford and Bern: Peter Lang, 107–22.

Horwath, A. (1991a) 'Die ungeheuerliche Kränkung, die das Leben ist. Zu den Filmen von Michael Haneke', in A. Horwath (ed.) *Der Siebente Kontinent. Michael Haneke und seine Filme*. Vienna: Europaverlag, 11–39.

____ (1991b) 'Wer war Edgar Allan?', in A. Horwath (ed.) *Der siebente Kontinent. Michael Haneke und seine Filme*. Vienna: Europaverlag, 181.

Hrachovec, H. (1996) 'Heimelektronik und Heimnachteil: Michael Haneke's *Benny's Video*', in G. Schlemmer (ed.) *Der neue österreichische Film*. Vienna: Wespennest, 286–99.

Jelinek, E. (1999) *The Piano Teacher*. Trans. J. Neugroschel. London: Serpent's Tail.

____ (2004) *The Nobel Prize Lecture*. On-line. Available at: http://nobelprize.org/nobel_prizes/literature/laureates/2004/jelinek-lecture-e.html (accessed 10 October 2008).

Jenny, U. and S. Weingarten (1997) '"Kino is immer Vergewaltigung": Regisseur Michael Haneke über Zuschauer als Opfer, die Obszönität brutaler Bilder und seinen neuen Thriller *Funny Games*', *Der Spiegel*, 38, 15 September, 146–7.

Johnson, J. (2004) *Pervert in the Pulpit: Morality in the Works of David Lynch*. Jefferson, NC: McFarland.

Johnston, I. (2007) '*Lost World*', *Bright Lights Film Journal*. On-line. Available at: http://www.brightlightsfilm.com/56/timeofwolf.htm (accessed 10 October 2008).

Kafka, F. (1978) 'To Robert Klopstock', 24 July 1922. *Letters to Friends, Family, and Editors*. Trans. R. Winston and C. Winston. London: John Calder, 344–5.

____ (1983 [1926]) *Das Schloß*, in *Franz Kafka. Kritische Ausgabe* (vol. 1). Eds J. Born, G. Neumann and M. Pasley. Frankfurt am Main: Fischer, 7–495.

Kagan, E. and J.-L. Einaudi (2001) *17 octobre 1961*. Arles: Actes Sud/Solin.

Kant, I. (1963) 'Perpetual Peace', in *On History*. Ed. L. W. Beck, trans. L. W. Beck, R. E. Anchor and E. L. Fackenheim. New York: Bobbs-Merrill, 85–132.

____ (1998) *Groundwork of the Metaphysics of Morals*. Ed. and trans. M. Gregor. Cambridge: Cambridge University Press.

Kellner, D. and H. O'Hara (1976) 'Utopia and Marxism in Ernst Bloch', *New German Critique*, 9, 11–34.

Kaplan, E. Ann (2005) *Trauma Culture. The Politics of Terror and Loss in Media and Literature*. New Brunswick, NJ: Rutgers University Press.

Kermode, M. (1998) '*Funny Games*', *Sight & Sound*, 8, 12, 44–5.

____ (2008) 'Scare us, repulse us, just don't ever lecture us', *Observer*, 30 March. On-line. Available at: http://www.guardian.co.uk/film/2008/mar/30/features.horror (accessed 28 March 2009).

Khanna, R. (2007) 'From Rue Morgue to Rue des Iris', *Screen*, 48, 2, 237–44.

Klinger, B. (2006) *Beyond The Multiplex: Cinema, New Technologies, and The Home*. London and Berkeley: University of California Press.

Knoop, H. (2005) 'Sexuality and Masculinity of Erika Kohut in Haneke's *The Piano Player*', in J. G. Reinelt (ed.) *Gender in Cultural Performances*. Berlin: Wissenschaftlicher Verlag Berlin, 117–27.

Kracauer, S. (1978) *Theory of Film: The Redemption of Physical Reality*. Oxford: Oxford University Press.

_____ (1995) 'Georg Simmel', in *The Mass Ornament: Weimar Essays*. Ed. T. Y. Levin. Cambridge, MA: Harvard University Press, 225–57.

Kuhn, E. (2002) '*Die Klavierspielerin*: über den Film von Michael Haneke', unpublished M.Phil thesis, University of Vienna.

Lacan, J. (1986) *The Ethics of Psychoanalysis, 1959–1960*: Book VII. Ed. J.-A. Miller, trans. D. Porter. New York: W. W. Norton and Company.

Laine, T. (2004) '"What are you looking at and why?" – Michael Haneke's *Funny Games* (1997) with his audience', *Kinoeye*, 4, 1. On-line. Available at: http://www.kinoeye.org/04/01/laine01.php (accessed 28 March 2009).

Lane, A. (1999) 'Robert Bresson: A Man Entranced', *New Yorker*, 25 January, 82–6.

Le Cain, M. (2003) 'Do the Right Thing: The Films of Michael Haneke', *Senses of Cinema*. On-line. Available at: http://www.sensesofcinema.com/contents/03/26/haneke.html (accessed 17 January 2008).

Lederle, J. (1997) 'Mit Kafka im Kino', *film-dienst*, 6/97, 11.

Levi, P. (1989) *The Drowned and the Saved*. Trans. R. Rosenthal. London: Abacus.

Levinas, E. (1963) *De l'existence à l'existant*. Paris: Vrin.

_____ (1969) *Totality and Infinity: An Essay on Exteriority*. Trans. A. Lingis. Pittsburgh: Duquesne University Press.

_____ (1978) *Existence and Existents*. Trans. A. Lingis. The Hague: Martinus Nijhoff.

_____ (1981) *Otherwise than Being or Beyond Essence*. Trans. A. Lingis. Pittsburgh: Duquesne University Press.

_____ (1983) *Le Temps et l'autre*. Paris: Quadrige Grands Textes.

_____ (1989a) 'The other in Proust', trans. S. Hand, in S. Hand (ed.) *The Levinas Reader*. Oxford: Blackwell, 160–5.

_____ (1989b) 'Reality and Its Shadow', trans. A. Lingis, in S. Hand (ed.) *The Levinas Reader*. Oxford: Blackwell, 129–43.

_____ (1989c) 'Martin Buber and the Theory of Knowledge', in S. Hand (ed.) *The Levinas Reader*. Oxford: Blackwell, 59–74.

_____ (1990a) 'Messianic Texts', trans. S. Hand, in *Difficult Freedom*. Baltimore: The Johns Hopkins University Press, 59–95.

_____ (1990b) 'Signature', trans. S. Hand, in *Difficult Freedom*. Baltimore: The Johns Hopkins University Press, 289–95.

_____ (1996a) 'Truth of Disclosure and Truth of Testimony', trans. I. MacDonald and S. Critchley, in S. Critchley, R. Bernasconi and A. T. Peperzak (eds) *Basic Philosophical Writings*. Bloomington and Indianapolis: Indiana University Press, 98–107.

_____ (1996b) 'Essence and Disinterestedness', trans. A. Lingis, with revisions by S. Critchley and A. T. Peperzak, in S. Critchley, R. Bernasconi and A. T. Peperzak (eds) *Basic Philosophical Writings*, Bloomington and Indianapolis: Indiana University Press, 109–27.

_____ (2000) *God, Death and Time*. Trans. B. Bergo. Stanford: Stanford University Press.

_____ (2002) 'Beyond Intentionality', in D. Moran and T. Mooney (eds) *The Phenomenology Reader*. New York: Routledge, 529–39.

Liauzu, C. (2005) 'Une loi contre l'histoire', *Le Monde diplomatique*. On-line. Available at: http://www.monde-diplomatique.fr/2005/04/LIAUZU/12080 (accessed 10 October 2008).

Lyotard, J.-F. (1984) *The Postmodern Condition: A Report on Knowledge*. Trans. G. Bennington and B. Massumi. *Theory and History of Literature 10*. Minnesota: University of Minnesota Press.

_____ (1989) *The Differend: Phrases in Dispute*. Trans. G. Van Den Abbeele. Minneapolis: University of Minnesota Press.

Ma, J. (2007) 'Discordant Desires, Violent Refrains: *La Pianiste*', *Grey Room*, 28, 6–29.

Macallan, H. and A. Plain (2007) '*Hidden*'s Disinherited Children', *Senses of Cinema*. On-line. Available at: http://www.sensesofcinema.com/contents/07/42/hidden.html (accessed 11 November 2008).

Maltzan, C. (2002) 'Voyeurism and Film in Elfriede Jelinek's *The Piano Teacher*', in M. Lamb-Faffelberger (ed.) *Literature, film and the culture industry in contemporary Austria*. New York: Peter Lang, 98–108.

Marx, K. and F. Engels (2005 [1848]) 'Manifesto of the Communist Party', *Marxist Internet Archive*. On-line. Available at: http://www.marxists.org/archive/marx/works/download/manifest.pdf (accessed 19 April 2008).

Massumi, B. (1992) *A User's Guide to Capitalism and Schizophrenia*. Cambridge: MIT Press.

Matthews, P. (2003) '*The Time of the Wolf*', *Sight & Sound*, 13, 11, 64–5.

McKay, E. N. (1996) *Franz Schubert: A Biography*. New York: Oxford University Press.

Mecchia, G. (2007) 'The Children are Still Watching Us, *Hidden/Hidden* in the Folds of Time', *Studies in French Cinema*, 7, 2, 131–41.

Metelmann, J. (2003) *Zur Kritik der Kino-Gewalt: Die Filme von Michael Haneke*. Munich: Wilhelm Fink.

Miller, D. (2005) *Women Who Hurt Themselves*. London: Basic Books.

Miller, J.-A. (2000) 'On the Semblances in the Relation Between the Sexes', in R. Salecl (ed.) *Sexuation*. Durham, NC: Duke University Press, 13–27.

Mulvey, L. (2006) *Death 24x a Second: Stillness and the Moving Image*. London: Reaktion.

Nevers, C. (1993) 'L'oeil de Benny', *Cahiers du cinéma*, 466, 66–8.

Nietzsche, F. (1961) *Thus Spoke Zarathustra*. Trans. R. J. Hollingdale. London: Penguin.

_____ (1973) *Beyond Good and Evil*. Trans. R. J. Hollingdale. London: Penguin.

Noys, B. (2008) 'Is Boredom Always Counter-revolutionary? On Michael Haneke's *The Seventh Continent* (1989)', *Kinofist: Boredom*. On-Line. Available at: http://kinofist.blogspot.com/2008/03/is-boredom-always-counter-revolutionary.html (accessed 19 April 2008).

Nussbaum, M. (1990) 'Love's Knowledge', in *Love's Knowledge: Essays on Philosophy and Literature*. Oxford and New York: Oxford University Press, 261–85.

Orr, J. (2004) 'Stranded: stardom and the free-fall movie in French cinema, 1985–2003', *Studies in French Cinema*, 4, 2, 103–11.

Pallasmaa, J. (2001) *The Architecture of Image: existential space in cinema*. Helsinki: Building Information, Rakennustieto Oy.

Pamuk, O. (2006) 'My Father's Suitcase', Nobel Prize Lecture. On-line. Available at: http://nobelprize.org/nobel_prizes/literature/laureates/2006/pamuk-lecture_en.html (accessed 22 November 2008).

Pekkilä, E. (2006) 'Introduction', in E. Pekkilä, D. Neumeyer and R. Littlefield (eds) *Music, Meaning and Media*. Hakapaino, Helsinki: The International Semiotics Institute, vii.

Peucker, B. (2000) 'Fragmentation and the Real: Michael Haneke's Family Trilogy', in W. Riemer (ed.) *After Postmodernism: Austrian Film and Literature in Transition*. Riverside, CA: Ariadne Press, 176–87.

_____ (2004) 'Effects of the Real', *Kinoeye*, 4, 1. On-Line. Available at: http://www.kinoeye.org/04/01/peucker01.php (accessed 19 April 2008).

_____ (2007) *The Material Image: Art and the Real in Film*. Stanford, CA: Stanford University Press.

Phillips, A. (1998) *A Defense of Masochism*. New York: St. Martin's Press.

Pier, J. and J.-M. Schaeffer (2005) 'La métalepse, aujourdhui', *Vox Poetica*. On-line. Available at: http://www.vox-poetica.org/t/metalepses.html (accessed 16 June 2008).

Price, B. (2006) 'Pain and the Limits of Representation', *Framework*, 47, 2, 22–4.

Prince, S. (1998) *Savage Cinema: Sam Peckinpah and the Rise of Ultraviolent Movies*. Austin: University of Texas Press.

Rea, S. (2006) 'A chilling spin on guilt, lies and videotape', *Philadelphia Inquirer*. On-line. Available at: http://www.philly.com/philly/entertainment/movies/16112872.html (accessed 29 September 2008).

Reader, K. (2000) *Robert Bresson*. Manchester and New York: Manchester University Press.

Rebhandl, B. (1993) 'Bilder aus dem beschädigten Leben', *Der Standard*, 25/26 October, 10.

_____ (1997) 'Fluchtbewegungen am Gartenzaun', *Der Standard*, 2 April, 10.

_____ (2005) 'Kleine Mythologie des Schwarzfilms', in C. Wessely, G. Larcher and F. Garber (eds) *Michael Haneke und seine Filme: Eine Pathologie der Konsumgesellschaft*. Marburg: Schüren, 79–86.

Reik, T. (1941) *Masochism in Modern Man*. Trans. M. H. Beigel and G. M. Kurth. New York and Toronto: Farrar & Rinehart.

Renov, M. (2004) *The Subject of Documentary*. Minneapolis: University of Minnesota Press.

Riemer, W. (2004) 'Michael Haneke, *Funny Games*: Violence and the Media', in M. Lamb-Faffelberger and P. S. Saur (eds) *Visions and Visionaries in Contemporary Austrian Literature and Film*. New York: Peter Lang, 93–102.

Romney, J. (1999) *Notes to Funny Games*. Artificial Eye VHS release.

_____ (2006) '*Hidden*', *Sight & Sound*, 16, 12, 64–5.

Rose, G. (1996) *Mourning Becomes the Law: Philosophy and Representation*. Cambridge: Cambridge University Press.

Rose, S. (2006) 'Unspeakable acts', *Guardian*, 16 November. On-line. Available at: http://www.guardian.co.uk/film/2006/nov/16/1 (accessed 8 June 2010).

Roth, J. (1956 [1932]) *Radetzkymarsch*, in *Joseph Roth. Werke* (vol. 1). Ed. H. Kesten. Cologne and Berlin: Kiepenheuer & Witsch, 1–311.

_____ (1956 [1924]) *Die Rebellion*, in *Joseph Roth. Werke* (vol. 2). Ed. H. Kesten. Cologne and Berlin: Kiepenheuer & Witsch, 287–374.

Roud, R. (1980) *Cinema: A Critical Dictionary*. London: Secker & Warburg.

Rousseau, J.-J. (1994) *Discourse on Inequality*. Trans. F. Philip. Oxford and New York: Oxford University Press.

Saxton, L. (2007) 'Secrets and Revelations: Off-Screen Space in Michael Haneke's *Caché*', *Studies in French Cinema*, 7, 1, 5–17.

_____ (2008) 'Close Encounters with Distant Suffering: Michael Haneke's Disarming Visions', in K. Ince (ed.) *Five Directors: Auteurism from Assayas to Ozon*. Manchester: Manchester University Press, 84–111.

Sharrett, C. (2004a) 'The Horror of the Middle Class', *Kinoeye*, 4, 1. On-line. Available at: http://www.kinoeye.com/ (accessed 20 December 2007).

____ (2004b) 'The World that is Known: Michael Haneke Interviewed', *Kinoeye*, 4, 1. On-line. Available at: http://www.kinoeye.org/04/01/interview01.php (accessed 19 April 2008).

____ (2005) '*The Seventh Continent*', *Senses of Cinema*. On-line. Available at: http://www.sensesofcinema.com/contents/cteq/05/34/seventh_continent.html (accessed 10 October 2008).

____ (2006) 'Michael Haneke and the Discontents of European Culture', *Framework*, 47, 2, 8–15.

Silverman, K. (1988) *The Acoustic Mirror: The Female Voice in Psychoanalysis and Cinema and Literature*. Bloomington: Indiana University Press.

Silverman, M. (2007) 'The Empire Looks Back', *Screen*, 48, 2, 245–9.

Simpson, D. (2006) *9/11: The Culture of Commemoration*. Chicago and London: University of Chicago Press.

Sontag, S. (1967 [1964]) 'Spiritual Style in the films of Robert Bresson', in *Against Interpretation, and other essays*. London: Eyre and Spottiswoode, 177–95.

____ (2003) *Regarding the Pain of Others*. New York: Farrar, Straus and Girou.

Sorfa, D. (2006) 'Uneasy Domesticity in the Films of Michael Haneke', *Studies in European Cinema*, 3, 2, 93–104.

Speck, O. (2008) 'The New Order: The Method of Madness in the Cinema of Michael Haneke', in R. Thomas (ed.) *Crime and Madness in Modern Austria: Myth, Metaphor and Cultural Realities*. Cambridge: Cambridge Scholars Press, 462–76.

Stewart, G. (2007) *Framed Time: Towards a Postfilmic Cinema*. Chicago: University of Chicago Press.

Strong, M. (1998) *A Bright Red Scream. Self-Mutilation and the Language of Pain*. New York: Penguin.

Tai, H.-T. Ho (2001) 'Remembered Realms: Pierre Nora and French National Memory', *American Historical Review*, 106, 3. On-line. Available at: http://www. historycooperative.org/journals/ahr/106.3/ah000906.html#REF2 (accessed 26 March 2009).

Tarkowskij, A. (1996) *Die versiegelte Zeit: Gedanken zur Kunst, zur Ästhetik und Poetik des Films*. Frankfurt/M: Ullstein.

Thompson, R. J. (1998) '*Pickpocket*', *Senses of Cinema*. On-line. Available at: http://www.sensesofcinema.com/contents/cteq/00/7/pickpocket.html (accessed 11 November 2008).

Toles, G. (2004) 'Auditioning Betty in *Mulholland Drive*', *Film Quarterly*, 58, 1, 2–13.

Toubiana, S. (2006) 'Interview with Michael Haneke', *Funny Games*, Kino Video.

Truffaut, F. (1978) *The Films in My Life*. New York: Simon and Schuster.

Turk, E. B. (2007) 'Isabelle Huppert; or, The Gallic Valkyrie Who Bewitched Brooklyn', *Camera Obscura*, 65, 22, 2, 158–63.

Ulmer, G. (1983) 'The Object of Post-Criticism', in H. Foster (ed.) *The Anti-Aesthetic: Essays on Postmodern Culture*. Port Townsend, WA: Bay Press, 83–100.

Valentine, D. A. (1998) 'Prepared statement of Debra A. Valentine, General Counsel for the U.S. Federal Trade Commission on "Pyramid Schemes" presented at the International Monetary Fund's seminar on current legal issues affecting central banks, Washington, D.C. May 13, 1998'. On-line. Available at: http://www.ftc.gov/speeches/other/dvimf16.shtm (accessed 15 October 2007).

Vangeim, R. (1983) *The Revolution of Everyday Life*. London: Left Bank Books and Rebel Press.

Vicari, J. (2006) 'Films of Michael Haneke: Utopia of fear', *Jump Cut*. On-line. Available at: http://www.ejumpcut.org/archive/jc48.2006/Haneke/index.html (accessed 11 November 2008).

Vincendeau, G. (2000) *Stars and Stardom in French Cinema*. London and New York: Continuum.

_____ (2006) 'Isabelle Huppert: The Big Chill', *Sight & Sound*, 16, 12, 36–9.

Vogel, A. (1996) 'Of Nonexisting Continents: The Cinema of Michael Haneke', *Film Comment*, 32, 4, 73–5.

Wheatley, C. (2006a) 'Unseen/Obscene: The (Non) Framing of the Sexual Act in Michael Haneke's *La Pianiste*', in M. Seabrook, A. Lewis, L. Bolton and G. Kimber (eds) *Framed!* London: Peter Lang, 127–44.

_____ (2006b) 'Ideology, Ethics and The Films of Michael Haneke', in B. G. Renzi and S. Rainey (eds) *From Plato's Cave to the Multiplex: Contemporary Film and Philosophy*, Newcastle: Cambridge Scholar's Press, 63–73.

_____ (2006c) 'The masochistic fantasy made flesh: Michael Haneke's *La Pianiste* as melodrama', *Studies in French Cinema*, 6, 2, 117–27.

_____ (2006d) 'Secrets, lies & videotape', *Sight & Sound*, 16, 2, 32–6.

_____ (2009) *Michael Haneke's Cinema: The Ethic of the Image*. Oxford: Berghahn.

Wood, R. (2002) '"Do I Disgust You?" Or, tirez pas sur *La Pianiste*', *CineAction*, 59, 54–61.

_____ (2003) 'In Search of the *Code Inconnu*', *CineAction*, 62, 41–9.

Wrye, H. (2005) 'Perversion Annihilates Creativity and Love: A Passion for Destruction in *The Piano Teacher*', *International Journal of Psychoanalysis*, 86, 1205–12.

Wyatt, J. (2006) 'Jouissance and Desire in Michael Haneke's *The Piano Teacher*', *American Imago*, 62, 4, 453–82.

Žižek, S. (1989) *The Sublime Object of Ideology*. London and New York: Verso.

_____ (2001) *The Fright of Real Tears: Krzysztof Kieślowski between Theory and Post Theory*. London: British Film Institute.

_____ (2004) *Revolution at the Gates: Žižek on Lenin, the 1917 Writings*. London: Verso.

_____ (2006) *How to Read Lacan*. London: Granta.

_____ (2007) 'Why is Every Act a *Repetition*?', in *Enjoy Your Symptom!: Jacques Lacan in Hollywood and Out*. London: Routledge, 69–112.

INDEX